# Value Negotiation

## How to Finally Get the Win-Win Right

Horacio Falcão
INSEAD

**Prentice Hall**

Singapore  London  New York  Toronto  Sydney  Tokyo  Madrid
Mexico City  Munich  Paris  Capetown  Hong Kong  Montreal

Published in 2010 by
Prentice Hall
Pearson Education South Asia Pte Ltd
9 North Buona Vista Drive
#13-05/06 The Metropolis Tower One
Singapore 138588

Pearson Education offices in Asia: Bangkok, Beijing, Hong Kong, Jakarta, Kuala Lumpur, Manila, New Delhi, Seoul, Singapore, Taipei, Tokyo

Printed in Singapore

17 16 15
19 18 17

ISBN 13    978-981-06-8143-2
ISBN 10    981-06-8143-7

---

**Copyright © 2010 by Pearson Education South Asia.** All rights reserved. This publication is protected by copyright and permission should be obtained from the publisher prior to any prohibited reproduction, storage in a retrieval system, or transmission in any form or by any means, electronic, mechanical, photocopying, recording, or likewise. For information regarding permission(s), write to: Rights and Permissions Department.

**Prentice Hall**
is an imprint of

www.pearsoned-asia.com

# dedication

*To Camila, Luca and Mateus*

*The three most fun, enriching and loving negotiations of my life. That our lives together continue to be the most meaningful value we can exchange.*

# contents

| | | |
|---|---|---|
| | **Foreword** | viii |
| | **Preface** | x |
| | **Acknowledgments** | xv |
| **01** | **Introduction** | **1** |
| | On Choices and Focus | 1 |
| | Why Value Negotiation | 2 |
| | A Book for Negotiators | 3 |
| |     A Textbook, but Different | 4 |
| |     Value Negotiation's Basic Assumptions | 6 |
| |     'Never Accept Their First Offer' | 6 |
| |     Reading is Readying | 7 |
| |     A Few Words on Practicing Skills | 8 |
| | How This Book is Organized | 8 |
| | Part 1 – Become a Negotiator | 9 |
| | Part 2 – Prepare for the Negotiation | 9 |
| | Part 3 – Negotiate | 9 |
| | **PART 1: BECOME A NEGOTIATOR** | **11** |
| **02** | **Understanding Negotiation** | **13** |
| | Negotiation Defined | 13 |
| |     What is Negotiation | 13 |
| |     Why Negotiations? | 15 |
| | So How did Negotiation Come to Be? | 15 |
| |     It All Began with Darwin | 15 |
| |     Win-Lose Then Became the Default Approach | 16 |
| | The Future of Negotiation in the Making | 18 |
| |     Tit-for-Tat Opened the Way | 18 |
| |     Win-Win – What Does the Future Look Like? | 23 |
| |     The Ultimate Test: Win-Lose vs. Win-Win | 24 |
| | *Summary* | 26 |
| | *Questions* | 27 |
| | *Scenarios* | 28 |
| **03** | **Challenge Your Negotiation Foundations** | **29** |
| | Value Foundation | 30 |
| |     Zero-Sum Negotiations and Monsters | 30 |
| |     A Brief Negotiation Introduction to the Pareto Frontier | 31 |
| | Relationship Foundation | 33 |
| |     The Trust, Chicken and Egg Problem | 33 |
| |     Short-term or Long-term Relationships | 35 |
| | Communication Foundation | 37 |
| |     But I Never Said That. Did I? | 38 |
| |     First Impressions Matter. A Lot. | 39 |
| | *Summary* | 42 |
| | *Questions* | 42 |
| | *Scenarios* | 43 |

## PART 2: PREPARE FOR THE NEGOTIATION!     45

### 04   Choose Our Goal     49
When Winning is Losing     50
Avoiding the Relative Goal Trap     53
The Pros and Cons of Complexity     54
The Seven Elements of Negotiation     55
Defining an Absolutely Great Deal     56
    Improve the Working Relationship Between the Parties     58
    Result from an Effective Two-Way Communication     59
    Satisfy Interests, not Positions     59
    Choose the Best of Many Possible Options     60
    Be Based on Legitimacy so that All Parties Believe it to be Fair     60
    Be a Well-Planned Commitment     61
    Be Better than Our BATNA     61
*Summary*     62
*Questions*     62
*Scenarios*     63

### 05   Choose Our Strategy     65
Win-Lose Strategies     65
    The Bargaining Process     66
    The Bargaining Styles: Hard or Soft     67
    The Bargaining Tension     67
Win-Win Strategies     69
         69
Win-Win Processes
More Than One?     70
    The Three Negotiations     71
    The Three Win-Lose Negotiations     72
    The Three Win-Win Negotiations     74
*Summary*     83
*Questions*     84
*Scenarios*     85

### 06   Anticipate the Critical Moments     87
Initiating the Interaction (Relationship)     88
Defining the Process (Communication)     91
Talking about Value (Interests)     92
Coming Up with Solutions (Options)     94
Making the Opening Offer or Counteroffer (Legitimacy)     96
Accepting or Rejecting an Offer (Commitment)     98
Deciding to Walk Away (Alternatives)     100
*Summary*     103
*Questions*     103
*Scenarios*     104

| | | |
|---|---|---|
| **PART 3:** | **NEGOTIATE!** | **107** |
| | Step 1 – Build the Bridge | 112 |
| **07** | **Relationship** | **115** |
| | Relationship Redefined | 115 |
| | Promote Interdependence | 117 |
| |     Interdependence: From Enemies to Partners | 118 |
| | Build Trust | 127 |
| |     Understanding Trust | 128 |
| |     Be Unconditionally Constructive | 135 |
| | *Summary* | 142 |
| | *Questions* | 143 |
| | *Scenarios* | 144 |
| **08** | **Communication** | **147** |
| | Information Asymmetry: The Source of (Almost) All Evil | 150 |
| |     Perceptions: Capturing and Storing Data | 151 |
| |     Attributions: Sharing Data | 152 |
| | The Dialogue Pattern: From Two- to Three-Way Communication | 154 |
| |     Ask to Lead and Learn | 159 |
| |     Listen: Proactive Learning | 168 |
| |     Talk: Transparent Advocacy | 180 |
| | *Summary* | 181 |
| | *Questions* | 182 |
| | *Scenarios* | |
| **09** | **Powerful Openings: Building A Solid Bridge Quickly** | **185** |
| | Relationship | 187 |
| |     Prepare a Conducive Environment | 187 |
| |     Small Talk | 189 |
| |     The Opening Statement | 190 |
| |     Share What is at Stake | 191 |
| | Communication | 192 |
| |     Negotiating the Four Ps | 192 |
| |     On Body Language | 195 |
| | *Summary* | 199 |
| | *Questions* | 200 |
| | *Scenarios* | 201 |
| | Step 2 – The Value Pursuit | 203 |
| **10** | **Value Discovery** | **205** |
| | Understanding Value | 205 |
| |     On Value and its Discovery | 205 |
| |     Value Discovery vs. Value Tension | 207 |
| | Discovering Value | 211 |
| |     Issues | 214 |
| |     Interests | 231 |
| | *Summary* | 232 |
| | *Questions* | 233 |
| | *Scenarios* | |
| **11** | **Value Creation** | **235** |
| | Understanding Value Creation | 235 |
| |     What is Value Creation? | 235 |
| |     Does Value Creation Create Real Value? | 236 |

| | Creating Value | 237 |
|---|---|---|
| |     *Be the Tailor! Make Options Suit Interests* | 237 |
| |     *Value Comes in Packages* | 246 |
| | Overcoming Value-Creation Enemies | 252 |
| |     *Internal Enemies* | 252 |
| |     *External Enemies* | 255 |
| | *Summary* | 261 |
| | *Questions* | 262 |
| | *Scenarios* | 262 |
| **12** | **Value Claiming** | **265** |
| | The Most Dangerous Step? | 265 |
| |     *Is It All About Numbers?* | 267 |
| |     *Value-Claiming Risks* | 272 |
| | Claim Value, not Numbers! | 276 |
| |     *A Journey for Meaning* | 276 |
| |     *Claiming Value Through Reason, Not Numbers* | 287 |
| |     *It is About Value, Not Power* | 292 |
| | Summary | 294 |
| | Questions | 295 |
| | Scenarios | 296 |
| | **Step 3 – Make the Best Possible Decision** | **299** |
| **13** | **Commitments** | **301** |
| | Making a Decision | 301 |
| |     *The Rational Side* | 302 |
| |     *The Emotional Side* | 306 |
| | Yes or No? | 308 |
| |     *Saying Yes!* | 308 |
| |     *Saying No!* | 309 |
| |     *Getting Them to Yes* | 311 |
| |     *Overcoming an Impasse* | 315 |
| | *Summary* | 321 |
| | *Questions* | 322 |
| | *Scenarios* | 323 |
| **14** | **Alternatives** | **325** |
| | The All-Too-Powerful BATNA | 325 |
| |     *Handling Their BATNA* | 327 |
| |     *Using Our BATNA* | 332 |
| | BATNA as a Win-Win Tool? | 340 |
| | *Summary* | 342 |
| | *Questions* | 343 |
| | *Scenarios* | 344 |
| **15** | **Conclusion: On Power and Ethics** | **347** |
| | Negotiation and Power | 348 |
| |     *Power in Negotiation vs. Negotiation Power* | 351 |
| |     *Power in Negotiation* | 351 |
| |     *Negotiation Power* | 352 |
| | Negotiation Ethics | 364 |
| |     *From Value to Skills* | 365 |
| | *Summary* | 371 |
| | *Questions* | 372 |
| | *Scenarios* | 373 |
| | **Bibliography** | 375 |
| | **Index** | 386 |

# foreword

Not knowing how to negotiate is no longer an option – for anyone. On a daily basis, negotiating is a way to succeed and survive. Ranging from dealing with an apartment landlord to thinking about how to ask for a pay raise to dealing with clients to introducing a new product in the market to merging multinational corporations to settling a border dispute among two nations, it is all about the same objective – finding the way forward.

To succeed, we all need a set of basic communication tools that can help us get to where we want to go. In this book, Horacio Falcão illustrates how to put these tools to use and, therefore, how to thrive. Throughout his book, Falcão writes with the great talent that he has successfully applied to complex negotiations and training sessions through the years. He honed his skills while working with governments, corporations and international institutions and organizations, and is now one of the most successful negotiators in the field.

These were the inherent qualities that Horacio displayed when he came to work for me as my first employee fresh out of Harvard Law School more than a dozen years ago. The techniques he takes to the next level in this book are the ones I myself have used in part to facilitate multinational transactions, including projects that involved working with international energy corporations, finding new business opportunities worth millions of dollars and working with governments.

The processes elaborated in this book were particularly pivotal in resolving a border dispute between Peru and Ecuador that had been languishing for 53 years. To finally usher in a peaceful settlement between Peru and Ecuador, our team focused on identifying the common interests of their governments, including discussing the millions of dollars in defense spending as a result of the tensions between the two countries. We then brainstormed on how a resolution of the conflict would unlock the support of international organizations that would invest in each country. To come to terms, we were thus able to bring the parties to question the most fundamental assumptions that had kept the two nations apart for more than five decades.

Central to this book is that negotiating is a process that creates and finds value, and gets individuals as much of what they want as is possible in a realistic world. Yet deep within, where nuances and subtleties combine at times to make a situation far different than it first appears, negotiations can also change the reality so that new areas of agreement are possible. A good negotiator will have studied the areas of concern and aims to leave all parties open to new possibilities. The objective is to turn a possible competitive situation into a collaborative effort in which value can be created.

From the start, parties share their interests with each other, and in reacting to those interests, we begin to understand, create value, and move forward toward an agreement. Understanding the interests of all involved is at the core of successful negotiations. A negotiator must ask, "Are we looking at this from every angle?" If one is not fully aware of the interests of the other party, one cannot possibly know what might satisfy that person or understand the lines beyond which someone will not go.

At any point in life successful negotiations can be highly rewarding. They can culminate in a situation in which everyone wins, often through personal growth. Being creative and resourceful, negotiators can give rise to so much. They can bring into being new atmospheres for progress. They can generate hope. They can leverage personal power to raise the creative capacities of individuals in constructive ways. In doing so, those engaged in negotiations also become more aware of their surroundings.

However complicated and competitive the world might have become in our lifetimes and regardless of how more extraordinary the times ahead might surprise us, these techniques can help improve the conditions around us. Well-executed negotiations can make for a better future. This is the promise of improving your negotiation skills. You can do good and do well! You owe it to yourself and to those with whom you will interact to be the best negotiator you can be. Get started today. In so doing, you help yourself to be a better person and make the world a better place.

Francisco Sanchez<br>
Former Special Assistant to the President of the United States &<br>
Former US Assistant Secretary of Transportation

# preface

In 1981, Roger Fisher and William Ury published *Getting to Yes* (GTY) and started a negotiation thinking and practice revolution. For the first time, the basic win-win process ideas were laid out for the common person. The book defined a common terminology that allowed many to dive into the field with much interest and care.

Since then negotiation became a mainstream course in all respectable law or business schools around the world. Naturally many articles and books followed by numerous negotiators and academics. As expected, not even Fisher or Ury's later texts aligned themselves 100% behind GTY, since their thinking about negotiation also evolved. Nevertheless, for the past 30 years, many new ideas on win-win and other approaches to negotiation were produced.

As new articles and books came along, a lot of ideas were either building up or correcting the original GTY theory. As academics, we do have a mission of helping the world to become a better place through knowledge. Our negotiation knowledge is built for the betterment of society and human relationships through value creation and superior conflict management. And indeed, negotiation academics are working really hard in generating new ideas to improve negotiation on a daily basis. So what is the problem?

The field of negotiation is already starting to get too broad and complicated for those who devote ourselves to studying it. What to say of the normal businessperson, lawyer or politician who negotiates everyday? How can they take the time to understand the connections and trade-offs of all different negotiation advices? How can they read over 50 books and twice as many articles to improve their negotiation effectiveness? The answer is they *cannot*. We, academics, are starting to build our negotiation ivory tower and isolating ourselves from the world.

As expected, in building our own ivory tower, our effort were uncoordinated. Some of our advice conflicts with one another. Some were produced under different assumptions or understandings. Some were very good but incoherent when paired together. Some were just too specific and thus unimportant in practice. In sum, like a Babel tower, we are all reaching for the skies, but we are starting to speak different languages.

So, for all our effort in generating new knowledge, there were not many who devoted themselves to make sense of all that was there. For all the advice and improvements on win-win negotiations, no one took the time to connect the dots into a coherent and consistent picture. This book aims to do just that: scan the negotiation advances since GTY to produce a coherent system that can be easily learned and applied by negotiators. We call this the Value Negotiation system.

## Value Negotiation

This project started as my students from the MBA, EMBA and executive education course repeatedly asked for book recommendations and additional readings. My answers usually indicated either too much reading or missed the mark. The truth was that there was no single book that satisfied their needs. The few who endured a long list of readings returned with questions on inconsistent and conflicting advice. Some were even more confused then before. Many asked me to write a book based on what they saw in my classes. Inspired and encouraged by them, I decided to take the first step.

Soon after, I found myself asking how could I add something new to the field and satisfy the needs of my students. First, the students' request was to consolidate the latest research and technology on negotiation in a single book. Second, many other basic negotiation books or textbooks were excellent repositories of theory, but the students were asking for something more pragmatic. Third, many negotiation books show negotiation as a single scientific truth and yet seemingly oscillate between win-lose and win-win advice. This oscillation reduces strategic focus and makes it harder for those who want to learn how to consistently negotiate win-win.

But why Value Negotiation? This project initial idea was to consolidate the GTY theory after 30 years of developments in a *"Getting To Yes II"*. However, it soon became apparent that this could neither be done nor titled as such. First, not being one of the original authors of GTY, there was no legitimacy to take on this responsibility and use this title. Additionally, the further the book developed, the more the fundamentals were tweaked and adjusted to enhance focus, coherence and impact.

After learning and teaching negotiation and interacting with some of the best negotiation experts in the world for about 15 years, several gaps and contradictions as well as new ideas within principled negotiation became apparent. Further research revealed some answers from different authors or disciplines. However, the more I wrote of the book, the more I realized that some of the holes and gap and even inconsistencies, required a whole step back and rethink. It was only after I was forced to look deep into them that I realized that a new system was evolving. Together with the reasons above, it was just fair to call it something else, while acknowledging its principled negotiation origins.

So what is Value Negotiation? First of all, it is no attempt to reinvent the wheel. Think of it as Principled Negotiation 2.0, which evolved through further practitioner experiences, reflective thinking and academic research. It is a new branch of win-win which is hopefully the best current response to negotiation challenges. Value negotiation uses win-win processes (or strategies) to give negotiators a clear and relentless focus on value.

> *"Value Negotiation aims to be the negotiation system that focuses on delivering the most possible value at the lowest possible risk in the widest range of situations."*

Value Negotiation raises awareness of our different process choices and assesses their risks/rewards to avoid blindly following absolute (and often mistaken) advice.

# The Book

This book aims to help negotiators learn and consistently negotiate win-win. To do so, many difficult choices were needed. Probably the hardest one was to exclude the more complex topics such as difficult behaviors and conversations, multiparty or cross-cultural negotiations, etc. But to include them here would have meant to either write an intimidating 1000-page mammoth or to superficially gloss over them. Since we wanted a book that people would read, learn and apply, we chose to stick to the basics.

We then chose to organize it in the most intuitive possible way:

**Become a Negotiator ➡ Prepare for the Negotiation ➡ Negotiate!**

## Part 1 – Become a Negotiator

**Become a Negotiator** is to set our assumptions and our mind to the task. If we do not understand how we think about ourselves and about negotiation, we are not ready to master either ourselves or negotiation. This also means challenging the way we currently think so that we can either consolidate or change some of our fundamental thinking structures. To become a negotiator, we need to think as one.

## Part 2 – Prepare for the Negotiation

**Prepare for the Negotiation** has us set the right goals and develop solid strategies. The right goals will keep us focused in the middle of the turmoil of some negotiations. Solid strategies will help us make trade-offs when tough choices present themselves. And yet, no preparation would be complete without anticipating critical moments, so that we can prepare an even safer and more potentially successful negotiation.

## Part 3 – Negotiate!

In **Negotiate!**, we face the moment of truth. To negotiate is to act and thus we examine which actions will give us the best possible results. First we look at the building of the bridge or the opening moment when negotiators establish a relationship and communication pattern. Second, negotiators engage in pursuing value through: value discovery – when you find out the raw material to generate value; value creation – the transformation of the raw material into higher value to the negotiators; and value claiming – the definition of the distribution of the value on the table among the negotiators. Then, we go into the Best Possible Decision phase, where the negotiators are pretty much left with a decision to close (commitment) or walk away (alternatives).

Finally we conclude by raising a discussion on negotiation power and ethics to summarize the book while adding a twist on the use of power and the role or value of ethics in negotiations.

# Instructor's Package

We designed and wrote this book to allow the instructor to deliver a complete negotiation course. The instructor's package also comes with an instructor's manual and a set of 15 PowerPoint presentations.

## Instructors' Manual

The instructor's manual will contain suggested class plans and activities that will include how to use the book's chapters, as well as the end-of-chapter questions and scenarios to their fullest. It will also suggest how to use the PowerPoint presentations.

## Teaching Slides

A set of ready-to-use PowerPoint presentations that summarize each chapter is available. Though they can be used directly without any adaptation, they intend to serve as a basis to facilitate the instructor's preparation and implementation of this book in the classroom. With time, we hope that each instructor will evolve and interact with the presentations as to develop his or her own version of the materials.

For university professors, adopting the Value Negotiation book entitles you to request a login and password through your local Pearson representative to access them via http://www.pearsoned-asia.com/falcao, or in the Instructor Resource Centre (IRC) at http://vig.pearsoned.co.uk/home.

This instructor's package will greatly aid negotiation instructors in delivering a world-class negotiation session every time he or she walks into the classroom. Please write to us with suggestions on how to improve these materials or what else could be of help. Thanks for choosing this book and good luck!

# Conclusion

**Value Negotiation: How to Finally Get the Win-Win Right!** filters, organizes and consolidates a vast body of knowledge into a simple and practical win-win negotiation system. This book aims to assist instructors in teaching negotiation and help students everywhere become empowered and responsible negotiators to negotiate a better world one negotiation at a time. Thanks for joining us!

# acknowledgments

This book has been a dream for many years. And yet a book is never the work of a person, but rather a combination of experiences and exchanges with different people and ideas. Hence, I would like to acknowledge the direct and indirect contributions of those who helped me and this book.

First and foremost, I want to thank my wife Camila and my two sons Luca and Mateus, who shared their husband and father with this book for over one year. They donated their time because they share the dream that this book can make a difference.

The African proverb "It takes a village to raise a child" could not be any truer in my case. My large extended family provided numerous social interactions as an early laboratory for the development of varied negotiation skills. Of greater influence were my mother Evangelina and my father Horacio as well as my two brothers Felipe and Fred. My grandparents were role models, who shaped my moral compass: Lou, Marina, Corintho and Bi.

But my village was much larger than that. I have always felt fortunate that I can count on my more than 15 uncles and aunts who, on many occasions, stepped up and were like a father or mother to me. Just as important are my more than 20 cousins who made me feel part of a very large and close-knit family and are like siblings to me. After getting married, my village grew even larger as my wife's family welcomed me as one of their own. Each of you taught me something, and for that I will always be grateful.

A few of my personal friends were extremely influential in supporting my dreams, goals, and choices, whether good or bad. I was also lucky to have been introduced to negotiation within an extraordinary community of people around and connected to the Harvard Program on Negotiation, CMI, CMG and MWI. I am proud to be able to call many of them colleagues and friends. Our years together have shaped much of my ideas and beliefs on negotiation. I appreciate your continued support and our enriching exchanges.

Within the negotiation community, there are a few people whom I would like to highlight. Firstly, I would like to specially acknowledge the influence of Professor Roger Fisher, who was a dedicated mentor and continues to be an inspiration. He showed me that we can believe in, are responsible for, and can work towards a better world through people, relationships and negotiation. This book is a tribute to his life's work, and I cannot thank him enough.

Second, I would like to acknowledge Francisco Sanchez; once a boss, then a partner, and always a friend. Where Roger was the guru and at times too far away to emulate, Francisco was the senior colleague, closer and still inspiring. He showed me that we can still make a difference even when times are dire and others do not care, and that courage is not the absence of fear, but instead comes from caring despite the odds and being willing to confront our fears.

Thanks also to INSEAD, who took a chance on me at the beginning of my career. Since then my colleagues and the institution have continuously invested in and helped me disseminate Value Negotiation around the world. Many of my INSEAD colleagues helped me by providing an article, raising an issue or answering a question on their field of expertise. The easy access to so much knowledge was a blessing that certainly raised the quality of this book.

Thanks also to Pearson Education, who stood by me during all the time that it took to write this book. Their support included many things, least of which was their openness and flexibility to negotiate a win-win contract with a unique value proposition to support this book.

Thanks to my clients and students who gave me the courage to pursue win-win solutions where most would not look or dare to go. You inspired me to constantly return to the drawing board and research new questions, think of new ideas and test new solutions. You contributed enormously to this book. I wish I could list you all by name, but fortunately you are so many that I cannot do it.

Thanks to those who devoted considerable time to turn my drafts into much better drafts and then a book: Andrew Lee, Boyd Fuller, Ayse Onculer, Wei Lian, Lo Hwei Shan, Monica Gupta, Nuno Delicado and Charley Bush. Thanks for your time, effort, ideas, attention to detail, careful feedback and candidness.

To all of you listed above, thank you very much. I truly hope this book is proof enough that your influence was and will continue to be important to me and to our readers as well.

Finally, thanks for those who came before us and helped shape the better world we live in. A world where win-win is possible and a necessary evolutionary step.

**Horacio Falcão**

# 01 Introduction

## On Choices and Focus

In the movie *Fearless* (2006), Jet Li plays Huo Yuanjia, founder of the Chin Woo Athletic Association, a kung fu school. Based on a true story, the movie fictionalizes some of Huo Yuanjia's famous successes in the early 20th century. He is claimed to have defeated US, European and Japanese fighters in publicized events at a time when China's power was seen as eroding. He became a national hero who is still remembered to this day.

In the movie, Huo Yuanjia accepts an invitation to join his Japanese challenger, Anno Tanaka, for tea. While there, they have a debate over the value of martial arts. Tanaka believes the goal of a martial artist is to defeat an opponent. Huo replies that the goal of studying martial arts is self-improvement. He argues that challenge matches were less about winning or losing but more about providing a practitioner with feedback on where to focus future learning.

Tanaka asks Huo which martial art is the best, to which he explains that he does not believe in such a thing. There is no best martial art, just different ways to become a master. The two fighters leave their meeting with a newfound respect for each other before an exciting fight scene.

Why start a negotiation book talking about a Chinese martial artist and his philosophy? First, negotiation is also wrongly seen by many as a way to beat an opponent; instead, it is a process to pursue value which involves other people. Second, as much as it is an activity, learning to negotiate is also a journey of self-improvement. Negotiation requires people to become negotiators, masters of themselves, so as to naturally master this process.

Finally, there are many great negotiation systems out there and thus many different ways to become a great negotiator. We claim nothing different. We do believe that different people can better learn and thus benefit from different negotiation schools. Having several schools gives people choices. Readers can hopefully find one that better aligns with their values, personalities and learning styles. This book is a proposal of a new choice.

Though there are various paths, we believe that choosing and sticking to one is important to get results. If we follow several diets and exercise programs, we actually follow none. If we swim all strokes at the same time, we sink. If we speak several languages at once, no one understands us. We believe in choosing and focusing on one negotiating system, then practicing it as well as we can. Like Huo Yuanjia said, it is not the school that makes the difference, but how good we become within it.

Of course, we believe that the value negotiation system which this book introduces is an excellent way for many to become master negotiators. Value negotiation is a flexible, robust, comprehensive and practical system, though not necessarily an easy one. Value negotiation is a process approach. Whenever appropriate, it coherently incorporates lessons from other approaches into its system.

If these values make sense to you, then we want to invite you to join us in learning our system: the value negotiation approach.

# Why Value Negotiation?

Value negotiation aims to be the negotiation system that focuses on delivering the most possible value at the least possible risk in the widest range of situations.

Value negotiation is not an attempt to reinvent the wheel, neither does it claim to be a revolutionary change in negotiation theory. It is a new branch of win-win negotiation, more specifically of the Principled Negotiation approach introduced in the bestseller *Getting to Yes* from Fisher, Ury and Patton. Value negotiation is intended as a step forward from principled negotiation and thus relies heavily on it. Think of value negotiation as principled negotiation 2.0. In that light, value negotiation and this book in particular benefit from standing on the shoulders of giants which came before us.

The value proposition of this book is not too ambitious in its innovative content, but aims to be an evolutionary step in the "right" direction. It draws from and attempts to consolidate the theory, thinking and practice of many, many others. To this end, we had to eventually make choices among dissenting views or fill in gaps when a single theory fell short of answering a question. This meant that we were forced to evolve. Value negotiation originated from further practitioner experiences, reflective thinking and academic research in adding new questions, tensions and solutions to principled negotiation.

As could be expected, this book benefits from several ideas found in other publications. Thus, one added value of this book is to present such advice in a summarized and coordinated system that is easy to use. The system was then named "value negotiation". This book presents the value negotiation system in a comprehensive yet simple way. Value negotiation aspires to be an international, theoretically sound and practitioner-friendly system that facilitates the study, learning and practice of negotiation.

- **Comprehensive yet concise** – After reading *Getting to Yes*, many ask: "What should I read next?" The answer is not obvious. Principled negotiation, for example, is not contained in one book only but spread over hundreds of books and articles. The reader is alone in bundling and sorting the different and sometimes conflicting advice into a single and hopefully coherent process. Most people have no time to invest in such an endeavour. If you are one of them, this book aims to help you.

- **International** – Most modern negotiation theories originated in some of the best US universities. Helpful as they are, their values are US-centric. As negotiation teaching spreads around the world, there is a clear need for a more internationally robust negotiation system. Value negotiation aims to fill this need.

  From line to country managers, from homemakers to CEOs, from buyers to sellers, from NGOs to governments, from small entrepreneurial start-up to large multinationals: this book covers the negotiation basics across different industries, levels, cultures, etc. Tried and tested, value negotiation is relevant, scalable and applicable to most negotiations we will ever face. Wherever you are from and wherever you negotiate, this book can help you.

- **Theoretically sound, practitioner-friendly** – Value negotiation is a theory for practitioners, thus it uses both theory and practice to deliver negotiation advice. Practical advice is grounded on theory to ensure that other practical moves consistently build on one another; theoretical advice is required to have broad and simple real-life applicability.

# A Book for Negotiators

This book was written to help anyone who wants to become a better negotiator. It raises awareness of different negotiation-process choices to promote better understanding and practical solutions to different challenges. This book aims to improve our ability to craft faster, better and more sustainable outcomes.

To achieve this goal, we believe a book needs to be:

- **Simple, but applicable** – This book is the simplest, most direct and readily-actionable route to make you a better negotiator that we could come up with. We focus on broad process steps and questions, while going deep into their application.
- **Short, but to the point** – Though we wrote over 1,000 pages at the start, we have summarized and revised them to keep the book as short as possible. This meant sharing what was essential and useful in the largest number of negotiations. It also meant not sweating the small details that only occur in very few cases. Most people cannot remember or use 1,000 negotiation moves, so we have focused on the essential principles.
- **Serious, but informal** – We chose to keep an active, conversational and personal style, so as to make reading a simpler and more fluid exercise. We often ask questions, tell stories and illustrate ideas with real negotiation dialogues to help learning. For the questions, we recommend trying to answer them mentally before continuing to read. This will help you form your opinion, prepare to engage in a dialogue, argue with the book and even with yourself. At the end, you learn more.
- **Analytical, but also prescriptive** – Many books try to explain what or why things are the way they are. They teach us how to craft and understand questions. They teach us how to think within a field. Other books give advice on how we should act. They provide us answers to commonly-held questions. They instruct us on what to do in different contexts. This book attempts to help us in both thinking and acting.

- **Helpful for us, but also for them** – This book is not a secret weapon; it is publicly available after all. Instead, it aims to benefit all parties. As with nearly all win-win approaches, value negotiation is most effective if all parties apply the same advice. Thus if they learn our "tricks," everybody can negotiate better.

## A Textbook, but Different

When writing this book, we had several choices to make. Some choices led us to seek a different positioning for the book. This in turn changed some expected priorities and consequently the best way to write it.

The most important and difficult choice was to write this book for the student, not the professor. The challenge is that it is the professor who ultimately recommends the book to the student. Our assumption however is that professors already understand negotiation, but need a tool to help their students learn. We did everything we could to make this book a powerful learning tool.

We wish to highlight several key features of the book. First, it is not a textbook, but rather a mix of a textbook and a business book. **This is a workbook.** A textbook helps us learn the theoretical foundations and systems that equip us to think on our own within a given field such as negotiation. A workbook tries to teach the basic applications of a field in a pragmatic way. A good workbook is supposed to make complicated concepts and terminologies quick to understand, easy to remember and simple to use.

Second, **this is a basic negotiation workbook**. As such, we do not cover difficult behaviors and conversations, multi-party negotiations, agency problems, cross-cultural negotiations, management of negotiation teams, etc. Though we started off trying to cover all these topics in one book, we quickly realized we would have to keep them superficial. Therefore, we decided to retain such topics for a second book.

Third, **we wrote for accessible learning.** So students everywhere could learn from this book, we sought out stories and examples from around the world. These contain international names, locations and currencies to demonstrate the cross-cultural applicability of this book. We also chose stories or examples that most students would have seen in their lives such as negotiations over a car, an apartment or salary. Most of us are not CEOs and thus cannot relate to such examples found in so many negotiation books. We have kept it close and relevant to most people so that more can learn.

Fourth, **we wrote for pragmatic learning.** This workbook is for the student of negotiation who needs to negotiate tomorrow, be it an MBA or law graduate, an undergraduate or an executive. This book was written to help them become negotiators, which meant taking away what added less value to them when learning how to negotiate.

- We consistently chose a simple and direct language. Many definitions and terminologies were changed to something simpler and more accessible. As a criterion, we looked for pragmatic explanations that could be mentioned in a real negotiation. This means that some definitions may seem less theoretically precise.

- We do not extensively name academics or describe research done. Of course, credit is given to them in the bibliography. We found students to be less interested in this information and we did not want anything affecting their attention from learning negotiation.
- At the end of the day, most students want to know what and how do we negotiate. We try to answer these questions as directly as we can.

Fifth, we **wrote to make learning easy and simple.** Most students struggle with too many readings from too many topics. This workbook makes negotiation a quick, fun and memorable part of their homework. It illustrates concepts and breaks down theory for quicker understanding, more profound learning and easier application.

- **Dialogues** – These were summarized to emphasize key learning points and to avoid wasting unnecessary space and reading time. It is true that many negotiations will not necessarily be as direct as some examples. Many dialogues also have a Diagnostics column to assist the reader in following the different negotiation moves behind what is said. Through this, students can develop their own diagnostic ability.
- **Summaries** – We believe in learning through repetition. And while we would be naïve not to think that some students may only read the summary, we prefer that to not reading at all. However, for the vast majority that will read in detail, our one-page summaries help to refresh what was just covered. It may be too much to expect a student to read the same chapter twice. But students can refer to these summaries after reading a chapter or just before the next lesson as a refresher.

Finally, **we learn less by only reading text**. This book is not intended as an intellectual exercise, but as a learning partner with whom we interact and work. We learn better by tackling the material through a combination of reading, class discussions, videos, exercises, role-plays, etc. This book has several exercises to invite the student to revise and rethink what was discussed in the chapter:

- Questions – These have various difficulty levels (easy, medium and difficult) so professors can tailor the assignments to the level of their students. They are used as revision to clarify concepts and ideas for application.
- Scenarios – These also have several difficulty levels. They have less simple or straightforward answers than the questions, and invite us to rethink or challenge what we have learned in the chapter. Scenarios can also be used to stimulate debates in class.

In sum, this workbook was written to maximize the learning for negotiation students around the world.

## Value Negotiation's Basic Assumptions

Value negotiation is based on a few core assumptions that we need to be aware of. Every analysis or recommendation will be made with these in mind:

1. **Negotiation is everywhere** – Negotiations go beyond formal business transactions or political meetings. They include interactions with friends and family, meetings with colleagues, casual corridor conversations, etc.
2. **Negotiation is a skill** – Some wrongly believe we are either "born with it or not!" Even those without what could be called a "natural talent" can improve their negotiation skills with the proper training and practice. Anyone can.
3. **We can try to negotiate everything** – It is not that we will always succeed, but at least we can try. We do not want to miss on golden opportunities by assuming they are non-negotiable before even trying.
4. **Negotiation is not a magic pill** – Despite the benefits negotiation can deliver, no single process can solve all problems. The goal is to increase our success rate. Knowing when to stop and pursue other courses of action is also important.
5. **There is no single, universal "best" way to negotiate** – Each person is different. Each negotiation is different. There is no single right answer, but several choices available and many potentially good answers.
6. **From strategy to implementation** – A chain is only as strong as its weakest link. The best strategic idea is only as good as the negotiator's ability to implement it. Conversely, great implementation has little impact if not part of a sound strategy. Negotiation strategy and implementation go hand-in-hand.

These are the broader assumptions behind value negotiation. Across the chapters, many other specific assumptions will be shared in their particular contexts. Another assumption holds special importance in value negotiation: every move in a negotiation has potential risks and potential rewards.

## 'Never Accept Their First Offer'

We strongly believe that negotiation advice containing words such as "always" or "never" are misleading in two ways:

1. They prevent negotiators from thinking intelligently and behaving appropriately about the particular situation in front of them; and
2. They are *always* wrong!

How do we choose among the different options? How can we know the best possible negotiation move? We like to think about negotiation based on a "Risk and Reward analysis" to help us:

- Remember to **analyse every element** of a negotiation and their risks and rewards;
- Assess **our (and their) risk appetite** within the particularities of each negotiation;
- Realize that there are **no necessarily right or wrong answers**;

- Accept that there are **trade-offs** between the different strategies and actions; and
- Appreciate that **different people** will react differently even if we diagnose and behave in a similar way.

This book concentrates on helping us think in terms of risk and reward and provides best practices based on them: strategies and techniques with the highest potential reward at minimum risk in the widest range of situations. These low-cost moves can be attempted numerous times with a high success rate. Even if they fail, we are not exposed to big risks or setbacks. But we do not stop there. We also look into other strategies and moves to reduce risks further.

The use of risk and reward is a big part of the international aspect of this book. By thinking in terms of risk and reward, we are preparing our minds to appreciate the nuances of different negotiation moves. Different moves will carry different risks and rewards in different settings and cultures. As a result, the value negotiator is culturally aware and prepared to negotiate inside and outside his or her cultural box.

## Reading is Readying

Reading this negotiation book will raise anyone's intuition and preparedness on how to negotiate better. It is the beginning step to really improving oneself as a negotiator. By reading up, we are but readying ourselves to learn more. It is helpful to use this book as a central tool in a learning journey, which includes:

- **Reading** – Read; but argue with the text, challenge and write notes and questions, summarize concepts, pages and chapters, list different ways to communicate the examples and dialogues, do the exercises. Make this book unique!
- **Lecturing** – Approach a professor, mentor or facilitator to clarify or go deeper on particular topics. Listen to their way of presenting them, their logic, their divergences and convergences with the book. Ask them or even ourselves: What is different? Why? How do I apply it? How does it relate to my experiences?
- **Doing** – For each chapter, try to do exercises, role-plays or apply the concepts to a real-life negotiation. If possible, take risks, do different things and worry less about the outcome at first. Develop the ability to diagnose the specific negotiation process at any given time.
- **Observing** – Watch, listen and learn! Watch dialogues in movies, read them in books, listen to people talk. Gain an awareness of why things are being said, their impact, good and bad ways of saying the same thing, the meaning between-the-lines, etc.
- **Discussing** – If you are at a forum where discussions are welcome, participate! Invite further discussion on interesting points, ask to understand better, include examples of successes and failures, and interact — the energy of participating helps to conserve learning.
- **Reflecting** – Action without reflection is just repetition without learning. After different exercises, role-plays or real negotiations, it helps to sit back and reflect on what was done and why. Think about what worked well and consciously repeat it. Think about what to change so as to improve on it.

## A Few Words on Practicing Skills

When reading this book, beware of the temptation of thinking "I've already heard about this" or "I already know this," and then skipping or paying less attention to it. Because true as such thoughts may be, do we put them in practice? And if we do, are we satisfied with how we are doing so? If not, it may be because there is a difference between knowing how to do it and actually doing it. The latter requires a lot more effort and practice to become part of our negotiation skills toolbox. Instead of dismissing the topic, make a point of revisiting and practicing it as soon as possible.

Neil Rackham, in his book *Spin Selling*, gives us a few pointers on practicing. He tells us to (1) **pick one new skill at a time to practice**. We need to resist the temptation to try too many things at once. When learning to juggle, most people start with one ball. To start with more prevents us from focusing on the basics before moving on to complex moves.

Next, (2) **focus on quantity, not quality**. Perfection is our worst enemy at first. To only do something new when we expect perfection from it is to never do it. Pick as many opportunities to practice as possible, because with quantity comes more opportunities for reflection and learning. The more we do, the more aware we become, the more our mental muscles strengthen, the more progress we see. Quantity creates a fertile environment for quality to emerge.

Wearing new shoes may hurt our feet. Instead of throwing them away, the advice is normally to break them in. Over time, they mould around our feet and may become our most comfortable pair. The same goes for negotiation skills: if at first a new suggestion seems awkward, (3) **stick to it at least three times**. Give a chance for it to be broken in and to become second nature. If we still see no improvement, then discard the suggestion.

To do something for the first time in front of many people and with a lot of money at stake is a challenging situation, to say the least. So finally, (4) **practice new skills in safe environments first**. In the same way that pilots use flight simulators, negotiators use role-plays. In the same way that young athletes enter minor competitions first, new skills are best practiced in small-stakes negotiations first.

## How This Book is Organized

Almost everyone who picks up a negotiation book is looking for better results. However, we do not improve results just by concentrating on them. Results in negotiation are usually consequences of our actions. Actions are often chosen based on a strategy. The chosen strategy is thought to be the best way to achieve a certain pre-defined goal. The goal is usually set based on our assumptions or implicit view of negotiations.

We are usually trying to get the best possible result when we negotiate. To achieve this, we need to look at and do our best towards our assumptions, goals, strategies and actions. This book takes that into account and is organized in hopefully the most intuitive way possible:

# Part 1 – Become a Negotiator
- Chapter 2 – Understanding Negotiation
- Chapter 3 – Challenge Your Negotiation Foundations

We believe that we should first ready ourselves to negotiate. *Become a negotiator* is to set our assumptions and our mind to the task. The unprepared land may not grow even the best of seeds. If we do not understand how we think about ourselves and about negotiation, we are not ready to master either. To become a negotiator, we need to think like one.

This also means challenging the way we currently think so that we can either consolidate or change some of our fundamental thought structures. If we do not set the right foundation, no matter the amount of correct technique, we will not attain success. It is like driving down the wrong road: no matter how fast or skilfully we drive, we will not get to our desired destination. Once we are ready as an individual, it is time to prepare for the various negotiations.

# Part 2 – Prepare for the Negotiation
- Chapter 4 – Choose Your Goal
- Chapter 5 – Choose Your Strategy
- Chapter 6 – Anticipate the Critical Moments

*Prepare for the Negotiation* has us set the right goals and develop solid strategies. The right goals will keep us focused in the middle of the turmoil of some negotiations. Solid strategies will help us make trade-offs when tough choices present themselves. Without proper preparation, we are but flags that drift with the wind — our outcomes are more a result of luck than skill.

And yet, no preparation would be complete without anticipating critical moments, the times in which a negotiation is most at risk. Critical moments allow us to foresee danger so that we can prepare an even safer and more potentially successful negotiation.

# Part 3 – Negotiate!
- Build the Bridge
  - Chapter 7 – Relationship
  - Chapter 8 – Communication
  - Chapter 9 – Powerful Openings
- Value Pursuit
  - Chapter 10 – Value Discovery
  - Chapter 11 – Value Creation
  - Chapter 12 – Value Claiming
- Make the Best Possible Decision
  - Chapter 13 – Commitment
  - Chapter 14 – Alternatives
  - Chapter 15 – Conclusion: On Power and Ethics

Then, the time comes to *Negotiate!* This is indeed the moment of truth, when all our awareness and preparation is tested. To negotiate is to act. The understanding of which actions will give us the best possible results is examined at great length to cover all relevant aspects of the negotiation process. Naturally, this forms the largest part of the book.

We start by covering what is often the first part of a negotiation, the building of the bridge. This is the opening moment when negotiators establish a relationship and communication pattern. After that, the negotiators engage actively in pursuing value. The main phases of pursuing maximum value with minimum risk are: value discovery (when you find out raw materials to generate value); value creation (transforming the raw materials into higher value for the negotiators); and value-claiming (distributing the value on the table among the negotiators).

Finally, we proceed to the Best Possible Decision phase, where the negotiators are pretty much left with a decision to close the deal or walk away. We discuss how to ensure we arrive at this stage with a maximum chance of obtaining positive commitment. We also cover how to protect ourselves from and manage effectively the possibilities of either party walking away.

We close with a discussion on negotiation power and ethics to bring together the learning of all prior chapters.

But enough with the introductions already. Let the negotiations begin!

# PART 1
# BECOME A NEGOTIATOR

Everyone negotiates! This, however, does not make us all negotiators. In order to become a negotiator, we need to ready ourselves for the new role. First, we need to better understand what negotiation is. Then, we have to revisit our current thinking about negotiation to either confirm or renew it.

To help in this process, we will walk through negotiation's past, present and future. Then, we will revisit some basic assumptions surrounding negotiations so that we can check our own. Finally, we recommend some assumptions that will give us a fresh and positive start.

# VALUE **NEGOTIATION:** A MAP

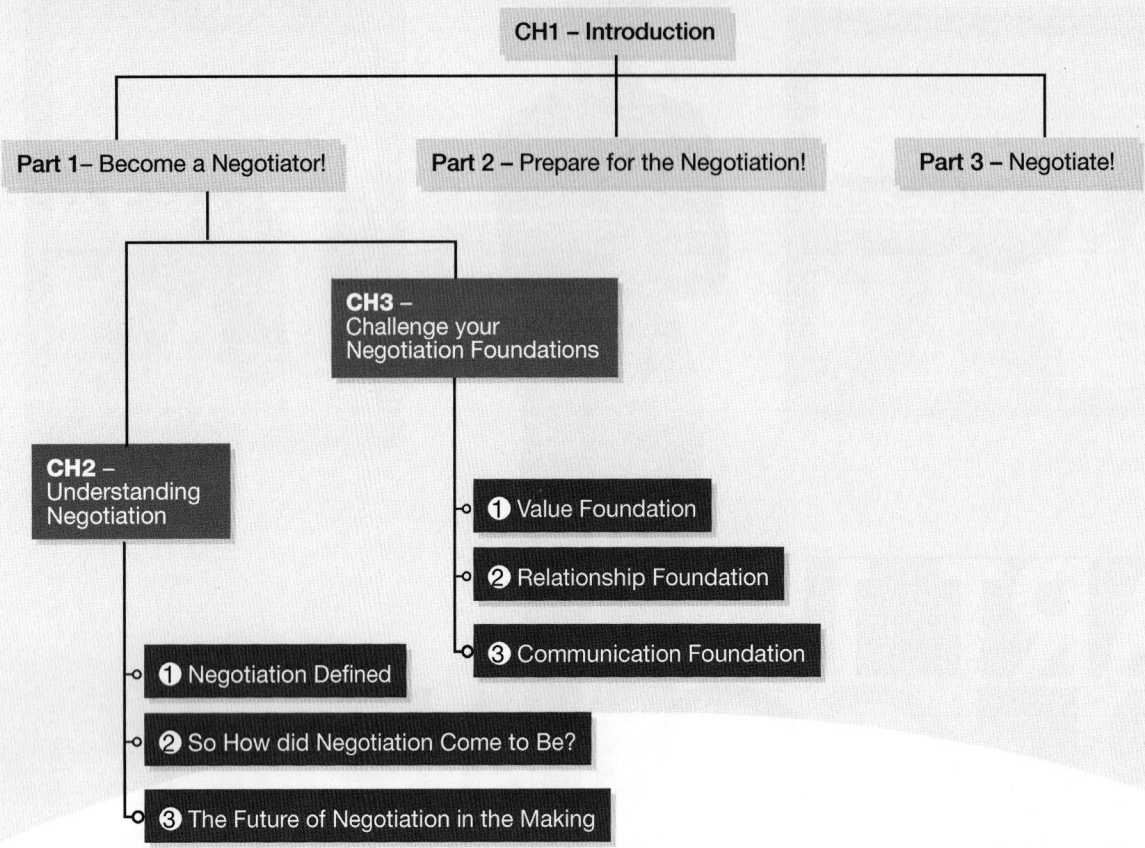

# 02 Understanding Negotiation

**Learning Objectives:**
- What negotiation is and is not
- How the win-lose and win-win strategies emerged
- What win-lose and win-win (their risks and rewards) are
- Which is better: win-lose or win-win

## Negotiation Defined

### What is Negotiation?

While shopping at the cereals aisle in a supermarket, I picked up my favorite brand, while my girlfriend picked a new one. I then curiously asked:

- *"Are you taking this cereal?"* pointing to the box she was holding.
- *"Yes, I think so,"* she answered somewhat hesitantly.
- *"Are you sure? You've always bragged that your favorite brand was the very best one and that you could not have anything else,"* I asked, trying to prevent her from regretting her decision afterwards.
- *"Please do not negotiate with me on cereals!"* she answered humorously.
- *"But I was not negotiating. I was just asking a question,"* I argued.
- *"Yes you were negotiating. And you are still negotiating with me right now. Stop it! I will take whatever cereal I want,"* she pressed and took the cereal.

She had a point. Knowingly or not, I was negotiating. Similarly, whenever I visit my parents, as soon as I say anything slightly different, my mom complains: "You are NOT using your negotiation tricks on me right now, are you? Remember that you do not negotiate with your mother." She then stares at me menacingly to remind me she is still my mother and the boss.

The pleasures of being known as a negotiator… Everything we do or say can be interpreted as a negotiation move. And so it should be. But why? What is negotiation after all?

**Negotiation is a process that happens whenever at least one person is trying to get another to do or not do something for him or her.** It could be to get money, influence a decision or a way of thinking, have someone perform a specific task, give them a present, prevent them from staying out late, gain recognition, be seen as trustworthy or caring, etc. With such a broad definition, it is not surprising that my girlfriend and my mom think that I am always negotiating (and I normally am).

As a natural consequence from the definition above, we can conclude some important aspects about negotiations:

- Negotiation is **everywhere**. It is in almost every single communication between two or more people (a discussion, a meeting or a simple conversation among friends) and not just in formal business or political settings.
- Negotiation has a purpose, and as such it is neither a skill nor a talent, but a **process** that requires several different (learnable) skills in action for one to be successful.
- As a consequence of the interaction of two or more people, **every negotiation entails a relationship**, short- or long-term, within which the process takes place.
- There are **numerous ways to negotiate**. Negotiation is a dynamic exercise that changes with the different people, relationships and context. Negotiation can take an almost infinite number of forms, methods or strategies **with their own potential risks and rewards**.

Would activities such as sales, marketing or even a war be considered negotiation? Under the above definition, our answer is yes. Sales is a process where one party tries to get another to buy its product or service. We do not limit our definition of negotiation to the price discussion, but we expand it to the whole process. Marketing is a one-to-many negotiation, where a company tries to get several people and companies to believe in its brand.

Even the extreme example of a war could be seen as a negotiation, where each side tries to get the other to accept their views and demands. War is not a violence exercise for its own sake, but usually a purposeful though extreme way of getting a country or a group of people to change their behavior or views.

So is negotiation everything? What is it not? Actually, negotiation is not about many things normally associated with it, such as game theory, psychology, leadership, decision analysis, conflict resolution, economics, deal-making, etc. Negotiation can benefit from these subjects, but it is not limited to any of them. A negotiator can adopt a game theory perspective, i.e., if we do A, they will probably do B or C, to which we then should... But people always surprise you, thus negotiation is not just game theory. Negotiation can benefit from psychological insights, though it is not psychology. In sum, negotiation benefits from the application of several fields of knowledge but is not defined by any of them.

Finally, Professor Michael Watkins takes **"a more expansive view of negotiation as creating and capturing value in a network of relationships."** Though one could argue that not all negotiations necessarily engage in a value creation exercise (they could), the ideas of a more expansive view of negotiation, the focus on value and the relationship context are fundamental. The expansion of the definition of negotiation increases the negotiator's playing field and thus the chances of getting the most possible value.

## Why Negotiations?

Okay, so we know what negotiation is, but why do people do it? Why do they bother? If people could get everything they needed or wanted on their own, they probably would not bother. But we cannot. That is why human beings evolved as social animals: we need one another. As a result, we have to negotiate to get what we need or want. **We negotiate to increase value for ourselves.**

What is value then? As the Dalai Lama says: "Everyone wants more pleasure and less pain." Negotiation is more than just a process to get material gain such as food, money or services. It <u>is also a process to seek emotional gratification such as personal satisfaction, trust or love</u>. Value is a relative word with various specific meanings to different individuals at different times. No two people will see value exactly the same way all the time. What brings us pleasure or avoids pain is not necessarily the same for other people.

To easily identify the two major categories of value, we use the terminologies of "<u>substance value</u>" and "<u>relationship value</u>." Substance value is whatever a negotiator wants that could be priced in a market. Relationship value is normally intangible, associated with a feeling and cannot be priced. Every negotiation move has an intention, positive or negative, conscious or not, of generating substance and relationship value to someone.

# So How did Negotiation Come to Be?

## It All Began with Darwin

Imagine two of the earliest cavemen meeting and only one has food. The first caveman, Strug, is very hungry and realizes that he is much stronger than the second caveman, Wik. He runs towards Wik and takes the food from his hands. Wik fights for his food with all his strength but to no avail. Strug not only takes the food, but seriously injures Wik, who dies from his wounds. Strug walks away happy with his food and his victory, but not without his share, though lesser, of injuries.

This is survival of the fittest, the law of the jungle or evolution at work. The fight for survival, an effective natural selection process, has a high cost and creates little value. Injuries abound, a serious risk of death, destruction of relationships, and all just for our next meal. It is hard to imagine how stressful and fearful a day in Strug or Wik's life was. Strength or power meant almost everything.

But even greater strength did not guarantee the winner all rewards at no cost. While Strug did have his meal, injuries from the fight with Wik weakened him for days. He was not as fit to hunt and almost died of hunger in the subsequent weeks. He then decided to do something different the next chance he had. So when a third caveman, Nul, passed by, the dialogue went somewhat like this:

- *Can I have your food?*
- *No! It's mine.* (Nul keeps the food away from Strug)

- *But I am very hungry.*
- So am I. It took me a lot of time to hunt this down. So I can't give you anything. I don't have enough for the two of us.
- *But I am really, really hungry.*
- Sorry! No can do.
- *Just a little bit, please?*
- I said no! (Turns around and begins to walk away)
- *Well, you can see that I am bigger and stronger than you.* (Showing flexed arms and chest muscles) *So, you either give me your food now or I will take it from you by force. It is your choice: hungry or dead. What will it be?*
- Okay. (Gives his food and walks away in hope of finding food somewhere else)

Now Strug feels electrified. He has found out how to get the food and walk away without any injuries. This seems to be the best thing ever. Strug just found a quicker and "cleaner" method to have it all. He has evolved from a fighter to a negotiator.

Darwin's evolutionary theory tells us that we are somewhat genetically wired to compete for the allocation of resources and ultimately for the evolution of the species. Most species, including humans, started competing over resources through fights. So what does Darwin have to do with negotiation? Strug and humans in general found negotiation to be a better process to allocate resources and yet survive as a species. Negotiation evolved from fighting as a method to solve differences.

Anyone is sure to have seen on TV or read about animal behavior in disputes over food, territory or status. Most of them do not jump straight into a fight like Strug did in the first example. Animals usually initiate a display of their power through noises, poses, dances, looks or demonstrations (baring teeth or standing up tall). Eventually, one animal realizes it is smaller and likely to lose, and yields to the stronger animal.

These animals learned the same lesson as Strug: even for the stronger one, engaging in a fight over resources has a potentially high cost. Thus, avoiding the fight altogether is a better strategy for both parties. But if they avoid the fight, how can they solve their dispute? And there lies the necessity that invented negotiation. It was initially a simple process that allocated resources through predicting the potential winner of a fight.

Negotiation then started as an all-or-nothing process far from producing optimal or ideal outcomes. Yet this simple power-measuring exercise reduced the risk of death to both members in the dispute. Species that adopted negotiation developed an evolutionary advantage over those that continued to fight (and die) over every little problem. Negotiation as a process for demonstrating power was passed down the generations as a successful evolutionary trait.

## Win-Lose Then Became the Default Approach

Win-lose or bargaining is the prevalent negotiation approach worldwide today, and for many it is the only one. It directly evolved from fighting, as seen above. **A win-lose approach happens when one party attempts to get what they want in a negotiation by demonstrating or using power over the other.**

Like in a fight, the expression "win-lose" indicates an intention to solve the conflict by winning **over** the other. As a result, it usually leads to results where we have a winner and a loser." Like Strug, the winner normally convinces the other of having more power. Meanwhile, the loser normally walks away empty-handed from the virtual fight. As a consequence, the parties focus on **power as the most important resource to win in a win-lose approach**. Power in a win-lose negotiation equals the ability to get what one wants independently of the other party's will.

The success of the win-lose approach is largely due to its simplicity and partial effectiveness. But it is also due to ignorance of better methods. Most negotiators nowadays focus on accumulating power to win. Indeed, a win-lose approach to negotiation can work very well for the more powerful party under two circumstances:

1. **Big power difference** – When one party is clearly much more powerful in the eyes of the other party, like how Strug appeared to the third caveman. In such a case, the weaker party prefers to yield than to challenge the power status.
2. **Short-term concern** – When the more powerful party doesn't care about the longer-term relationship, but only about getting what it wants immediately. If Strug were concerned with being able to take food from Wik for weeks to come, he would have to hold back in the fight so as not to kill Wik. Unfortunately, in the process, he would also reduce his chances of success at obtaining food.

In a scenario of a big power difference and short-term concern, a win-lose approach can prove successful. The more powerful party can easily overcome the other party's resistance today (power difference) or not be concerned about facing resistance tomorrow (short-term concern).

Nonetheless, the win-lose approach is not devoid of risks and problems. Its main issue is the **resistance** it naturally generates. Once a party applies power indicating their win-lose approach, most other parties will resist to avoid losing—a case of action meets reaction.

Resistance is less of a factor, however, when faced with a big power difference and short-term concern. However, life and negotiation are seldom so simple and resistance will generate high risks. As a result, the win-lose approach may cause negotiators to either lose or win less than they could. Below are some examples of the risks of win-lose negotiation and its power focus:

- **Lose certainty** – Are we really the most powerful party? Power comes in many forms, making it hard to predict the winner. We may be bigger, but they may be faster and stronger. It is never 100% guaranteed.
- **Lose focus** – Under resistance, many shift their focus from "winning" to "not losing" or from value to power. A common result is a lose-lose or lose more/lose less outcome.
- **Lose value** – Resistance may force us to invest more resources or take more risks. Even if we overcome their resistance, we may have done so by incurring higher cost than planned (like Strug's injuries after Wik's resistance).
- **Lose potential future value** – As we press our power over them, they will not only resist us today, but may also resist entering a negotiation with us tomorrow.

- **Lose tomorrow** – In overpowering them, we set a pattern to our negotiation. Tomorrow, they may return stronger and, under the same pattern, overpower us.
- **Lose our ethics** – If resistance becomes desperate, we may appeal to extreme measures which we consider unethical, such as lying or manipulating.
- **Lose control** – Once we realize they are more powerful, there is little left to do. The outcome will naturally reflect our power difference. Better luck next time!
- **Lose peace of mind** – Though a few enjoy the win-lose combative approach, most find it a dreadful exercise filled with fear and anxiety.

With so many risks, why is win-lose negotiation so popular? Indeed, damage is minimized compared to a fight or going to court. Sometimes, a win-lose strategy can produce some very big wins as well. Still, its popularity is mainly a consequence of it being the current standard way of thinking and talking about negotiation. Most people do recognize that win-lose is a poor and volatile method to build value and relationships. Yet most still use this approach due to ignorance of better methods rather than ignorance of its risks.

# The Future of Negotiation in the Making

## Tit-for-Tat Opened the Way

A few decades ago, negotiation was given an evolutionary jump—interestingly enough from within a competition. In the early '80s, Anatol Rapoport entered his software Tit-for-Tat in a computer-simulated competition for value-maximizing strategies.

In short and for simplicity's sake, the competition matched one software (A) against another (B) and gave them two possibilities: collaborate or defect (not collaborate). Notice that both software have to choose at the same time so that no software learns about the other's move before its own. If both software collaborate, they get a point each. If both defect, then no points are given. But if one collaborates and the other defects, then the defector gets two points. See **Table 2.1** for illustration:

**Table 2.1** Competition payoff

|  | B Collaborates | | B Defects | |
|---|---|---|---|---|
| A Collaborates | A = 1pt | B = 1pt | A = 0pt | B = 2pts |
| A Defects | A = 2pts | B = 0pt | A = 0pt | B = 0pts |

Tit-for-Tat always starts with an initial collaboration move. In subsequent rounds, it responds with the same action that the other software (opponent) uses in the previous round. For example, if the opponent collaborates in round 1, Tit-for-Tat remains collaborative in round 2. But if the opponent defects in round 2, Tit-for-Tat would defect in round 3. If the opponent persists in defecting in round 3, Tit-for-Tat would do the same in round 4. However, if the opponent collaborates again in round 4, Tit-for-Tat would reward that and collaborate in round 5. And so on and so forth. The representation of this example follows in Table 2.2:

|  | Round 1 | Round 2 | Round 3 | Round 4 | Round 5 | Round 6 |
|---|---|---|---|---|---|---|
| Tit-for-Tat | Collaborate | Collaborate | Defect | Defect | Collaborate | ? |
| Opponent | Collaborate | Defect | Defect | Collaborate | ? | ... |

**Table 2.2** Illustration of Tit-for-Tat moves

For more than two decades, Tit-for-Tat beat far more complex strategies created by economists, psychologists and other experts to continue winning the subsequent iterations of annual computer simulation tournaments. Tit-for-Tat did not win all matches, but in all tournaments, after several matches, it held the highest average score per match and the highest final score of the game. The software became widely recognized as a very robust and flexible approach to maximizing value in any long-term dynamic between two parties.

Many examples of Tit-for-Tat's strategy are also found in nature, known in biology as "**reciprocal altruism.**" In evolutionary biology terms, reciprocal altruism happens when an organism's intentional behavior benefits other organisms. Reciprocal altruism involves risk-taking, since it is done even at a potential cost or lower gain to the organism. Much of its success comes from its positive message and subsequent value reciprocation. Tit-for-Tat and reciprocal altruism show that negotiators can generate better value acting for their collective good (Collaborate/Collaborate) than selfishly (Defect/Defect).

It was impossible for negotiation to ignore these tournament victories along with increasing evidence of reciprocal altruism as a successful evolutionary strategy in nature. For many people, Tit-for-Tat became the optimal strategy to maximize value and showed that collaboration pays off in the long run. The road was paved for the emergence of a win-win approach.

## What can Negotiation learn from Tit-for-Tat?

There are many lessons to draw from Tit-for-Tat on how to lead a negotiation towards a successful collaboration. Axelrod, one of the first to link Tit-for-Tat to negotiations, says that its success comes from being nice, provocable but forgiving:

- **Nice** (at first) – Cooperates on the first move or is never first to defect.
- **Provocable or retaliatory** – Reduces an opponent's gain and increases its cost for defecting at once, in response to its defection. More than a punishment of the past, this is an attempt to influence the future.
- **Forgiving** – Immediately returns to cooperation if the opponent does so.

In sum, Tit-for-Tat is **positive**, but **not naïve**. Tit-for-Tat sends a positive message of collaboration to lead the other party into doing the same. However, if the other party fails to reciprocate, Tit-for-Tat is not naïve. It will do what it takes (retaliate) to lead the other party back into a collaborative dynamic. Once it succeeds in leading them back, it goes back to being positive again (forgiving).

The result is value maximization.

And there is more to Tit-for-Tat than meets the eye. Its success also comes from communicating:

- **Proactively** – It sets the tone it believes will bring the biggest value (i.e., collaboration). It takes the risk to send the right message and leads by example.
- **Clearly** – Tit-for-Tat benefited from the very clear messages the game offered. To collaborate or to defect meant just that: collaborate or defect. Clarity was reinforced by the strategy's:
  - **Simple process** – Easy to understand and quick to recognize as a strategy (they defect now, we defect next time) facilitate reciprocation if desired.
  - **Consistent pattern** – Tit-for-Tat's consistency gives predictability and reliability, which facilitate parties' engagement without fear or surprises.
- **Interdependence** – If the other party could independently get what it wanted, why collaborate with Tit-for-Tat? If it could unilaterally force Tit-for-Tat to collaborate (dependence), why not defect and score more? In sum, the parties need one another to score (interdependence) and that generates a motivation to collaborate.
- **Quick feedback** – Tit-for-Tat could quickly see the impact of its actions and adjust their communication and actions to better influence and lead.
- **Focus on Value** – The constant and unemotional focus on value helps Tit-for-Tat to keep moving forward. It motivates change if value drops (retaliate) or forgiveness if value returns.

In sum, Tit-for-Tat teaches negotiators to be proactive in sending a positive (but not naïve), clear and consistent message of focusing on value, based on a simple, interdependent and quick feedback process.

## Tit-for-Tat meets Real Life

Despite all of its lessons, as a computer experiment run in an artificial environment, Tit-for-Tat has its limitations in real life. Especially when applied to the richness of real-life negotiations, Tit-for-Tat's shortcomings require adaptations.

Many argue that Tit-for-Tat is not well prepared to handle some real-life negotiation challenges. The most common criticisms are:

- **Single round negotiations** – As Tit-for-Tat invariably starts collaborating, without a future retaliation threat, the other party becomes encouraged to defect.
- **Last round betrayal** – Likewise, no ensuing round annuls the retaliation threat, allowing the other party to defect while Tit-for-Tat repeats their previous move.
- **Communication imperfections** – If in real life the other party intends well but communicates poorly, Tit-for-Tat may misunderstand and mistakenly retaliate.
- **Emotional escalation** – Tit-for-Tat is void of emotions, but humans are not. After a few defections, humans are likely to react emotionally (seek revenge or take longer to forgive) even at risk of sacrificing value in the process.

- **Alliances or coalitions** – Despite its dominance, in 2004, Tit-for-Tat lost to another strategy known as the "Southampton team." This strategy was based on peer recognition and cooperation. Once two Southampton players met, one would sacrifice itself so the other could win repeatedly. But against a non-Southampton player, the Southampton player would only defect to hurt the "outsider." As a result, Southampton players were among the top three but a majority of them were among the worst performers. Though some beat Tit-for-Tat, their team average was well below Tit-for-Tat's. Still, the Southampton team victory highlights the importance of friendship and alliances inherent in a more realistic human environment with strong social and relationship components.

Indeed, because of the controlled computer environment within which Tit-for-Tat operated, it did not "evolve" to handle all possible scenarios. But real-life negotiations can handle most of Tit-for-Tat's shortcomings precisely because they are not within the same controlled environment. The real-life negotiator can actually be more creative and overcome most of these challenges, for example:

- **Single round negotiations** – Communication in real life is not simultaneous and we can almost always talk. We can start cautiously positive and adjust behavior based on feedback from the other party.
- **Last round betrayal** – If we anticipate a risk of last round deception, we can negotiate a guarantee or penalty to align incentives and avoid the betrayal.
- **Communication imperfections** – Tit-for-Tat may retaliate too quickly, but we can ask questions to clarify a point before acting on it.
- **Emotional escalation** – We can always take time off to calm down or discuss the impact of the defections, and be able to refocus on value once again.
- **Alliances or coalitions** – In real life, we do not have to negotiate with just anyone. Thus as we identify the Southampton team, we can refuse to negotiate until they are ready to collaborate.

Next, we look into a typical short-term negotiation conducted in a win-lose fashion, using many of the principles from Tit-for-Tat stated above.

## A Tit-for-Tat Negotiation

Many believe that buying a used car has to be one of the clearest forms of win-lose negotiation we can undertake. This assumption is likely based on the experiences and stories of the millions of used car negotiations that turned out in such a way. Still, the real-life account below shows how even a used car negotiation need not be a win-lose engagement.

In 2000, after years of bike-riding, Gunter decided to buy a used car that he hoped would fit his budget. Shortly after starting his research, Gunter saw a leaflet advertising a 1993 Toyota Tercel in a Japanese store. He called and arranged for a viewing of the car.

Not knowing much about cars, Gunter researched the Internet extensively to learn more about buying a used car. He came up with a 20-item checklist to inspect at the garage. He also looked at the *Kelley Blue Book*, a reliable US guide on used car prices. He found that US$3,800 was the recommended price for this car model and year if indeed in excellent condition.

On the agreed date and time, Mr. Hiroshi, the car owner, brought the car to Gunter's garage. Gunter greeted him as soon as he came out of the car.

- "Mr. Hiroshi, thank you for bringing the car here. It is very kind of you to do so."
- *"No problem. I will leave for Japan soon, and I want to sell this car quickly."*
- "Sure, let's be quick then. I have a checklist for verifying used cars. It should take 15–20 minutes. Is that okay? By the way, I brought you a copy." Gunter handed him the printed checklist.
- Mr. Hiroshi browsed through the checklist mildly surprised and then said, *"That's okay. I believe it's good that you check the car. But let me tell you that it is in excellent condition."*
- "I agree it looks very nice. It seems you took great care of it. Let me get started to not waste your time." Gunter proceeded to inspect the bumpers, engine, etc., and as he went along, all of the items seemed to be in great working condition. Halfway through the list, Gunter complimented him once again on keeping a more than seven-year-old car in such good shape.
- At the end he said, "Your car seems to be in excellent condition. I am very impressed."
- *"Indeed, I like it a lot. Thank you. It's a pity that I have to sell it to return to Japan."* He commented with a mild smile underneath his Red Sox baseball cap.
- "I can imagine that. The car looks good. Is there anything that I should know?"
- *"Yes! The electrical part is old and I never changed it."*
- "Thanks for that. Could we go for our test drive now?"
- *"Sure."*

After the test drive, they stopped in front of Gunter's apartment. He thanked Mr. Hiroshi once again for his time and patience with all the tests. It was time to talk about price. He then said,

- "Your car seems to be in great condition. You took great care of it and it shows. That is why I am interested in buying it. How much are you asking for?"
- *"I was asking for US$3,500,"* he paused. *"But you were the only one out of 10 potential buyers who did not try to say how bad my car was. Hence, I am willing to sell the car to you for US$3,200."*
- "Well, this is good. I believe that your price is very generous. Thank you so much. Now if you do not mind me asking, when are you going back to Japan?"
- *"In a couple of weeks. Why?"*
- "I was thinking that since you are used to having a car, how will you manage these two weeks?"
- *"Well, this is a problem for me. I am thinking of renting a car during this time."*
- "How much would that cost you?"
- *"Around US$400."*
- "You see, that makes me think of an idea that could save us both some money. I have lived five years without a car; I can surely manage another two weeks. Would you want to keep the car for the two weeks, and in exchange, reduce the car price by half of your savings from the rental?"
- *"That would work for me, thanks. So we agree on US$3,000, is that right?"*
- "Exactly."

And the conversation continued for a little longer, as they found other opportunities to help each other. Since Gunter was away for most of the two weeks, Mr. Hiroshi took the car for a check-up and remained responsible for damages within that period. Gunter then drove Mr. Hiroshi to the airport when picking up the car. He also saved them time by returning their old plates when going to the Registry of Motor Vehicles to pick up his new plates.

The negotiation above seems easy, almost unreal. More like a dance than a fight. That is how negotiations are supposed to be. Next, we try to understand the elements that make a win-win negotiation, like the one above, a better process.

## Win-Win – What Does the Future Look like?

As Tit-for-Tat generates some solid foundations for a successful collaboration, many may ask: so is that the win-win approach? Yes and no. Though Tit-for-Tat is one form of win-win approach, it is not the only or even the best answer to our negotiation challenges. Win-win goes beyond Tit-for-Tat.

**The win-win approach happens when at least one party tries to get what he or she wants with the other party's consent and without the need to use or display power**. To gain someone's consent, the win-win negotiation can do a myriad of things: persuade, exchange, appease, compensate, etc. As seen above, Gunter did not try to take advantage of Hiroshi when he found that he only had two weeks to sell the car. Gunter had the power there to use time against Hiroshi. Instead, he found a way to make both of them better off with the extra information.

At the end of the day, **the secret of win-win lies in making resistance unnecessary** for the other party. If no one resists, the risks of win-lose disappear. Normally, this is achieved by communicating that a win-win negotiation with us needs no losers. Consequently, they do not need to fear or resist losing and power becomes somewhat irrelevant.

Had Gunter tried to pressure Hiroshi like the other buyers did, Hiroshi would most likely have resisted him. As a result, he would not have gotten the better price. By finding ways to help Hiroshi, resistance became unnecessary and Hiroshi reciprocated instead.

Once resistance is taken out of the picture, collaboration is possible and negotiators can work together towards greater value. This is easier said than done, we recognize. Don't worry, the rest of this book aims to help find the win-win choice in most situations. But one thing we can already mention: **the main tool of win-win is communication**, not power as in the win-lose approach. If done well, a win-win strategy renders power and resistance unnecessary for the negotiation.

Through good communication (positive and consistent), Gunter convinced Hiroshi that he was not trying to take advantage of him. That confirmation probably made Hiroshi feel comfortable to share more information with Gunter. As Gunter got more information, he was able to come up with ideas to create more value for them.

Finally, why did Gunter bother to engage in a win-win approach? It was not for the sake of a long-term relationship, as many would expect. Gunter knew he would never meet Hiroshi again (or the likelihood was minimal). Gunter engaged in a win-win approach to make resistance unnecessary. Without resistance, the parties can more efficiently use their effort and resources at lower levels of friction and pain. As a result, **win-win delivers higher value at lower risk**.

Win-win is an approach that fosters collaboration to deliver more value, and thus it can occur even amongst competitors. For example, Coca-Cola and Pepsi compete fiercely for market share, yet both collaborate in their distribution to some remote markets to reduce costs and remain profitable. Even in wars, all sides often collaborate in accepting the Red Cross and Red Crescent to intervene and take care of the injured.

Make no mistake; win-win also carries risks. Most risks come from its complexity and novelty. Most people do not know what win-win looks like or how to do it well enough. Unfortunately, failure becomes the result and many then stop trying. So before we run the risks, here is a list to prepare us for our win-win attempts:

- **Complexity** – As opposed to the win-lose approach, win-win is a much more complex and delicate process. There is much room for mistakes for the unprepared negotiator.
- **Hardwired** – If we fail to see win-win reciprocation after one or two moves, many go back to win-lose ways. This unfortunately erodes whatever credibility built around our initial win-win efforts and intentions (lack of consistency).
- **Being nice** – Many negotiators mistake collaboration efforts with being nice. If we try to be nice to a hyena, we will probably end up being bitten. Being collaborative and nice are two different things. Remember: positive, but not naïve.
- **Fairness as a 50/50 split outcome** – Many negotiators expect win-win to produce outcomes that split the value in two equal parts (50/50). If not, they get frustrated and walk away from what could be a good deal. A 50/50 split is not necessarily fair. Different needs, resources and potentials may grant different shares of the value produced. There are many ways to look at fairness.
- **False sense of security** – Reciprocal altruism or Tit-for-Tat does not work 100% of the time. Tit-for-Tat did not win all the matches and not everyone reciprocates an altruistic act just because we would.

With greater knowledge and experience, most of the risks above become smaller obstacles to success. Practice makes perfect.

## The Ultimate Test: Win-Lose vs. Win-Win

Which is better after all? Put simply, **win-win is better than win-lose because it can bring more value on average**. Another win-win advantage is that it can actually reverse many of the risks of win-lose and turn them into advantages as seen below:

- **Higher certainty** – Since it is not about power and if the outcome turns out to be win-win, no matter where we stand we are sure to gain.
- **Keep focus** – Without resistance, there will be fewer distractions from our main objective of securing value.

## POINT OF INTEREST

**Outcome or Attitude?**

While most talk about win-win or win-lose outcomes, we believe this to be a misleading use of the terms. Win-win and win-lose are first and foremost intentions, attitudes and eventually processes.

A win-win negotiator is not someone who secures win-win outcomes, but rather someone who has a win-win belief and attempts to negotiate in a win-win way. There is, however, no guarantee of success.

Though we can also use the terms to define outcomes, they give us little insight into the reality of the negotiation. A win-win outcome does not mean the parties negotiated with a win-win attitude. Maybe only one of them did. A win-lose outcome may have been the result of the parties' inability to negotiate win-win, despite their best efforts.

- **Create value** – Without resistance, all the extra resources may be invested in creating more value at lower risks.
- **Preserve potential future value** – A win-win agreement is no guarantee of repeated interactions. And yet, people prefer to negotiate again with whom they shared positive experiences or heard positive things about.
- **Win value tomorrow** – If we close a win-win deal today, even if they have more power tomorrow, they are more likely to reciprocate.
- **Remain ethical** – Without resistance, there are fewer instances where we may feel the need to resort to extreme measures.
- **Keep control** – Being independent from power, it does not matter if we are weaker. We can still lead the process towards higher value for all involved.
- **Enjoy peace of mind** – Win-win feels more like a dance in which the parties are working together towards something good for all. The lower chances of losing reduces the overall fear and anxiety normally associated with negotiations.

The above, however does not mean that we should only negotiate win-win, but rather that we should always investigate the possibility to do so. A good negotiator understands that there are always choices. For example, in situations where we find ourselves with a big power difference and short-term concern, win-lose may well be our better choice.

We do not expect the whole world to enter into one big win-win collaboration, though we would love to see it happen. Until then, adopting the win-win approach can give negotiators a competitive (and evolutionary) advantage. By negotiating more value with less resistance, both sides generate higher returns from their relationships. As a result, they become more competitive than those who negotiate win-lose.

This book is an attempt to help negotiators better master the complexity of win-win negotiations to tap into the greater value potential negotiations have.

# summary

Negotiation is a process that happens whenever at least one person is trying to get another to do or not do something for him or her.

1. Negotiation is **everywhere**.
2. Negotiation is a **process** with a purpose.
3. Negotiation requires a **relationship**.
4. Negotiation has **numerous ways with their own potential risks and rewards**.
5. Negotiation is not game theory or psychology, but benefits from these and other fields to create the right process moves towards a successful outcome.
6. We negotiate to increase substance or relationship value for ourselves.

Win-win and Win-lose are not outcomes, but intentions, attitudes and processes (approaches).

## Win-Lose
- A win-lose negotiation approach uses or demonstrates power over the other.
- **To win** – It is easier if we have a big power difference; and a short-term concern.
- **Risks** – It generates resistance and risks losing certainty, focus, value (today and tomorrow), potential future value, our ethics and peace of mind.

## Tit-for-Tat
- Reciprocal altruism has real strategic advantages for survival or competition.
- Tit-for-Tat is nice (at first), provocable or retaliatory, and forgiving.
- **To win** – Start sending a positive (not naïve), clear and consistent message of focusing on value, based on a simple, interdependent and quick feedback process.
- **Risks** – Real life situations such as single round negotiations, last round betrayal, communication imperfections, emotional escalation, alliances or coalitions. These, however, can be handled in real-life mostly through win-win moves.

## Win-Win
- A win-win negotiation approach gets the other party's consent without the use or display of power.
- **To win** – Communicate to make resistance unnecessary.
- **Risks** – Becoming weak or returning to a win-lose process by mistake due to win-win's higher complexity, confusion with being nice and false sense of security. Additionally, many negotiators are hardwired for win-lose and mistakenly believe that fairness is a 50/50 split outcome.
- **Rewards** – Win-win approaches, on average, bring more value than Win-lose approaches, including higher certainty (less volatility), stronger focus on value, higher value outcome today and in the future, increased future deals, conducive to ethical behaviors, sense of control, lower conflict and anxiety.

# questions

## Easy

1. Why do people negotiate?
2. What is the difference between substance and relationship value?
3. What is the difference between win-win and win-lose?
4. What is the key advantage of win-win?
5. Why is win-lose so prevalent?
6. What do big power difference and short-term concern mean?

## Medium

1. What is negotiation?
2. Is a war a negotiation? Why or why not.
3. Why is negotiation everywhere? Give examples.
4. What are the benefits of believing that negotiation is everywhere? Any risks?
5. Give examples in nature, in your culture or in your life of reciprocal altruism.
6. In your own words, compare the evolution from fighting, to win-lose to win-win.

## Difficult

1. When we say that negotiation is a process, does it mean that negotiation does not require an outcome?
   - Does it mean that negotiation is only one process?
   - Does negotiation have a right answer?
2. Some people say that negotiation is a part of the sales process. Here, we argue that sales is one negotiation process.
   - What is the difference?
   - Which one do you believe in and why?
3. Win-win and win-lose are not outcomes. Do you agree? Why?
4. What are the advantages of thinking about negotiation in terms of risk and reward?
5. Can the more powerful party negotiate win-win? Is it easier or harder for them to do so?
6. How about the weaker party? Can they negotiate win-win against someone very powerful? If so, what do they have to do well?

# scenarios

### Easy

Do you agree with the statement below? Why? What is the logic behind it?

*While power distance is almost a requirement for success in a win-lose negotiation, it is one of the biggest enemies in a win-win negotiation.*

### Medium

Describe the dialogue of one of your recent or memorable negotiations.
1. Was it a win-win or win-lose negotiation? Why?
2. What did you do well?
3. What would you have liked to do differently?
4. How did you feel at the beginning, at the middle and at the end? Why do you think you felt that way?

### Difficult

Revisit the dialogue from the beginning of this chapter.
- *Can I have your food?*
- *No! It's mine. (Nul keeps the food away from Strug.)*
- *But I am very hungry.*
- *So am I. It took me a lot of time to hunt this down. So I can't give you anything. I don't have enough for the two of us.*
- *But I am really, really hungry.*
- *Sorry! No can do.*
- *Just a little bit, please?*
- *I said no! (Turns around and begins to walk away.)*
- *Well, you can see that I am bigger and stronger than you. (Showing flexed arms and chest muscles.) So, you either give me your food now or I will take it from you by force. It is your choice: hungry or dead. What will it be?*
- *Okay. (Gives his food and walks away in hope of finding food somewhere else.)*

Can we make it into a win-win negotiation? How? What would we need to change? Do it for Strug first and then for Nul.

# 03 Challenge Your Negotiation Foundations

**Learning Objectives:**
- Some ideas about negotiation that we usually take for granted
- How some ideas about negotiation prevent us from negotiating win-win
- Several concepts around negotiation value (Pareto Frontier, zero-sum, etc.)
- Do we need trust to negotiate or to negotiate win-win?
- The impact of short- and long-term relationships on negotiations

> "We have met the enemy, and he is us."
> Walt Kelly

Think about a time when we lost something, say our home or car key. We probably went looking for it as soon as we realized it was lost. We looked and looked, but we could not find it. We looked in all of the places we could have left it and in some others just to make sure. We double-checked all the same places and still, no key! Eventually we gave up and, swallowing our pride, we asked for help. We then probably said something like: "I've looked everywhere and I could not find my key. Could you please help me find it?"

Our friend (or partner or child) then starts looking. And, many times, after a short while, they come back with the key in their hands and a smug smile on their faces. We look at them astonished. How could they find it? We were just in that room minutes ago. We looked everywhere. Where was it? And the answer is usually that our key was in some silly place at the top of a shelf, inside a drawer or underneath a magazine.

Now what is the connection between our key and negotiation? None! The story of the search, though, has an important message. We believed we looked everywhere and yet it is clear that we didn't. We were fully and sincerely convinced that we tried everything we could. We were not even lying to ourselves yet the truth is that we didn't try everything. As soon as someone with a different perspective came in, they were able to find our key. What prevented us from finding our own key?

One answer is that someone kept it where we would never find it. Another, and more common, reason is that we probably just assumed that it had to be in a certain number of places. Once we exhausted these possibilities, we simply gave up. The number of possibilities we could think of became the total number of possibilities in our mind. Once these were exhausted, there was nothing else to do. Very logical, but unfortunately this is one of our blind spots. It is not a problem of how smart we are, because it happens to even the smartest among us.

Interestingly, as soon as a person fresh to the problem joins with potentially different assumptions and looks in different places, the result is often success. This doesn't mean that we did not find their keys for them in other instances either. It is a two-way street.

The heart of the matter is that we act within the confines of our assumptions and fundamental beliefs about something. These assumptions can be about where we lost our keys, the meaning of a word or sentence, if human beings are inherently good or bad, where to find the best noodles or about the process of negotiation. Built from direct experience or passed down by others, these assumptions become the foundations of how we think, who we are and what we do. No improvement in negotiations can be achieved without revisiting our assumptions.

Accordingly, we will look a little deeper into three main foundations or beliefs that people have on negotiation: value, relationship and communication. Since we believe that most people built their negotiation assumptions in a win-lose context, it is our goal here to revisit these assumptions from a win-win perspective. Now that we know what negotiation is and can be, we want to start with the most powerful foundations.

As Mr. Miyagi said in the famous movie *Karate Kid 3*:

> "If roots strong, tree survives."

If our thinking is set out right, we will be ready for any negotiation.

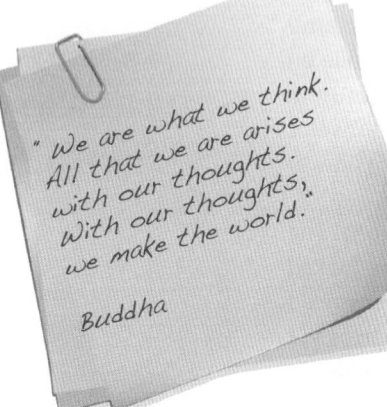

> "We are what we think. All that we are arises with our thoughts. With our thoughts, we make the world."
>
> Buddha

# Value Foundation

## Zero-Sum Negotiations and Monsters

Most people, including many negotiation experts (professors and practitioners), would say they believe that: "Many, if not most, negotiations are zero-sum." "Zero-sum" is a term from economics. Say we find ourselves in a negotiation where for us to get an extra €1 (win), the only way is to take that €1 from the other party (lose). This would be a zero-sum transaction. No matter what we do, value just goes from one hand to another. Nothing is added. Nothing is created. One side's win is another side's loss. The overall result is zero (€1 for me – €1 for the other party = €0 created in the negotiation).

Notice how the zero-sum belief forces a win-lose process. It makes us wonder if such a belief contributed to the widespread adoption of the win-lose approach.

Now that we know the meaning of "zero-sum," we may be asking ourselves: But isn't this the case in negotiations? Not really! But let's be specific. We do agree that **many negotiations do end up being zero-sum**. Most, if not all, negotiators that engage in a win-lose approach end up with a zero-sum outcome. But the fact that they ended with a zero-sum outcome does not mean that the parties could not have done anything else, right?

In other words, to end with a zero-sum outcome does not necessarily mean that the negotiation is zero-sum from the beginning. However, if we believe that many negotiations are zero-sum affairs, we may assume that negotiations have an inherent trait of being zero-sum. As a result, if we find ourselves in a negotiation that seems zero-sum, we will automatically believe that there is nothing we can do about it. It is out of our hands and the only thing left is to take value away from them and towards us. Negotiations require that we behave in a win-lose way. There is no other way.

On the other hand, if we believe that a zero-sum is only one of the ways negotiations can end, our assumption is completely different. For us, a negotiation will only be zero-sum if at least one of the parties behaves in a win-lose manner. But, more importantly, we also believe that the negotiation can potentially be a positive-sum affair if we find ways to make it happen.

Positive-sum happens when for us to get an extra €1 in a negotiation (win), we do not have to take it from the other party (not lose). Or they can get more as well (win).

If we believe that all negotiations have a positive-sum potential, then every negotiation can be approached in a win-win way. It means that by working together, we may find ways to enrich at least one side without forcing the other side to lose or resist. Before we get carried away, let's remember that we may still fail to find a win-win outcome or just choose not to achieve it. But at least we would have maximized our chances for more value or made our appropriate strategic choice. The responsibility and the choice are ours. It is in our hands.

If we believe that we looked everywhere for our key, then we will stop trying. If we believe in monsters guarding the treasure, we will not even go there. But if we believe that there may be places we have not yet looked and that there are no monsters, we may keep on looking. We may need to ask for directions and ideas, but eventually we will find our key or treasure.

So if we believe that **all negotiations can be positive-sum affairs**, we may well find ways to make it so. With a few more practical ideas to help us do this, we will be in a completely different position to pursue value when negotiating.

# A Brief Negotiation Introduction to the Pareto Frontier

To better understand the debate over zero- or positive-sum negotiations, the concept of the Pareto Frontier can be quite helpful. It gets a little technical so if we are already "sold" on the positive-sum potential of negotiations, feel free to jump to the next section.

The Italian economist Vilfredo Pareto defined as "optimal" an outcome in which no one could be better off without making someone else worse off. This definition of optimal outcome became known as **Pareto efficiency** or **Pareto optimality**. However, if someone could still improve the deal for themselves, without making it worse for someone else, the outcome was not optimal. The outcome could still be improved and that became known as **Pareto improvement**. Notice how Pareto improvement follows the win-win approach: we improve the outcome for us (win) at least without making them lose or even helping them win as well.

Why are these concepts important? Because it is widely accepted that Pareto efficiency can be used to measure the success of a negotiation's efficiency in generating maximum value. In theory, if a negotiation still has room for Pareto improvements, then they should be pursued. To do otherwise would be to waste potential value from the negotiation.

But, of course, life is not that simple. In a negotiation with many variables, there can also be many Pareto-efficient outcomes. For example, we may be indifferent whether we get a better product for a higher price or a worse product for a lower price. These different but equally valid Pareto-efficient outcomes can be lined up together in a graph to create a **Pareto frontier: a representation of all Pareto-efficient or best possible outcomes**. This representation in Figure 3.1 can help us understand the three different possibilities.

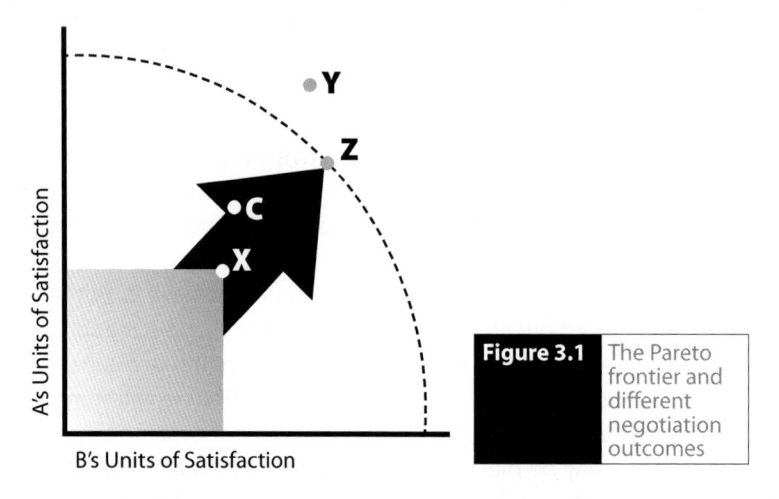

**Figure 3.1** The Pareto frontier and different negotiation outcomes

If a deal (X) falls short of the Pareto frontier, then it is still suboptimal. The parties can still seek Pareto or win-win improvements.

A deal beyond the Pareto frontier (Y) does not allow Pareto improvements since in the real world resources are limited. Only unilateral improvements can be made, usually through win-lose moves: we become better off by making them worse off.

At the Pareto frontier itself (Z), the parties have the best possible deal they could put together and could just stop here.

The Pareto frontier is not just a technicality. It becomes a powerful concept for negotiations if combined with another piece of information. Consider the following: the moment we find a solution such as X that seems good for all, we normally close the deal. The problem is that when we do so, we stop. **Our first deal is most likely Pareto-inefficient**, since chances are quite slim that our first solution lies right at the Pareto frontier.

The Pareto frontier idea should remind us that our first potential deal is not optimal, but rather a good start or safety net. With a potential deal like X in our hands (safety net), we can relax a little and **focus on Pareto improvements** (such as C or D). Such improvements can hopefully carry the final deal all the way to the Pareto frontier (Z).

Now, many of us may be eager to learn how to calculate the Pareto frontier. This would allow us to know when we have maximized the value of our outcomes from every negotiation. Though mathematically possible, we would need to know all the variables in a negotiation to do so. Unfortunately, many of these variables are unknown, complex, subjective or temporary. Consequently, calculating a Pareto frontier for negotiations is an often time-consuming, frustrating and possibly fruitless exercise from a practical standpoint.

But if we do not know where the Pareto frontier is, how can we know when to stop trying to maximize value? It is not about knowing when to stop as much as about wanting to. Although we are responsible for maximizing value, we can stop when we run out of time or get all we wanted. Another hint is when every idea to maximize value makes one of the parties worse off. This probably indicates that the Pareto frontier has been crossed. But like everything else in a negotiation, it is up to us when to stop.

The Pareto frontier helps us see that:

- Every negotiation has a positive-sum and a zero-sum potential.
- It is up to the parties to negotiate in a positive-sum (win-win) or a zero-sum (win-lose) way.
- A positive-sum or win-win approach can happen through Pareto improvements.

# Relationship Foundation

## The Trust, Chicken and Egg Problem

There may be no more commonly accepted truth in negotiation than that its most important element is trust. People from all cultures tend to come together behind this one statement. And even more so if we are talking about a win-win negotiation. However, we are almost afraid to say, this statement is not true. Actually we would go as far as stating that **trust is not needed at all in a negotiation**, win-win or otherwise.

Before we raise the ire of readers with such a statement, let us clarify that we do believe trust makes negotiations easier. Negotiating with someone we trust and who trusts us in return does make for smoother sailing. The crux of the statement is the belief that one needs trust to negotiate, when in fact trust is merely nice to have. Trust alone cannot be responsible for the success or failure of our negotiation.

If our job is like most people's jobs, with the following things: office, desk, clock, phone, salary, deadlines, targets, ties, boss (maybe more than one), clients, suppliers, colleagues, not-so-nice colleagues, etc.; then we, like most people, probably cannot afford the luxury of only negotiating with those we trust, right?

In this case, how often do we enter negotiations knowing very little or nothing at all about the other side? We assume that it is more often than not. So if we do not know much about them, consequently we cannot trust them. If we do not trust them, then we should not be able to negotiate with them. But we do. How?

By building trust along the way? Potentially. And we are still confused because trust is built over time. Trust is not like microwave popcorn that is ready in two minutes. Because it takes time, while we are building it, we find ourselves negotiating already. Actually time and again, people decide to trust someone by how they behave in the negotiation, so parties have to be negotiating already. This alone indicates that many people can negotiate without trust.

An interesting question that follows is: how do people normally negotiate with someone they do not trust? The answer is usually through a win-lose approach, because we need to be extra careful with such a person. But now we are even more confused, because in a win-lose negotiation, aren't the parties at opposite sides behaving like enemies in a fight? How can we build trust with someone we are trying to beat or defeat, usually at any cost? The truth is we can't.

We hope it is becoming increasingly clear that **the need for trust to negotiate is the very thing that pushes trust away**. To require trust before negotiating win-win is to relegate ourselves to a life of win-lose negotiations. So if we do not trust, we negotiate win-lose; but if we negotiate win-lose, we do not build trust. Here is negotiation's own version of the famous chicken-and-egg question. Negotiation, however, does have a solution to its version of the riddle.

The idea is to start without trust and to avoid the win-lose approach. No chicken or egg—we reject them both. We already know that we can negotiate without trust, but we still need to build a relationship, even if short-lived, to negotiate. And to avoid the win-lose approach means the hard task of adopting a win-win approach with someone we do not trust. So what do we do? Like Tit-for-Tat, we should start positive, but not naive.

Why interdependence?
- **Independence** happens when we do not need anyone else. Therefore, we do not need to negotiate. Even if we trust them, we can just do whatever we want on our own.
- **Dependence** happens when we need them or vice-versa. Therefore, neither us nor them need to negotiate. Even if we trust each other, they can just order us to do what they want or vice-versa.
- **Interdependence** happens when there is a mutual need or benefit in working together. It requires negotiation. Even if we do not trust each other, if we need something from one another, we negotiate to make it happen.

*[Margin note: Communicate this.]*

Interdependence is more quickly communicated than trust. It can actually be done in two minutes. When there is a negotiation, there is at least some level of interdependence. All we need to do is identify it clearly.

Once established, interdependence works as a reminder of the basis of and the need for this negotiation relationship. This reminder creates a safer environment as the parties' incentives become better aligned towards a win-win approach. Any party can then initiate a win-win negotiation like Tit-for-Tat. As the negotiation evolves, the parties can observe each other's behaviors and make up their minds about whether to trust.

Most of us would prefer to have trust in our negotiations. The funny thing is that once our negotiation relationships start relying more on interdependence we end up building more trust. Let's explain. As interdependence makes the parties more likely to negotiate win-win, it becomes much easier to develop trust with someone who is working with us; as opposed to people working against us in a win-lose approach.

## Short-term or Long-term Relationships

Late at night, Samia called a pizza delivery place. The dialogue went somewhat like this:

- "Thanks for sharing the choices with me, but I do not want any of them. Could you please do a pizza with only onions, peppers and olives?"
- *"Sorry, we can't do that," the attendant answered.*
- "Why not? You have the pizza; you have the onions, peppers and olives. Why not put them together?" Samia protested.
- *"Do you want the vegetarian pizza then?"*
- "No! I hate the pineapple in the vegetarian pizza. And it comes under the cheese, so I cannot take it off."
- *"Well as I said before, there is nothing we can do."*
- "What do you mean 'nothing we can do?' This is stupid! Do you want to sell me the pizza or not?" Samia threatened.
- *"No! Not to you anymore," the attendant answered before hanging up.*

All other delivery places were closed and Samia had to settle for some unappetizing leftovers in her refrigerator. The pizza restaurant also lost a sale to a willing but more demanding customer.

We could point out several mistakes in the story above, but all in due time. For now, we shall concentrate on Samia being a victim of another bad assumption, an issue that plagues even experienced negotiators. Many negotiators believe that:

- If it is a **short-term** relationship, I apply the win-lose approach; but
- If it is a **long-term** relationship, I use the win-win approach.

This actually seems very consistent with one of Tit-for-Tat's strengths as seen above. The multiple rounds of negotiations made Tit-for-Tat's strategy more successful. In the long term, the risk of retaliation and a lower score encourages people to collaborate. It also seems consistent with the short-term-concern condition for a successful win-lose approach, as there is less fear of retaliation.

Once again, we want to say that these two statements are wrong, but not entirely wrong. It all goes back to the element of choice. It is not necessarily wrong to use the win-lose approach in a short-term relationship. But it is wrong to assume that the relationship will be short term and that one has to use win-lose. Because one never knows the future, therefore what seems a short-term relationship could turn out to be for a longer term.

Of course, if we behave in a win-lose fashion towards them, they are unlikely to want to negotiate with us again. The relationship may have become short-term as the result of our behavior. In believing it was going to be a short-term affair, we chose to act in a win-lose fashion. As a result, we created too much resistance and friction in the relationship, destroying any long-term potential it could have. The relationship became a victim of our self-fulfilling prophecy.

Negotiations are not only zero-sum, but have the potential for both zero- and positive-sum. In the same spirit, relationships are not short term or long term before they begin, instead they have the potential for both. A relationship will only be confirmed as short term or long term at the end as a result of how one negotiates.

If relationships are not predefined, but rather a consequence of how one negotiates, then **the length of a relationship is a choice** — one that we can make before the negotiation. But why would we do so? Deciding that a negotiation is short term before it starts limits our ability to identify the potential for future negotiations. The contrary is also dangerous. Deciding on a long-term relationship before the negotiation makes us underestimate signs that it should actually be a short-term engagement.

However, like Samia, most negotiators ignore that choice. We do not even process it. We simply see a negotiation before us and assume that it is either short term or long term. Then, more like a reaction than a plan, we act in accordance with the "recommended" negotiation approach: short term = win-lose or long term = win-win.

If the length of the relationship is a choice, so is the approach adopted. Wal-Mart, Carrefour and Tesco have long-term relationships with a large number of suppliers. Many of these suppliers claim that their negotiations consistently follow a win-lose process with them on the losing end. Why do they not walk away? Some suppliers just can't afford to leave or to retaliate, so they take the beating. Then again, most people or companies lack the power distance of Wal-Mart, Carrefour or Tesco. In any event, the conclusion is that **relationship length and negotiation approach are choices independent of each other**.

Since most of us are in a different position from Wal-Mart, Carrefour or Tesco, the choice of a win-lose approach even for the short term is riskier. Back to Samia's story, had she treated the pizza attendant with a little more patience and respect, she might have found someone more willing to help. It could even have led Samia to become a regular customer of the pizza delivery place. However, her aggressive win-lose behavior, in a Tit-for-Tat style, invited an abrupt end even to the short-term interaction.

# Communication Foundation

Let's start by reading the email message below:

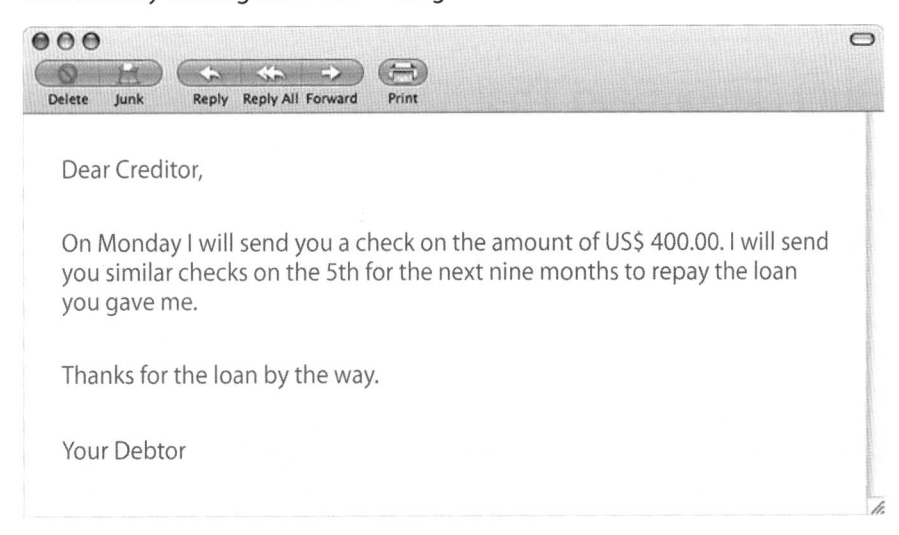

> Dear Creditor,
>
> On Monday I will send you a check on the amount of US$ 400.00. I will send you similar checks on the 5th for the next nine months to repay the loan you gave me.
>
> Thanks for the loan by the way.
>
> Your Debtor

Seems like a nice and harmless email, doesn't it? It probably was intended as such. Now here was the answer:

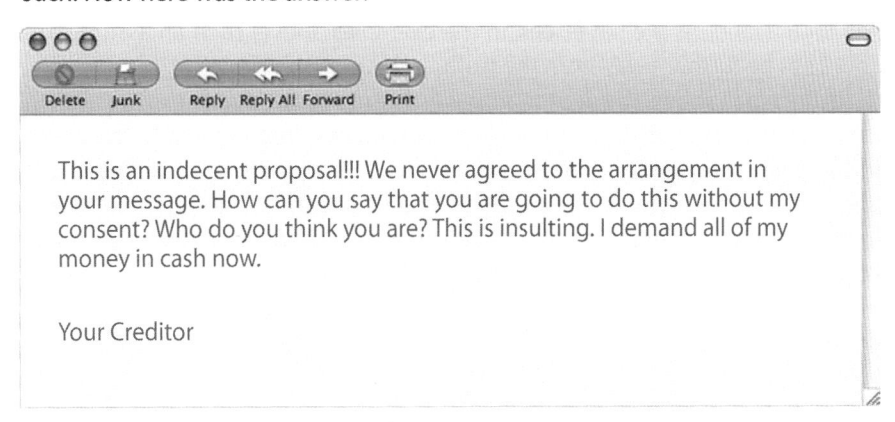

> This is an indecent proposal!!! We never agreed to the arrangement in your message. How can you say that you are going to do this without my consent? Who do you think you are? This is insulting. I demand all of my money in cash now.
>
> Your Creditor

We are all aware of the mysteries and traps behind email communication. Most of us probably have a similar experience to the above. Let's look at another example.

Together with some colleagues, we ran and collected the results of several rounds of a negotiation exercise with people from all over the world. The exercise was similar to the computer tournaments which Tit-for-Tat competed in and provided clear choices too. In addition to the choices of collaborating or defecting, the players could also choose to play neutral. Room for misunderstanding was minimal unlike the email above.

Around 80% of the players indicated they wanted to start with a "wait-and-see" strategy. These players defined wait-and-see as the strategy of reciprocation. They wanted to start not making any moves (wait) until the other side made a positive or negative move (see). Then they would just reciprocate: positive with positive or negative with negative.

Curiously, at closer look, most of their first moves were defections and not neutral as one would expect. How does that make sense? Should they not, consistent with their intended strategy, start with a neutral message to wait and see what the other does first?

## But I Never Said That. Did I?

When asked, the players justified their defection move as a means of protection. While they wanted to wait-and-see, they also wanted to avoid a loss from the start. If on their first move they collaborate or wait (neutral), but the other side defects, they start with a loss. Thus to avoid a bad start, most negotiators defected, not intending to gain over the other, but as protection from losing.

The unfortunate consequence is that the other side is unaware of the defector's true motivation. The first-move defection is mainly interpreted as a win-lose attack. Since the other party also does not want to lose, they get afraid and defect in the next round. A death spiral of defections ensues in what economists call a "prisoner's dilemma". No one has the incentive to stop defecting or even knows how this death spiral really started. Trust and value are destroyed in the process.

Why do bad things happen to good people? Why do so many negotiations go wrong like the ones above even when people have positive intentions? One of the reasons is that most people believe that what they say is what the other side will understand. As we have seen in the examples above, such an assumption could not be further away from the truth.

In the email above, the debtor probably meant and believed he expressed his message as a proposal. Unfortunately, he was unclear in it. Limited to the words in the email, the creditor had no way to know what the debtor really meant. She then (mis)interpreted the message as a unilateral decision by the debtor. In the negotiation exercise, the players who intended to wait-and-see most hoped the other side would show they wanted to collaborate. But despite their best intentions, they ended up sending a message of defection that indicated aggression.

Here are some conclusions that follow from the examples above:

- What I say ≠ what they understand (A ≠ B).
- What I say ≠ what I think I said (A ≠ $A_1$).
- So what I think I said ≠ what they understand ($A_1$ ≠ B).

In sum, **my intended message and the impact it generates are not necessarily the same.** In negotiation, this is called the "**intent-impact gap.**"

Why does this happen? Because people are much less aware in their communications than they think. Because when we speak, we have a context in our head that is rarely communicated. But also because as the singer Sting croons:

> "Every move you make, every breath you take, I will be watching you."

Scary thing, isn't it? Even more so if we recall that Sting was in a band called The Police. As they watch us, they interpret whatever they want. We may not even know they are watching. So how can we possibly tell what they are interpreting?

Which leads us to another conclusion: **everything we say, do, don't say or don't do, sends a message.** Not necessarily the one we intended. Maybe we intended nothing at all or did not realize we were communicating. It doesn't matter. They are still watching us. And as they watch, they interpret the messages we do not even know we are sending. Because we send so many signals in our communication, we need to get better at it both in quantity and quality.

## First Impressions Matter. A Lot.

Let's go back to the negotiation exercise example described earlier. Remember the 80% who said they would wait-and-see including those who defected in the first round? Well, guess what? In the second round, many of them repeated the other side's first move. So if the other party defected, collaborated or went neutral in the first round, the original party did exactly the same in the second round. But what do we think the other parties mostly did in the second round (Table 3.1)?

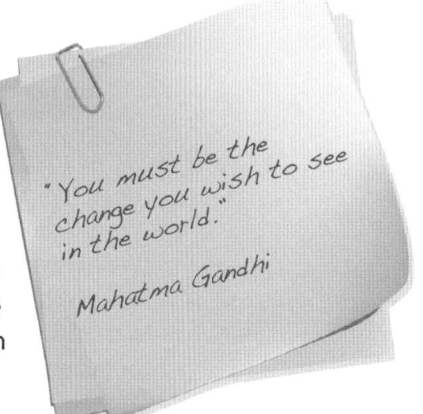

*"You must be the change you wish to see in the world."*
*Mahatma Gandhi*

|  | Round 1 | Round 2 |
|---|---|---|
| Wait-and-See Party | Defect | Collaborate, Defect, or Neutral |
| Opponent | Collaborate, Defect, or Neutral | ? |

**Table 3.1**
"What will they do?"

They defected. Imagine that the Opponent saw a defection come in the first round. What would they think? As seen before, they probably believe the Wait-and-See party is actually a win-lose negotiator who would maintain this tactic in the second round. So the logical thing for the Opponent to do is to protect themselves or retaliate by doing the same: defect.

The perverse effect of this logical reaction by the Opponent is the impact on the third round and beyond. We probably can foresee what is about to happen (Table 3.2).

|  | Round 1 | Round 2 | Round 3 |
|---|---|---|---|
| Wait-and-See Party | Defect | Collaborate, Defect, or Neutral | ? |
| Opponent | Collaborate, Defect, or Neutral | Defect | ? |

**Table 3.2**
"Can I see the future?"

Indeed, more defections. Let's try to understand why. After a defection in the second round, the Wait-and-See party will probably think along one of the following lines:

- If Opponent did 1st round defection + 2nd round defection (which means that they could very well be another Wait-and-See party), then they are clearly going for defection in the 3rd round so we also need to defect.
- If Opponent did 1st round neutral + 2nd round defection, we do not really know why they went neutral at first. But it doesn't matter because we are now winning and to continue our advantage we need to defect in the 3rd round.
- If Opponent did 1st round collaboration + 2nd round defection, then they were not very smart and probably feel that we took advantage of them. They are probably angry and are clearly going for defection in the 3rd round so we also need to defect.

All told, no matter what we think, we seem stuck with defecting. This is the death spiral of defections (prisoner's dilemma) mentioned a few pages ago. We are caught in a process that neither side ever wanted. How did this happen? Well, we now know how. We just saw it above. But how did we let this happen? We may have figured out by now that it all started with our very first move. A big part of the problem is the wait-and-see strategy. Another is the fear of losing and of taking risks in the first round.

The wait-and-see strategy is based on the hope that someone else will take the risk of initiating collaboration. In other words, we hope to get lucky. Since most people share this outlook, the end result is continual defections. A common example of this behavior in highly competitive industries is engaging in price wars. The wait-and-see strategy is not a reciprocation strategy as many believe it to be, but rather a fear-based, reactive strategy.

What is the difference? Reciprocation is a rational response to another person's moves, while reaction is an emotional response. When we reciprocate, we do so with a clear intent of supporting or influencing their future behavior. When we react, we are just responding to something past. Reciprocation means we are still in control if we decide the direction taken does not serve us, while reaction means giving control away. The significance of this is reciprocation's success as a strategy as seen before with reciprocal altruism.

Tit-for-Tat owes something else to its success: proactivity or the initiative to collaborate in the first move. Tit-for-Tat is actually a **proactive reciprocation strategy**. It is neither passive nor reactive. Tit-for-Tat takes the opportunity and the risk of the first move to show the way and lead the other party into collaboration.

Indeed, collaborating in the first move is risky. Leadership is risky. And there are about 80% of people willing to wait-and-see. If our message makes sense to them, these people will likely follow our lead. They will probably welcome our intention to collaborate any day, over defection. And so our leadership is quite likely to succeed.

Though we all know that leadership has risks, have we ever asked ourselves about the risk of not leading? The risks are many: no control, defection spirals, less deals and lower value. Plus, in real life, it is not only about our first negotiation move.

Within a negotiation, there are several new process moments (new beginnings) where the parties will wonder how to continue. If one is not well aware and fails to act proactively, many opportunities that lead towards value will just pass by. So **the risk of not leading tends to be much greater than that of leading**.

Being positive does not mean being naïve. There is a real risk in being proactive and we should try to reduce it whenever possible. Thus, we can adapt how we communicate our collaborative message without changing what we want to say.

One last word: when emotions run high and misunderstandings are a possibility, we may not want to reciprocate as fast. Remember, the other side's defection in Round 2 may have been a mistake or just out of fear. Consistency in a positive process can send a message that it is safe to follow us. It increases the chances that they will change their behavior. And if this happens, we just got them to follow the process we wanted. We then have succeeded in our first negotiation challenge. Congratulations!

# summary

There are several assumptions that guide our negotiation behavior. Some are more helpful than others.

## On Value, Zero-sum and Positive-sum

The Pareto frontier shows how many, if not most, negotiations are probably not zero-sum, though they may end up being zero-sum. Every negotiation can be approached in a win-win way.

- Every negotiation has a positive-sum and a zero-sum potential.
- It is up to the parties to negotiate in a positive-sum (win-win) or zero-sum (win-lose) way.
- A positive-sum or win-win approach can happen through Pareto improvements.

## On Trust and Interdependence

- Trust is not needed at all in a negotiation, but rather it is nice to have.
- Trust is neither as present, nor can be built, as fast as we would like.
- The mistaken need for trust to negotiate makes trust harder to build.
- Interdependence is the real source of good relationships in negotiation.
- The relationship length (short-term and long-term) and negotiation approach (win-win or win-lose) are choices that are independent of each other.

## On Communication and Process

- Intent-impact gap = my intended message and the impact it generates are not necessarily the same.
- Every thing we say, do, don't say or don't do sends a message.
- Tit-for-tat is actually a proactive reciprocation strategy.
- The risk of not leading tends to be much greater than that of leading.
- We can adapt how we communicate our collaborative message without changing what we want to say to increase persuasiveness and align our impact.

# questions

## Easy

1. What is the Pareto frontier?
2. What are Pareto efficiency, Pareto optimality and Pareto improvement?
3. What does the Pareto frontier teach us?
4. What is the difference between dependence, independence and interdependence?
5. What is the intent-impact gap?
6. What is a proactive reciprocation strategy?

## Medium

1. Why does a negotiation that ends zero-sum not necessarily mean it is zero-sum from the beginning? What is the difference? Can every negotiation potentially end zero-sum?
2. Why is our first deal most likely to be Pareto-inefficient?
3. How do we know when to stop creating Pareto improvements?
4. How does the intent-impact gap affect our negotiations?
5. Why should we lead our negotiations? What is the risk of not leading?
6. What exactly should we lead in to prevent running unnecessary risks?

## Difficult

1. Can all negotiations really be positive-sum affairs?
2. Why can every negotiation be approached in a win-win way? Would that be helpful? Why?
3. Why do we not need trust in negotiations? Why does it push trust away?
4. Why does game theory link short-term with win-lose and long-term with win-win? Do you think it is correct? Why?
5. What is the problem with the assumption: *"What I say is what they will understand?"* What should I do?
6. Why does "everything we say, do, don't say or don't do" send a message?

# scenarios

## Easy

*Game theory is just that! It is a game and thus it operates with a nice and stable set of rules. It is a theory and thus it has no commitment to practical applicability. Negotiation operates within a messy and noisy environment where the rules are constantly rewritten. Thus game theory helps to explain tendencies, but not finalities.*

Do you agree with the paragraph above? Why? What are the consequences?

## Medium

*As negotiators we are communicators. As communicators, we communicate 100% of the time, thus in a negotiation we have to be attentive to everything we say, do, don't say or don't do.*

1. Do you agree?
2. Why?
3. How should we do it?
4. If not, what should we do instead?

## Difficult

Recall the earlier e-mail conversation in this chapter. How would you have responded to the second email message?

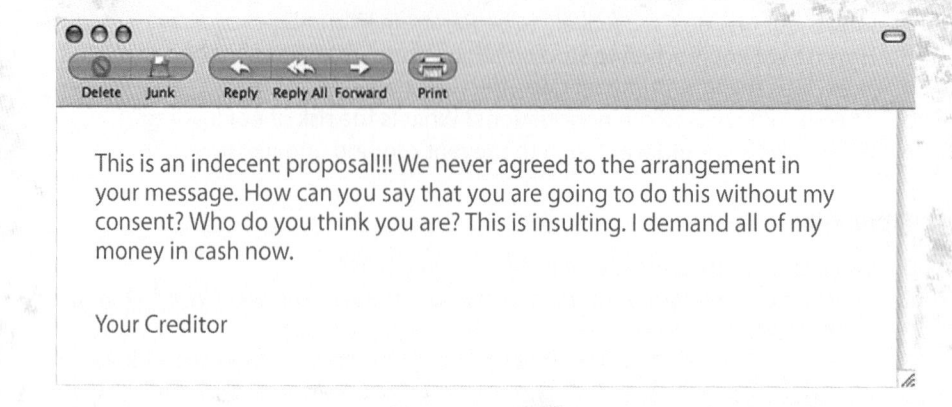

> This is an indecent proposal!!! We never agreed to the arrangement in your message. How can you say that you are going to do this without my consent? Who do you think you are? This is insulting. I demand all of my money in cash now.
>
> Your Creditor

# PART 2
# PREPARE FOR THE NEGOTIATION!

By now, we understand better what negotiation was, is and can be. We also have the right thinking foundations or assumptions about some of the most important elements of a negotiation: value, relationship, trust, communication and leadership. We are now ready for the next phase. In Part 2, Prepare for the Negotiation, we intend to help you do just that: prepare!

Okay, so now we are excited about the car we bought from Mr. Hiroshi. It is still just an old Toyota Tercel, but it is red like a Ferrari and it is running pretty well. We decide to go for a road trip. What would we do to prepare for this trip?

We would probably start by figuring out where we want to go. Once this is sorted out, we will look at a map for the best route to the chosen destination. We may choose the fastest route, the easiest, the most scenic or even one with a stop somewhere exciting. All these choices are fine. It's our road trip after all. Let's pack our bags and go!

Well, wait a minute! Knowing where to go and how to get there is not enough. Ours is still a small, fragile car. No matter how good our car is, any road trip carries risks. Most risks are common, such as running out of gas or oil, low amount of brake fluid, a flat spare tire, wrongly pressurized or worn tires, the engine doesn't start, etc. With a little extra preparation, we can easily prevent most of them. After all, we do not want to be caught unprepared in the middle of the journey and ruin all the fun!

So, we drive to a gas station and fill our tank, check the oil, the condition of the tires and their pressure, the battery, the wipers, the brakes, etc. We buy some snacks and drinks to make the trip more pleasant. We withdraw some money from the ATM machine since, as my Dad has always told me, it is better to have cash in a crisis. We quickly think if we need to go to the toilet before we leave, then off we go. We are now ready to enjoy our road trip!

We recommend preparing for a negotiation following the same steps for a road trip. This preparation involves three steps (Table P2.1):

Table P2.1

| Road Trip | Negotiation |
| --- | --- |
| Choose our destination | Choose our goal (vision) |
| Choose the best route | Choose our strategy |
| Anticipate common problems | Aniticipate critical moments |

And before we ask: why not just buy a GPS? There is no GPS for negotiations yet. I am sorry. We will have to learn how to read maps. So let's get started!

# VALUE **NEGOTIATION:** A MAP

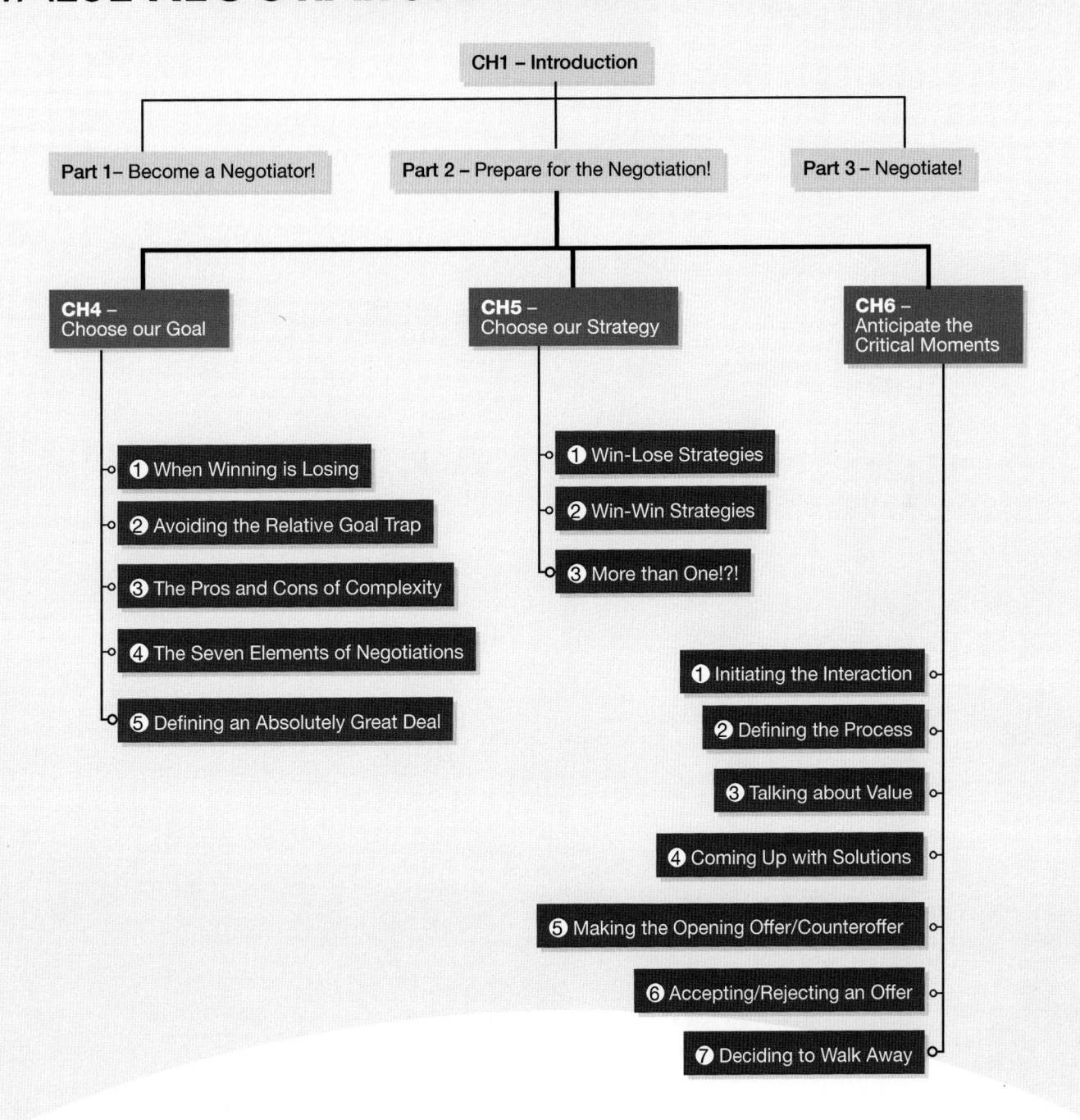

- **CH1 – Introduction**
  - **Part 1** – Become a Negotiator!
  - **Part 2** – Prepare for the Negotiation!
    - **CH4** – Choose our Goal
      1. When Winning is Losing
      2. Avoiding the Relative Goal Trap
      3. The Pros and Cons of Complexity
      4. The Seven Elements of Negotiations
      5. Defining an Absolutely Great Deal
    - **CH5** – Choose our Strategy
      1. Win-Lose Strategies
      2. Win-Win Strategies
      3. More than One!?!
    - **CH6** – Anticipate the Critical Moments
      1. Initiating the Interaction
      2. Defining the Process
      3. Talking about Value
      4. Coming Up with Solutions
      5. Making the Opening Offer/Counteroffer
      6. Accepting/Rejecting an Offer
      7. Deciding to Walk Away
  - **Part 3** – Negotiate!

# 04 Choose our Goal

**Learning Objectives:**
- Why we should care if our goal is relative or absolute
- How complexity impacts a negotiation
- What the different body parts of the negotiation anatomy are (Seven Elements framework)
- How to best set our goal to get what we want

Jean Pierre (JP) long wanted to vacation in Cancun, Mexico, to experience the Mayan culture and pyramids. On his second day there, after visiting some impressive ruins, he came across a few shops. They were clearly tourist traps, but JP spotted in one of them a fascinating Mayan artifact. Since he always fancied himself as a good negotiator, he decided to go for it. He entered the store and with his beginner's Spanish asked:

- "How much does this cost?" pointing to the artifact.
- *"250 pesos."*
- "Wow! That is too expensive."
- *"Okay then, how much do you want to pay?"*
- "Well, I am willing to pay… 20 pesos."
- *"What? 20 pesos! There is no way I can sell it for 20 pesos. Have you seen how finely crafted this is? This was done by a local artisan, who died a few years ago. It is one of a kind."*

And for about 10 minutes they discussed how good or bad the artifact really was. Eventually, the shopkeeper said:

- *"Okay, you seem to really want this, so to help you out, I can offer you a special one-time-only discount: 200 pesos."*
- "Sorry, it is still too expensive. I can pay 25 pesos."
- *"This is an insult! I come down 50 pesos and you only come up five?! Do you know how long it takes to carve such a piece?"*

And the discussion went on again for another 10 minutes. But JP would not give in so easily and eventually the shopkeeper realized that and said:

- *"Alright then. I am willing to go as low as 150 pesos. I am only doing this because you are my first client of the day. But this is as far as I can go."*

JP paused for a short while, shook his head and said:

- "I am very sorry, madam, but it is still too expensive."

The shopkeeper then paused. Not a two-second pause, more like a two-minute pause. JP stood there, feeling awkward, but knowing he was getting somewhere. Finally, the shopkeeper broke the silence:

- *"Okay then, sir. If 150 is still too expensive, how much do you want to pay?"*
- "I said I wanted to pay 20 pesos, but since you are being flexible I believe I can pay 30 pesos."

The shopkeeper shook her head unhappily. She suddenly stood up and went through a door at the back of the shop. JP could hear some vivid conversation going on, but couldn't understand it. After a few more minutes, the shopkeeper returned and said:

- *"Okay, my husband told me that I can offer this for 50 pesos."*
- *"But I offered you 30."*
- *"I know, but 50 is the best I can do. If you do not want it, it is okay, you can leave."*
- *"Fine then. Fifty pesos!"* JP answered after the threat of the shopkeeper.

JP left the store triumphant. He got a 250-pesos artifact for only 50 pesos. He negotiated an 80% discount. That was even beyond his initial expectation. He felt great.

# When Winning is Losing

As JP returned to his hotel with his prized artifact, he did not know if he was happier with the artifact or with his success in negotiation. Later that day, as he went for the first time to the city center, the first shop he saw had a basket filled with the exact artifact he just bought. The only difference was a sign announcing, "Three for 30 pesos!" What a blow! Worse still, every souvenir shop he saw had exactly the same basket with the same artifact at the same price.

Every time he walked by one of those signs, it was like an Mayan spear piercing through his heart. Suddenly, the trip was not as fun anymore. It was not so much the money paid, but rather his feelings of failure and being manipulated. To think for a second there, he felt guilty for taking advantage of the poor shopkeeper. How quickly the sweetness of victory can turn bitter, JP thought to himself.

After JP returned home, he agreed to an interview. The interviewer's goal was to try to understand and learn more about his story.

> Dear JP, we know that your story was very painful. So thank you for agreeing to this interview. We believe that many of our readers can empathize with your story.

> You are welcome. Indeed it was very, very painful. I want to share my story so that others don't have to suffer like I did.

> Thank you once again. Let's be frank; had you not seen the artifact in other stores, you would still be happy, wouldn't you?

> Possibly. But being happy and closing a good deal are two different things. And I was probably happier for believing I had gotten a good deal. I could keep on believing that, but it would have been an illusion. I got a bad deal.

> Was she able to fool you because she knew you wanted the artifact?

Not really. Everyone who asks about the price of products indicates interest. Asking the price or even negotiating doesn't mean a willingness to pay more than its real value.

> So was it your lack of preparation or information then?

That surely contributed. Normally, I would have thanked her for her first price and looked around more to check prices. I had the time, but I am not sure now why I didn't do it.

> Maybe because she has more experience than you in these kinds of negotiations?

Possibly. She surely does have a lot more practice with bargaining than I have. But if I realized she was fooling me I could have walked away. This doesn't explain why I did so poorly.

> So when do you believe you really lost the negotiation?

Right at the very beginning. As soon as she asked for 250 pesos and I replied with 20 pesos.

> Why? Was it because you were already offering more than the market price?

Well, yes, but it was also the message it sent. As I reacted to her price and followed her lead in bargaining, she confirmed I had no idea of the real value of the artifact. She understood, even if intuitively, that I would feel successful by how many concessions I managed to extract from her, if I would get her to go below her bottom line, how low I would get her to go, and how uncomfortable she would feel towards the end.

> But how does knowing this help her?

> By knowing my goal or how I measure it, she can fake concessions to manipulate me. She could make me feel like I won, when I was actually grossly overpaying for it.

> How exactly did she manage to manipulate you?

> It was actually my fault. I had a relative goal: bring the price as low as possible from 250 pesos. This meant that I relied on a reference outside of my control: her price instead of, for example, how much I wanted to pay. By manipulating the reference, she manipulated me. My success depended on her which gave her power over me.

> Was there anything you could have done differently?

> Sure! Lots of things. I could have avoided reacting to her price. She invited me to haggle and I accepted, without realizing that I was entering a win-lose game in a losing position. I could have proactively suggested a new process where I had better chances of winning. Like I said before, I could have just thanked her for the price and looked around. Tell her that I would be back if I found her price to be competitive.

> Anything else?

> Sure. The first and best thing I could have done was to reject my own relative goal. Instead of feeling successful by how much I took from her or how much she lost, I should have negotiated for the fair market value of the artifact.

> So should one always reject relative goals?

> Not necessarily. If I negotiate for something small such as the artifact, I may decide that 50 pesos doesn't represent much in the larger scheme of things. I may not care. However, if I go into a more important or complex negotiation, I will be careful with relative goals as the risks of mistakes or manipulation increase dramatically.

> JP, thank you once again for your time. I believe your experience will benefit thousands of readers and negotiators.

> Anytime. It was fun actually. Bye now.

> Can I see the artifact by the way?

> Yes. I keep it here as a reminder. Here you are.

> But it is beautiful.

> I know! I know.

# Avoiding the Relative Goal Trap

If we have a relative goal, the trap is that we will likely negotiate win-lose even if we do not want to. We will inevitably compare how well we do in relation to the other party as in a competition. We will only see our success at their expense. As JP's interview shows, this is a dangerous trap.

Each day, sellers around the world increase prices just so they can give discounts to unaware buyers with relative goals. Though dangerous, the relative goal is quite a simple trap—one we create for ourselves without thinking. Many of us fall into this trap more often than we would like to admit. If a party makes more than the other, they feel like a winner and regard the other as a loser.

So what should we do instead? We should **seek absolute goals**. And even that is not so easy. Imagine we want to buy a special book and research to find out it is worth $100. Our goal is to buy it before the end of the week and pay no more than $100. We go to a small bookstore and say:

- "I am interested in the book on display. I have no time for hassle and I already researched its fair price. I am willing to take it now for $80. Deal?"
- "Yes!" replies the bookstore owner without any hesitation.

How do we feel now? We should feel great. We got it cheaper and faster than our goal. Most people, however, can't enjoy this. They feel they have lost something as a little voice inside them whispers: "It was too easy. I paid too much. The product has a problem." Maybe they are right or maybe, just maybe, the shop's policy is to give a 20% discount for books on display. We don't know because we never asked. But what we can see is the trap from making our goal a relative one. Why is it so hard for us to avoid this trap?

Part of the answer comes from a long, long time ago. Humans evolved in small, social environments, where every negotiation meant a gain or loss in status, then a matter of life and death. Status is a naturally relative element as it is measured by comparing ourselves to others. Since every negotiation was a competition for status, it is not surprising that after centuries they became closely associated.

Let us disagree with Einstein for a few moments, shall we? Not everything is relative. He is likely right in physics and we defer to him in that area. But as the human race evolved into larger societies, daily negotiations do not impact status half as much. As we saw with Tit-for-Tat, trying to beat every opponent actually leads to a lower average outcome. Nowadays, it is gaining value rather than defeating someone that ultimately defines status. So what worked a long, long time ago, may actually be the opposite of what works in today's radically different social environment.

An absolute goal protects us from manipulation as it becomes harder for them to know and exploit our limits. An absolute goal gives us a clear milestone for success and makes it easier to explain our outcome to third parties. It reduces second-guessing and regret. In decision theory, there is the distinction between Satisficers and Maximizers:

- **Satisficers** – Good enough is good enough. Satisficers have an objective in mind and feel happy when they get it.
- **Maximizers** – Good enough is not good enough. Only the best will do. Maximizers are only happy if they get, have or are more than their neighbor.

Absolute goals make us satisficers. The good news is that decision theory found satisficers to be happier than maximizers and, as seen above, more successful as well. While we may still carry relative goals of the maximizer within us, the discipline of absolute goals can help us focus and succeed on what really matters: value.

# The Pros and Cons of Complexity

As JP said above, one does not need to always reject relative goals, only when it matters. So if we are in a simple negotiation with little value at stake, the risk of a relative goal may not be as high. But most of the negotiations that bring real value in our life are not as simple as JP's story. On the contrary, they are often quite complex.

If a relative goal is already a risk, it becomes even riskier as the negotiation grows in complexity. With more external references, a negotiator becomes even more exposed and vulnerable to manipulations. Therefore, as the negotiation complexity increases, so does the importance of absolute goals.

On the positive side, the higher the complexity, the higher the negotiation's potential for value. It can be much easier to reach agreement in a complex negotiation as it inherently provides more possibilities than a simpler negotiation.

So while complexity is bad for negotiations with relative goals, it is actually good for negotiations with absolute ones.

For the above reasons, a negotiator will do well to recognize negotiation factors that increase its complexity. Complexity in a negotiation increases in layers with one or more of the following characteristics:

- **Repeated interactions** – A negotiation with multiple rounds or different negotiations with the same parties.
  - *Complexity* – Trade-offs between short-term and long-term risks and rewards, i.e., future consequences of current actions.
- **Multi-party** – A negotiation with more than two people either present at or absent from the negotiation table.
  - *Complexity* – More individuals trying to pull the negotiation in different directions.
- **Intra-organizational** – Interconnected or linked negotiations such as internal negotiations on a strategy to negotiate with a big supplier.
  - *Complexity* – The limitations one negotiation imposes on the others as well as ensuring communication flow.
- **Multi-issue** – A negotiation with more than one topic to discuss.
  - *Complexity* – Keeping track of all issues' potential risks and rewards, avoiding oversight or information overload.
- **Tangible and intangible issues** – The existence of tangible issues we can put a price on (price, benefits, volume, time, quantity, quality, etc.) and intangible issues that we can't (trust, reputation, precedent, pride, etc.).
  - *Complexity* – The lack of similar currency to evaluate the value of both tangible and intangible issues makes trading between them harder.

### POINT OF INTEREST

**Cross-Cultural & Complexity**

We believe cross-cultural is a terminology that, when applied to negotiation, goes well beyond nationality. Cross-cultural relates to nationality, gender, age, religion, profession, education, social, and marital status, family, etc. Thus, every negotiation is a cross-cultural exercise since no two people will have a similar combination of cultures.

This does not mean that the cross-cultural nature of negotiation is not complex; just that it is not specific to some negotiations.

# The Seven Elements of Negotiation

In the seminal book *Getting to Yes!*, Fisher, Ury and Patton defined the seven elements of a negotiation. These seven elements work as the anatomical parts of the negotiation body. Every negotiation has them all, and each negotiation move can be classified into one or more of these elements. The seven elements divide a negotiation into smaller pieces so we can more easily understand, discuss, prepare, conduct and learn about negotiations.

We believe that the seven elements are as helpful to negotiation as supply and demand is to economics and anatomy to medicine. Hence, this book will use the seven elements terminology extensively and we have defined them below:

1. **Relationship** is built through the combination of intangible factors such as behaviors and emotions (trust, respect, friendship, family ties, status, etc.) that take place when two or more people interact.
2. **Communication** is the conduit for everything that takes place in a negotiation. Used to send and receive messages, it is also referred to as the element of process: the way in which things are communicated during a negotiation.
3. **Interests** are all the reasons that motivate someone to negotiate. These can be positive (needs, wants, hopes and desires) or negative (fears and concerns).
4. **Options** are all the proposals, suggestions, recommendations and possibilities put forward within a negotiation to satisfy interests towards an agreement.
5. **Legitimacy** is the basis for any argument made to persuade the other party that an option is or isn't acceptable, appropriate, right or fair.
6. **Commitments** are any agreement, oral or written, explicit or implicit, partial or final, made in the course of or at the end of the negotiation.
7. **Alternatives**, or walk-away alternatives, are the opportunities that any party has independently from their counter-parties. One important concept within alternatives is the BATNA (Best Alternative to a Negotiated Agreement), commonly known as "plan B." BATNA is the best one can do if they walk away from the deal.

### POINT OF INTEREST

**Options vs. Alternatives**

Although options and alternatives have a similar meaning in various languages, for negotiation purposes, it is helpful to separate them: alternatives are potential solutions to the interests **outside** of the negotiation, while options are potential solutions to the interests **inside** the negotiation.

# Defining an Absolutely Great Deal

When the CEO of a great multinational company called his best corporate development executive, Maziar, into his office, Maziar was very excited. Upon entering, the CEO went straight into business:

> Hi Maziar! Thanks for coming. Do you remember Project One Million?

> Sure!

PART 2 • PREPARE FOR NEGOTIATION!

> Well, I need you to take over. And before you get too happy about it, you should know it is not going well. So you are to go in and secure $1 million to make some sense out of this project for us before we shut it down.

> So you want me to go there and negotiate it with our partners?

> Yes!

> I have a few questions...

> Just ask.

> Okay. You said you wanted $1 million out of the negotiation, right?

> Yes!

> So if they offer $800K and I help the project save us another $200K, is that okay?

> I think so.

> Now would you prefer me to get the $1 million at any cost, even if that means going to court?

> No, I do not want lawyers between us and our partners. Not for this.

> And what if they offer to pay $750K now or $1 million in six months or even $500K now and another $600K one year from now; which would you prefer?

> I am not sure. I need to think about this one. How many of these questions do you actually have?

> Actually, as I ask them I realize I have more and more. It seems that $1 million is just part of what we want, right?

> Yes, so?

> I am afraid that I do not understand what else is important for you and I fear I could sacrifice too much if I am just focused on the $1 million.

> Good point.

> How about I prepare a brief document with different possible outcomes for you to get your feedback? Would that work?

> Sure. Just let me know when you want to meet and bring the document then. Good luck!

Although the CEO offered an absolute goal ($1 million), Maziar suspected it was too narrow. Further conversation revealed that the CEO valued many other things, which led Maziar to negotiate for a more comprehensive objective. He went from a single bottom-line target to a Negotiation Balanced Scorecard (NBS). A balanced scorecard is a way to measure the success of achieving several different objectives which can be competing and of different relevance. The NBS aims to help negotiators secure the greatest possible value on all objectives without overly sacrificing one for another.

The NBS can give Maziar an absolute goal that takes into account all seven elements of the negotiation. As a result, he is less likely to make mistakes or overlook possibilities. The NBS can guide us to negotiate a great deal. Below we find the seven objectives that can help us prepare our NBS.

## Improve the Working Relationship Between the Parties

In a great deal, parties' behaviors during the negotiation leave their working relationship in better shape than when they started. By "working relationship," we do not mean friendship as many friends may not work well together or under crisis. We actually mean the parties' ability to work together productively and respectfully, even over their differences (conflicts, surprises, misunderstandings, etc.).

A strong working relationship usually allows the parties to arrive at a more efficient and profitable deal. With less suspicion and attrition, they are better able to explore value and mitigate risks. This, in turn, increases the potential for future deals, which may also have great value. After all, the most valuable negotiations are normally those involving repeated interactions (family, boss, employees, clients, etc.). And even if we walk away from a deal, we may want to keep the door open for the future.

## Result from an Effective Two-Way Communication

In a great deal, parties do not waste time or value through poor communication. When the parties talk without listening or listen without talking, they engage in one-way communication. This usually invites reciprocation. As the parties start to ignore each other, progress becomes very slow and frustrating. It usually breeds danger as well since the parties miss potential opportunities, and misunderstandings and conflicts increase.

Good communication should help negotiators minimize the time and effort to pursue maximum value while keeping risks under control. In two-way communication, the parties are listening as well as speaking with clarity and patience. A well-crafted message can minimize the need for repetition and the risk of misunderstanding. In the same way, active listening demonstrates respect and gathers information that can lead to favorable opportunities.

## Satisfy Interests, not Positions

In a great deal, parties focus their attention and resources on what really matters as opposed to what doesn't. This point is well illustrated in the "orange" anecdote from the book *Getting to Yes!*. Two sisters are fighting over the last orange in the house. The mother cuts the orange in half and gives each daughter one half. After she leaves, the younger sister peels her half, eats the fruit and throws away the peel. Meanwhile, her older sister peels her half, throws away the fruit and uses the peel to bake an orange cake half the size originally planned.

The mother fell into the trap of focusing on the daughters' positions (orange), instead of their real interests (fruit and peel). Positions are the parties' inflexible demands, usually a single, narrow and rigid view of what they believe they want. As seen above, the focus on positions usually leads to conflict and to a waste of resources. This, in turn, can either lower the value or destroy the possibilities of a deal. Fights over positions are at the heart of win-lose negotiations.

Beneath every position though are usually several interests that are the real motivations for the negotiation in the first place. The fact that positions are frequently opposing does not mean that interests are as well. As a matter of fact, most, if not all, negotiations involve non-conflicting interests. As the orange anecdote hints, the focus on interests opens new ways for the parties to agree and maximize value.

Value means different things to different people. The orange meant different things to the two sisters. Thus, a great win-win deal identifies the different interests behind the parties' positions. Then, through an efficient and intelligent use of resources, we should satisfy the parties' interests as best as we can.

## Choose the Best of Many Possible Options

In a great deal, parties discuss several potential solutions to combine and use their resources to produce the maximum value possible. Unfortunately, all too often negotiators just share their positions and fail to arrive at a great deal.

A position is the single (inflexible) option a party decides on: "Give me a 20% discount now!" This could be an option, but as the only possibility presented, it becomes a position. Consequently, the perverse effect is having negotiators bring only one option to the table believing it is **the** solution. Well, chances are that the other side will not think exactly alike and conflict will surely emerge.

Every negotiation has many potential solutions. To arrive at a great deal, we have to bring as many options as we can possibly imagine. This exercise greatly enhances the likelihood of finding at least one solution that works for all parties. Coming up with many options also has another advantage. A great deal requires negotiators to work to identify and create the best option. The best possible option, regularly a package of several different options, minimizes waste and realizes the highest value potential of a negotiation.

## Be Based on Legitimacy so that All Parties Believe it to be Fair

In a great deal, the parties do not use power to coerce one another, but agree on an outcome that makes sense and feels fair to them. Few things generate more resistance in a negotiation than feeling forced to accept an option that is seen as unfair. Though it is true that even win-win negotiations can produce unfair outcomes at times, almost everyone will be more easily persuaded to agree on and implement a particular option if they see it as fair.

Thus, basing an argument and a deal on legitimacy is a good idea because it works, not because it is nice to be fair. The latter is a side benefit of legitimacy. However, achieving legitimacy can prove to be harder than it seems. For any negotiation, there is always a potentially wide range of ways to understand what is fair, right or appropriate.

For example, some MBA students were given identical financial information on a sample company. Half of them had to come up with the seller's valuation and the other half with the buyer's. The difference in valuations went as high as 100%, though both groups sincerely believed that their numbers were based on fair and objective calculations.

Culture or even the side taken in a negotiation can alter people's perception of what is fair, right or appropriate. In practice, each negotiator can come up with several legitimate arguments per option to resist imposing their view only. This also enhances the chance that parties will work together to find the one outcome that can satisfy them all.

# Be a Well-Planned Commitment

In a great deal, parties agree to something that is sustainable. A well-planned commitment avoids falling apart at the implementation phase, be it for lack of transparency or flexibility, misunderstanding, unrealistic or undesired targets, etc. As the final goal of a negotiation, the commitment should be crafted with care.

It should develop a clear and coherent framework, yet remain open for future changes. Sustainable agreements are clear, sufficient and operational:

- **Clear** – A deal is clear when the parties share the same understanding on potential communication gaps and ambiguities. One technique is to ask if it can be understood by the person implementing it without reading between the lines.
- **Sufficient** – A deal is sufficient if it covers the negotiators' important issues, thus reducing the need for additional negotiations or future renegotiations.
- **Operational** – A deal is operational when the parties are sure of their abilities and resources to implement it. It also helps to implement a deal that is:
  - *Flexible* – As the unexpected is a fact of life, the deal must leave room for future changes, like the straw that bends with the wind and survives while the strong but rigid oak is torn apart.
  - *Verifiable* – Responsibilities and targets that can be monitored increase compliance as misunderstandings and opportunistic behavior are reduced.

# Be Better than Our BATNA

In a great deal, the parties only close if it is better than anything they can get elsewhere. If the potential deal is worse than that, then it makes little sense to accept it. Thus, before agreeing, it is always helpful to compare the deal at hand to our BATNA. This simple step helps us recognize if a deal is realistically good or bad and allows us to accept or reject it with greater peace of mind.

For example, we get thirsty during a concert and find the bar price for a bottle of water, soda or beer outrageously high. We can buy it; alternatively we can go thirsty, steal someone's bottle, leave the concert or try our luck with the toilet sink water. We may conclude that paying the price is better than our alternatives. It may not necessarily be a fair price, just the best we can do right then.

Ignorance of our alternatives is no excuse to close a bad deal. If we decide to do so, just consider the risk of it being as bad as JP's artifact deal. Though time-consuming, working on our alternatives tends to increase the quality of our deal as it helps us make better decisions.

# summary

## Relative vs. Absolute Goals

- Relative goals influence us to choose win-lose approaches, while absolute goals help us to choose win-win ones.
- Relative goals expose us to manipulation and power moves, while absolute goals protect us and enhance collaboration attitudes.
- Relative goals are particularly risky in complex negotiations, which include:
  - Repeated interactions
  - Multi-party
  - Intra-organizational
  - Multi-issue with tangible and intangible issues

## The Seven Elements of Negotiation

1. **Relationship** is the emotional or intangible link between negotiators.
2. **Communication** is the process of or messages within a negotiation
3. **Interests** are the reasons to negotiate.
4. **Options** are the potential solutions to interests.
5. **Legitimacy** is the argument or process used to promote or reject an option.
6. **Commitments** are the agreements.
7. **Alternatives** are what negotiators seek if they reach no deal.

The Negotiation Balanced Scorecard is a system of interconnected objectives which:

- Improves the working relationship between the parties
- Results from an efficient two-way communication
- Satisfies interests, not positions
- Chooses the best of many possible options
- Is based on legitimacy so that all parties believe it to be fair
- Is a well-planned commitment
- Is better than our BATNA

# questions

## Easy

1. When is winning actually losing in a negotiation?
2. What is the difference between relative and absolute goals?
3. What is the difference between alternatives and options?
4. What is the Negotiation Balanced Scorecard?
5. What is the difference between a working relationship and a normal relationship?
6. What is the difference between interests and positions?

## Medium

1. What is the difference between satisficers and maximizers? Which one are you normally? Give an example.
2. How did the shopkeeper manage to manipulate JP? How did he facilitate it? How could he have prevented it?
3. Why are relative goals so prevalent? What are their risks?
4. How do absolute goals help us negotiate better?
5. How do satisficers and absolute goals go together?
6. What are the pros and cons of complexity?

## Difficult

1. If JP had not seen the artifact being sold more cheaply in other stores, would he have thought that he had a good outcome? Why? Would he be right or wrong? Why?
2. What is culture in negotiation? Why is it not an element of complexity in negotiation?
3. What are the advantages of having a Negotiation Balanced Scorecard? To get a good outcome, do we have to satisfy all seven elements? And what if we don't?
4. What is the advantage of using legitimacy in a negotiation? Give an example.
5. Should we close a deal worse than our BATNA? Why?

# scenarios

## Easy

If someone asked you to work for their company for free, how can you respond to protect your interests by being paid in terms of:
- Interests
- Options
- Legitimacy
- Alternatives
- Commitment
- Communication
- Relationship

Give an answer that suggests you should be paid for your work.

## Medium

*Independently of how much we try to create absolute negotiation goals, if we see someone else getting a better deal in a similar negotiation we will always feel bad. If we close too fast or too easy, we will always feel that we could have gotten more.*

Do you agree or disagree with the statement above? Why? What can we do to help ourselves do better?

## Difficult

After entering a shop, we engage in the following dialogue:

> How much does this cost?

> Two hundred fifty pesos.

> Wow! That is too expensive.

> Okay then, how much do you want to pay?

> Well, I am willing to pay... 20 pesos.

> What? 20 pesos! There is no way I can sell it for 20 pesos. Have you seen how finely crafted this is? This was done by a local artisan, who died a few years ago. It is one of a kind.

What are we doing wrong? How can we change this dynamic? Give examples.

# 05 Choose our Strategy

**Learning Objectives:**
- Why win-lose strategies only have two styles: hard and soft
- How the negotiation tension became the bargaining tension
- Why there are several win-win strategies
- Why we should choose the value negotiation approach
- Why we actually need three negotiation strategies to succeed

Let's return to our road trip for a short while, shall we? After choosing our destination, it is time to get the roadmap and choose the best route to get us there. In the negotiation roadmap, we see two routes to get us to our chosen destination: win-lose and win-win.

These two routes may have several different variations, but it all boils down to the two of them. Let's explore each of them further so that we can better understand the consequences of choosing one over the other.

## Win-Lose Strategies

The win-lose process is also known as bargaining, haggling or positional bargaining since positions are at its core. Before we go any further, let's first recap what we have seen so far on win-lose:

- It happens when one party attempts to get what they want in a negotiation by demonstrating or using power.
- Power is the most important element, but it generates resistance as a reaction.
- Big power difference and short-term concerns are good conditions for win-lose.
- Risks of win-lose are many as compared to win-win.

But there is more. We want to know what win-lose looks like and how it impacts our trip. The win-lose road is interestingly tricky. It starts promisingly simple, straight and easy. "I will take the highway everyone else takes, as it has got to be the best one," we think to ourselves. We have heard several stories of people who succeeded going down that road. "That many people cannot be wrong," we conclude.

Looking at the map, we imagine this magnificent highway to be full of signs, light, space, nice pavements and no speed limit. A few kilometers down, we realize that this beautiful promise of a highway has given way to a narrow two-way mountainous dirt road in the middle of nowhere. There are absolutely no signs, lights, smooth pavements or stops. Instead we find holes, mud, sharp turns, icy patches, cliffs and a heavy rain. If that wasn't enough, cars are constantly coming from the opposite direction with their lights off and at full speed.

65

## The Bargaining Process

If it sounds so awful, why are there so many people who do it? Bargaining is a part of life. It is popular because **it is a simple, well-known and almost intuitive process** that, from time to time, delivers.

From as young as we can remember, we have bargained. We either cried for our mother's milk late at night or haggled to buy a souvenir in a foreign country. And it probably worked. Our mother may not have been very happy or we may not have gotten the best price for our souvenir, but it worked. Whatever "worked" means.

Strangely enough, there is also **a sense of familiarity and comfort around bargaining.** We gather this is probably due to its simplicity and the fact that everyone has experienced it. Everyone can relate to bargaining. Actually, enough people wrongly believe that bargaining and negotiation are one and the same. So what does bargaining look like?

**Figure 5.1** Positional bargaining process

An X-ray of a positional bargaining process resembles Figure 5.1. After some small talk, the parties share their positions, often by committing to a certain price. They go on to reject each other's positions and threaten to leave if their demands are not satisfied. Since no one really wants to leave, they concede value to move their positions linearly closer to one another. This position-threat-move dynamic repeats itself for a while. It ends when parties either find something in between their initial positions (compromise) or realize there is no room for an agreement.

As we can see, bargaining is an unsophisticated and simplistic process. It limits itself to only two of the seven negotiation elements: commitments and alternatives. On one side, the parties concentrate on positional offers and counter offers (commitments). Meanwhile, they implicitly or explicitly exchange threats to walk away (alternatives). Its one-size-fits-all approach ignores the specific risks and opportunities in the different negotiation scenarios. Bargaining is aptly captured in the famous saying "Take it or leave it" ("TioLi").

## The Bargaining Styles: Hard or Soft

There are as many bargaining styles as there are people. Everyone brings their personality into the bargaining process. However, on closer look, all of them fall into two categories based on their tactical focus: hard (alternatives) or soft (commitments). We characterize the two extremes below, knowing that most bargainers are somewhere in between.

*"If you only have a hammer, everything becomes a nail!"*

*Popular saying*

**HARD**

**SOFT**

Hard negotiators focus on the material value of the deal above all else. Power is constantly used to intimidate and dominate to secure a better deal for them. Hard negotiators don't say much more than their positions. They open with extreme offers, reject most other offers and make few but demand many concessions. They easily threaten to walk away (alternatives) to pressure the other party to give them more value.

Soft negotiators also want value but focus on the relationship of the deal above all else. The relationship is constantly mentioned as the source for long-term value. Soft negotiators appear open, friendly, helpful and fair in their positions. They open with what they believe is a fair offer, are uncomfortable saying "no" to other offers and give generous concessions. Soft negotiators easily claim their commitment or trust in the relationship to manipulate the other party into giving them more value.

Both hard and soft negotiators commit similar mistakes when they force their style into all negotiations. By treating every negotiation equally, they ignore its particularities, lose touch with reality and risk making worse negotiation decisions. For example, both negotiators ignore the role that BATNA plays in the decision to either continue talking or walk away. The hard negotiator may threaten to and actually walk away, even when her BATNA is bad, while the soft may never threaten to or walk away, even when his BATNA is good. They let their style, not reality, define their decisions.

## The Bargaining Tension

Have we ever found ourselves in a negotiation where for us to get more money, we felt we had to put pressure on the relationship? Or for us to build a better relationship, we had to sacrifice some of our monetary gains? And as a consequence we felt frustrated that we could not have everything we wanted? Well, we are not alone.

How does this happen? Figure 5.2 illustrates this. On one end, the hard negotiator squeezes the most possible value out of the other party. The relationship is normally damaged in the process and future value-generating potential becomes limited. On the other end, the soft negotiator negotiates to build a relationship, thus sacrifices value today for the longer term. Unfortunately, not only may future interactions never materialize, but even if they do they typically follow a similar low-value pattern. The soft negotiator will continue to sacrifice value whenever he perceives a risk of antagonizing the relationship with the other party.

**Figure 5.2** Styles of hard and soft negotiation

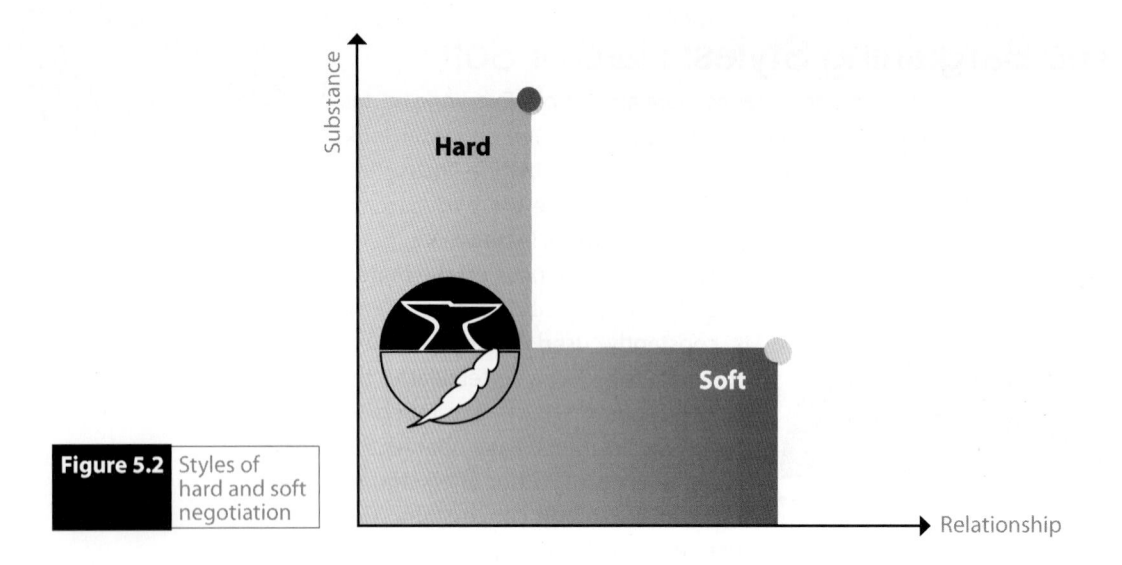

Most people do not see themselves in these two extreme styles. They believe they are somewhere in between and can be harder or softer depending on a number of factors: relevance (important versus trivial), context (professional versus personal), power (more versus less), duration of relationship (short term versus long term), nature of relationship (friend, foe, boss, employee, etc.).

Unfortunately, all factors raised above still share one common thing: we are still choosing a suboptimal combination of substance and relationship. Any combination of **hard and soft styles still forces negotiators to be reactive and sacrifices value** in the process. It is still take it or leave it.

Until recently, this was known as the negotiation tension: for us to make money we had to sacrifice the relationship or vice-versa. In other words, we could never have it all. The general perception is that the negotiation process inherently forces us to choose one over the other. Since most people negotiate with a win-lose mentality and associate negotiations with bargaining, linking this tension to all negotiations was natural.

However, this tension is actually rooted in the take-it-or-leave-it essence of the bargaining process. As bargaining styles focus on either relationship or substance, it is bargaining, not negotiation, that forces us to choose. So the negotiation tension is actually the bargaining tension. The good news is that we do not have to accept that tension in our negotiations. We just need to choose a process different from bargaining to have no tension at all. The door for more value and better relationships is open.

# Win-Win Strategies

What do we know about win-win so far?

- The win-win approach happens when at least one party tries to get what he or she wants with the other party's consent and without the need to use or display power.
- Win-win uses collaboration and communication to make resistance unnecessary.
- Tit-for-Tat shows that successful collaboration involves a proactive, clear and consistent communication of a simple, interdependent and value-focused process.
- Win-win delivers, on average, higher value at lower risk than win-lose.

Back to our road trip: the win-win roads are not without their share of problems. Looking at the map, we really have no idea what to make of them. There seems to be numerous ways to get where we want. The way these roads break away, split, cross each other and come back together again several times can seem complex. It is hard to figure out what they are like. One thing is for sure: it is not just entering a highway and only having to think about the exit close to our destination.

These roads are newer and somewhat promising of a better ride, but vastly unknown. They are less traveled and are essentially being built as we go along. There are several choices along the way, many of which take us back to bargaining. Indeed, there are few signs and fewer people around to give us directions. The landscape changes all the time and the choices are not so intuitive. These empty and unknown roads can be scary as they feel unfamiliar.

Why would anyone use roads like that? Being unexpected, they offer us **no false sense of security and keep us sharp** to make the many choices along the way. We stay alert and are less likely to sleep at the wheel. They give us **choices**; when one road has problems, we can always take another to reach our destination. They also give us **flexibility**; as interesting sights or locations appear unexpectedly, we may decide to take a detour or stop to enjoy them.

All win-win strategies bypass the bargaining tension and enable optimal-value outcomes. They are dynamic processes that consider the reality and particularities of each negotiation to come up with the best decision. They emphasize good communication and proactivity. They fully explore and combine the potential of all seven negotiation elements to avoid limiting our choices and possibilities.

## Win-Win Processes

Win-win strategies, due to their increased complexity and possibilities, can take many forms. Despite their many similarities, shifts in emphasis and nuances render them different. Some of the most well-known strategies are:

- **Interest-based** – Emphasizes rejecting positions for the benefit of focusing the negotiation on interests.
    - *Risk* – After discussing interests, this process may still fall into the bargaining trap of discussing only one or two unilateral options.

- **Mutual gains** – Emphasizes parties' creative efforts to generate options that will benefit everyone involved (mutual gain).
    - *Risk* – Many mutual-gains processes create several options only for parties to end up bargaining over them.
- **Principled** – Emphasizes seeking win-win choices and thinking through strategic win-win principles before making decisions.
    - *Risk* – Many principled negotiators get overwhelmed by the amount of win-win decisions to be made that they risk losing focus.
- **Value negotiation** – A system under the principled approach, it emphasizes making decisions based on win-win strategic principles with an unmistakable focus on value.
    - *Risk* – Value negotiations can tempt negotiators to adopt win-lose moves if they fail to consider other win-win avenues towards value.

The principled approach and consequently the value negotiation approach go one step beyond the previous two approaches and other win-win variations. With the principled approach, intelligent decisions are made throughout the entire process instead of being limited to a style that concentrates on a few repetitive behaviors. The principled approach creates more choices.

But too many choices can become overwhelming and reduce the quality of our decisions. The value negotiation system is an evolution of the principled approach as it gives the negotiator:

- A stronger clarity of purpose (focus on value); and
- A practical, quick and culturally-sensitive method to apply win-win principles (risk-reward analysis).

The value negotiation process aims to give us enough choices to expand our possibilities, while giving us tools to quickly manage them before they become too many to weigh us down. The improvements made on the value negotiation approach are many: some small, all significant. What they have in common is to help the negotiator choose the most valuable win-win move within a negotiation.

# More Than One?

Well, yes! Every time we negotiate there is more than just one negotiation going on. It is not like we have a choice whether they happen or not. They just will. That's why we may as well be prepared so that we can influence or lead them. Look at what happened to Lemuel Boulware, who seemed ignorant of that fact.

In the early 1950s, Boulware was responsible for labor relations at General Electric in the US. He was frustrated with how the labor management negotiations went. In typical bargaining fashion, the union asked for twice as much as it wanted. Management would reciprocate with an offer 50% below what it was prepared to agree on. Agreement always meant a compromise reached after five to seven weeks of intensive bargaining sessions over unimportant details.

The process was not only ineffective, but did little to improve relations between labor and management.

Boulware decided to change things and devised a negotiation strategy, later known as Boulwarism. His strategy had two main steps. First, he used his understanding of the parties' needs to determine, through advanced data analysis, the maximum GE could pay. Then, he would present the union leaders with his "first, last and best offer" on a "take-it-or-leave-it" basis. Noteworthy was Boulware's expressed willingness to change if anyone surfaced relevant and new information that could improve the deal for all. His offer was also made without favoritism to all unions and non-unionized employees alike.

Some argued that the offers were fair and among the best in the industry. Others accused Boulware of manipulating data and trying to bypass the unions. But all believed Boulwarism to be a rigid and inflexible, take-it-or-leave-it power play. Even after some successful agreements, the unions still hated Boulware for his approach which led to some very long strikes. Finally, in 1965, the US courts declared that GE was guilty of refusing to engage in collective bargaining. In 1969–70, the unions united on a large strike to make Boulwarism ineffective from that point onwards.

## The Three Negotiations

While we will never know the truth of Boulware's intentions, it remains important to understand the reasons why Boulwarism failed. If it indeed delivered the best possible value, why did the unions fight so hard against it? In our opinion, Boulwarism failed to consider the three negotiations.

As seen before, to build our bridge we need to negotiate both relationship and communication. So on top of negotiating value, we also have to prepare for these two other simultaneous and parallel negotiations. After all, we cannot avoid communicating or developing at least a short-term relationship with the other side. Hence, we may as well make sure that we can positively influence them.

As outlined in Figure 5.3, the value negotiation definitions of the three negotiations are:

- **Substance negotiation** – Parties pursue substance value.
- **Relationship negotiation** – Parties pursue relationship value including, but not limited to, interdependence and trust.
- **Communication negotiation** – Parties attempt to create the most efficient process to negotiate.

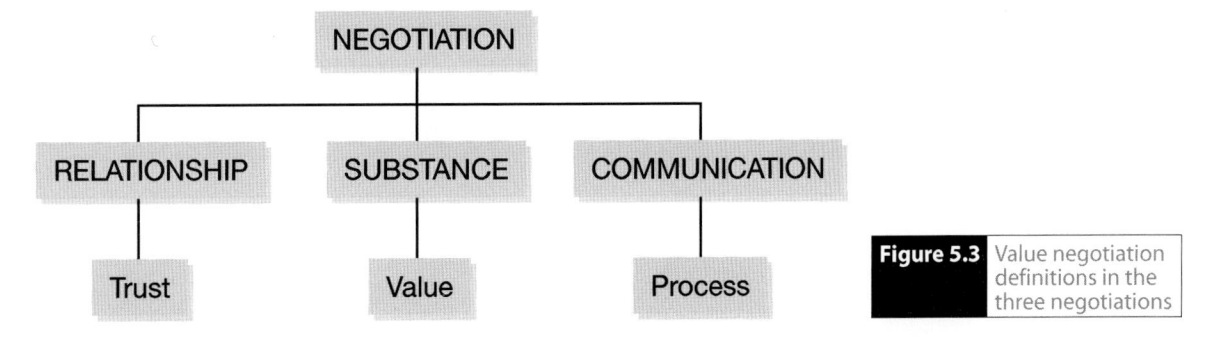

**Figure 5.3** Value negotiation definitions in the three negotiations

Like Boulware, almost every negotiator is aware of the substance negotiation and of the relationship as a relevant issue. Still, few treat the relationship as a separate negotiation in itself. And even fewer negotiators are aware that the communication is negotiated at all. Boulware fell victim to his focus on the substance negotiation and disregarded the relationship and communication negotiations.

### POINT OF INTEREST

**Is Every Negotiation Actually Three Negotiations?**
The substance negotiation is the only one that may at times be absent. In some particular situations, the parties may have no material value to negotiate. They may decide to only negotiate their relationship interests or emotional value. For example, when I negotiate for respect or for someone to stop a behavior I dislike. On the other hand, every negotiation has the relationship and the communication negotiations.

By offering maximum value for both sides, Boulware thought that the negotiation was solved. However, his lack of a relationship negotiation strategy deepened the lack of trust that customarily plagues labor management negotiations. He never listened to or engaged the unions as partners in finding the so-called "best possible deal." He named it the "first, last and only offer." And though he invited new information after the offer was made, his invitation was never taken seriously by the unions. Even his extension of the offer to non-unionized employees could have been perceived as an attempt to bypass the unions.

His lack of flexibility or openness generated distrust, suspicion, fear and resentment. His behavior was in direct contradiction with his message of the best deal for all. In sum, Boulwarism's unilateral approach created a power play perception which ruined it.

Had Boulware engaged the unions early in better understanding their interests and in analyzing the data to craft the "first, last and only offer," would they have responded differently? Had he posed this offer as GE's first attempt to find the best possible solution and openly invited the labor unions to improve on it, would they have reacted differently? We believe he would have succeeded had he worked equally hard on all three negotiations.

## The Three Win-Lose Negotiations

Boulwarism is a great example of how win-lose strategies approach the three negotiations. If Boulware had a win-win mentality, as some argue, his choice of the take-it-or-leave-it process was utterly inconsistent. Together with his sole focus on the substance negotiation, Boulwarism turned into a version of bargaining.

Win-lose strategies do not approach the three negotiations as one, but rather treat each as a different power source (Figure 5.4).

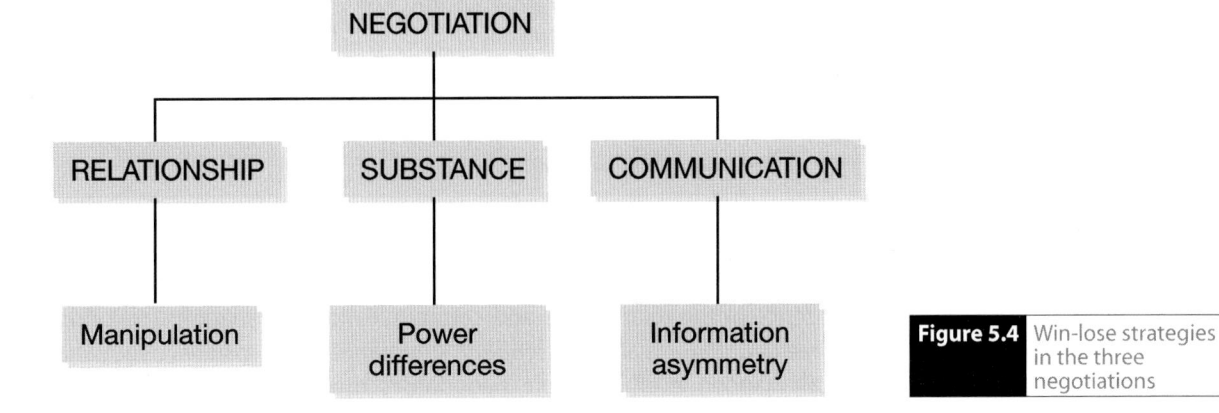

```
                    NEGOTIATION
          ┌──────────────┼──────────────┐
     RELATIONSHIP    SUBSTANCE     COMMUNICATION
          │              │              │
     Manipulation      Power        Information
                    differences     asymmetry
```

**Figure 5.4** Win-lose strategies in the three negotiations

1. **Substance negotiation** is a search for power or resource differences to be used against one another in a competition for value.
   - *Boulwarism* – We are the only ones with all the data and who understand all the detailed analysis behind our "first, last and only offer."
   - *Example* – Since we are much richer than them, we can pay our lawyers to keep this in court for years. Even if they might win, can they wait that long?

2. **Relationship negotiation** is an opportunity to manipulate the parties' emotions and relationship (past, present or future) to extract value from one another.
   - *Boulwarism* – We will address the employees directly to make them feel valued but also obliged to accept our proposal as a goodwill gesture.
   - *Example* – Since we are friends, could they give us a discount?

3. **Communication negotiation** is an opportunity to use information asymmetry, the differences of information between the parties OR impose a communication process to take advantage of one another.
   - *Boulwarism* – We cannot reveal all the data from the GE side as some of it is confidential. OR, Here are the rules of the game. Take it or leave it!
   - *Example* – They have to bid for this company before we give them access to the books. OR, They can submit their bid within this format and deadline.

Interesting enough, the hard and soft win-lose processes choose one negotiation over another. The hard bargainer, of which Boulware is an example, concentrates on the substance negotiation. They might derive power from their higher status or deeper pockets. The soft bargainer, such as the negative stereotypes of a used car salesman or a phony politician, concentrates on the relationship negotiation. They might derive power from their charisma, false compliments or gifts.

Few concentrate on the communication negotiation as they seem to be unaware of it. That may be one of the reasons why bargaining is not a very creative process. The different forms are all variations of a take-it-or-leave-it process.

Nonetheless, both hard and soft styles do take advantage of information asymmetry through lies, threats, sweet talk or empty promises.

Bargaining does not seem to fully explore all three negotiations. Instead, it corners itself into a preferred negotiation and exercises power almost exclusively from there. As seen with the Boulwarism example, it is more likely that they will concentrate their efforts on one negotiation at the expense of the other two.

## The Three Win-Win Negotiations

Win-win strategies explore all three negotiations to unlock their value potential. The value negotiation process believes that all three negotiations deserve important attention. For example, the substance negotiation will likely fail in the absence of the relationship and communication negotiations (no bridge). The three negotiations are independent, simultaneous and parallel negotiations that can happen even with the negotiator's ignorance like in Boulwarism. But they are also interconnected, so:

- Though **all deserve attention**, the relationship and communication negotiations' ultimate purpose is often to pursue better value for the substance negotiation.
- Though **independent**, a move in one negotiation may impact the others.
- Though **simultaneous**, they move at a different pace and at different times, but if well managed usually in the same direction.
- Though **parallel,** their boundaries are not always clear, and they do not remain separate by their own right.
- Though **they just happen**, nothing guarantees that they will happen in ways that help us.

A value negotiator proactively monitors, advances, separates and leads the three negotiations to ensure that all are moving forward as desired. For example, we may be talking about value for a long while. We may decide to stop and run a routine check on the relationship and the communication: "So how are we doing so far? Is this negotiation going the way we want?"

### POINT OF INTEREST

**Relationship and Communication: Elements of Negotiation?**

For clarification purposes, relationship and communication are two negotiation elements but also full-blown negotiations with their own seven elements. For example, the relationship negotiation can have a relationship interest: "I want them to trust me more!" The communication negotiation can, for example, have a communication option and legitimacy: "Since I patiently listened to you, I believe it would be fair if you could now reciprocate [legitimacy] and listen to me for a few minutes [option]. Is that okay?"

How does a value negotiator approach the three negotiations? Below, we make strategic recommendations to manage the three negotiations. These recommendations are not meant to be rigid, but serve as directives with the potential for high rewards at low or manageable risks.

Any strategic directive requires trade-offs. So while these directives can help us succeed, they also limit our ability to engage in certain win-lose behaviors. However, since they do not eliminate our ability to act opportunistically, there will always be temptations to make win-lose moves. Falling for these temptations may destroy our win-win investment so far, as they generate resistance that reduces the value of the final outcome.

To help us be aware of the choices we are making, we will elaborate on the strategic directives, trade-offs and temptations of each of the three negotiations (Table 5.1).

|  | The win-win directive to | makes it harder to | and tempts us with | so we persistently |
|---|---|---|---|---|
| Substance | Focus on value | Focus on power | Easy power opportunities | Promote the dialogue pattern |
| Relationship | Negotiate three negotiations autonomously | Manipulate | Relationship over value | Avoid trading between negotiations |
| Communication | Promote learning | Exploit information asymmetry | Complacency | Proactively diagnose |

**Table 5.1**
Strategic directives, trade-offs and temptations of the three negotiations

## Substance Negotiation

In substance negotiation,
- The **strategic directive** is: Focus on value. Every move is directly committed to increase value, not power.
- The **trade-off** is: Focus on value reduces the negotiator's ability to make a unilateral power move.
- The **temptation** is: Identifying easy power opportunities. As the parties talk about value and their guard is down about power, easy power-grabbing opportunities may arise.

### Focus on Value

When Boulware tried to impose his deal, the unions reciprocated with long strikes and lawsuits against GE. As Boulwarism illustrates, even a perceived power move will invite reciprocation and initiate a fear-based power race. Most negotiators believe that without power they will be unable to secure the best deal for themselves. The weaker side will feel the need to catch up for fear of falling behind. The parties may get so deeply entrenched in the power race that they lose sight of value and destroy it.

Indeed in a bargaining process, we may as well go home if we lack power. We will get nothing at the end of the day. But if we do have power, we can always guarantee our share of the pie. Power is bargaining's insurance policy against fear. But insurance policies are not free. Translating power into value is not a given or even an easy task.

Most people may prefer not to invest in such an insurance policy if they perceive it may not be needed. In such a process with no significant power difference, no one needs to be excluded. Everyone is guaranteed a share of the pie. If no one fears a race for power, why not just invest all our resources into securing value instead? Our focus on value demonstrates to the other party that there is no need to initiate the power race. Our focus on value early on demonstrates that they will likely get what they want too.

Keeping our focus on value can be remarkably hard in two situations:

- When despite our best efforts, the only thing they concentrate on is power; or
- When easy power moves continuously present themselves to us.

It is precisely in these more difficult situations where the focus on value will make the most difference. Our task is to persist in making the negotiation independent of competitive power to avoid destroying or unilaterally allocating value. And before we think that this advice is too naïve, remember that we are aiming to be positive, not naïve. To help us do that, we recommend promoting the dialogue pattern.

## Promote the Dialogue Pattern

Every move a negotiator makes can be perceived as a value or a power move. Power moves are unilateral moves to benefit one party at the other's expense. Boulware could have avoided the power imbalance by reducing or eliminating his unilateral moves. He could have invited the unions to work together and give him feedback before his "first, last and only offer." These moves would have promoted a dialogue pattern.

The dialogue pattern promotes a balancing effort where no power difference is felt or created during the negotiation. To move away from power and towards value, the dialogue pattern turns every potential unilateral move into a bilateral one. The dialogue pattern can be summarized as proactive positive reciprocation: "If something goes their way, something should come our way and vice-versa." Some examples of how to promote it:

- If we talk, we want to give them time to talk so that we also learn. If they talk, we want to make sure that we talk so they can have the benefit of our information.
- If we ask questions, we want them to ask as well so they perceive that it is okay to continue answering our questions, just as we will continue to answer theirs.
- If they offer or demand a concession, we suggest something in return (trade).

A well-implemented dialogue pattern reduces or eliminates unilateral moves. When we reciprocate value-focused moves, **we reward good behavior** and inspire similar moves in the future. The balanced reciprocal moves enhance the sense of interdependence and fairness among the parties and prevent extreme behaviors. A negotiator promoting the dialogue pattern would hardly embark on a monologue without listening or fire off an interrogation without sharing. As they work together, the mutual control and inclusion eases the fear of losing and desire for power. A virtuous cycle initiates where power becomes harder to implement, while value becomes increasingly the focus.

But what if we find ourselves in Kumar or Ananda's shoes as in the dialogue below?

> Thanks for listening, Ananda. Would you like to share your story now?

> Not really? I can't do it. It's confidential! Sorry!

> But I just told you my story!

> I know! And thank you for that. I never told you I was going to tell you mine. You just started telling your story so I listened to it. Very interesting indeed!

What is likely to happen next? Kumar stops sharing information, but the damage is already done. Though Ananda now knows Kumar's story, his power move limited future information flow and consequently the potential for further value. But it is not all Ananda's fault. This power move was made possible because Kumar blindly jumped in first and then hoped Ananda would follow his example. Such unprotected moves usually end up in frustration and disappointment. So if we were in their shoes, what could we do? Actually, either of them could have taken responsibility for the dialogue pattern.

Before his story, Kumar could have proactively introduced the dialogue pattern:

> I will be glad to share my story first if that works for you. But before I do it, can I also expect to hear your story after I am done with mine?

Kumar would learn that Ananda cannot share his story; he could then stop and decide what to do next. Through the dialogue pattern, he created a safe step-by-step approach that allowed him to be positive while protecting himself. Ananda, on the other hand, could have anticipated that Kumar wanted reciprocation. So Ananda could say:

> Kumar, I appreciate you are telling me your story, which I believe to be important and helpful to the negotiation. Before you continue, I want you to know that I am not authorized to share my story. Is that a problem for you? What should we do?

05 • CHOOSE OUR STRATEGY

Rejecting such an easy power move is not an easy thing to do. However, Ananda's statement reduces any perception of a powerful move since the story was not yet shared. With no damage done, there is no need for a power race. His move demonstrates honesty and concern for Kumar while inviting him to work together towards value.

# Relationship Negotiation

In the relationship negotiation,

- The **strategic directive** is: Negotiate the three negotiations autonomously. The negotiator seeks independent solutions for each of the three negotiations.
- The **trade-off** is: By negotiating substance and relationship separately, the negotiator limits the ability to mix, manipulate or trade elements of one negotiation for the other.
- The **strategic temptation** is: Relationship over value. As the parties attentively improve the relationship, they say "yes" more quickly or are afraid to say "no," even to the wrong requests.

## Negotiate the Three Negotiations Autonomously

In 1998, guerrillas and para-military groups abounded in Colombia with the Revolutionary Armed Forces of Colombia (FARC) leading the way. In that year, Andrés Pastrana was elected president backed by strong public support for his peace platform.

The FARC, however, imposed a condition to participating in the process. It required the government's previous demilitarization of a particular region roughly the size of Switzerland. Once demilitarized, it was clear the FARC could invade and control the region without resistance. The president decided that a goodwill gesture was a small price to pay for peace. Unfortunately, after the demilitarization, the FARC did not honor its commitment and demanded further demilitarization. Pastrana then rejected the new demands.

Pastrana made a mistake that negotiators around the world repeat on a daily basis: he **mixed the three negotiations**. He gave away a piece of land (substance) in the hopes of starting a relationship or at least a communication process. Surely, his substance concession seemed small if his move were to succeed. But the odds that the demilitarization would have succeeded in bringing the FARC to negotiate were quite slim.

Even if the FARC had honored their commitment, the president had established a negative negotiation pattern of unilateral substance demands. If Pastrana resisted the smallest of demands, they could just threaten to leave the process. The demilitarization signaled a willingness to give tangible, substantive value in exchange for no substance but only a relationship promise. And the demilitarization did nothing good for the relationship either. After the perceived weak or desperate move, the FARC probably lost any respect they may have had for him. Unfortunately, throughout his four-year mandate, Pastrana made little advances in peace and the FARC occupied more territory.

This example demonstrates how mixing the three negotiations only **rewards bad behavior** and invites more of it. It does not improve any negotiation and it still unilaterally costs us money. However, negotiating the three negotiations autonomously is not an easy concept to put in practice. Not only are their boundaries hard to identify, but they are also hard to respect. After all, most of us have been trained for years or even all our lives to do just the opposite. To help us keep the three negotiations autonomous, the best thing is to remember to persistently avoid trading between them.

## Avoid Trading between Negotiations

Consider that the three negotiations, like different countries, have their own currency each. Although a currency has value in its country and abroad, in negotiations there is no official exchange rate among them. Therefore, trading elements of one negotiation for another can be done but is a risky move. The negotiator would be better off avoiding trades between them altogether.

Conglomerates normally hold different accounts to better control and understand their separate companies. If instead they held a single account, they would not know which company makes money and which does not. As a result, we would never know if a particular move resulted in an absolute value gain or loss. Threatening to walk away to one's BATNA is such an example. It may get us more money today, but at the expense of a future relationship and potentially more money tomorrow.

All three negotiations are important and are better satisfied when handled separately. Value negotiators separate people concerns (trust, respect, emotions, etc.) from value or substance ones (price, product, service, contract duration, etc.). The value negotiator satisfies relationship interests with relationship options, substance interests with substance options and communication interests with communication options.

At times, this could even mean separating meetings for the relationship or substance negotiation to clearly distinguish their boundaries. Separate meetings create the appropriate environment to reduce the temptations to mix the negotiations.

But what if Ananda and Kumar continue with their negotiation?

> Come on Ananda. We've known each other for years now. Can't you give your friend even a small discount?

> Sorry Kumar, I can't. But because of our relationship, I am ready to spend more time and effort to explore transaction cost reductions that can help you.

> That's good. But Ananda, you did not share your story with me, remember? The least you can do now is give me a discount here.

> Dear Kumar, if my inability to communicate my story is hurting this deal, I am glad to add whatever other information I can to improve it. Can we try that?

Notice how Kumar first insisted on mixing relationship and substance and then communication and substance. Ananda avoided trading between the negotiations. However, because Kumar's arguments on long-term relationship and limited information exchange were valid, Ananda sought solutions along the same negotiations.

### POINT OF INTEREST

The famous negotiation saying: "hard on the problem, soft on the person" uses bargaining terms ("hard" and "soft"), but conveys the idea of separating and treating the substance and relationship negotiations differently.

## Communication Negotiation

In the communication negotiation,
- The **strategic directive** is: Promote learning. The negotiator constantly seeks to increase the amount of information available as this increases the value potential of a negotiation.
- The **trade-off** is: In negotiating for a learning process, the negotiator reduces the ability to use information asymmetry for unilateral advantage.
- The **strategic temptation** is: Complacency. As the parties start trusting each other's information, data or processes, they may become less proactive in communicating or double-checking.

### Promote Learning

This is where Boulwarism probably failed the most. Boulware did try to learn as much as possible from the available data, however the data used was biased or limited. He limited himself to his own understanding of the unions' interests, thus failing to learn what they truly were. He also presented his "first, last and best offer" on a take-it-or-leave-it basis. In doing so, Boulware failed to learn the union's feedback of the proposal on the table. By limiting or biasing the data analyzed, Boulware limited value possibilities and the quality of his conclusions.

In bargaining, the decisive factor in winning is the difference in power. One source of bargaining power is information asymmetry, i.e., difference of information available to each negotiator. Since **information asymmetry can be found in different levels in all negotiations**, many negotiators try to profit from it. The presence of information asymmetry is often used as an excuse for unethical behavior.

Many negotiators rely on the other's ignorance to threaten, hide, conceal or lie about important aspects of the negotiation. Even when unintentional, information asymmetry is the origin of many misunderstandings and conflicts. This partial to total withdrawal of information clearly impairs efficient communication and good decision-making. Having guesses, biases and perceptions instead of solid data reduces anyone's ability to find the best possible outcome.

As power is to win-lose negotiations, good communication is to win-win negotiations. Hence, the value negotiator needs to proactively promote learning through the broadest possible information exchange in all three negotiations.

The learning reduces information asymmetries and bargaining temptations while enabling good value-based decision-making. The best way to promote it is to constantly and relentlessly diagnose whenever the negotiation presents ambiguities, assumptions, indecisions or lack of information.

## Proactively Diagnose

Stock markets rely on the assumption of market efficiency, where reliable asset information will be efficiently distributed and priced. However, stock markets are also plagued with the information asymmetry of insider trading. Insider trading gives insiders information to buy or sell stocks at a better price than outsiders could. Since traders only negotiate stock price and quantity, they fail to recognize and defend themselves against insiders with privileged information. Because insider trading can undermine the confidence in the fairness and integrity of the trading process, most governments treat it as a highly regulated or illegal activity.

In most other negotiations, however, governments will not intervene. Unfortunately, this means that we are on our own against the negative impact of information asymmetries. Opportunely, in most negotiations we can ask for and seek further information whenever something is suspicious, unclear, ambiguous or assumed. The value negotiator has the strategic duty to diagnose which information to clarify before proceeding to a decision.

To diagnose is "to recognize by signs and symptoms" or "to analyze the cause or nature of." For negotiation, it is how we learn as much as possible about the situation and the parties in the negotiation. Good diagnostics allow negotiators to fill communication gaps with as accurate information as possible to negotiate the best possible outcome. And now, Ananda and Kumar return to illustrate this with their negotiation:

> Dear Ananda, I understand you cannot share your story. Can you tell me why?

> Well, some of it is confidential. Don't you trust me?

> Because I do trust you, I am not challenging it. I just want to know more, because not hearing your story may make it harder for us to reach an agreement. Is it okay to at least say why it is confidential?

> Because it contains sensitive information our competitors would die to learn.

> I would never want that. Correct me if I am wrong, but since you said only some of it was confidential, do you mind sharing what's not? What I need may actually be non-confidential information. Does that work for you?

> Sure! I can at least try.

Kumar did an excellent job of seeking all possible information he could while promoting a safe learning environment. He argued why learning was important for the negotiation in ways that could motivate Ananda to expand the information flow.

One risk novice negotiators run when diagnosing is to turn it into a unilateral interrogation process. To avoid that risk, diagnostics also happen under the dialogue pattern, so we share information while learning. Transparent communication rewards the openness of the other party motivates them to share more.

## POINT OF INTEREST

**Short of Words?**
Many negotiators confess that at times in a negotiation, they are short of words. These are the times a negotiation is "telling" us not to say anything and to diagnose instead.

# summary

**Win-lose** strategies are usually implemented through bargaining processes. Bargaining processes are widely adopted probably because they are familiar and almost intuitive. They are, however, simplistic and unsophisticated, and thus they:
- Limit negotiations to only two of the seven negotiation elements: commitments and alternatives.
- Forces the parties into zero-sum choices ("Take it or leave it!").
- Limit negotiators into two main styles: hard or soft.
- Impose the bargaining tension between substance and relationship.

**Win-win** strategies can be implemented through several processes such as the value negotiation approach. They do not give us a false sense of security, while also developing choices to give us flexibility.
- They attempt to explore the possibilities of all seven elements.
- They allow for positive-sum choices (value creation).
- They allow for many styles beyond hard and soft.
- They free us from the bargaining tension between substance and relationship.

Every negotiation contains three independent, parallel and simultaneous negotiations:
1. **Substance negotiation** – Parties pursue substance value.
2. **Relationship negotiation** – Parties pursue improved relationships.
3. **Communication negotiation** – Parties attempt to create the best process.

The three negotiations can be addressed in a win-lose or win-win way. If win-win, we have to make trade-offs to extract maximum rewards at minimum risk.

|  | The win-win directive to | makes it harder to | and tempts us with | so we persistently |
|---|---|---|---|---|
| Substance | Focus on value | Focus on power | Easy power opportunities | Promote the dialogue pattern |
| Relationship | Negotiate three negotiations autonomously | Manipulate | Relationship over value | Avoid trading between negotiations |
| Communication | Promote learning | Exploit information asymmetry | Complacency | Proactively diagnose |

05 • CHOOSE OUR STRATEGY

# questions

## Easy

1. What is the difference between win-lose negotiation, bargaining and positional bargaining?
2. Why is bargaining so prevalent and popular?
3. What are the two main styles of bargaining? Please describe.
4. What are the advantages of the value negotiation approach over other win-win processes?
5. Define the three negotiations and their likely goals.
6. What is the dialogue pattern?

## Medium

1. What is the typical bargaining process like? Please describe and elaborate on its pros and cons.
2. What is the bargaining tension? How do we get out of it?
3. Which one is the most important of all three negotiations? Why? What problem does that create?
4. Is every negotiation actually three negotiations? Why?
5. What were the good and bad things about Boulwarism from a win-win perspective?
6. How does win-lose operate within the three negotiations?

## Difficult

1. Does a win-win strategy limit possibilities for the negotiator? Why? Why would this be bad? Why would this be good?
2. The win-win success may eventually put us in places where we are tempted to change our course. Do you agree? What moments could these be? What are the temptations? How do we overcome them?
3. When is it hard to focus on value? To negotiate the three negotiations autonomously? To promote learning? What can we do to help us keep our focus?
4. What is information asymmetry? Is it different from the intent-impact gap? If so, how?
5. Why is mixing relationship and substance bad? Should we never do it?

# scenarios

## Easy

Imagine Boulware comes to you for advice when he realizes that Boulwarism is not working well as a negotiation strategy. He shares with you that he really wants to do the best for the unions and GE at the same time. He asks you to improve on his "first, final and last offer" strategy. Please prepare your best advice to give to him.

## Medium

*Most people negotiate win-lose, but few people are hard or soft bargainers altogether. Most people are somewhere in between and fluctuate closer to one or the other extreme as the context changes. As a result, most people compromise, which can be considered a lose-lose negotiation since both parties walk away with less value than they expected and many times with frustrated relationships as well.*

- Plot a compromise point in the graphic below.
- Do you agree with the statement above? Why?
- What are the consequences?
- What needs to be done to improve?

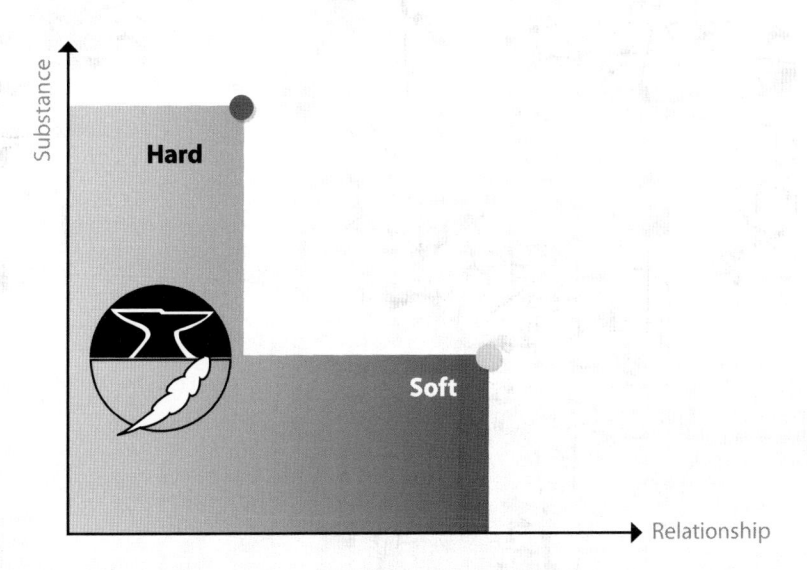

## Difficult

> Thanks for listening, Ananda. Would you like to share your story now?

> Not really. I can't do it. It's confidential! Sorry!

> But I just told you my story!

> I know! And thank you for that. I never told you I was going to tell you mine. You just started telling your story so I listened to it. Very interesting indeed!

Imagine you are Kumar, what do you say or do now? From a win-lose perspective? From a win-win perspective?

# 06 Anticipate the Critical Moments

**Learning Objectives:**
- What a critical moment is
- What the seven critical moments of any negotiation are
- Why these particular moments are critical
- What their dangers are
- What the best moves during critical moments are

Let's recap our preparation for our road trip:

> Choice of destination?

> Check.

> Choice of best route?

> Check.

> Anticipating common problems such as a flat tire or battery?

> Let's get to it now.

Now we enter our last preparation stage: trying to anticipate and be ready for potential problems, known in negotiations as critical moments. Critical moments are **moments when the negotiation process is in a state of flux** before it enters a new stage. Critical moments are not necessarily more difficult, but they do raise the stakes in terms of risks and rewards. Thus, how we handle critical moments can shape the new stage or even the rest of the negotiation process. Consequently, they demand heightened awareness.

Knowing the critical moments is of great help to negotiators. As we already discussed, everything we say, do, don't say or do sends a message. This means an impossible responsibility to be 100% aware of what we communicate. Negotiation would be a miserable process indeed if it required this from us. Recognizing critical moments allows us to increase our communication awareness only when needed most and to avoid wasting energy elsewhere.

Accordingly, critical moments make negotiations either a very forgiving or unforgiving process. A mistake made during a non-critical moment may have no impact whatsoever on the negotiation as a whole. But even a small slip-up during a critical moment could derail the entire negotiation process, erode the relationship or reduce the value potential.

A well-prepared negotiator can go through them without even noticing the extra pressure they carry. Performing skillfully at these times is just a matter of being ready for a few extra risks and rewards. Unfortunately, it is impossible to predict all the critical moments a negotiation can have. Some of them are specific to the context and parties involved. However, it is possible to know the ones common to almost all negotiation processes.

The predictable critical moments happen when a negotiation shifts its focus from one of the seven elements to another. During a critical moment, it is common for us to tap into our own learned win-lose behaviors. Thus, our biggest risk is to instinctively react in a win-lose way and derail the negotiation. Against this risk, we need to proactively ensure the establishment or continuation of a value negotiation approach. In Table 6.1, we elaborate further on the critical moments, our goal and the strategic advice to better manage them.

| Critical Moment | Element | Goal at Hand | Strategic Advice |
|---|---|---|---|
| 1. Initiating the interaction | Relationship | Improve the working relationship | Negotiate independently from trust, while promoting interdependence |
| 2. Defining the process | Communication | Achieve efficient two-way communication | Transparently lead the communication process |
| 3. Talking about value | Interests | Satisfy interests | Consider all parties' interests |
| 4. Coming up with solutions | Options | Finding the best of many possible options | Initiate with mutual-gains options |
| 5. Making the opening offer/counteroffer | Legitimacy | Argue based on legitimacy | Seek and use objective, external and neutral criteria |
| 6. Accepting/rejecting an offer | Commitment | Close a well-crafted commitment | Commit late to substance, but early to process |
| 7. Deciding to walk away | Alternative | Close a deal that is better than our BATNA | Use our BATNA as a strategy of last resort |

**Table 6.1**

Elements, goals and strategic advice in critical moments

# Initiating the Interaction (Relationship)

When negotiating parties first interact, there is usually much expectation and anxiety about how the others will behave. Negotiators may involuntarily make quick conclusions about each other to define status and formulate expectations. This makes initiating the interaction a critical moment.

To achieve the goal of improving the working relationship, many negotiators mistakenly focus on trust. Unfortunately, the sole emphasis on trust, when initiating the interaction, invites a bargaining pattern. Negotiators may start off with an all-or-nothing trust assumption which leads us to either trust (soft) or distrust (hard) others. This bias can be a dangerous trap when initiating our interaction. As we lean towards bargaining strategies, we can damage the negotiation in two main ways:

- **Hard bargainers** – Inherently distrust people and believe that trust doesn't matter. They are ready to sacrifice trust for value. As they cheat, lie, manipulate and threaten, the other party resists by withholding information or reacts in kind. Value is limited or even eliminated.
- **Soft bargainers** – Revere trust and sacrifice all under its altar. Consequently, many forget to prepare a substance negotiation strategy. Limited to appealing to trust to justify value, a soft bargainer can only trade between negotiations. This can lead to less persuasive arguments, less ambitious options or even coming across as manipulative. Consequently, few get the desired value.

To manage the critical moment of initiating the interaction, we **negotiate independently of trust while promoting interdependence**. Though trust improves relationships, to base our relationship strategy on this alone is risky. Not only is trust hard to build, but as seen above, negotiators have a trust bias that may lead to bargaining. Negotiators are better off focusing on the real objective of improving their ability to work together, not their trust. Interdependence is the best way to build a strong working relationship. Trust will be the consequence. Trust me!

Interdependence means that negotiators need or are better off dealing with each other to get what they want. Being more objective and concrete than trust, it is easier to convey the advantages of working well together. Interdependence quickly establishes a positive relationship negotiation environment within which the parties can prove they are trustworthy. Through interdependence, we can build a stronger relationship faster as we resist choosing between trust or distrust armed with little information.

In Table 6.2, we illustrate how to negotiate independently from trust, while promoting interdependence. We created a hypothetical follow-up dialogue between former Colombian president Andrés Pastrana and the FARC leader from the previous chapter. Pastrana initiated the interaction:

| NEGOTIATION DIALOGUE | DIAGNOSTICS |
|---|---|
| I see your potential interest in the peace process, which can benefit both of us. Can we discuss your demilitarization request and some other issues? | Uncovering interdependent interest in the peace process and then inviting to start the process itself |
| *No, you do not understand. We will only sit down to negotiate if you demilitarize the region.* | *Trading between relationship (sit together) and substance (demilitarization commitment)* |
| Sorry, if it seemed that I did not understand you at first. I do not believe your request is a good move for me, and I feel it may set the wrong tone and precedent to the peace process. | Committing to invest in relationship without giving up the substance; demonstrating that the trading between the negotiations is a unilateral power move |
| *What do I care if this is not good for you? That is your problem, not mine.* | *Ignoring interdependence; trying to instill a sense of dependence on the president* |

| NEGOTIATION DIALOGUE | DIAGNOSTICS |
|---|---|
| Well, I believe it is our problem, because if a move is a bad one for me, I am not likely to accept it, meaning neither of us gets what we want. | Promoting interdependence: one will only get something if the other also does |
| *So are you telling me that you are not going to do it? Are you threatening me?* | *Misunderstanding or trying to twist the interdependence as a power move* |
| No. I am saying that I am committed to working with you towards a deal that satisfies us both, not just one of us. | Clarifying interdependence's focus on value, not power (dialogue pattern) |
| *So why don't you give me what I want first?* | *Insisting on dependency: if I get it first, then you are in my hands afterwards* |
| What guarantees will I have that you will not take the demilitarized area yourself, that you will negotiate and seriously seek a good solution for everyone involved? I want to ensure that we both negotiate with a sincere intention to end this long-lasting conflict. | Demonstrating the potential unilateral dependency that can originate from the FARC's request and sharing an interest in working together (reinforcing interdependence) through a dialogue pattern |
| *Well, we are saying that we will come to the table, isn't that enough? Don't you trust us?* | *Asking for a commitment on substance based on trust alone, without giving any guarantees* |
| I do not know. This is the first time we have met, and we have not discussed anything yet. We are on opposing sides of a war, which indicates that I should not trust you. However, I would prefer for us to trust each other, as you seem to prefer that as well and get what we both want. Could we try to talk about what we both want for a while? | Showing that trust is not something that happens but that is built together, and thus, it is not given, but earned; then showing a willingness to work towards it |
| *What do you mean? Do you not trust us?* | *Insisting on trust to get the demilitarized area with no guarantees or value in exchange* |
| Well, not yet. You have given no reason for me to trust you until now, but I'm glad to work with you on both our issues while we get to know each other and learn to trust each other in the process. So tell me why the demilitarization is so important for the FARC. | Resisting the request to trust with no data (no trading between negotiations); explaining why and inviting to build trust through an exercise of interdependence; attempting to initiate the substance conversation |
| *Well, we need the demilitarization because…* | *Recognizing that trading between negotiations is not working and moving on* |

**Table 6.2**

Negotiating independently from trust

Initiating the interaction independently from trust, while promoting interdependence is a powerful strategy because it:

- *Avoids trading between negotiations* – Negotiating independently from trust forces the parties to base substance decisions on legitimacy, rather than trust.
- *Promotes a dialogue pattern* – When interdependent, the parties are more likely to work together for value instead of risking power moves that could backfire.
- *Proactively diagnoses* – When we trust their information too much or not at all, our mind is made up. If trust is not an issue, we focus on real understanding.

# Defining the Process
## (Communication)

No matter when the negotiation begins, through a phone call, in a face-to-face meeting or by email, negotiators seek control as early as possible. Because this control struggle usually happens when the parties are defining the negotiation process, this is a critical negotiation moment.

Many negotiators ignore the goal of efficient two-way communication and mistakenly use communication to control the other. Hence, at the critical moment of defining the process, a struggle for communication control becomes another bargaining struggle for power. Negotiators will either give unilateral commands to impose control (hard), or accept how things evolve to avoid conflict (soft). The control then veers towards the relationship instead of the process in two possible ways:

- **Hard bargainers** – Attempt control by talking over the other party and ignoring or rejecting their every proposition. While they may effectively intimidate the person and extract a few concessions, they will also generate resistance that results in fewer deals with lower value.
- **Soft bargainers** – Concede control by limiting themselves to listening and accepting every proposition. These behaviors can communicate a lack of process responsibility or weakness, and invite either process chaos if the other also avoids responsibility or stronger power moves from a hard bargainer. The lack of control reveals the soft bargainer's reliance on luck to obtain value.

To manage the critical moment of defining the process, we **transparently lead the communication process** towards a value-maximizing outcome. Our leadership searches for the best possible communication process to focus on value as opposed to power. We do not lead for the sake of leading alone, but rather to proactively ensure a value-focused dialogue pattern. As a leader, we should be prepared for three scenarios:

- If no one leads, then we take charge.
- If someone leads poorly (bargaining), then we intervene.
- If someone is already leading well (value negotiation or other win-win process), then we simply reward good behavior. At all times, we keep an eye on any signs of misappropriation of the leadership towards power.

Transparent process leadership involves explaining how our process options, among other possible options, lead to a better negotiation for all. Transparency keeps the leadership value-focused as it surfaces any attempt to unilaterally control the negotiation. Thus, our leadership becomes inclusive and presents choices for those being led. Transparent process leadership not only reduces suspicion but it also encourages working together and a shared sense of control.

Table 6.3 shows an example of how to transparently lead the process when they use a time limit argument to put pressure towards a better price:

| NEGOTIATION DIALOGUE | DIAGNOSTICS |
| --- | --- |
| So what is your best price? | Forcing the process towards positions early and an opening offer from the other party |
| For me to be able to give you my best price, I need to gather some information from you. Do you mind if I ask you some questions first? | Transparently explaining the need to take another process step and then inviting comment on that (dialogue pattern) |
| Well, I am in a hurry. Just give me a ballpark figure or a range to help me find out if I can afford you or not. | Insisting on their strategy by putting time pressure and hinting at alternatives: I am in a hurry = I may walk away if I do not get what I want right now |
| Without some answers from you, I will have to give you a wide range that may mean nothing to you. The lower end may be inapplicable to you and raise wrong expectations. To avoid wasting your time, I can keep my questions to a minimum so as to give you at least a rough estimate. Do you have a few minutes for that? We can also talk another time if you prefer. | Demonstrating the negative consequences of adopting the process suggested by the other and trying to come up with a new process option to satisfy a perceived process interest of moving fast, then posing the process choices explicitly |
| I do have a few minutes, but please be fast. | Understanding that insisting on the position without answering the questions will probably not work |

**Table 6.3**
How to transparently lead the process

Transparently leading when defining the process is a powerful strategy because it:

- *Avoids trading between negotiations* – Transparent explanation of process steps limits the ability to trade between negotiations due to ignorance or ill intention.
- *Promotes a dialogue pattern* – Transparent process leadership invites value-focused ideas as it is harder to justify an idea just for unilateral benefit.
- *Proactively diagnoses* – Again, the need to explain the benefit of a process idea surfaces more information on the assumptions or interests behind it.

# Talking about Value (Interests)

In any negotiation, there is a time when the parties share what they want or value. Unfortunately, most negotiators jump straight to offering the solution to their problems and needs. In doing so, they distance the conversation from what value really is and position it as a power contest. That is why talking about value is a critical moment.

Considering the goal of satisfying interests, most negotiators are not even aware of the concept of interests. At the critical moment of talking about value, most negotiators believe they know what they or the other side wants. To make bargaining efficient, they present their position as soon as possible to go straight to the point. Negotiators will focus only on their positions (hard), or assume what the other wants to craft their position (soft). If the position is satisfied, then the negotiation is quickly over. Unfortunately, life is rarely that easy.

- **Hard bargainers** – Ignore what the other party wants and demand a position that unilaterally maximizes their value. While this creates a sense of clarity and control, it actually reduces flexibility and possibilities of agreement. The alienation of the other party also invites resistance that forces concessions, a compromise or no deal.
- **Soft bargainers** – Create positions to please the other party but are ignorant of their true interests. Thus, these positions offer more value than needed at a lower satisfaction rate as they are not tailored to what the other side wants. This strategy is of poor quality, not to mention expensive. Finally, soft bargainers start with a position that partially sacrifices interest to avoid conflict.

To manage the critical moment of talking about value, we **consider all parties' interests** instead of positions and assumptions. We diagnose their interests as proactively as we share our own in a dialogue pattern. This includes relentlessly rejecting to offer or discuss options until as many interests as possible have been revealed. Considering interests helps avoid the unilateral bias of positional bargaining and the temptation to solve problems before understanding them.

Though this sounds simple, it can be a deceptively difficult task. In Table 6.4, we show how a negotiator under positional pressure can consider all parties' interests:

| NEGOTIATION DIALOGUE | DIAGNOSTICS |
|---|---|
| I want your presentation ready within one hour. | Positional statement |
| *Could you help me understand why this has become so urgent? I thought we had a full day to do this.* | *Diagnosing the position and seeking the underlying interests* |
| I am your boss, and I am telling you to finish it within an hour, so just do it! | Using hierarchical power to pressure the other into his initial position |
| *It may be hard to get it done within an hour, even if I wanted to. If you help me understand the nature of the urgency, I may be able to help you find alternative solutions. Would that work for you?* | *Explaining why the focus on position is detrimental and sharing an intention to work together* |
| Well, my deadline was moved from tomorrow afternoon to the end of today, so I need your part now. | Elaborating on his interests, but insisting on his position |
| *So you would like to have my part to be able to do yours, is that right?* | *Surfacing assumption over the previous explanation* |
| Not really, I just want to make sure that as I prepare my part, it will be coordinated with yours. | Correcting partially mistaken assumption and thus further explaining their interests |
| *Would it be helpful if I told you now the major elements of my part of the presentation so you could already refer to them? I am assuming that this would allow you to start right away with your part instead of having to wait a full hour, and it will give me more time to finish my part as well. Does that work for you?* | *Coming up with a new option to satisfy both their urgency and coordination interests while allowing her to satisfy her interest of having more time* |
| Actually, it is even better. Thanks. Tell me then, what are the key risks in this project? | Recognizing that his interests are now better satisfied with the new option |

**Table 6.4**
How a negotiator under positional pressure can consider all parties' interests.

Considering all parties' interests when talking about value is a powerful strategy because it:

- *Avoids trading between negotiations* – Understanding interests identifies which of the three negotiations each belongs to and what options are consistent.
- *Promotes a dialogue pattern* – Moving away from positions removes the need for power and invites an inclusive value conversation to satisfy all interests.
- *Proactively diagnoses* – The need to find the interests underlying positions encourages negotiators to ask for and produce as much information as possible.

# Coming Up with Solutions (Options)

After discussing value, it is time for the parties to come up with solutions. This is when both sides can profit the most from a safe environment where they can explore ideas creatively. However, this is also when they start shaping the deal, which can make them quite edgy. No one wants to even consider something they dislike, but wants to immediately secure what they like in the deal. It is hard to be creative or see the big picture in an environment of fear and pressing decisions. This is why coming up with solutions is a critical moment.

To achieve the goal of finding the best of many possible options, many negotiators ignore the idea of "finding" for "securing" the best possible options for them only. At the critical moment of coming up with solutions, negotiators exchange proposals in a similar way they would exchange positions. Old habits die hard. Negotiators put forward an extremely good proposal for them (hard) or a very good one for the other side (soft).

- **Hard bargainers** – Put forward proposals only benefiting them, which sends messages of indifference and selfishness. The unilateral and extreme nature of the proposal resembles power moves to prepare for bargaining. The other side may not take it seriously or fear that they need to reciprocate to satisfy their interests. In the end, escalation or lack of credibility deteriorates the deal.
- **Soft bargainers** – Propose solutions that are very good for the other party without being clearly good for them. This can generate suspicion and distrust as the other party thinks: "This is too good to be true. Are they desperate? What is the catch?" This misunderstanding may result in rejection of the proposal or increased attempts to exploit the soft bargainer's perceived desperation.

To better manage the critical moment of coming up with solutions, we **initiate** the options conversation with **mutual-gains options**. Mutual-gains options satisfy common interests of all parties, even if not to the same extent. Initiating with mutual-gains options sends a consistent message of working together and sets the right value-creation tone. Firstly, we demonstrate concern for the interests of all parties. Secondly, we show our efforts to satisfy everyone. Finally, we eliminate any suspicion of our motives.

Table 6.5 examplifies how to introduce mutual-gains options when coming up with solutions:

| NEGOTIATION DIALOGUE | DIAGNOSTICS |
|---|---|
| *It seems that we have a good understanding of what both of us are looking for. Do you agree?* | *Getting commitment on successfully concluding the interest conversation* |
| Yes, I think so. | |
| *I would like to start sharing some ideas on how we could satisfy both our interests. Would you like to do that?* | *Inviting the other party to engage in an options conversation* |
| Yeah, I am okay with that. If you want to start, go ahead. | |
| *Okay. From what I understood from your interests, among other things, you would like to promote your image as well as contribute to society. Is that right?* | *Checking correct understanding of their interests before suggesting options based on them* |
| Yes. Among other things, of course. | |
| *Well, I hope I clearly expressed that I am also interested in promoting our image and contributing to society.* | *Ensuring my interests are remembered and showing they are common* |
| Yes, it was clear. | |
| *So in the event that we succeed in closing a deal together, I would like to start by suggesting something small that we could do together: both of us could dedicate some of the proceeds of our joint product launch to charities of our choice, as well as invite them to participate in the event to promote their causes. I believe this would help promote both our images in ways that also give back to society. Is that something that points in the right direction?* | *Introduction and explanation of mutual-gains option without asking for firm commitment* |
| That sounds like a good start. | *Keeping the conversation open from commitment* |

**Table 6.5** How to introduce mutual-gains options

Initiating with mutual-gains options when coming up with solutions is a powerful strategy because it:

- *Avoids trading between negotiations* – It eliminates the temptation to generate a substance option just to create relationship goodwill with the other party.
- *Promotes a dialogue pattern* – The intrinsic mutual nature of the option avoids feelings of exclusion or opportunities for building up unilateral power.
- *Proactively diagnoses* – To confirm the mutual-gains nature of an option, the parties are likely to discuss its ramifications to identify the value for themselves.

# Making the Opening Offer or Counteroffer (Legitimacy)

Making the opening offer or counteroffer happens when the parties exchange numbers. Once a number is on the table, most negotiators find it hard to discuss anything else. This similarity with bargaining can fool or tempt many into power behaviors. That is why making the opening offer or counter offer is potentially the most critical moment of a negotiation.

In an effort to claim value, many negotiators forget the goal of arguing based on legitimacy. The critical moment of making an opening offer or counteroffer is normally brought up too early in the process. When coming up with solutions, negotiators should limit themselves to idea generation. Instead, negotiators instinctively exchange numbers and frame options as offers to claim value, like positions. Combining the value-creation and value-claiming phases reduces the effort put into creation. With less value available, the parties concentrate on guaranteeing their share, not on legitimacy offers.

The lack of concern with legitimacy when making an opening offer or counteroffer opposes relationship and substance in the negotiation. Negotiators either make a unilaterally aggressive offer to maximize value (hard), or a seemingly reasonable one to preserve the relationship (soft).

- **Hard bargainers** – Open with an extremely aggressive number then use power or coercion to force the other party to commit early without knowing more. It can send the message that the party is not serious or not concerned about fairness. Unfortunately, this can push the other party to resist or just walk away from what seems to be an unreachable deal.
- **Soft bargainers** – Open with a seemingly reasonable number to persuade the other party of wanting to be fair to improve the relationship. Hopes that the party will trust them and not ask more about the offer. However, the other party can still believe this is a bargaining position with more to gain if pressure is exerted.

Both bargaining approaches may be perceived as unfair, be resisted and result in fewer or lower-value deals. To better manage the critical moment of making the opening offer or counteroffer, we seek and use objective, external and neutral criteria. Our effort helps to legitimize the different offers on their fairness and appropriateness. These criteria encourage offers that can be fair for all, and have a better chance of being accepted. By promoting data-driven decision-making, rational persuasion reduces coercion or manipulation of the relationship for price advantages.

Why are we likely to be persuaded that an offer is fair, right or appropriate if it is objective, external and neutral?

- **Objective** – A rationally produced standard. An argument supported by subjective or no explanations will be less persuasive then one based on objective criteria, such as laws, regulations, industry standards, current or best practices, valuations, mathematics, logic, statistics, evidence, academic research or general principles like reciprocity or precedent.

- **External** – A standard produced by someone external to the negotiation. A company's valuation done by an external party is less likely to be biased towards any side, thus reducing suspicion and increasing its perceived fairness.
- **Neutral** – A standard produced outside the sphere of influence of the negotiators. The external author may want to please one of the parties or see the deal closed in a particular way. If uncovered, this bias can destroy the power of any argument.

Following are three examples that illustrate which choice sounds more persuasive:

1. I want to paint the wall green. (*Option without any criteria*)
2. I want to paint the wall green, because I like green better. (*Option supported by subjective and personal reason, thus individually biased*)
3. I want to paint the wall green, because there is extensive research proving that green soothes people and helps them become more productive in the workplace. (*Option supported by objective data, externally produced by people neutral to the negotiation*)

In the salary negotiation in Table 6.6, the candidate persistently **seeks and uses objective, external and neutral criteria** towards a legitimate opening offer or counteroffer:

| NEGOTIATION DIALOGUE | DIAGNOSTICS |
|---|---|
| *I am happy to hear that you are glad to join us. Your salary will be R$20K/month. Is that okay?* | *Opening with a low offer* |
| Where does this number come from? | Seeking legitimacy |
| *What do you mean?* | *Confused or trying to make the person uncomfortable for asking* |
| Can you share with me how you came up with this number? | Persisting in gathering more data |
| *Do you think it is not good?* | *Trying to get an early commitment* |
| I am not saying if it is good or not. I do not know since I do not know how you came up with this salary offer. | Avoiding early commitment without information |
| *What? Are you saying that my number is not fair then?* | *Offended, confused or trying to make the person uncomfortable* |
| I also did not say that. What I am trying to say is that my research shows this offer to be 30% below the market average. | Clarifying intentions and objective, external and neutral criteria |
| *This is a fair number. Believe me! Don't you trust me?* | *Trying to force a value decision based on relationship* |
| I trust you believe your number is fair. There is a reason for what you offered me and I would like to know it. It may be fair, but I do not know yet if it is. | Avoiding trade between negotiations and clarifying intention while persisting in seeking legitimacy |
| *If I were to say that this is our internal standard for the position, would you be happy?* | *Giving a tentative explanation and seeking commitment* |
| If that is the case, it is below my expectations. But maybe I am still missing something? Could you help me understand why people would accept 30% less than the market average? | Being honest about interests and seeking even more information, without compromising the deal |

| NEGOTIATION DIALOGUE | DIAGNOSTICS |
|---|---|
| Because we rely a lot more on variable pay than our competitors. Our people end up making, in a regular year, about 25% more than in competitive companies. | Sharing more details of why the base salary of R$20K/month is fair |
| So that is why only R$20K/month is offered as base salary, right? And is the base plus bonus the full compensation package? | Seeking confirmation and further criteria |
| No. You also get health, life and dental insurances, pension, sign-on bonus, performance bonus. The list goes on. | Sharing extra options. |
| Do you mind sharing more about those with me? | Seeking even more legitimacy. |
| Sure. So you are okay with the salary then? | Again seeking early commitment |
| I may be depending on what I learn about the rest. Do you mind if I answer you a little later then? | Making sure commitment will only come after all data is on the table |
| Okay. | Seeing that no early commitment will be made |

**Table 6.6**
Seeking and using objective, external and neutral criteria

To seek objective, external and neutral criteria when making the opening offer or counteroffer is a powerful strategy because it:

- *Avoids trading between negotiations* – Separating the number from the person makes the offer the sole subject of the substance negotiation and keeps the relationship intact.
- *Promotes a dialogue pattern* – The search to persuade them of the fairness of our offer helps us focus on fairness rather than power.
- *Proactively diagnoses* – As we reject just throwing numbers at each other, we insist on learning the reason(s) behind the offers and to argue based on merits.

### POINT OF INTEREST

**Legitimacy: Shield or Sword?**

Even many win-win negotiators and scholars say that legitmacy can be used as a shield and a sword. The shield protects us against bad offers while the sword advances our preferred offers. Though illustrative, this metaphor invokes the win-lose ideas of a battle. This shows how dangerously close to bargaining this critical moment is. Though the underlying point of the saying is valid, legitimacy can do much more.

# Accepting or Rejecting an Offer (Commitment)

What is the pattern around the last few critical moments? The recurring issue is the parties' eagerness to close the deal fast. When talking about value and coming up with solutions, many rush to offer a preferred position. This invites a reaction to either accept or reject it. After all, what else can we do? Our reaction invites the bargaining process, making this a critical moment.

To achieve the goal of closing a well-crafted commitment, negotiators will do well to remember to promote learning as much as possible. At the critical moment of accepting or rejecting an offer, negotiators feel the bargaining trap to say either yes or no. Commitments are seen as rare opportunities which create a false urgency to decide before understanding their consequences. Negotiators then either reject most offers (hard), or demonstrate a readiness to accept whatever is offered (soft).

- **Hard bargainers** – Systematically reject any offer made to push the other party to offer more. Saying "no" too quickly limits learning and risks rejecting potentially good offers with hidden value. Constant rejection of offers frustrates the other party who may reciprocate or escalate towards lower-value or no deal.
- **Soft bargainers** – Quickly accept whatever is offered to build a positive relationship. Besides the obvious drawback of accepting bad offers or offers that are too good to be true, it discourages collaboration. Saying "yes" too quickly communicates eagerness, desperation and ultimately weakness and limits the ability to walk away. The other party may attempt to exploit the situation.

To better manage the critical moment of accepting or rejecting an offer, we **commit on the substance only at the end of the process**. Commitments, like a mathematical equation, are the natural evolution of a process. We do not start with an equation, from the end, but rather get to it by working through the steps. We do not have to say "yes" or "no," but rather "let me learn more". Our responsibility is to discuss and learn as much as possible about the potential interests, options and legitimacy. Only then can we commit knowing that we have uncovered all the possibilities to improve a deal.

In Table 6.7, we show an example of how to accept or reject a substance offer only at the end of the process:

| NEGOTIATION DIALOGUE | DIAGNOSTICS |
|---|---|
| I can pay you US$1,200 in installments of US$300/week for crashing your car. | Making an offer |
| *Thanks for the offer. As I understand, you are now only making US$250/week. How will you pay US$300/week?* | *Expressing thanks for the offer and checking further on its implementation* |
| Oh, that's easy. I will ask my mom for money each week. | Explaining how the offer is feasible |
| *Do you mind if I ask how you intend to pay for your own expenses during this time, like food, transportation, etc.?* | *Investigating potential consequences of the offer implementation* |
| Well, I'll go live with my mom for a while until I finish paying you. It will be walking distance from school and work, and I can eat at her place. | Explaining further |
| *Is your mother aware of this potential arrangement?* | *Checking how realistic the deal is* |
| Not really, I just had the idea. Why do you ask? | |
| *What if she has no money or is unable to have you live with her right now? If that happens, what will you do?* | *Anticipating a worst-case scenario to plan for it* |
| Well, I am pretty sure that she will accept—she is my mom. She does everything I ask her to do. | Trying to dismiss the concern, may be denial of a bad situation |
| *I am sure she does. That's what moms do. I just want to know what to do if something unexpected happens.* | *Clarifying that this is not an attack, but a preventive implementation measure* |

| NEGOTIATION DIALOGUE | DIAGNOSTICS |
|---|---|
| Well, if she says no, which I do not expect at all, then I can only pay US$100/week. Would that be okay for you? | Coming up with a backup plan |
| That is fine, since you just said the chances of that happening are limited. Can you deposit the money in my bank account every Monday? | Accepting it as a backup plan, but not as a mainstream deal; moving on to another point of clarification |
| Sure. Do you mind if I start paying next week to give me time to set myself up at my mom's place? | Already in the mode of clarifying the offer towards better commitment |

**Table 6.7** How to accept or reject a substance offer only at the end of the process

Committing late in the substance negotiation when accepting an offer is a powerful strategy because it:

- *Avoids trading between negotiations* – Postponing substance commitment until full understanding reduces chances of accepting a bad offer for relationship's sake.
- *Promotes a dialogue pattern* – Committing late on the substance reduces opportunistic power moves, as there will be time to learn and reflect on the offers.
- *Proactively diagnoses* – Committing to substance late helps us develop the discipline to seek further understanding before we accept any offers.

### POINT OF INTEREST

**Process Leadership & Early Process Commitment**

To manage the pressure to close early, one can commit over the process early. By separating substance and communication, the negotiator can have separate commitment strategies: commit early to the process to ensure efficiency and commit late on the substance to ensure quality.

Early process commitment is a tool for transparent process leadership. Negotiators can quickly commit on a value-focused process and then direct their energies to the substance. Negotiating the process early initiates the relationship and a dialogue pattern before entering the substance negotiation. Making mistakes while discussing process risks less value than making mistakes on substance.

# Deciding to Walk Away (Alternatives)

Deciding to walk away is different from the other critical moments as it may never happen. But it also may happen for whatever reason at any time or even several times in a negotiation. If at every twist and turn negotiators waste energy on a go or no-go decision, less energy is left for everything else. The uncertainty alone seriously distracts the parties away from a good relationship, an efficient process or a higher-value outcome. That is why deciding to walk away is a critical moment.

Coherent with the goal of closing a deal that is better than the BATNA, negotiators walk away if nothing beats their BATNA. So before the critical moment of deciding to walk away, negotiators should discuss all possible options for comparison's sake. However, most negotiators treat BATNA as an all-or-nothing power source instead of an element of the decision to walk away. Negotiators then either talk about BATNA as early as possible (hard), or never talk about it or have one (soft).

- **Hard bargainers** – Disclose their BATNA early as a threat to force a desperate party to give in to their demands. However, this move runs four major risks:
  a) Being caught off-guard by the other party's better BATNA and now being in a weaker bargaining position.
  b) Warning the other party that whatever value created will be appropriated, thus causing them to become defensive and reduce their value collaboration.
  c) Setting the bar too high too early may derail the negotiation. It can lead the other party to quit before learning that they could do better than the BATNA.
  d) Setting the bar too low, thus allowing the other party to give us less value than they could.
- **Soft bargainers** – Never disclose or have a BATNA to preserve the relationship and focus the parties on joint action. Not having a BATNA means that only under extreme conditions will a negotiator decide to walk away. This vulnerability may force the negotiator to accept just about any deal, good or bad. By never disclosing their BATNA, they forego a powerful tool to obtain value if the situation requires.

To avoid the risks above, we **use the BATNA only as a strategy of last resort**. We should have a BATNA, but only disclose it if needed and even then only late in the process. This way, we avoid the temptation to use the BATNA as a bargaining tool, while protecting ourselves from accepting just any deal. And if our deal happens to be better than our BATNA, we may not even discuss it at all. Deciding to walk away or to disclose our BATNA are two very different decisions and should be carefully thought through.

In Table 6.8, we demonstrate an example of how to negotiate under pressure to share our BATNA early, so as to maintain the use of the BATNA as a strategy of last resort:

| NEGOTIATION DIALOGUE | DIAGNOSTICS |
|---|---|
| So what other offers do you have? | Probing for BATNA and power |
| Do you mind if I ask why this is relevant to our negotiation? | Asking for the legitimacy of this process move/question |
| I just want to know. | Avoiding the question |
| Well, I would prefer to focus on what offer we can work on together. Is that possible? | Suggesting a new process that avoids BATNA |
| Sure, we can do that, but do you have other offers? | Ignoring the suggestion and insisting on the BATNA conversation |
| As I said, I would prefer not to talk about this right now. | Resisting the pressure to give in |
| You are just saying that because you do not have any, right? | Threatening to assume that there is no BATNA |

| NEGOTIATION DIALOGUE | DIAGNOSTICS |
|---|---|
| *I am not saying anything, because I fear that no matter what I answer it could be negative to our conversation.* | *Explaining the reason to prefer a different conversation* |
| What do you mean? | Confused, curious or challenging |
| *If I say I have other offers, it may sound as if I am trying to put pressure on you. If I say I don't, then you may be tempted to reduce your offer to me. So I prefer if we focus on what is the best the two of us can do together.* | *Further elaborating on the risks of a BATNA conversation* |
| Alright, but I need to know if I will be able to afford you. You know, I do not want to waste my time if I can't. | Sharing an interest, thus giving a reason to learn about the BATNA |
| *That is reasonable. I promise that if at any point it seems that our proposals are too far apart and no deal is achievable, I will let you know as soon as possible. I have no intention of wasting your time, and I do strongly believe that we can cut a deal together.* | *Reframing the interests as concerns on time and affordability; reassuring to work towards satisfying them* |
| Alright then, what do you want to talk about? | Opening up to a new conversation since the interests were satisfied |

**Table 6.8**
How to negotiate under pressure and share our BATNA early

Using the BATNA as a last resort when deciding to walk away is a powerful strategy because it:

- *Avoids trading between negotiations* – The BATNA is not used as a pressure tool on the relationship for substance gain nor ignored to please the relationship at a potential substance sacrifice.
- *Promotes a dialogue pattern* – By postponing the decision to walk away, we are more likely to pursue value to overcome everyone's BATNAs.
- *Proactively diagnoses* – The absence of an early BATNA conversation encourages information sharing without the fear of having it used against us.

# summary

As we can see, critical moments share many similarities:

- They tempt us to fall into bargaining and if we do, the risks are high.
  - The hard bargainer uses them to increase power.
  - The soft bargainer uses them to improve relationships.
  - They all seem to jump steps to rush towards alternatives or commitments.
  - The solution is beyond the limited "yes" or "no" vocabulary of bargaining.

- The value negotiation strategy to manage critical moments involves:
  - Being true to our seven-elements goal.
  - Being proactive to avoid reacting to the temptation of bargaining.
    - Defining the process (communication)
  - Being objective to avoid trading between negotiations.
    - Initiating the interaction (relationship)
    - Making the opening offer or counter offer (legitimacy)
  - Avoiding unilateral moves to focus on value.
    - Talking about value (interests)
    - Coming up with solutions (options)
  - Pacing the process correctly to promote learning.
    - Accepting or rejecting an offer (commitment)
    - Deciding to walk away (alternatives)

# questions

## Easy

1. What is a critical moment?
2. What normally makes a moment critical in a negotiation?
3. What are the advantages of knowing at least a few critical moments?
4. Why are negotiations stimultaneously very forgiving and very unforgiving processes?
5. What are the similarities and differences between "Initiating the Interaction" and "Defining the Process"?
6. Why is "Deciding to Walk Away" not always a critical moment?

## Medium

1. How can we use critical moments to prepare ourselves?
2. Why is it important to link the common critical moments to the seven elements and to their respective goal?
3. How do bargainers normally behave in a critical moment? Hard? Soft?
4. To avoid the bargaining trap, do we always have to avoid "yes" or "no" answers? Why?
5. What are the similarities and differences between "Coming up with Solutions" and "Making the Opening Offer or Counteroffer"?

6. Why did we verify if each of our critical monemts' recommendations were consistent with
   - Avoiding trading between negotiations;
   - Promoting a dialogue pattern; and
   - Proactively diagnosing?

## Difficult

1. Are there other critical moments that you can identify from your negotiation experience?
2. Is there an order to the critical moments? If so, please put them in the order that makes most sense to you and list the reason for it.
3. What are the similarities and differences between "Deciding to Walk Away," "Rejecting an Offer" and "Making the Opening Offer or Counteroffer"?
4. How can we use the critical moments to lead the process transparently?
5. Which critical moment is most difficult for you to manage? Why? Describe three statements (or ideas) to help you manage the negotiation next time you find yourself in this critical moment.

# scenarios

## Easy

It seems that the predictable critical moments have some common themes and handling them could be summarized to the following pieces of advice:
- Being proactive to avoid bargaining.
- Being objective to avoid trading between negotiations.
- Avoiding unilateral moves to focus on value.
- Pacing the process correctly to promote learning.

Do you agree? Why? What else could be done?

## Medium

*Reviewing the dialogue examples for each critical moment, we notice the value negotiator talks more than the win-lose minded counter-party.*

Do you agree with the statement above? If so, why do you think that is?
What are the risks? How could it be different? Choose three win-win statements from any of the dialogues in this chapter and rewrite them using your own words.

## Difficult

We have changed the text in the table below (with the exception of the first column) and moved some of it into different cells. Please fix the table without referring to the original one.

| Critical Moment | Element | Goal at Hand | Strategic Advice |
|---|---|---|---|
| 1. Initiating the interaction | Communication | Improve our working ability | Negotiate two-way communication |
| 2. Defining the process | Commitment | Achieve efficient commitment | Transparently commit to a process |
| 3. Talking about value | Options | Options that satisfy interests | Satisfy all parties' interests |
| 4. Coming up with solutions | Alternatives | Finding the best solution | Initiate with many-gains solutions |
| 5. Making the opening offer | Interests | Close a good deal | Avoid positions |
| 6. Accepting/rejecting an offer | Relationship | Be fair | Commit to the substance and the relationship |
| 7. Deciding to walk away | Criteria | Close a better deal than our BATNA | Walk away whenever the deal at hand is worse than our BATNA |

# PART 3
# NEGOTIATE!

Let's do a quick recap of what we have covered so far, shall we?

We now better understand negotiation and its foundations, including the proper assumptions to have in terms of value, relationship and communication. Beyond understanding these, we can prepare our goal based on the seven elements and our strategy for the three negotiations. To finalize our preparation, we can anticipate and get ready for the seven critical moments. In sum, we ready ourselves as negotiators and then for the specific negotiation ahead of us.

We have covered a lot of ground already. We started to negotiate even before we first interacted with the other side. But at some point, we will interact with the other side. For a few, this is when the fun starts. For most, this is when the negotiation gets difficult. In Part 3, we will help you know how to manage the negotiation each step of the way. Consequently, this is the largest and most pragmatic part of the book. Let's start by laying down what we consider to be the three main process phases of a value negotiation.

# The Value Negotiation Process

Once again, let's go back to our road-trip metaphor. Let's assume that our destination is in another city. We look at our country or region map to find the major roads to take us there. Then we realize we also have to figure out a couple of important details:

- First, how do we get out of our city?
- Next, how do we get to our address in the destination city from the major roads?

The answers to these questions can be quite simple and thus are usually overlooked or taken for granted. Yet many times they are the most intricate, frustrating and time-consuming part of our trip. How many times after entering our rented car do we realize that we are unsure how to get to the highway? Or when we drive for hours just to spend another exhausting 15–30 minutes trying to find parking and the right address?

In a very similar way, the value negotiation process has three main phases (Table P3.1):

| Road Trip process | Value Negotiation process |
|---|---|
| Get out of our city | Build the Bridge |
| Drive through the highway | Value Pursuit |
| Arrive at our desired destination | Make the Best Possible Decision |

**Table P3.1** Three main phases for road trip and negotiation

Though value negotiation is not as linear a process as the road trip, as a framework it helps to think about these stages in the sequence below. Unlike bargaining that pushes us straight and only into alternatives or commitment, value negotiation helps us cover all elements. Each process stage covers some of the seven negotiation elements in a sequence where the previous step facilitates the next. Of course, this is the ideal case!

**1 - Build the Bridge**

COMMUNICATION    RELATIONSHIP

INTERESTS / OPTIONS / FACTS / LEGITIMACY

**2 - Value Pursuit**

If 'yes'    If 'no'

COMMITMENT    ALTERNATIVES

**3 - Best Possible Decision**

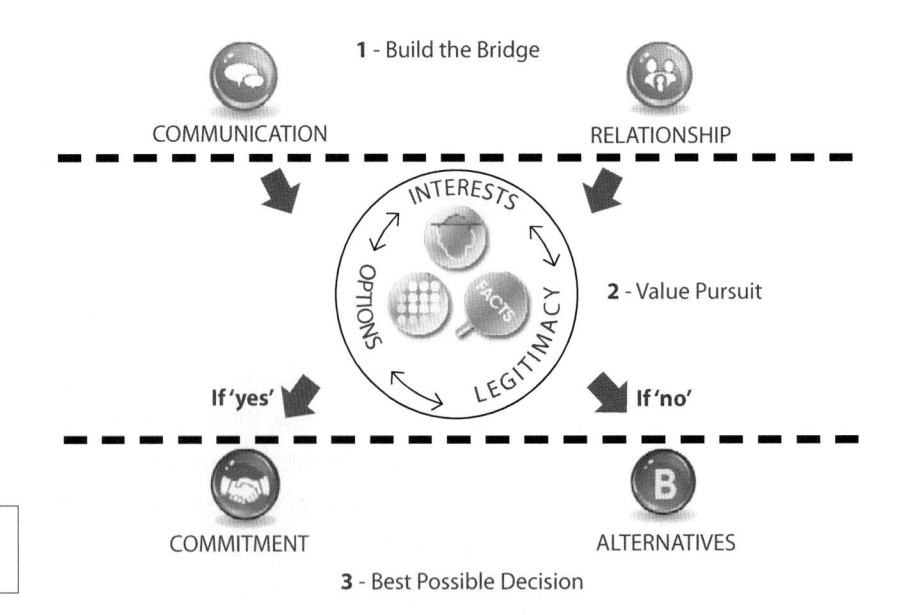

**Figure P3.1** The value negotiation framework

As negotiations take on a life of their own, we may need to move faster, jump or return to a certain stage. Feel free to move around! It is our negotiation after all. The process map offers guidance when negotiators are asked to move at different times, directions and speeds. When that happens, we have to know where we are and what our best next step should be.

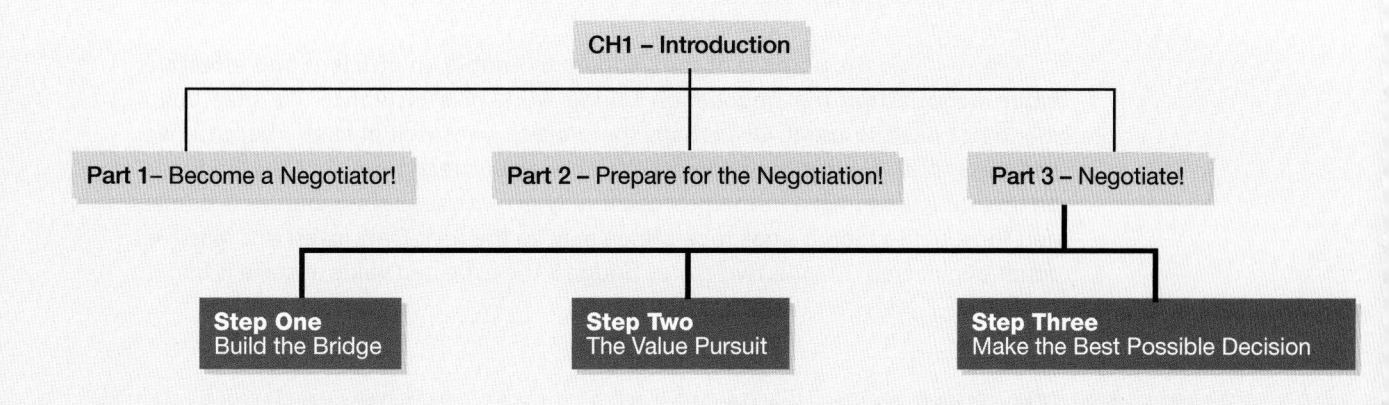

```
                        CH1 – Introduction
        ┌───────────────────────┼───────────────────────┐
Part 1 – Become a Negotiator!   Part 2 – Prepare for the Negotiation!   Part 3 – Negotiate!
                                                            ┌───────────────┼───────────────┐
                                                      Step One         Step Two         Step Three
                                                    Build the Bridge  The Value Pursuit  Make the Best Possible Decision
```

## Build the Bridge

Negotiators are like people on different sides of a river trying to trade goods. Without a bridge, the best we can ever achieve is to throw goods from one bank to the other. Alternatively, we can try to swim across the river. But how much value will be able to throw or carry with this method? Let's see the dialogue below:

> Sorry I am late. But now that I am here we can get started. How can I help you?

> No problem! Good morning! My name is Bruno. And you are?

> Sorry again! My name is Caio. Caio Barbosa. So what do you want?

> Are you in a hurry? If you are, I can work with it. I just want to know. You see, this is an important meeting for me and as I understand for you as well. I wanted to get to know you a little better before we jump into doing this.

> That makes sense! Okay, what would you like to know about me?

**PART 3 • NEGOTIATE** 109

Building a negotiation bridge, as Bruno insisted on doing, creates the right foundations for a high-value, win-win outcome. Jumping this stage create a shallow environment that can easily lead to bargaining. The negotiation bridge is built through the negotiation of both **relationship and communication elements**. With relationship, we seek to build at least a civil and respectful environment for the parties to negotiate. With communication, we negotiate the process within which the parties would like to conduct the negotiation: the rules of the process, the time, the purpose, the people involved, etc.

Keep in mind the purpose of the bridge is **to enable an efficient and effective value negotiation**. The negotiation bridge works like insurance. We may build it and not need to use it. Or perhaps the process went well precisely because we had insurance? We may never know the answer, but recognize that the bridge is an investment we make in the process. It may go without saying, but for a simple and short transaction, a small rope bridge may do the trick. Only invest in a massive, super-engineered, 12-lane, two-storey bridge if the expected value at stake is huge.

## The Value Pursuit

Once the bridge is appropriately built, only eventual maintenance may be necessary. The parties can now concentrate on pursuing value, which is the reason for the negotiation in the first place. The value pursuit supported by the interests, options and legitimacy elements has three phases:

- **Value discovery** (interests) – Negotiators first need to discover and understand all parties' interests, which is what the parties truly attribute value to.
- **Value creation** (options) – Once all interests have been identified, negotiators can come up with options to create the value or satisfy the interests.
- **Value claiming** (legitimacy) - Once value is created, the parties can work on figuring out who is taking what or how much out of the available value.

*"A wise man's question contains half the answer."*

*Popular saying*

The expression "value creation" is more about finding and satisfying the parties' interests. Actual creation is little; rather it is about putting options together in a creative and hopefully satisfying way. Consequently, the value discovery becomes the most important phase as a mistake here can "snowball" into the following phases. However, remember that the discovery and creation phases share the single goal of generating maximum value. This way, negotiators can more easily claim value without having to take it from the other (i.e., Pareto improvements).

# Make the Best Possible Decision

Once the negotiators discover, create and claim all the value they want or can have, what do they do?

| **Popular assumption**: So when it's all said and done, I close the deal as I came here to do. ||
|---|---|
| The feeling the other party has from how we negotiate | **They may think that** we, as negotiators, are desperate, have no good alternatives and will close the deal 'no matter what'. |
| Risk | The other party becomes tempted to charge a premium under the belief that the deal will still be closed even if it is unfair. |
| Reward | The other party will be happy! And we will have a deal (though it may be lousy). |
| **Preferred assumption**: So when it's all said and done, I compare the deal on the table with my BATNA and decide what is best for me (and for those I represent). ||
| The feeling the other party has from how we negotiate | **They may think that** we want what they have to offer, but if they charge an unfair price, we may walk away. |
| Risk | The other party may be upset if the deal is not good enough for us and we decide to walk away. |
| Reward | The other party may offer us more value or at least not feel that they can get away with an unfair deal. |

**Table P3.2**
Making the best possible decision

We should remember that negotiation is a decision-making process. As such, it should help us make the best decision considering both the commitment and alternative elements. If the deal laid out is better than the alternatives, then commit; but if it is not, walk away.

Some deals may have poor alternatives or seemingly none at all, but it is still important to realize we can walk away. One reason is that a deal can eventually turn out so badly that you may prefer to do nothing. Another is to ensure the other party does not charge a premium, as seen above.

So here it is: the value negotiation process, our bridge to a value decision. Next, we will examine each of these three steps within the negotiation in more detail to you. At the end of this section/part, we will hopefully gain the ability and confidence to engage in and lead any negotiation.

# Step 1 - Build the Bridge

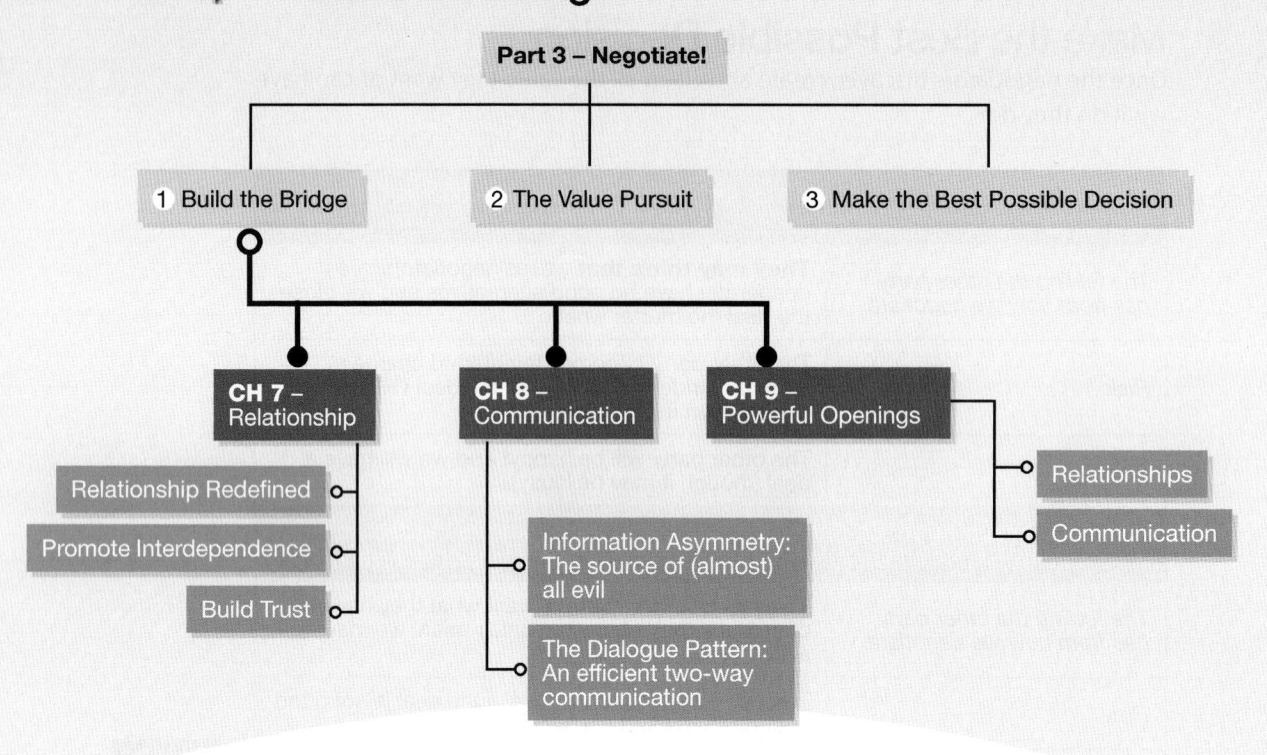

```
                    Part 3 – Negotiate!
        ┌───────────────┬───────────────┐
   1 Build the Bridge  2 The Value Pursuit  3 Make the Best Possible Decision
        │
   ┌────┼────┐
 CH 7 –  CH 8 –    CH 9 –
Relationship  Communication  Powerful Openings

Relationship Redefined                                    Relationships
Promote Interdependence                                   Communication
                    Information Asymmetry:
                    The source of (almost)
                    all evil
Build Trust
                    The Dialogue Pattern:
                    An efficient two-way
                    communication
```

Most people negotiate under a win-lose mentality where negotiation is a battle:

- My *position* is…
- I will do *whatever it takes to win*.
- I will *defend* my arguments.
- I *attacked* his *weak* points.
- I *resisted* and never *gave in*!
- I *took* everything he had!
- I *fought* until my *last breath*.

Under such a mentality, no one tries to build a relationship or communicate better with the other. In a battle, building a bridge to allow our enemy to get closer is clearly stupid.

However, imagine that instead of a battle, the negotiation is seen as a Joint Problem-Solving Process. In this case, getting to know each other and improving the communication are vital for the negotiation's success. Building the bridge creates the necessary infrastructure to work together. Through a positive relationship and efficient communication, we greatly enhance our potential to maximize value.

Unfortunately, due to reasons such as little time or a win-lose mentality, many plunge directly into the value pursuit. Though plunging can work, this adventure is as exciting as swinging on the trapeze without a safety net. With no (relationship and communication) bridge, we risk falling into bargaining as if only substance matters. Any negotiation move here is risky and unstable. Hence in a value negotiation, there is no greater urgency than to build a bridge early on. So we start with learning how to establish a solid relationship and an efficient communication process in our negotiations.

## POINT OF INTEREST

**Distributive and Integrative Negotiations**

Many books refer to negotiations as "distributive" and "integrative". Distributive negotiations are the ones where value can only be distributed and not created (zero-sum). Integrative negotiations are those where value can be integrated or created.

We prefer the more colloquial terms "value discovery," "value creation," and "value-claiming."

We also believe that every negotiation has integrative and distributive components.

Parties may ignore the integrative negotiation potential to concentrate only on the value-claiming.

Nevertheless, ignoring the value-discovery and value-creation potential does not mean that the negotiation was only distributive to begin with. It is rather a choice, conscious or not, to only explore part of its potential.

# 07 Relationship

**Learning Objectives:**
- Why most people mix and trade between the three negotiations
- How to establish interdependence
- What the five components of trust are
- What zero-trust is and how to use it
- What an unconditional contructive behavior is
- Why concessions are very dangerous moves

To build a good working relationship in our negotiations, we need to know how to answer three basic questions:

1. What are we really trying to build to begin with?
2. How do we start building it?
3. How do we strengthen it?

Thus, this chapter is organized to help us do just that:

1. **Define Relationship** – Better define what a relationship is so that we can be sure of working towards the right goal and avoid mixing relationship and substance;
2. **Promote Interdependence** – Positively frame the relationship among the parties to allow them to quickly yet safely adopt a value negotiation process; and
3. **Build Trust** – Make every behavior count towards building trust, while avoiding power differences.

In sum, we want to create an interdependent and sustainable relationship that enables negotiators to better pursue value.

## Relationship Redefined

Every day, thousands if not millions of negotiators give discounts and sacrifice value today to create a long-term relationship. This is a classic example of trading between negotiations by mixing relationship and substance. Why do so many smart people commit such a seemingly basic mistake?

### POINT OF INTEREST

**Relationship with Organisations?**
When World War II veterans were interviewed, they shared that they felt unbearable fear every time they entered a battle. Only one thing made them charge forward anyhow: their desire to not let their fellow soldiers down. It was not orders, a sense of duty, patriotism or even survival. It all boiled down to their relationships. We consider organizations when developing long-term transactions, but we limit long-term relationships to people. We do not have relationships with organizations, but with the people in them.

Our belief is that most negotiators misunderstand the very definition of a relationship for negotiation purposes. When parties talk about a long-term relationship, many times they refer to the repeated number of transactions between similar parties. Well, experiencing several transactions or having a long-term contract does not mean that the parties have a good relationship. **Relationships are built by how we behave and feel towards one another, not by the substance we exchange.**

Thus, to avoid confusion going forward, we want to clarify and define these concepts:

1. Substance (positive or negative depending on the material value generated)
    a) *Short-term transaction* – The value of the present transaction.
    b) *Long-term transaction* – The present value of all past, present and future transactions with the same person or organization.

2. Relationship (positive or negative based on the parties' ability to work together)
    a) *Short-term relationship* – The behaviors and emotions among the people during a specific meeting or interaction.
    b) *Long-term relationship* – The behaviors and emotions among the same people during a series of meetings or interactions.

### POINT OF INTEREST

**When is Relationship the Substance of a Negotiation?**
Never. Even by definition, the relationship will never be the substance value. We can choose to exclusively focus the process on the relationship negotiation, such as a meeting to initiate the relationship with a new client, to improve my relationship with my girlfriend after a discussion, or to build a better relationship with my boss for the future. However, even when only trying to satisfy relationship interests and pursue relationship value, the relationship is not the substance.

These definitions help separate relationship from substance moves to avoid trading between the three negotiations. So, for example, we can have a positive long-term transaction while having a negative long-term relationship. In other words, we made money, but we may never want to see the other party again.

Back to the first example. A negotiator can give a discount today (negative short-term transaction) to close a longer-term contract (positive long-term transaction). However, this negotiator understands that it is a pure money or substance negotiation trade, not a relationship one. This approach helps the negotiator giving the discount to remember the dialogue pattern and pair the discount with a guarantee. This way, we avoid giving value today for a future relationship that may or may not bring future value.

Now we may be left wondering: If my negotiation goal is to maximize value, then what I actually want is positive short- and long-term transactions. Why should I care about the relationship?

Audacious as this question is, we believe it is a very good and relevant one. After all, good relationships require a lot of effort and no one should invest so much without knowing why. We can think of three very value-pragmatic reasons to devote time and attention to building good relationships:

1. **Relationship value** – Found within relationship interests, some examples are to feel like part of a group, be close to someone we know, feel respected, be trusted, etc.

2. **Source of potential future negotiations** – A positive network of relationships expands the resources available. The association with someone of high status or with a specific expertise can come in handy. More people will listen to and do something for us or have us in their radar if they see an opportunity. These relationships increase our potential for future transactions and therefore future value.
3. **Facilitates material value creation** – A good relationship generates interdependence or trust that keeps emotions under control and allows for more rational behaviors. This safe value negotiation environment enables and protects the pursuit of short- and long-term substance value.

Without positive relationships, negotiators are less likely to collaborate, exchange information or pursue maximum value. The investment in relationships increases the short- and long-term overall potential value in a negotiation. Next, let's see how we can best build solid relationships in negotiations through the promotion of interdependence and trust.

# Promote Interdependence

In the previous chapter, we saw that to improve the working relationship, we needed to initiate the interaction promoting interdependence. Interdependence means that negotiators need or are better off dealing with each other to get what they want. Instead of questioning if this relationship is the right one, we can ask: How can this relationship be the right one?

Interdependence is different from dependency or independence (Figure 7.1). Both dependency and independence lead to unilateral dynamics of power. In dependency, they either believe they have power over us (or us over them). In independence, they may believe they do not need us and can do it all on their own. Neither creates an incentive to work together.

Promoting interdependence allows the universal value of reciprocation to surface. Reciprocation is one of the strongest motivators for collaboration in humankind and the animal world.

Interdependence reduces negotiation power dynamics because when we need one another we are less tempted to use power. A very powerful negotiator, who understands his interdependence with a less powerful one, will have a stronger incentive to collaborate. Our job early on is to help them understand our interdependence. This quickly focuses them on the value we can pursue together, instead of on the power that separates us. As a result, interdependence improves our ability to work together and normally builds stronger working relationships.

**Figure 7.1** The various types of dependence

Interdependence quickly builds the initial good working relationships necessary for us to start the negotiation. Interdependence is particularly important if we expect a short-term relationship, as we may never have enough time to build trust in the negotiation. But even for expected longer-term relationships, interdependence creates the initial positive atmosphere for us to work together. As we work together, we experience each other's behaviors and learn if we can trust one another.

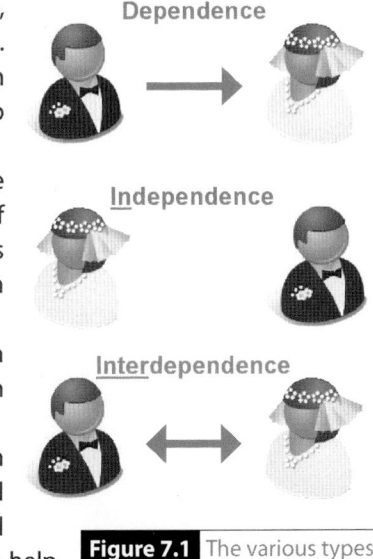

Being faster and easier to establish than trust, interdependence is particularly appropriate as an **early relationship strategy**. We can communicate our need or the advantages to work together faster than persuade someone to trust us. We can argue the logic in working together, but we need evidence to be trusted. Early on, with little data on one another, accepting interdependence is an easier decision than trusting someone.

That is not to say that we should promote interdependence only at the beginning. During critical moments, power temptations are strongest and the relationship is usually most at risk. It is interdependence that will likely keep negotiators collaborating. Thus, we consistently promote interdependence to avoid the feeling of power imbalance among the parties. If dependence becomes the pattern, the negotiation easily falls into a win-lose dynamic.

## Interdependence: From Enemies to Partners

In win-lose negotiations, relationships usually:

- Happen within a battle frame.
- Focus on them as the enemy or the problem.
- Shape an "us vs. them" mentality.
- Create subordinated roles and labels.

As seen at the beginning of this chapter, negotiations are often metaphorically understood as battles. Within a battle frame, negotiators are enemies with an "us vs. them" mentality that encourages power behaviors to subjugate the other.

We aim to substitute the negotiation frame from a battle to a joint value pursuit. First, we erase power distances in the relationship between the parties. Then, we refocus the parties towards value.

Consequently, the problem or opportunity between the parties becomes the value challenge. The enemy is now externalized and dissociated from the parties. This frame develops a "we" mentality so negotiators identify each other as partners instead of enemies. Negotiators can sit side-by-side to productively address the common challenge that brought them together in the first place.

Frames create reality in people's minds. If the other party agrees to our desired frame and we consistently reinforce it, they are more likely to behave differently. More importantly, if we truly see negotiation as a joint value pursuit exercise, we are more likely to behave accordingly.

Interdependence requires a balanced relationship, where no one comes across as trying to dominate the negotiation. We seek collaborative relationship roles as opposed to hierarchical or dependent ones to reduce the power distance between us.

In sum, to build interdependence, the value negotiator will negotiate for:

- A joint value pursuit frame.
- A joint focus on a common opportunity or challenge.
- A "we" mentality.
- Coordinated relationship roles or labels.

# Joint Value Pursuit Frame

Instead of a battle-linked vocabulary, we would like to reframe negotiation so that power has no or almost no use. Value negotiators see negotiation as a value-creation opportunity and thus make statements such as:

- My interests are…
- We will invest our best efforts to maximize our value.
- We will be firm in our intention to build a fair deal for all.
- We explored options to satisfy as many of our interests as possible.
- We avoided concession to create value-enhancing trades and exchanges.
- We maximized the potential value on the table.
- We worked as hard and creatively as we could to generate a collaborative environment.

The value negotiation joint value pursuit (JVP) frame dissipates early win-lose fears and promotes strong interdependence. It helps to keep the focus on collaboration and learning towards value. The JVP frame clarifies early on that our negotiation is not a win-lose game, but rather a partnership invitation in a value-focused collaborative game.

### POINT OF INTEREST

**Joint Value Pursuit vs. Joint Problem Solving?**
The two expressions have very similar goals and attempt to move away from the battle frame. We prefer the Joint Value Pursuit expression to give the negotiation an even more positive and optimistic frame as it focuses on value rather than on a problem.

Similarly, another famous win-win expression is to "focus on a common enemy" to externalize this problem from the parties. Here, we believe that the word "enemy" is still too close to the battle frame, whereas the expression "common opportunity or challenge" is linked closer to a positive teamwork experience.

Normally, disbelief or perceptions of weakness are the bigger risks of the JVP frame. Disbelief normally dissipates under the consistency of our behavior, which demonstrates the truthfulness of our intentions. The perception of weakness can be overcome by proving our resilient focus on value, not power.

The JVP frame should be communicated as early as possible to enhance the chances that it will be accepted. Otherwise, the parties may adopt the default battle frame and the reframing into a JVP becomes a much harder task. Some examples of generic JVP statements are:

- I am glad to meet with you and see what we can do together.
- I am excited with this opportunity to work with you towards creative solutions.
- I am sure that by working together we will be able to come up with lots of valuable ideas.
- I am here today so that we can all overcome this challenge in front of us.

All the above statements have a few aspects in common: working together (not for one another or alone), the frame evolves towards "we" (not "I" or "you" only), a transparent explanation of intentions and normally a focus on value, solutions, opportunity or challenge. Next, we will elaborate on these common aspects to help build interdependence in negotiations.

## Focus on a Common Challenge or Opportunity

The advice "Don't shoot the messenger" was first attributed to Shakespeare in both his works *Henry IV*, part 2 (1598) and in *Antony and Cleopatra* (1606–07). Though a popular saying in many parts of the world, this "shooting" is still done by many negotiators.

Are we saying that negotiators are just messengers? Not necessarily. And yet, many times we treat the other parties as enemies when they bring us bad news or reject our requests. After all, in a battle frame, only our enemies prevent us from getting what we want. This behavior contradicts the popular saying "Attack the problem, not the people," which many know intuitively or from experience to be wise advice.

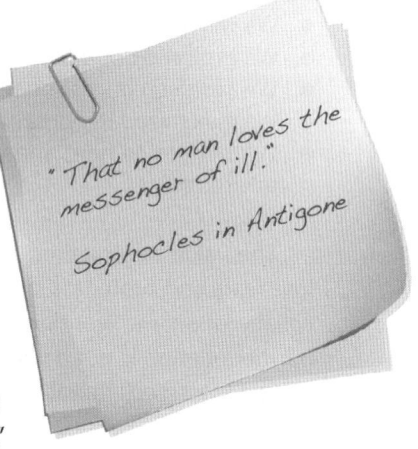

*"That no man loves the messenger of ill."*

*Sophocles in Antigone*

### POINT OF INTEREST

**Attack the Problem?**
- So, what is your problem?
- I don't have any problems.
- Sorry, what do you believe is the problem between the two of us?
- I already told you, I do not have a problem! Maybe you do!

The expression "attack the problem, not the people" reminds us not to be negative to the people in a negotiation. However, many people associate the idea of a problem with something negative. Many negotiators react against the idea of a problem as they may perceive it as a weakness. Hence, we prefer to use the terms "challenges" and "opportunities" as they are more value-focused and more commonly associated with something positive.

Messengers of bad news may actually be our best allies. They are the ones helping us to prepare for the worst or to understand what the real value limitations could be. And when we believe and demonstrate that other negotiators are not our problem, they are much less inclined to defend themselves. As we are not attacking them, their resistance fades and they start to investigate solutions or focus on the real issues.

Within a JVP frame, we first shift our focus to an external challenge or opportunity. Following the spirit of the Arabian proverb: "The enemy of my enemy is my friend", an external "enemy" can simultaneously suspend the parties from seeing each other as enemies and create a sense of unity. Here, we seek anything that gives the parties reason to need each other and to eventually come together to address it. Thus, we should choose the challenge or opportunity which most strongly encourages collaboration to maximize the incentives to work together.

So which challenges and opportunities would do this? Are resources scarce? Are we up against a limiting or unfair rule? Do we lack authority to solve a problem?

The answer is whatever pitches one party against the other as enemies. In a value negotiation, the most important challenge or opportunity is overcoming value-creation obstacles. There are three categories which normally limit value creation:

- **Resource constraint** – The negotiation cannot create enough value due to a real or perceived scarce resource (such as money). Consequently, we are seen as competition for this resource in a positional bargaining.
  - **Suggestion** – Invite them to search together for more or alternative resources.
- **Artificial limit** – We cannot create value due to a law, policy, rule, tradition, habit, assumption, agreement or any other external human-made limitation. Obstacles to value can be unfair even if they come with good intentions.
  - **Suggestion** – Invite them to either jointly renegotiate the externally imposed artificial limit or to find options that respect the limit while allowing the pursuit of extra value.
- **Narrow scope** – At least one party has a limited mandate or view of the negotiation due to lack of authority, preparation, time, courage, willingness, vision, etc. It limits the negotiator's ability to see or go beyond their initial goals.
  - **Suggestion** – Invite them to explore ideas without the need to agree on them today or include conditions, guarantees and safety nets.

Positional negotiators believe their team is "us" and the others are "them." This frames the negotiation as opposing groups. The JVP frame emphasizes the negotiation's shared nature, where "us" represents all parties and "them" common challenges or opportunities. However, to strengthen the sense of interdependence even further, we can go beyond just reframing the "us vs. them" mentality.

# The "We" Mentality

The "us vs. them" mentality makes negotiators see each other as enemies and creates obstacles in building good relationships. If others appear too different from us and we do not identify any connection, it becomes easier to dehumanize them. If we are different, then they do not deserve the same respect or standards we give ourselves. It becomes easier to treat them poorly or to justify any bad acts against them.

In extreme cases, dehumanization has been used to justify genocides, including Nazis towards Jews or Hutus towards Tutsis in the 1994 Rwanda conflict. A report on the Rwanda conflict clearly registers this issue:

There are psycho-political phenomena of demonization and dehumanization, which transform the opponent into a non-human and dangerous being, which should be killed if one wants to survive. The purpose of this is to change violence against him into a redeeming action, which, at the same time, constitutes a justification… It is within that logic that the Tutsis, in particular in Rwanda, in times of the successive crises and conflicts, were given the names of insects such as "Inyenzi" (cockroaches) or "Inzoka" (snakes) and the Hutus who were unfavourable to violence were persecuted.

Fortunately, in most negotiations, the dehumanization risk is much smaller. However, the need to bridge the "us vs. them" gap remains. As seen above, one way to do so is to refocus on a common challenge or opportunity. To avoid the temptation to label the others as "them," it is helpful to apply that label to something else altogether. In Rwanda, it could have been to refocus on overcoming the resource scarcity that plagued the country then.

Nevertheless, this refocusing may not be enough to humanize us in each other's eyes. Thus, to build strong relationships, we also promote the "we" mentality. Once we see ourselves as equals, we are more likely to believe we can partner together independently of the reason. We are also less likely to believe that we have a right or power over them. In sum, we need to believe that we are similar at some level.

## POINT OF INTEREST

**We Who? Us Who?**
One inherent risk when attempting to develop a "we" mentality is linguistic in nature. The ambiguous use of "we" or "us" may lead the other negotiators to believe we are referring only to our team or company. Therefore, though a small detail, it is important to make the reference explicit to them. We can say, for example, "all of us here today" or if there are six negotiators, "the six of us together."

Referring to all negotiators as "we" or "us" sends an implicit message that we are one group. Former president of Ecuador, Jamil Mahuad, and former president of Peru, Alberto Fujimori, met to negotiate the Twinza conflict. Mahuad's first move was to sit beside Fujimori with a document in hand that described their conflict. He then pointed to the document and said: "Fujimori, we have a problem!" This was the beginning of what then became a strong friendship.

With this statement, Mahuad externalized the problem and refocused the negotiation towards a common challenge: solving the Twintza conflict. His "we" mentality statement, simple as it was, acknowledged Fujimori as a partner, not as the problem. It facilitated working together and invited Fujimori's ideas to overcome the challenge.

To create an even stronger "we" mentality, Mahuad could have added: "As presidents of two neighboring nations, we have a problem." This would clarify their common identity link for that particular negotiation. Mentioning "neighboring nations" instead of "nations at war" highlights what brings them together, instead of what separates them. The label of "we = presidents" places them in roles of equal power. His action to sit beside Fujimori probably enhanced the sense of working together and collaboration.

As seen in the example above, there are two main techniques to build a "we" mentality: sit side-by-side and invoke collaborative relationship roles.

## Sit Side-By-Side

The metaphor "sit side-by-side" opposes the idea of sitting as enemies on opposite sides of the table ("us vs. them"). This metaphor is so powerful that it can be followed literally like Mahuad did when negotiating with Fujimori. Value negotiators often sit on the same side of the table and in front of a flipchart, board or document. Sitting in this manner signals that we are ready to work together as a team ("we" mentality). However, to sit side-by-side is not to be only taken literally.

Negotiators may disagree on some issues, but they normally agree on many others. Unfortunately, the latter usually go assumed or unspoken. When developing a "we" mentality, persuade and remind them that on the more relevant topics, we sit side-by-side.

> **POINT OF INTEREST**
>
> **Yes, BUT vs. Yes, AND**
> Fewer small things seem to put people on opposing sides more than the expression "Yes, but". It is considered as the great eraser in negotiation. The "but" erases any positive message you may have sent with your "Yes". Imagine if after supporting your case for 20 minutes, the other party says "Yes, but…," or "Your idea is good, but…," you know a disagreement is coming, even if they liked 99% of it. However, the focus is on the 1% concern they have. Many times, what we really want to say is. "Yes and" such as in "I like your idea and I see some minor risks. Would you like me to share my concerns?"

Actually, many negotiators by instinct or otherwise attempt to sit side-by-side by saying:

- Before you continue your argument, please remember we are on the same side.
- I am on your team. I am with you on this one.
- I am not against you here. I am just trying to…
- I think we are saying the same thing in different ways.

These statements generally try to convey the message that we are here to help or to work together. It conveys our perception, and more importantly our intention, of being on the same side. It does accept the existence of differences but with a belief that we can overcome them.

Other statements that can help negotiators sit side-by-side are:

- Your interests are also important for me.
- I am here with a strong intention to help you maximize your value as well.
- I believe that if I help you satisfy your interests, you are more likely to help me do the same.

A metaphorical "sitting side-by-side" can happen when we share our intention or belief that their interests are also important to us. Though talking about their interests, we are showing that we are by their side. They do not need to be afraid or look over their shoulders at every critical moment of the negotiation anymore. Our transparency of intentions helps them understand, and more importantly, believe that we perceive this as an interdependent situation. We are likely to be better off if we help them be better off.

Two risks can take place when making statements to sit side-by-side: the statement may be perceived as a unilateral commitment to help or as insincere. On the aspect of unilateral commitment, notice that the three statements above were carefully aligned with the dialogue pattern principle:

- Your interests are *also* important for me. (Not necessarily more than or at the expense of mine.)
- I am here with a *strong intention* to help you maximize your value as well. (But with no unilateral commitment if you are not willing to do the same.)
- I believe that if I help you satisfy your interests, *you are more likely* to help me do the same. (Keeping action conditional to the reciprocation.)

The insincerity aspect can be a perception due to their disbelief about what we say or even our own disbelief. To manage the latter, we need to remember that eliminating resistance is a key enabler of value negotiation and maximization. And that is unlikely to happen, if we do not attempt to help them win as well. Thus, we have no reason to be insincere about our intentions to help, if not for magnanimous reasons then at least for selfish ones like maximizing our own value.

If the other party is suspicious, we can transparently share our belief that helping them is the easiest way to help ourselves. Few negotiators believe those who claim to care for others in a negotiation out of the goodness of their hearts. But most will see, and therefore believe, the value logic behind reducing or eliminating resistance. Funnily enough, in situations of suspicion, it is sometimes easier to believe the selfish than the selfless.

## Choose Collaborative Roles

The relationship that we choose defines rank, power and ultimately what we can or cannot say or do. Imagine the following conversation at work with the boss:

> Boss, could you help me out here?

> As your boss, I am not supposed to do your job for you. However, as a colleague, I am more than glad to lend a helping hand.

> As your employee, I have to thank you. As your colleague, I can say that this was weird...

As seen above, the roles we choose in any given negotiation can have great impact on how we behave. Normally, negotiators try to choose roles from hierarchies or contexts that carry the most power: client instead of seller, father instead of son, boss instead of employee. However, these roles create a power or top-down temptation to engage in a win-lose negotiation. Since these hierarchies and contexts are fluid in time, eventually things change and so will the power: monopoly seller instead of buyer; independent son instead of ailing father; star talent employee instead of struggling boss.

The problem with these choices (or lack of) is that they consistently increase the power distance between the parties. Let's look at the following dialogue between Melissa and the manager of her university gym:

> Hi! I am a student here at the university and a frequent user of the gym. Do you have a few minutes for us to talk?

> Hi! Sure. How can I help you? Is there a problem?

> As your client, I have several ideas to improve the gym.

> But we just went through a significant renovation a few months back. Didn't you notice it?

> I know. I know. The renovation was okay.

> Okay? We tried to implement everything that the customer survey asked us to. We spent lots of time, effort and money on it.

> Yeah. I know. Please do not take this badly, but there are still some minor things that could have a great impact if changed.

> I do not know if anything can be done at this point. It would have been great to have your ideas one year back when we were planning the renovation.

After a neutral introduction, Melissa framed herself as a client entitled to be heard and attended to. The gym manager started believing there was a problem, since that was why clients normally sought him out. The power Melissa had being the client already generated some resistance. Add the unilateral improvement "demand" and the lack of acknowledgement of the gym's renovation, and we can imagine why Melissa did not come across as an ally. The manager was left to defend himself against an "enemy," which he did to the end.

Now, Melissa probably did not think that by calling herself a "client," all these bad consequences would happen. Her intentions were probably good and motivated by the desire to share ideas to improve a gym she already liked. Her use of "as your client" was probably just to legitimize that she knew what she was talking about. Unfortunately, independent of her intentions, the act was perceived as a power play and thus rejected. Roles can frame our relationship with their own baggage. Thus we need to understand what these roles are to manage what they bring to our negotiation.

Instead of leaving it to chance and falling prey to the power temptation, value negotiators choose roles that promote collaboration. These questions can help us do so:

- What roles are relevant for our conversation and consistent with the JVP frame?
- What roles will more likely eliminate the power difference or temptation between us? (Focus on common challenges and opportunities.)
- What roles connect us and bring us a closer relationship? ("We" mentality — whatever makes us similar can bring us closer.)
- What roles better allow us and them to express ourselves and to show that we care? (Sit side-by-side.)
- What roles make them feel good about themselves? (After all, no one likes to be the bad guy unnecessarily.)

Some general examples are mentor-mentee, colleagues, team members, business partners, friends, etc. Notice that collaborative roles normally only require one word compared to the two-word dichotomy of power roles (e.g., buyer-seller). When invoking collaborative roles, the seller who usually fears the power of the buyer, can say: "As two players in this very cyclical yet volatile market, I would like to explore how the two of us can reduce our risks together. What do you say?"

Collaborative roles usually promote the dialogue pattern more naturally. This way, the negotiators feel the roles are balanced between them. In a JVP frame, all parties are supposed to be participating. There should be no unilateral impositions made or concessions demanded. Thus, it will also be helpful to ask:

- Which roles avoid dominating the conversation?
- Which roles create more opportunities for joint activities? (Doing things together increases trust and a sense of partnership.)

For example, instead of coming up with a list of ideas, we can invite them to contribute ideas pertaining to a certain issue. If we have an idea, we can ask for suggestions on how to improve it.

Now imagine Melissa using a value negotiation approach in her conversation (Table 7.1):

| NEGOTIATION DIALOGUE | DIAGNOSTICS |
|---|---|
| Hi! I am a student here at the university and a frequent user of the gym. As such, I noticed the recent renovations and I wanted to say that I liked them a lot. | Made a general introduction to legitimize why she can praise the work done. Adds a positive tone to the conversation (sits side-by-side) |
| *Really. It's kind of you to share. We spent a lot of time, money and effort in doing so and it is great to see that you enjoyed it.* | *Appreciating the recognition and further explaining the effort. Accepting and sharing the sitting side-by-side* |
| Indeed. It became clear to pretty much everyone that you are committed to improving the gym services and experiences. | Confirming assumption of collaborative relationship role: you are an individual committed to the institution |
| *We are! After all, if we do not do it, people will complain or stop coming altogether and we do not want that. Besides, as a fitness enthusiast myself, of course, I enjoy working out in a nice place.* | *Confirming assumption and further explaining it, including a personal note that explains the professional interest* |
| I couldn't agree more. You may not know that I am also one of the members of the Student Council, and like you I am constantly trying to improve overall services and experiences in our university. | Finding and explaining the collaborative role that connects them: we are individuals committed to this institution ("we" mentality) |
| *Good to know. Is there something else that you would like to share?* | *Appreciative, but trying to now know where this is going* |
| Actually, I do. Once the renovations were done, we had some new ideas that we are glad to share with you that we believe could potentially improve the services and experiences even further. Would you like to hear them? | Focusing on a common opportunity. Acknowledging that the renovation generated new ideas/opportunities which will be shared only if he wants = not a complaint |
| *Sure. Ideas are always good. I do not know if we will be able to make them all happen, but I would love to hear them out.* | *Open, but still making clear that there are no commitments, just listening so far. Not trusting but starting the interdependence* |
| I agree. We just wanted to learn your reactions to them. We do not have all the information, but we thought it would be a waste or even selfish to not share them with you. | Accepting the non-committal process and their less knowledgeable point-of-view and explaining motivations to share. Making the manager feel secure and in control, no power struggle. Again sitting side-by-side |
| *I am all ears.* | *Probably seeing her as a potential ally that could lead to a good opportunity* |
| Well, there are three main ideas: first... | Starting on the substance of the negotiation |

**Table 7.1** Using a value negotiation approach

This is a completely different negotiation, where Melissa actually gets the gym manager to listen and probably consider her ideas. The gym manager might not trust Melissa yet, but feels positive and confident enough (interdependence) to work with her. She managed to develop the sense of interdependence through a Joint Value Pursuit frame, a common opportunity (or challenge), a "we" mentality, sitting side-by-side and choosing collaborative roles. Next, we build trust to strengthen relationships further.

# Build Trust

In Chapter 6 (Anticipate the Critical Moments), we discussed how one should negotiate independently of trust while promoting interdependence. Before we continue, we would like to make a very serious statement: Trust is very important for negotiations! If anyone thought that we did not believe in trust, we just wanted to clarify that we do. Good! We just needed to get this out of the way. Now we are clear.

Negotiating independently of trust is important when initiating the interaction. However, trust can also generate several negotiation benefits. Trust generates positive expectations about the other parties, thus limiting the worst-case scenario or fear-based thinking. As a consequence, negotiators are more open to exchange or provide information about their interests. In turn, negotiators learn more and increase the value-creation potential. For example, with trust, chances are that the parties will talk about and identify options to trade. Trust is also persuasive, since requests made by someone trustworthy are more likely to be accepted.

However, there can be too much trust, since trust can create contentment and blind the parties from learning further. Trust increases the chances that a negotiator will accept what is said by the other side without any legitimacy to back it up. To maintain a "nice" relationship, we may fail to double-check what is being said. That is not to say that the parties will necessarily lie to or mislead one another. Eventually, someone may make a mistake, and in an environment of trust, this may unfortunately be accepted and acted upon.

Furthermore, too much trust may tempt us to trade relationship arguments for substance gains. Thus, it is important to avoid relying on trust alone as a short-cut to success in the substance negotiation. After all, trust is not the end, but the means to create the best conditions for the value pursuit (substance negotiation). Trust, for example, is no substitute for a good process (communication negotiation) however easier and better it makes the negotiation.

Next, we explore the concept of trust in more depth and try to understand its many dimensions and levels. Then, we look at how we can use unconditionally constructive behaviors to build a strong, trust-based relationship.

## Understanding Trust

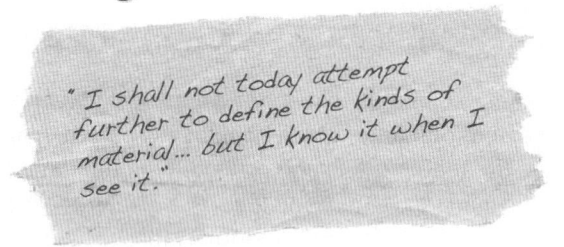

> "I shall not today attempt further to define the kinds of material... but I know it when I see it."

Some may recognize this quote as belonging to Potter Stewart (Associate Justice, US Supreme Court) when referring to obscenity. Hopefully no one will take offense with this comparison, as the same could be said by many when asked about trust. Can trust be defined? What do we really mean when we talk about trust?

Indeed, trust is like the Holy Grail — everyone pursues it, but only a few seem to really grasp its meaning. Consequently, most negotiators leave trust-building to chance, which is understandable if we do not know what trust really looks like.

The bad news is that trust represents different things to different people. The good news is that these different meanings are like layers of trust, which do not contradict one another. Below we dissect the trust layers to better understand and proactively build trust in our negotiations.

## The Anatomy of Trust

Consider the normal steps involved in most hiring processes:

1. First, the company examines CVs for information on the candidates' ability to perform the work.
2. Second, candidates whose CVs have established credibility on the required skills and experience are invited for an interview. The interview checks on the honesty of the information sometimes by testing some of the skills and experience.
3. Third, the company then asks for references, which are contacted to double-check on the ability and honesty. The references also inform on the candidate's reliability in a long-term relationship.
4. Finally, the candidate returns for more subjective, though no less important, interviews. The interviews become intimate one-on-one conversations, where the team looks for the cultural fit or connection with the candidate. The company is more likely to answer questions and to persuade the candidate to join.

Devised to hire the best person for the job, the interview process is not just about skills. Job candidates try to prove they can fit in and be trusted to deliver better than other candidates.

Hiring is a serious trust-building exercise (relationship negotiation). The hiring process phases illustrate the different trust categories as defined below:

- **Ability** – To trust someone's skills, knowledge or credentials to deliver on a promise.
- **Honesty** – To trust someone's good intentions to deliver on a promise.
- **Reliability** – To trust someone's consistency and availability to deliver on a promise.
- **Intimacy** – To trust someone's similar emotion or perspective on issues important to you.
- **Caring** – To trust someone also has our best interests at heart to deliver on a promise.

Intimacy is the more subjective, emotional and personal part of trust. For example, if two people like butterflies, there may still be no intimacy between them. But if liking butterflies partially defines who they are, this may well be a door to intimacy between them. Fortunately or unfortunately, there is no single formula to develop intimacy.

Caring normally does not have its separate behavior, but is intertwined within each and every other aspect of trust. Even if money is a candidate's main motivation, we prefer one who also cares about the job and the organization. It is harder to trust an employee who only works for the money. Similarly, a salesperson who only wants to sell will probably not be trusted. The buyer wants a salesperson that cares about the buyer choosing the best product and making a fair deal.

Finally, do notice that these five components of trust can happen alone or in pretty much any combination: we trust them as honest, but we may not care about them; we believe we are able and care about them, but we may never be there when they need us. The strongest trust happens when all five categories come together, but this is usually not realistic or even necessary.

## Trust Different People Differently

Now that we understand the different trust components, we can define our relationship negotiation goals. We cannot invest the time and effort to build all five components with everyone we meet or deal with. Imagine the following dialogue taking place on a bus:

> Tickets, please.

> How are you doing sir? Nice to see you again. Do you remember me? I take this bus every day at the exact same time. I am sure I have seen you before.

> Tickets, please.

> What is your name? Mine is Albert. Do you take this bus often? What are your favorite bus stops?

> Sir, do you have a ticket at all?

> Of course I do. What do you think I am? By the way, I am actually an accountant at KLO Accountants. Do you know it by any chance?

> Sir, you either show me your ticket right now or you'll have to leave the bus.

> Okay, then. Having a bad day are we? No worries, I take this bus every day, so I am sure to see you around. I hope your day gets better. Bye!

A little overkill, maybe? Hopefully the dialogue above illustrates how we need to adapt our trust-building efforts to the relationship at hand. In the case above, the relationship hardly merits any trust-building investment at all.

How do we calibrate our trust-building efforts to the relationship at hand? Normally, we look into two interactive variables: the depth of personal relationship and the breadth of business issues. If we expect major interactions, we check the status of our relationship and invest in trust accordingly. If our relationship is already strong, we may only need a small trust maintenance effort to conclude a big transaction.

We can focus our trust-building efforts on the missing components necessary to strengthen the relationship. This targeted approach makes the relationship strong enough to support the interaction we desire, but not more than necessary. The relationships can fit broadly into four categories:

- **Transactions** – The simplest and most ritualized relationship; transactions are part of daily routine, like buying a newspaper or taking a bus. They only require trusting someone's **ability** to perform a certain task efficiently. We normally make a request, pay for it and only expect it to be fulfilled. Positions, not interests are the norm here.
- **Needs** – Needs-based relationships represent the majority of our important negotiations. In a fancy restaurant, we may ask: "What is the chef's recommendation?" Instead of being positional, we ask for options. Our ignorance risks them recommending the expensive fish that will be disposed of if not served today. Thus, we need to trust the waiter's **honesty**.
- **Partnership** – We not only convey our needs, but also potential joint opportunities. We may need more time and, due to its higher complexity, risk greater variability and information asymmetry. Thus, **reliability** to weather the tough moments is a trust requisite. Partnerships share responsibility for options.
- **Trust** – The broadest and most complex business issues are better supported within the robustness of a trust relationship. As in partnerships, we trust them with our needs and opportunities, and jointly engage in finding options. However, the trust relationship is one we often control less but respect more. They can, even if unsolicited, share their critical opinion. A trust relationship stimulates an **intimate** appreciation for and a deep understanding of one another.

Why was the caring component not linked to a specific relationship category? Caring is the trust component that we want in appropriate amounts in every relationship we engage in. At a fast-food restaurant, transactional as it may be, I want them to be able to deliver a hamburger. But I also want them to at least care if I found the hamburger any good.

As we increase the relationship complexity (i.e., more issues and deeper relationship), we require additional trust layers to better support it. For example, the needs-based relationship requires ability from the transaction relationship plus honesty. The amount of caring probably increases as well. So when deciding what relationship we want to develop in a negotiation, we should take that extra investment into account.

The trust-based relationship can be seen as the pinnacle of trust, though it cannot be the goal of every relationship. No one can have or even desire all their relationships to be trust-based. Think about the time and energy needed to achieve and maintain such relationships! Only very few trust-based relationships can generate a decent return on the time and energy invested. We have to balance relationship and substance goals before committing to invest more in them. Many times, managing a few partnership-based relationships well can be just as good and profitable as handling trust-based ones.

On the other hand, many negotiations fail for lack of relationship investment. For instance, many major negotiations are supported only by a transactional-based relationship. Consequently, negotiators resort to win-lose tactics or fail to reach agreement. The value negotiator proactively chooses to invest in the appropriate relationship support to enable a better substance negotiation.

## Zero-Trust
### Starting with Trust

As the fourth and last day of their romantic trip to Prague came to an end, Mr. and Mrs. Wang sadly went to check out of the Hotel Bellagio. They carefully reviewed the bill but before they could pay, a beautiful picture book on Prague caught their attention. They decided to buy it. Mr. Wang then received and signed the new bill. They deposited their luggage in the luggage room and left to enjoy their last hours in Prague.

After an enjoyable afternoon, the Wangs returned to pick up their luggage and board a taxi to the airport. As they entered the hotel, the same receptionist approached them, looking horrified, and said:

> I am so glad you have not left yet. I am so, so sorry! Please forgive me!

> Okay, we are here. What happened?

> Well, when I added the book to your bill, the total came up to Kč27,000, but I pressed the "000" button once by mistake, so you signed on a bill of Kč2,700,000. I am very sorry! I am glad I caught you before you left. Please let me have your credit card to cancel the last bill and issue a new one with the correct price.

> Sure. Here it is.

Conversely, imagine if the Wangs had left directly to the airport. They would have received a massive credit card bill and probably gotten very angry and suspicious, even though the establishment just committed a honest mistake without any ill intentions. Actually, the receptionist double-checked the bill and found the mistake, which she subsequently brought up and rectified. So after this experience, can the hotel be trusted? Yes and no. Good intentions aside, there is always human error to account for.

This then begs the question: can anyone be trusted 100%? No one is perfect and we sometimes make mistakes, just like anyone else. By trusting someone 100%, we put unjust pressure on them by expecting them to never make a mistake. Even if they have good intentions, they cannot live up to that level of expectation.

Trust gives us a subjective sense of safety and understanding about each other's interests. Trusting 100% makes us believe we know more about each other's interests than we actually do. Consequently, the curiosity to ask, listen and learn diminishes until it all but stops. In sum, as trust increases, so does the risk that the negotiation will advance based on more assumptions and less data.

## Starting with Distrust

In Koh Samui, Thailand, Andre walked into a resort seeking his most esoteric adventure ever. Despite his ex-girlfriend's recommendation, he still wanted to learn more before signing up for this one-week fasting program. Since he never believed or did anything like this before, he was a little guarded about the whole experience. As he arrived, he sought the manager who had a thick Australian accent:

> **Hugh:** Hi, mate! I'm Hugh. You are interested in our fasting program, is that right?

> **Andre:** Yes. I would like to learn some more. I have never done anything like it before.

> **Hugh:** No problem. Where are you from? What do you do?

> **Andre:** I'm a banker in Hong Kong.

> **Hugh:** Coming here to de-stress from the financial big-city life, right? No problem at all, let me explain the program... (Hugh gives a detailed explanation)

> **Andre:** Thanks for sharing the good, the bad and the ugly. So how much would it cost?

> **Hugh:** Well, as you can see here in the list, the price is 31,000 baht. Since you mentioned that you already have housing here on the island, we will give you the take-away package, which is right on this page here. (He flips a binder to a page which reads "Take-Away Fasting Program: 19,000 baht") Well, this is not really the same program for you. Actually... (he flips the binder quickly back to the original page) the package for you would have a 10% discount, so the total would be around 27,000 baht.

> **Andre:** Thank you. I will think this through and come back to you later.

Andre felt Hugh tried to overcharge him. He decided he would not go through such an important experience under the guidance of someone he distrusted. As a result, he never asked about the differences between the 19,000-baht and the 27,000-baht packages. Andre never returned.

As Andre demonstrated, distrust does not guarantee deeper probing. On the contrary, many times the distrusting negotiator assumes the worst-case scenario and just gives up. Instead, Andre could have asked and learned that the 19,000-baht package was shorter than the initially discussed seven-day program. Even if Hugh was overcharging, maybe he was expecting some bargaining from a potentially aggressive banker. Checking his assumption could have led Andre to choose a shorter program or find room to negotiate the price. If Hugh were indeed overcharging, Andre could still leave afterwards.

### Starting with Zero-Trust

Value negotiators believe that more information improves the quality of the communication and the resulting value creation. But how can we avoid starting with trust or distrust since they reduce learning? Start with zero-trust instead.

"Zero-trust" derives from the term "suspicion" which happens "when one entertains multiple, plausibly rival, hypotheses about another's motives." In zero-trust, we hold off judgment to come up with alternative interpretations why someone would say or do something. Unfortunately, in less academic environments, instead of neutral ambiguity, suspicion has a negative connotation. As seen in the following Merriam-Webster definition, suspicion can indicate distrust, an assumption of wrongdoing and a need to investigate:

> SUSPICION (\-\ - noun)
> 1 a: the act or an instance of suspecting something wrong without proof or on slight evidence
>
> MISTRUST: a state of mental uneasiness and uncertainty: DOUBT

We prefer the term "zero-trust" to promote unbiased learning as it is void of positive (trust) or negative (distrust) connotations. Assuming knowledge of the parties' interests, the trusting negotiator tries to save time by not asking many questions. Assuming the worst, the distrusting negotiator may give up and just walk away. However, the zero-trust negotiator holds back on assumptions, is more curious and motivated to learn. Consequently, we seek more information and, in the process, improve the quality of the communication and of the deal.

A challenge in zero-trust is to withhold judgment while proactively attempting to build trust. Zero-trust is just the best starting point for the trust-building exercise. As soon as new information arises, we proactively start building trust. In such an environment, negotiators eventually feel safe to share information and create more value together.

Is zero-trust actually possible? Not really. When two people meet, they are already outside of zero-trust as an intuitive trust or distrust immediately emerges between them. In zero-trust, we try to not let trust or distrust run rampant and expose us to unnecessary risks. It is then helpful to ask ourselves: "Am I trusting or distrusting without data to back this feeling up? If so, why?"

Zero-trust is a discipline to promote increased information exchange, rational trust efforts and value-creation decisions based on legitimacy. The zero-trust discipline has us ask ourselves at an early stage: "If trust were not an issue in this negotiation, how would I behave? What should I do to build a good environment, keep learning and create value?"

## Be Unconditionally Constructive

So far we have learned what trust is, what we want out of it and where to start building it. Now, we just need to learn how to build it. Trust is built by our dozens, hundreds or thousands of behaviors in any given interaction. To be aware of and align our many potential moves, we need a very simple rule: be unconditionally constructive.

An unconditionally constructive behavior (UCB) is any behavior that is simultaneously:

- Good for the relationship between the parties;
- Good for them; and
- Good for us, even if they do not reciprocate our action (the "unconditional" part of the strategy).

It is easy to fall into one of two main mistakes when negotiating the relationship: reacting to their unproductive behaviors with similar actions and creating a vicious circle; or mistaking unconditionally constructive for unconditionally nice and becoming a pushover.

Many soft bargainers fail precisely at this step. They often make unilateral substance concessions to the other side, in hope of reciprocation. However, we cannot consistently bet our relationship-building efforts on potential reciprocation alone. What happens if our unilateral move goes unreciprocated? Though the other party may have never signaled or intended to reciprocate, we will most likely feel betrayed. As a result, our relationship suffers.

### POINT OF INTEREST

**Can Power Build Trust?**
Though possible, it comes at a high cost! For example, in the article *Risky Business: Trust in Negotiations* by Deepak Malhotra, the author lists six trust-building moves. Two moves in particular could be interpreted as power moves, namely "make unilateral concessions" or "make dependence a factor." While these moves can increase trust, we believe that they do so while risking value. The trade between the relationship and substance negotiations can generate the unintended consequence of a power imbalance between the parties. The unilateral or dependency moves can result in a non-reciprocal and unsustainable trust, not to mention the potential value loss.

**How About Substance?**
Maximizing joint gains to build trust is one advice to use substance to generate trust. We agree that negotiators feel better about each other when they achieve a joint-gains outcome. We just believe they may not necessarily trust each other for it. What if next time they are not able to build joint gains? Should they stop trusting each other then? It is the working and caring for one another within the process of developing joint gains that builds trust.

To avoid falling into the above bargaining traps, the value negotiator thinks before acting in a certain way:

- *Will that increase the trust among the negotiators? (Good for the relationship)*
- *Will they appreciate it? (Good for others)*
- *Will I benefit without sending a sign of or exposing a weakness? Will I feel good about it even if they do not reciprocate? (Unconditionally good for me)*

Constructive behaviors take every possible opportunity to strengthen a relationship (high reward). When unconditional, they minimize the expectation of reciprocation and thus the temptation to make unilateral substance moves to build relationship (reduced risk of trading between the three negotiations). This in turn allows us to lead the relationship negotiation independently of their intentions or behaviors. With guessing minimized, the high-reward/low-risk equation of UCBs makes them ideal relationship-building moves.

UCBs could be considered as being built on the old Brazilian adage: "One thinking head is better than none!" Every person in a relationship has a potential share of responsibility and control. Being unconditionally constructive means taking this share to improve the relationship. Even if the other side does not reciprocate, the relationship will still be better off because we are doing our part.

In sum, UCBs do not put a negotiator at risk or leave us any worse off than before. On the other hand, they build better relationships even if reciprocation does not follow. With their unconditional nature, UCBs lead by example, which often encourages positive reciprocation. When reciprocated, UCBs then have an even stronger ability to build trust. Below, we share six examples of UCBs.

## Be Rational

People have emotions. However, it is risky to either ignore or depend on emotions in a negotiation. Being rational is the **controlled and balanced management of emotions**, rather than total inclusion or exclusion of them. Instead of reacting angrily, the negotiator can communicate the feeling and seek ways to deal with the situation:

> For the last few minutes, your comments consistently hinted that my age is a problem. As you can imagine, this is not something enjoyable to me. Since I believe you have no intention to insult me, can you please tell me why my age seems to bother you so much?

We do not focus on the emotion so as not to inflate it. Instead, we focus on its source to dissipate it. Instead of dwelling in anger, we focus on what made us angry to begin with.

If the other side is under strong emotions, we can still bring rationality in. We can say: "It seems that you are frustrated with how things are going. Is that right? [Pause and if no answer then] Is something bothering you?"

Rational behavior is:

- *Good for the relationship* – Fewer emotional outbursts or repressed emotions make for a clearer and more honest conversation.
- *Good for them* – If talking about feelings is okay, they will likely be more at ease.
- *Unconditionally good for us* – Even if they are not rational, we increase our chances of being heard, handling feelings productively and focusing on the substance negotiation faster.

Another aspect of being rational is resisting short-term, quick-gain opportunities at the expense of the other side. Such temptation can tarnish our reputation; we can be regarded as greedy (more for us at their expense) and untrustworthy. Here is when rationality invites us to **balance value benefits over time**. Instead of greedy, be ambitious (more for us or both sides, but never at each other's expense).

## Understand

More than just listening, we aim to **understand how they see and feel things**. It is not enough to understand, but also to show that we understand. Even if they are not helping, it is our responsibility to initially increase understanding towards learning.

> Thanks for explaining your point-of-view to me. I want to be sure that I fully understand it. Do you mind if I ask a few questions on something I am still a little confused about?

Understanding is:

- *Good for the relationship* – It increases the chance that the negotiation will deal with the real issues and thus be more efficient.
- *Good for them* – Most people like to feel heard and even more so to be understood, especially in a negotiation when they need to get their point across.
- *Unconditionally good for us* – Even if they do not understand us, understanding them gives us information to better manage the negotiation.

At this point, many negotiators ask: "But if I see their side of the story so well, will I not end up agreeing with them?" No. Understanding and even **empathizing with their situation does not mean agreeing** to their request. Understanding them does not mean that they are right. We may understand and empathize with someone's fear-based decision to strike another person coming from behind in a dark alley. That however may not justify to us not trying to run, talk or ask for help before resorting to violence.

## Communicate

When two countries go to war, they usually close down their respective foreign embassies. The communication cut-off is normally a cause for the delay in potential resolution of the conflict. To avoid this mistake, the recommendation is to keep the communication channels open, and **whenever possible, to consult before deciding.**

> I am in charge of presenting a plan on our Indonesian operations by the end of this week. As you are our Indonesia expert (or since this may impact you), I would like to share my main ideas and hear yours before I decide on the final plan.

- *Good for the relationship* – Communication reduces surprises and misunderstandings while surfacing negotiation risks and opportunities.
- *Good for them* – Since they now know what may impact them, they feel less nervous or afraid as well as more confident to talk freely and make decisions.
- *Unconditionally good for us* – Even if they do not communicate with us, our communication increases potential buy-in and learning.

Communication enables learning which can lead to a better proposal or anticipation of future risks. It does not mean sharing everything with everyone, but rather consulting those with information or who may be impacted by our decisions. Many negotiators fear that in consulting others, they share their decision-making power. Sharing information (and asking for more) is different from sharing authority. To make this clear, we can state that after considering their inputs, we will be the ones deciding (not them).

## Be Trustworthy

It is important to **follow through on our promises and only promise what we can deliver.** Being trustworthy includes voicing when something cannot be shared or admitting what we do not know. Even if the other party is untrustworthy, responding in the same manner may tarnish our reputation and not necessarily yield the desired results.

> Though my costs rose significantly, I am not touching our agreed prices. However, if we decide to do this again, I need you to know I will have to raise my prices accordingly.

- *Good for the relationship* – A trustworthy environment has lower levels of disruption, betrayal and surprises, and consequently lower transaction costs.
- *Good for others* – Everyone prefers to deal with someone they know will act on their words and not cheat or betray them.
- *Unconditionally good for us* – Even if they are untrustworthy, they will more likely believe and accept our promises without demanding guarantees.

Though being trustworthy gives us power to persuade others, we should only **trust based on risk analysis**. Similar to the zero-trust attitude: promote trust, but only trust them based on evidence. If the value at risk is small, we may trust quicker, but be conscious that there is still risk. However, if the value at risk is high, we either invest time on building trust or on crafting a deal independent of it.

Besides being trustworthy, we build trust through **small, slow and verifiable steps** based on risk analysis. These steps allow trust-building with minimum risk as they give opportunities for the negotiators to reciprocate and prove their trustworthiness. In contrast, large, quick and unilateral steps create power distance and win-lose temptations.

For example, many cease-fire agreements fail when they demand a complete and immediate stop of hostilities. This is too much too fast, thus making complying and verifying extremely difficult. A better approach creates a demilitarization schedule that leads to a complete cease-fire. Each party can see the other side fulfilling their small commitments as both move together towards the cease-fire. No one becomes an easy target for unilaterally enacting the full cease-fire.

# Persuade

No one likes to be coerced or threatened into changing a decision. Generally, people want respect and to change their minds only if convinced that it is the right thing to do. Therefore, we are better off if we convince people based on persuasion.

> I am not asking you to stay home tonight as your father, but because your sister is sick. I want your help to take care of her. She needs more attention than I can give alone.

- *Good for the relationship* – It substitutes the power or authority dynamic for a rational conversation of what is the right thing to do.
- *Good for them* – Instead of feeling bullied into a decision they dislike, they feel their right to make up their minds is being respected.
- *Unconditionally good for us* – Even if they coerce us, we are more likely to change their minds through persuasion than coercion.

Persuasion indicates respect in the relationship negotiation while trying as hard as possible to convince the other on the substance negotiation. Persuasion, not coercion, helps to **attack the problem, not the people**.

Persuasion is especially powerful if we are also **open to being persuaded**. If we come across as not open, our so-called logical persuasion arguments are just disguised unilateral coercion moves. If we cannot accept that they can also have valid points and arguments, why should they believe in ours? Somtimes by sharing what may persuade us, we can prove that we are not just being positional. It is then up to them to produce the evidence that can indeed persuade us.

> There is nothing I can say that can convince you, right? You own the truth! You never came here to negotiate, only to tell me what to do. This is unacceptable.

> I am sorry to have given you this impression. It was not my intention. I am open to changing my mind, but I have not yet heard anything that has convinced me. However, if you prove that he was at fault, then I will probably change my mind.

## Accept

We want to remind the reader that we are separating the relationship from the substance. By "accept," we mean to accept the relationship or **accept negotiators' rights to think, feel or just be different**. We need to accept that their differences are as worthy of consideration and learning as our own. This is very different from accepting the substance, which should only happen if there are very good reasons to do so (legitimacy). By "accept," we think of "respect," but not "commit."

> I understand that you support the death penalty and, though I still disagree, I am sure you have reasons for it. Before sharing my views, I would like to learn some more on your views about the benefits of the death penalty. Do you mind sharing them with me?

- *Good for the relationship* – When people feel accepted, they tend to be less aggressive or defensive, thus allowing them to focus on the real issues.
- *Good for them* – They will appreciate being accepted (even if they do not say it) and will feel more at ease during the negotiation.
- *Unconditionally good for us* – Even if they do not accept us, by accepting them, we reduce or eliminate their resistance.

Accepting alone does not guarantee a perfect risk-free working relationship. Many times, we fear addressing risks and spoiling the positive relationship momentum. Much like sweeping the dirt under the carpet, things get ugly when the dirt comes out. Though not at the beginning, but certainly before the end, those who **jointly identify and manage risks** solidify their relationship.

Parties can then define incentives or penalties together, or exchange personal or institutional guarantees to ensure the desired behaviors. After all, risks are part of any relationship; it is how we deal with them that makes a difference.

> I agree that this is a great project. I am excited about the possibility of working with you. Do you mind if I share some of my fears?

> What? Is there something wrong?

> No, nothing wrong if all goes well. You and I have developed a great relationship so far. I am just concerned that if, for example, you are headhunted to another company, this could set the project back quite a bit.

> Don't worry. I have no plans of leaving. Still, I have a very capable direct report who will be aware of everything. In the rare event that I leave, I will ensure that the transition is quick and smooth. Does that help?

### POINT OF INTEREST

**Six Unconditionally Constructive Behaviors & Seven Elements**

The six unconditionally constructive behaviors could relate to the seven elements in the following way:
- Be rational when talking about relationship
- Understand the interests of all parties
- Communicate our options before committing
- Persuade based on legitimacy
- Be trustworthy on our commitments as agreed
- Accept their communication will be different

The reason for no link to alternatives is due to an almost unconditional negative impact on relationship. Although it is good for a negotiator to be rational when deciding to take up their alternatives, this is clearly not unconditionally constructive for the relationship.

In sum, first we understand what relationship is to avoid trading it for substance. Second, we promote interdependence through a Joint Value Pursuit frame, a common challenge or opportunity, a "we" mentality, sitting side-by-side and choosing collaborative roles. Third, we enter a negotiation with a zero-trust mentality and a clear trust-building goal in mind. Finally, we consistently behave in unconditionally constructive ways in the negotiation to build and strengthen the trust independently of substance.

# summary

To better handle the relationship negotiation, we need to be able to:

1. Define relationship;
2. Promote interdependence; and
3. Build trust.

## Define Relationship

Relationship is built by how we behave and feel towards one another, not by the substance we exchange. It is important to differentiate:

1. Substance: Short- or long-term transaction; from
2. Relationship: Short- or long-term relationship.

Investing in the relationship negotiation is valid because it generates:

1. Relationship value;
2. Sources of potential future negotiations; and
3. Material or substance value creation.

## Promote Interdependence

Interdependence is an early relationship strategy based on positive reciprocation, which is built through five main techniques:

1. **Joint Value Pursuit frame** – Distinguish negotiation from battle.
2. **Common opportunity (or challenge)** – Find something external that unites us.
3. **"We" mentality** – Identify points we have in common.
4. **Sitting side-by-side** – Show that we are working together.
5. **Choosing collaborative roles** – Invite behaviors away from power temptations.

## Build Trust

While interdependence is our early relationship strategy, trust can then help strengthen the relationship further. There are five layers of trust:

- Ability
- Honesty
- Reliability
- Intimacy
- Caring

And four relationship categories that require different layers of trust to safely operate.

- Transactions
- Needs
- Partnership
- Trust

Relationship negotiations are more successful if they start with a zero-trust discipline and then promote trust through unconditionally constructive behaviors (UCBs) which are:
- Good for the relationship between the parties;
- Good for them; and
- Good for us, even if they do not reciprocate our action.

There are six well-known UCBs:
- Be rational
- Understand
- Communicate
- Persuade
- Be trustworthy
- Accept

# questions

## Easy

1. Why should we build a good and solid relationship in a negotiation? Give three reasons.
2. What is the difference between a short-term relationship and a short-term transaction?
3. Why is interdependence more important than trust in a value negotiation?
4. What are the goals of promoting interdependence?
5. What are the five layers of trust?
6. What makes a behavior unconditionally constructive?

## Medium

1. Why is the difference between a short-term relationship and a short-term transaction important for negotiation purposes?
2. Why not just call it "business relationship" and "personal relationship"?
3. What are the differences between a Joint Value Pursuit frame, a common challenge (or opportunity), a "we" mentality, sitting side-by-side and choosing collaborative roles? Briefly describe what each of them brings to the table.
4. What is a good response to someone who asks you: "Don't you trust me?"
5. What are the differences between the five layers of trust? Why should we care about them?
6. Is zero-trust possible? Why? How can it be helpful in a negotiation?

### Difficult

1. Can we rely on trust alone as a short-cut to success in the substance negotiation? What is the potential reward and potential risk?
2. What is the difference between the focus on a common challenge or opportunity and scapegoating?
3. Name a new unconditionally constructive behavior (besides the six listed above) and explain why it fits the category. Give two examples of uses of this behavior.
4. Trust is not gained by doing things for people, but rather by doing things with them. Do you agree with this statement? Why? What is the logic behind it?
5. Why is an unconditionally constructive behavior consistent with the value negotiation approach?

# scenarios

### Easy

Some may say that the following statement is too evasive:

*I am here with a strong intention to help you maximize your value as well.*

To strengthen the commitment to working together, is the following statement acceptable? Is it better or worse?

*I am here to help you maximize your value as well.*

What is the difference between the two statements? What are two alternative ways of conveying the same message (keeping the risks as low as possible)?

### Medium

Fisher and Shapiro mention that making ourselves indebted to the other can help improve the relationship between the parties, as the debtor now feels better for having been generous and helpful as well as more committed to the indebted. Indeed, politicians often use this technique by asking people to donate time, money or other resources to a campaign. Once the person commits the time or money, the politician knows that he or she is hooked and more can be solicited for. What are the rewards of this move? What are the risks? Why might it work?

## Difficult

Please identify and explain how Melissa developed interdependence through:

- Joint Value Pursuit frame;
- Common opportunity (or challenge);
- "We" mentality;
- Sitting side-by-side; and
- Choosing collaborative roles.

| NEGOTIATION DIALOGUE | DIAGNOSTICS |
|---|---|
| Hi! I am a student here at the university and a frequent user of the gym. As such, I noticed the recent renovations and I wanted to say that I liked them a lot. | |
| *Really. It's kind of you to share. We spent a lot of time, money and effort in doing so and it is great to see that you enjoyed it.* | |
| Indeed. It became clear to pretty much everyone that you are committed to improving the gym services and experiences. | |
| *We are! After all, if we do not do it, people will complain or stop coming altogether and we do not want that. Besides, as a fitness enthusiast myself, of course, I enjoy working out in a nice place.* | |
| I couldn't agree more. You may not know that I am also one of the members of the Student Council, and like you I am constantly trying to improve overall services and experiences in our university. | |
| *Good to know. Is there something else that you would like to share?* | |
| Actually, I do. Once the renovations were done, we had some new ideas that we are glad to share with you that we believe could potentially improve the services and experiences even further. Would you like to hear them? | |
| *Sure. Ideas are always good. I do not know if we will be able to make them all happen, but I would love to hear them out.* | |
| I agree. We just wanted to learn your reactions to them. We do not have all the information, but we thought it would be a waste or even selfish to not share them with you. | |
| *I am all ears.* | |
| Well, there are three main ideas: first... | |

# 08 Communication

**Learning Objectives:**
- Why communication is so important for negotiations
- What communication's main enemies are
- What three-way communication is and how it is different from two-way communication
- What makes for good communication
- How to listen, and ask questions to learn and lead
- How to talk and increase our power of persuasion

Communication is the conduit for everything that takes place in a negotiation. Used to send and receive messages, it is also referred to as the element of process: the way in which things are communicated during a negotiation.

Under the goal of developing an efficient two-way communication, negotiators aim to develop both their listening and advocating skills. To achieve this goal, negotiators also transparently lead the process to reduce power distances and information asymmetries. The combination of effective communication and process delivers a successful communication negotiation.

Though the communication negotiation deals with both, there is a difference between communication and process. Communication is how, while process is when, something is said or done. The communication goals are effective learning and persuasion; the process goal is to develop an efficient and fair process to maximize value while minimizing risks.

Since everything in a negotiation is expressed through communication, even a small improvement can largely impact the whole negotiation. For example, unconditionally constructive behaviors (UCBs) show how relationship and communication are intertwined. To communicate (or talk) and understand (or listen) are two UCBs. Two others are directly related to communication: rational discussion of emotions and persuasiveness. How and what we say have a great impact on interdependence and trust. This makes us wonder if sound communication and process could be even more important and resilient than trust.

To improve our communication skills, we first need to understand communication's biggest enemy: information asymmetry. Then, we will explore a value-focused process and the key communication skills: listening, advocating and asking.

## Information Asymmetry: The Source of (Almost) All Evil

Paola was finally getting married! After years of seeing all her best friends get married before her, it was her day at last. She had over 500 guests between friends and a very large family in a beautiful wedding ceremony and party. Her parents presented her a wonderful gift: a brand new apartment. She was ecstatic!

Since Paola's parents lived out of town, they got her an apartment in front of her divorced aunt. After all, it is always good to be close to family in case you need some help, right? During the wedding party, her aunt said:

> I am so happy that I will have you as a neighbor! I am looking forward to having you around. Please enjoy your honeymoon. I will take care of your place for you.

> Oh, dear auntie! This is so kind of you. I am looking forward to living close to you too. I will come to see you in a week as soon as I return from my honeymoon.

Paola had a wonderful honeymoon but could not contain her excitement in anticipation of all her wedding gifts. For Paola, opening wedding gifts was probably the least spoken about and yet most satisfying part of the whole wedding package. However, as she stepped in her apartment for the very first time, she was in shock: the apartment was spotless!

It was neither empty nor with a pile of gifts at a corner of the living room as she expected. No! Everything was already organized, in its proper place, tucked away or beautifully displayed. All the paper wrappings were already thrown away and the apartment cleaned of any gift-opening vestiges. On a table, there was a list of names of the people matching their gifts so that thank-you cards could be sent to them. Everything was taken care of.

Paola was furious! She stormed into her aunt's apartment. Her aunt came to greet her:

> Paola! I am so glad you are back! Have you seen your apartment yet?

> Yes! How could you do this to me?

> Do what? I wanted to show you how happy I am to have you as my neighbor. Knowing how busy you are professionally, I decided to help you out. I organized your place as I promised during your wedding so that everything was ready when you arrived. It took me five days, but you are my favorite niece. I hope you liked it!

> You had no right to do it! I was looking forward to opening my gifts for months now. I had been living in anticipation of this moment as well. How could you do this to me?

> What are you talking about? Do this to you? I told you that I was going to take care of everything while you were gone, didn't I?

> No, you said that you were going to take care of my place, not my gifts.

> But I was trying to help you out! I did not know that this was so important for you. My mom also opened all of my wedding gifts.

> This was not helping out! You had to know that this was not right. You did it on purpose!

The conversation lasted for another hour, until Paola left her aunt's apartment promising never to talk to her again. For over six months, they ignored each other even in the elevator.

Now let's assume that the aunt really meant well as she claimed. She put a lot of care into preparing the house and even leaving a list for the thank-you cards. She also mentioned at the wedding party that she would take care of things. Indeed, she was not specific and Paola probably could have never imagined this kind of "help". The heart of the matter is that neither meant bad. Both sincerely liked each other. The good intentions just did not survive a terrible communication process. But why did that happen?

Consider assisted negotiation, such as mediation, where a neutral third party helps the parties to settle their differences. Most mediators do nothing more than ensure that parties in conflict engage in an efficient communication process towards agreement or resolution. The mediator is like a communication doctor.

Now add to that the following data: the success rate of mediation can be quite high. It can go from 47% in Ghana, to 85–90% in the US and UK, up to 95% in Singapore. The large variation is due to service quality, local culture, mediation style, type of disputes, etc. Moreover, almost half of failed cases can be due to absence or lack of preparation by a party. This information suggests that many, if not most, conflicts are communication problems.

Now the big enemy in such communication problems is normally information asymmetry. **Information asymmetry is the gap of information, and subsequently of understanding, between the parties**. No negotiator has all the relevant information from all sides. That, on its own, would not be a problem if the negotiators were aware of information asymmetry. They could then proceed to learn as much as possible from one another to narrow the information gap.

In reality though, negotiators usually unconsciously fill in information gaps with their assumptions. This mix of information and assumptions generates a false sense of understanding and security. Information asymmetry can also create a power imbalance and tempt negotiators to extract advantages from each other. As a result, every negotiation is at risk of having misunderstandings, disagreements or, at its worst, conflicts. It operates on two main levels:

1. Perceptions (assumption of understanding)
2. Attributions (assumption of intention)

# Perceptions: Capturing and Storing Data

Paola assumed that her aunt would only take care of minor tasks. Meanwhile, the aunt assumed that Paola gave her a blank check to do whatever she wanted. Victims of a very vague conversation, both of them filled in the blanks with their own ideas. Based on very little data, they drew conclusions on their perceived reality and acted upon it. Now with the conflict in place, both of them sincerely believed that they were right. Why would two intelligent women make what seems to be such basic mistakes?

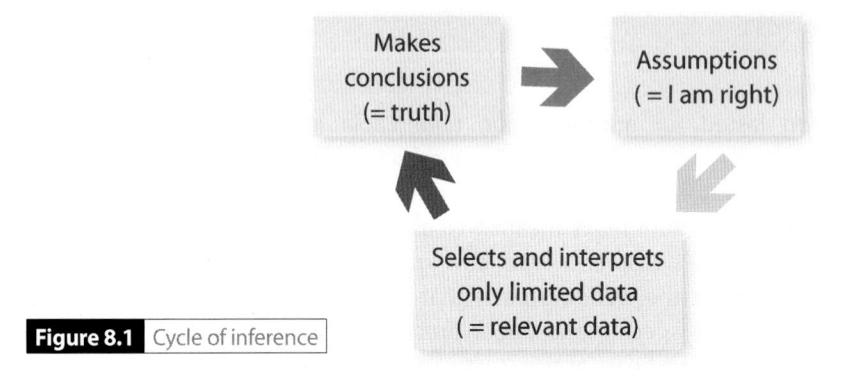

**Figure 8.1** Cycle of inference

The conflict between Paola and her aunt originated in the way our minds have evolved to absorb and process information. Our senses capture only a small fraction of the world around us at any given time. Even then, our senses are not exact machines, but rather interpreters of our interaction with the environment. For example, a dish that is spicy for us may be just right for them. We focus on different data (external and internal) and generate different conclusions (Figure 8.1). As a result, we end up experiencing different worlds. The meal we had was good for us but terrible for them.

Are our conclusions doomed to rely on partial information? Yes! If not, we may not have survived as a species. Imagine a caveman pondering over all possible information before choosing to fight or run from a wild animal. Even the smallest decision would have too much to worry about. So we evolved to be able to make decisions even without all the information.

The problem begins as we are hardwired to believe our perception to be the truth. We believe it so much that when faced with opposition, our instinct is to attack their views or their supporters. After making a conclusion, humans tend to collect more supporting evidence, while ignoring or undervaluing disconfirming data.

Again, the roots of this habit may be found in evolution. Once a caveman decided to attack, certainty rather than doubt increased the chances of success. In a fight, having second thoughts was not the best way to win it. In academia, scholars are familiar with the temptation to conclude before they have all facts. In their commitment to scientific truth, it is necessary to withhold judgment until opposing views have been heard. But once they reach a conclusion, it is rare that any of them will change it without a fight.

Perceptions impoverish our communication not only through a biased input, but also through an imperfect storage system. We just do not have the capacity to keep all the data we want. To maximize our storage, we group the data based on similarities with previous references. This categorization process simplifies the information but also cuts some out. The data is further impacted as our memory of it fades or changes. Finally, when we want to use that stored data to communicate, we can only remember parts of it.

## Attributions: Sharing Data

When Paola heard: "I will take care of your place for you," she heard a harmless and generous statement. What she could not have heard was what her aunt assumed inside her head. The aunt truly believed that Paola understood her intention to take full charge of Paola's place.

Information asymmetry gives room for assumptions. Assumptions in turn create perceptions by making us believe that we have successfully captured and stored information. They also create attributions by making us believe that we have successfully shared what is on our minds. Attributions make it harder to know if we have truly communicated, as we assume that they fully understood us. Since we know what we want to say, we assume our message perfectly conveyed it. If our message was perfect, then it is logical to assume that they fully understood it.

However, if we say the word "elephant," most people would probably visualize a different elephant: male or female, adult or infant, African or Asian, etc. If we narrow the interpretation by saying "male elephant," this can still refer to several sizes. So the images in our heads will almost always vary, even if not in significant ways. Figure 8.2 illustrates how the things we see at the start can differ from what the other party understands in the end.

1. We see    2. We perceive    3. We memorize    4. We say    5. We understand

**Figure 8.2** The communication flow and the attribution trap

The attribution trap makes us believe that they see the same elephant that is on our mind. The perception trap makes them believe that the image in their mind is exactly the one meant by us. The likelihood of an exact match is actually quite small.

In all fairness, words just represent the data, much like a map represents a territory. It describes a territory, but it is not the territory. The map and the territory are actually very different objects. Similarly, any word carries different meanings to different people.

The intent-impact gap is the simplest representation of attribution. It reminds negotiators of the distance between what is thought or intended and what is understood or its impact. Table 8.1 illustrates the gap more clearly:

**Table 8.1** Intent-impact table

| IF WE SEND A MESSAGE | Know the INTENT | Know the IMPACT |
|---|---|---|
| WE | YES | NOT FOR SURE |
| THEY | NOT FOR SURE | YES |

Though we know the intentions of our messages, we cannot be sure of their true impact on others. They, however, know exactly the impact of our messages on them, but cannot be sure of our true intentions.

The most accurate communication of our idea would happen if we brought an elephant into the room. Then we could say: "This is what I mean — I am talking about this elephant and not any other one." But elephants as well as abstract concepts are hard to carry around. It is a miracle that we manage to communicate successfully at all.

Fortunately, most conversations only seek a basic understanding of a general concept, i.e., a broad idea of an elephant. There are, however, two main situations in which we need to improve our communication: first, when our basic understandings may vary significantly; or second, when we need a more specific common understanding of a concept. To overcome information asymmetry, we need greater awareness and sophisticated communication skills and processes.

# The Dialogue Pattern: From Two- to Three-Way Communication

Two-way communication is a great negotiation process where the parties talk (share or advocate) and listen. If more negotiators did it, negotiations would maximize value and minimize conflict.

However, two-way communication may indicate that we lead when talking and are passive when listening. Consequently, negotiators put their best efforts in talking to control the negotiation and sacrifice listening in the process. The negotiation quickly becomes a one-way communication battle for an opportunity to talk. The desire for control and power deviates from the goal of an efficient two-way communication. So what is really an efficient two-way communication?

Could the telephone dialogue below be understood as such communication?

> Alessandro, I want you to come to the meeting room right now!

> Sorry, Inès, I can't, because ...

> Alessandro, I don't think that you understood me. I am telling you that you need to come to the meeting room right now.

> I understand that you want me there right now, but I can't come, because ...

> I don't care why you can't. You just need to come right now. No excuses!

> Sorry, as I told you I can't, because ...

> Alessandro, if you do not show up in the meeting room in five minutes I will personally come to your office and drag you down here.

> Dear Inès, you are welcome to try that but I fear that you will not find me in my office. This is what I have been trying to tell you. I am at home today on sick leave and as much as I would like to be in your meeting in five minutes, I just can't. I am sorry!

To some extent, the dialogue above was two-way as both spoke and listened. However, it is hard not to think of Inès as Alessandro's superior. This perception of power makes it an inefficient and somewhat unbalanced conversation. Efficient two-way communication requires balance between listening and talking for successful learning and persuasion.

For a balanced two-way communication, listening has to become as active a skill as talking. The concept of active listening was created to make listening easier and motivate us to talk and listen in equal measure. Despite its advantages over normal or passive listening, most who learn active listening still find it difficult to implement. For example, it is hard to listen to something which is, in our opinion, irrelevant or negative. If we listen to whatever they say, then we are still being reactive to them.

Active listening frequently becomes (re)active listening. Without a purpose, listening is not an active skill as it lacks direction. Without direction, active listening will not clarify how to lead the process towards success. Imagine a police investigator saying to a suspect:

> Well, I am listening!

> To what? I did not say anything.

> Still, I want to listen.

> I don't understand. What are you talking about? What am I supposed to talk about? I do not even know who you are. I find this very weird. I am leaving!

Efficient two-way communication is supposed to encourage collaborative processes, help us learn and steer (lead) our conversation. As we can see in the dialogue above, talking and active listening are not enough. So what is efficient two-way communication like, and how do we do it?

One example of this is the dialogue pattern. It is a balanced and purposeful communication process that allows parties to maximize learning and reduce the power imbalance to help them focus on value. The dialogue pattern adds two ideas not commonly present in two-way communication: asking questions and proactive learning.

Instead of active listening, we prefer the terminology "proactive listening" or, even better, "proactive learning." Proactive learning reminds us that listening is a proactive skill to direct the negotiation to a particular purpose: learning. With proactive learning, we take the initiative to narrow our information asymmetry to better surface value. Proactive learning prompts us to ask questions and direct the negotiation to the areas we want to learn about. Asking what interests us works as a natural mechanism to stir our curiosity to listen better and more often. The negotiation becomes more focused and efficient.

In sum, the dialogue pattern uses questions to improve listening and transforms it into proactive learning. With the inclusion of asking questions, what is called an "efficient two-way communication" now becomes a three-way communication. The value negotiator first asks, then listens curiously, and empowered with more or better information, talks. To avoid an interrogation, we invite the other to also ask and listen, thus creating our turn to talk once more. The dialogue pattern keeps us in diagnostic mode and reduces the power distance since everyone contributes. The rest of this chapter will cover how to implement a dialogue pattern.

## Ask to Lead and Learn

Questions are the pivotal communication tool. Asking promotes the dialogue pattern for better understanding and value creation. Asking reconciles perceptions and attributions. It also promotes a better relationship since asking, rather than imposing, is usually an invitation for collaboration. Both advocacy and listening are more successful when done jointly with questions. However, many struggle to increase the quantity and quality of questions asked.

How can we learn proactively? We believe that identifying simple and practical categories can make it easier to recall and use questions during negotiations. Despite the existence of several classifications of questions, we focus on their purpose to learn and lead a negotiation.

All questions aim to learn. When we ask: "Could you tell me more about this interest of yours?" or "What are your thoughts on what I just said?" we clearly want to learn more. On the other hand, when we ask: "Do you mind if we move on to our next topic on the agenda?" or "How about we take a 15-minute break before we continue into options?," the data-gathering intention is not as strong as the process-leading intention. The goal of the latter questions is to consult with them if moving in a certain direction is acceptable.

## Learning Questions

Learning questions are very similar to open questions, but are not the same. Learning questions are questions motivated to diagnose and learn. Open questions are also known as "W" questions since in English, interrogative words usually start with a "W": when, who, what, why, where, etc. They open the door for parties to reveal as much information on a topic as possible.

By asking "What is your view of the conflict?," we start to learn and reduce information asymmetry. As we gather more information, we are less likely to make a move based on perceptions or attributions.

The dialogues between Paola and her aunt, and Alessandro and Inès, show that omissions and generalizations create perceptions and attributions. When Alessandro said: "Sorry, Inès, I can't...", his omission allowed Inès to think that he was in the office. Based on that perception, Inès repeated her demands with little progress. Instead, she could have proactively asked a learning question: "Why can't you come now?" And all would have been solved much faster and with less confrontation. Learning questions normally double-check on omissions or narrow generalizations in the substance or relationship negotiations.

### POINT OF INTEREST

**Open vs. Learning Questions**
Though open questions normally are the best questions to promote learning, not all open questions have this goal. On the other hand, not all learning questions are open. Examples:
- "I believe that we all would like to stop talking about this right now. What would you like to talk on next?" (The question, though open, is more geared towards leading than learning.)
- "So if I understand you correctly, you feel that we are not valuing your contribution, right?" (The question, though not open, seeks information or learning.)

The following are some examples of learning questions:

1. Omissions – When the speaker fails to clarify the reality described.
    a) Nouns – "**They'll** never agree to this **proposal.**"
        i. Q: "Who are 'they' exactly? Could you name them for me?"
        ii. Q: "What part(s) of the proposal do they dislike?"
        ii. Q: "What would it take for them to agree?"

    b) Verbs – "We will **increase** profits by 12% this year."
        i. Q: "How do we intend to do that?"
        ii. Q: "Can you elaborate on that? Tell me more, please."
        iii. Q: "What risks do you anticipate?"

    c) Comparative – "This is a **smaller** matter."
        i. Q: "Smaller compared to what exactly?"
        ii. Q: "Smaller for whom?"

2. Generalizations – When the speaker assumes an interpretation of reality as a fact that reduces creative or fair thinking.
   a) Inflexible command – "We <u>have to</u> decide this today!" Or "Even if I wanted, I <u>could not</u> do this."
      i. Q: "What would happen if we did/did not?"
      ii. Q: "What exactly prevents us from doing it?"
      iii. Q: "What would it take to allow us to decide tomorrow?"

   b) Absolute quantifiers – "I have tried <u>everything</u>." Or "You <u>never</u> helped!"
      i. Q: "Everything? Never? Always? Everyone? No one?"
      ii. Q: "To which specific situation are you referring to?"

   c) Opinions – "This proposal <u>clearly</u> indicates the best way to do this."
      i. Q: "Clearly to whom?"
      ii. Q: "Why is it so clear?"

Some other examples of omissions and generalizations are more specific to the relationship negotiation, such as when negotiators:

- Simply eliminate information from a sentence
  - "I'm <u>worried</u>." (Q: "*About what?*")
- Make assumptions about people's behaviors or the cause and effect of an emotion
  - "If <u>you only knew</u> how angry that makes me, you would never say it again." (Q: "*What makes you think I don't know?*")
  - "<u>You make me</u> nervous." (Q: "*How exactly do I do that?*")

Though normally framed as an open question, learning questions can also be closed. When framed as closed questions, learning questions should come later in the negotiation, after much learning has already taken place. Closed learning questions serve a confirmation purpose to double-check the learning and clarify an assumption once and for all:

- "So if I understood you correctly, your interest is to avoid a negative precedent so that your other clients do not think you were unfair to them. <u>Is that right</u>?"
- "Yes, I suggested some dates. Do you prefer to meet on <u>Monday or Tuesday</u>?"

Finally, beware of the interrogation temptation when trying to ask more learning questions:

> As I was saying, I would like to know a little more about you.

> Why do you want to know more about me?

> Well, if we are going to do business together, I like to know whom I am dealing with.

> Why do you need to know?

> Because it is important for me to know if you are someone I can work with.

> Why is this important for you?

> I believe it will help us trust each other more. Don't you?

> Why do you believe that?

> I don't know; I just do. Maybe it's experience.

> Why does your experience tell you that?

No one would stay in a negotiation like that for long! When we recommend asking more questions, we are recommending a focus on learning to make better decisions. Thus, learning questions are aimed at the information you believe will better enable you to pursue value.

## Leading Questions

Leading questions are similar to closed questions, but very different in their purpose and use within a negotiation. Much like closed questions, leading questions often require answers that are "yes" or "no," or from a set of multiple choices. However, closed questions limit the negotiation to the parties' existing knowledge and assumptions. Consequently, they do little against information asymmetry and are less than adequate for learning purposes.

In addition to reduced learning, closed questions are usually statements disguised with a question mark at the end. They make a point or accusation, put words in others' mouths or are used to counter-argue. Such questions risk irritating people and undermining trust. Following are some examples of statements disguised as closed questions (Table 8.2):

| QUESTION EXAMPLE | DISGUISED STATEMENT | ALTERNATIVES TO LEARN |
|---|---|---|
| Don't you think that my idea is better than yours? | I believe it is! (However, the listener probably does not believe this, otherwise they would have said so themselves) | • Why do you believe your idea is better than mine?<br>• What elements of my idea do you think are weak or risky?<br>• What are, in your view, some positive points in my idea? |

| QUESTION EXAMPLE | DISGUISED STATEMENT | ALTERNATIVES TO LEARN |
|---|---|---|
| But don't you think that to use the inflation as an index like you suggested is dangerous? | I think it is dangerous, and you are dumb or treacherous to disagree! (The listener may actually believe there are dangers, but that it is still the best solution available) | • And in your view, are there risks with using inflation as our index?<br>• What risks do you anticipate if we adopt your idea?<br>• What risks are you aware of or what is the experience of others in having inflation as an index? |
| Why didn't you think of bringing a flashlight to the camp? | You are a moron for not bringing it! (Why did the asker not think of it?) | • What happened?<br>• Did you bring anything else?<br>• How can we find our way in the dark? |
| Who was the imbecile who prepared this memo? | If it was you, you are an imbecile. (Placing blame before trying to improve the memo) | • Who wrote this memo?<br>• What happened?<br>• What do you think of your memo?<br>• How can we improve it?<br>• Who would like to edit this memo before the end of the day? |

**Table 8.2**

Examples of statements disguised as closed questions

Although normally framed as closed questions, the last two examples above are open questions, though not for learning purposes. Thus, we prefer to categorize questions based on purpose (learning or leading), instead of frame (open or closed). Learning questions seek to learn and explore, while leading questions invite the participation of others in defining the process.

Leading questions do not need to be closed questions: "Since we just understood our interests, what would you like to discuss next?" Though framed as an open question and seeking information, this question has the clear purpose of leading the negotiation forward. Leading questions bypass the temptation to use power to impose our will. By proactively inviting them to participate in shaping the next step, leading questions nudge us towards transparent leadership. Transparent process leadership enhances collaboration, minimizes surprises and information asymmetry and focuses on value. Some examples of leading questions:

- Can we vote now?
- How would you like a 15-minute break right now?
- I scheduled one hour for our meeting today. Do you believe this will be enough?
- Would you like to continue talking about this issue? Would you prefer to set it aside for now and move on to the rest?
- Am I right to believe that we have less than half an hour left for our meeting? If so, can we take two minutes to select what to focus on for the rest of our time?
- If you do not mind, I want to sleep on the offer and respond tomorrow. Is that okay?

Leading questions are very important for the success of a negotiation as they advance or change the process. Consequently, they focus on the communication negotiation and are framed as an invitation or suggestion of a process option.

To increase their effectiveness, they can come supported by legitimacy and address the other party's interests. For example in Table 8.3:

| NEGOTIATION DIALOGUE | DIAGNOSTICS |
|---|---|
| So what's your best price? | Process position |
| Would you mind if we speak about price after I ask you some questions? | Process option – talk about price after questions |
| No! I want to know your price now. | Process position |
| I cannot give you my best price now, since I do not fully understand what you want. | Process legitimacy – my price depends on your wants, so I cannot give it without data |
| No problem! Just give me a range then. | Bargaining on process – from best price to a range |
| If you answer a few of my questions, I will more accurately know what you want. I can then quickly give you my best price. What do you think? | Process interest – help me to help you |
| Okay, let's try this for a few minutes. | |

**Table 8.3**
Supporting leading questions with legitimacy

Instead of the whole dialogue, a leading question could have been asked from the start:

> I will be glad to give you a price now, but since I do not fully understand what you want, I will not be able to give you my best price. For me to be able to do it as fast as possible, I just need to ask you a few questions first. Is that okay with you?

- Consider their process option as one potential option – "I will be glad to give you a price now..."
- Legitimacy and setting aside their position – "... but since I do not fully understand what you want, I will not be able to give you my best price."
- Speak to their interests – "For me to be able to do it as fast as possible..."
- Our process option – "... I just need to ask you a few questions first."
- Leading question – "Is that okay with you?"

Though the question is only in the last few words, the preceding statements create the context that renders the question effective. Hence, we consider the whole statement as part of the leading question as it helps to lead the process.

## Listen: Proactive Learning

Although most people recognize the value of listening, it is still an underutilized skill in negotiation for several reasons.

First, hard bargainers believe that talking controls the negotiation and persuades us. They believe that listening is a passive skill that at best leads to information to be used against us. Add to that the pre-negotiation anxiety and the fear of being misunderstood. These feelings lead many negotiators to want to talk first and repeat themselves until they feel heard and understood.

Besides unhelpful assumptions and feelings, we have internal voices that hijack our attention. These internal voices sound louder in our heads and talk while others talk. Actually, they represent several different roles: judge ("This is a stupid proposal!"); defense attorney ("On this point she is making, I have two counter-arguments."); victim ("I had no choice!"); savior ("You need to tell him to stop."); and daydreamer ("I wonder how the tennis game ended…").

As mentioned before, active listening is better than normal listening as it minimizes several listening obstacles. Active listening basically comprises three steps (Figure 8.3):

1. Listen to their emotional message (acknowledge the feeling – relationship negotiation);
2. Listen to their substance message (paraphrase the message – substance negotiation); and
3. Ask for clarification if something was not fully understood (inquire to clarify – relationship and substance negotiations).

Acknowledge the feeling → Paraphrase the message → Inquire to clarify

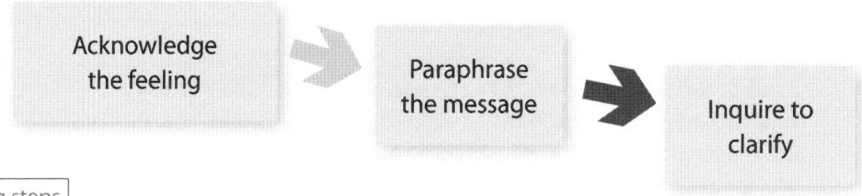

**Figure 8.3** Active listening steps

Active listening presents no clear step to lead the communication or the process. The inquire-to-clarify step is a small one in this direction, though it is reactive to the information received. Without proactivity, positional bargainers will still find active listening weak. Without balance, active listening may help us to ease their feelings, but we may not ease ours. Finally, without purpose, there is no way to shut up our internal voices. The lack of initiative, balance and purpose in active listening are liabilities when trying to handle listening obstacles.

Since we cannot turn listening off or remain 100% focused, we need to manage listening during critical and non-critical moments. Proactive learning gives us the purpose to recognize them so we know when to turn our learning on or off. Proactive learning is a robust listening skill as it promotes listening with a purpose. The best active listeners actually practice proactive learning.

Proactive learning promotes a process where learning leads to value. Confronted with arguments or information asymmetry, proactive learning instills the curiosity and discipline to listen, gather information and learn. Confronted with emotions, repetition or the urge to be understood, proactive learning allows the venting of emotions to cool down. Proactive learning goes on to show the other party they were understood so they can reveal the rational negotiator within.

Finally, proactive learning models good behavior and inspires positive reciprocity. If they feel heard and understood, they are more likely to listen to us in return. If they still refuse to listen, we can now more legitimately ask for our turn to talk.

Proactive learning includes three very similar steps to active listening. The steps are:

- Ask to listen (communication negotiation);
- Acknowledge the feeling (relationship negotiation); and
- Paraphrase the message (substance negotiation).

These steps compose a listening cycle that spins as many times as we believe necessary. Deceptively similar to active listening, proactive learning does much more than bring asking to the forefront of the process. It raises the role of asking to increase initiative, balance and purpose.

## Ask to Listen: The Four Cs

Listening is normally understood to begin when the other party starts talking. Proactive learning starts much earlier: when thinking of a question, we prepare ourselves internally to listen. Asking focuses the conversation on our topics of interest. Thus, we sincerely convey our interest in listening, which works as an invitation and reduces their inhibition or resistance to talk. Proactive learning helps them talk with more confidence and clarity to improve information exchange.

Even something as broad as "Would you like to share your side of the story?," "Do you care to share some more with me?" or "Let me know when you are ready to talk?" can initiate the listening cycle. When we ask to listen, we lead the negotiation into a learning phase. In listening, questions fulfill four different roles: conduct (lead), confirm, clarify and check-in (learn).

**Conduct** – Conducting questions lead the conversation towards our intended issue.
- "Can you tell me more about your interests?"
- "What else does this particular clause in the contract mean to you?"
- "Could you help me understand from your point of view why this is good for me?"
- "Before we talk about price, could you explore the timing you have in mind, as this also impacts my decision?"
- "Could you elaborate further on your concerns about the delivery date?"

**Confirm** – Confirmation questions check if our perception or understanding is correct.
- "If I heard you well, you are not interested in this proposal. Is that right?"
- "If I understood Samuel correctly, you are angry with me because I did not invite you to the meeting. Am I missing anything?"
- "Is the front page news true?"
- "Does it seem like I understood you so far?" (I believe I did, but let me confirm.)

**Clarify** – Clarification questions eliminate ambiguity and assumptions on what was said or done.
- "What do you mean by fair and respect?"
- "Could you please elaborate a little further on your side of the story?"
- "When you said you wanted a fair deal, were you referring to a 50–50 split?"
- "Can you help me understand why is this the case?"

**Check-in** – Check-in questions diagnose the three negotiations to see if they need attention.
- "How are we doing so far?"
- "Is everything okay?"
- "How do you believe we can do better?"
- "Does it seem like I am listening to you better now?" (I am not sure if you noticed my effort.)

Conducting questions lead to initiate or move the conversation. Confirmation questions during the "paraphrasing the message" step help to consolidate conclusions. Clarification questions happen at any time when omissions or generalizations pop up. Check-in questions are preventively asked from time to time or when anything seems wrong.

Conducting or check-in questions are more likely to take the form of a closed question and limit learning. Usually, people understand the spirit behind the closed question and share more:

> Are you okay?

> Not really, my car was stolen yesterday.

Nevertheless, in negotiations where mistrust or negative emotions are involved, closed questions make it hard for the other negotiator to open up:

> Is everything okay?

> Sure!

> Really?

> Sure!

> It doesn't seem like everything is really okay. Are you sure?

> Yes, I told you I am sure.

> Is there anything you would like to talk about?

> No. Let's continue.

> Okay then.

Therefore, focus first on open learning questions and only then move on to closed ones.

## Acknowledging the Feeling

Most times, negotiators take the trouble to communicate because they have an emotional need to do so. Emotions are an intrinsic part of a message and at times, the most important one. If left unearthed, these emotions can build up, explode and cause great damage to the negotiation. Thus, listening to words is only partial listening; we also need to listen for the "music," or the emotional tone. Acknowledging the emotion beneath the words shows we fully understood them.

Acknowledging the feeling is particularly important in more personal or emotional negotiations. The other side's tone of voice and tension in their speech are cues for potential emotions. Imagine the dialogue between two colleagues:

> Could you please change the date of your presentation since it coincides with mine?

> No! It is very important that I have my presentation on that day. If you want, you can change the date of your presentation.

> I already sent the invitations out and, as far as I know, I scheduled it first.

> You scheduled it first, but I still have the right to pick the day of my presentation.
> (Internal monologue: This is not going to be like last time. I always have to accommodate you. This time, if you want, you will have to accommodate me. Now you will know what it feels like to be in my position all the time.)

> But this is going to be bad for both of us!

> I don't care. This is your problem. If you want to, you can change.

The lack of listening to the emotions makes us believe that the other party's behavior is completely irrational. Indeed, their seeming irrationality may follow an underlying emotional logic which needs to be understood. Without acknowledgement and understanding, this behavior may never give way to a more rational and constructive conversation.

Acknowledging the feeling proves our understanding and makes insisting on expressing these emotions an unnecessary exercise. Once understood, their negative emotions will usually dissipate; all the more when they realize our serious commitment to listening.

## POINT OF INTEREST

**Emotional Need to Feel Heard**
The need to feel heard is a powerful emotional interest. So while someone speaks, it is important to listen and demonstrate that we are listening through words and actions. Normally, an open, attentive and relaxed body posture without interrupting or raising counter-arguments conveys our listening to them.

The hardest part of acknowledging the feelings is doing it without making conclusions or judgments. Such acknowledgement solely aims to show that the emotion was understood; no more, no less. So if someone is angry, it suffices to say: "I can see you are quite angry about this." If they are sad or frustrated, we can say: "This sounds frustrating!" If they are happy or excited about some news, we can remark: "Wow, this seems to have really made you happy!"

In more formal settings, we must be careful not to come across as unprofessional or taking liberties that can be seen as inappropriate behavior. Michel found this out the hard way:

> Hi boss, can I have a minute? (The boss looks at Michel with wide open eyes, surprised that he cannot see she is on the phone and answering emails at the same time.) Sorry, I can see that you are probably overwhelmed.

> Excuse me a minute (says the boss to the caller). Michel, who are you to tell me I am overwhelmed? I will talk to you when I need you. Now, get out of here.

Michel's use of the word "overwhelmed" could be seen as judging his boss's inability to cope. She felt this to be inappropriate and got angry. We need to exercise care in situations where talking about emotions is less conventional or a potential sign of weakness. For those circumstances, use neutral and indirect language. We can describe what we see, which can be a reflection of how they feel. If Michel were given a second chance, he would be better off choosing this technique:

> Hi boss, can I have a minute? (She looks at Michel with wide open eyes, surprised that he cannot see she is on the phone and answering emails at the same time.) Sorry, I can see that you are really busy right now. I will come back later.

> Sure, come back in 10 minutes.

In more formal or hierarchical situations, we may not be able to suggest that they feel anything. However, if the emotions are strong, we can suggest how upset (or other emotion) we might feel if it happened to us. Be careful not to make the conversation about ourselves. Remember, listening is always about them: it is their turn to talk.

## Paraphrasing The Message

Paraphrasing the message means repeating what the other negotiator said in our own words. The goal of paraphrasing is to communicate understanding. Paraphrasing has two benefits: it exposes where understanding needs correction; or indicates that they do not need to repeat themselves, since they were understood. Paraphrasing starts when they are talking. Before they stop talking, we should take notes (even mental ones) that allow us to summarize our understanding to them.

When our views and ideas conflict, we have to work harder to really understand their key messages. Paraphrasing requires holding back judgment and the temptation to interrupt and counter-argue. Anything else sends a strong message that we are not really listening and risks blocking the information flow.

A focus on learning what they believe to be important helps us concentrate on listening for:

- What comes across as key messages (interests or relationship issues);
- Whatever is surprising for us (alternatives, commitments or options);
- The merit of what is being said (legitimacy); and
- Whatever is repeated several times (communication).

At the end of their talk, our objective is to be able to state their views as well as they have. If done successfully, they cannot dismiss our ideas by claiming that we do not understand their concerns. Normally, paraphrasing is introduced as a confirmation question:

- "If I understood you correctly, your main concerns are…"
- "I heard you say that you have three priorities, is that right? And they are…"
- "Correct me if I am wrong in saying that you want…"
- "So is it right to say that you are really against…"

Many fear that understanding them makes us give in. But listening is not agreeing. Imagine a discussion over which team will win the soccer final. We can appreciate that their team won more games and scored a higher number of goals. We can see how they believe they will win the championship, but we may still disagree with that conclusion.

Afterwards, we explain that our team has the best defence and won only one game less than theirs, then add that our team won their last two confrontations. We can conclude that these factors will better predict the champion.

Besides emotions and words, we also listen to "meta-messages," or underlying messages often revealed through intonation. Inspired by Fisher and Shapiro, a sentence can convey several different meta-messages depending on which words are stressed:

- "**I** believe you should act now." (I believe, but no one else does.)
- "I **believe** you should act now." (I have a strong conviction, but I may not be able to rationally explain why.)
- "I believe **you** should act now." (You should do it before the competition.)
- "I believe you **should** act now." (Though I am not so certain if you have to do it.)
- "I believe you should **act** now." (Don't spend any more time thinking about it.)
- "I believe you should act **now**." (Now and not later, as this may be a unique window of opportunity.)

Paraphrasing usually raises new issues that stimulate the listening cycle: new questions, acknowledgement and paraphrasing. After the paraphrasing, we can ask confirmation, clarification or check-in questions until we fully learn from and understand them. Then, we can move the process forward with conducting questions.

## Adopting a Proactive Learning Stance

As proactive learners, we are responsible for preparing a setting conducive to listening. We saw how questions re-align our curiosity and reduce the interference from internal voices to create an authentic learning opportunity. However, even proactive learning may fall short of directing attention when we have complete apathy towards the substance. In such cases, two things can help capture our attention again:

- Anticipating the process consequences of not listening (communication negotiation); or
- Thinking about the relative importance of the relationship (relationship negotiation).

Marc, an ice-hockey supporter, was watching his team's match on TV as his wife arrived home:

> Hi, darling!

> Hi! (He doesn't turn around and speaks in a fairly distant voice, hinting that he is not available to talk as he is watching television – meta-message.)

> You have no idea what happened at work today! (Coming to his side and sitting down, showing an eagerness to talk.)

> Yeah, you're right, I have no idea! (Continues staring at the television, trying to get his focus back to the game as soon as possible.)

> Well, it was a terrible day. You will not believe what my boss did! (Pause) By the way, are you going to pay attention to me or to this stupid hockey match? (Insisting and trying to get his attention, her tone gets a little angrier.)

At that moment, Marc only cared about his ice-hockey match but his wife wanted to talk about uninteresting office politics. Marc thought about the consequences of not listening and imagined two possibilities: he could pretend to listen; or ask if she could wait until after the match. He quickly realized that neither of these would work and risked a huge argument. He was a little more inclined to listen now. He also realized that though he did not care about the topic, he did care a lot about his wife. He then confidently said:

> Darling, I'm sorry! I was too focused on the hockey match when you arrived. I have been waiting all season to see it, but I really want to hear about your day. Please give me a minute to start recording it and then we can talk. Is that okay?

> Sure, go ahead! Meanwhile, I will get us a drink. This may be a long talk.

If all else fails, we can negotiate for a better time, when we have the focus to listen.

# Talk: Transparent Advocacy

Transparent advocacy minimizes information asymmetry and increases persuasion. It aims for clear communication so others comprehend our message and avoid disagreement based on misunderstandings. The term "advocacy" reminds us that every opportunity to talk is equally an occasion to persuade. Negotiation is persuasion, so advocacy starts when the negotiation starts.

Many negotiators claim that advocacy should be assertive. We prefer to qualify our advocacy as transparent rather than assertive. First, advocacy as arguing is already close to asserting and thus may come across too strong. Second, it is hard to walk the thin line between assertiveness and aggressiveness, and even harder in relationship-based cultures. Third, assertiveness has two main parts: the ability to ask for what we want; and to say no to what we don't. Both can generate resistance if poorly executed. Transparency, on the other hand, has none of the risks above and assists assertiveness if one wants to.

The following story illustrates many elements of transparent advocacy. Olga invited Jan to a nice and private café, which she believed was an appropriate setting for their conversation.

> Jan, I asked you here today, because I am angry with you. In the past, you manipulated me and others. You always say what we want to hear, even if you don't believe it, just to get your way.

> Wow, Olga, let me just take 10 seconds to say that I am very surprised and also sorry to hear that you are angry. This is pretty important, indeed. I am glad you made the time to talk to me about it. Tell me more.

> Yes, I am angry because every time we complain or disagree about something, you always turn the topic around. I do not know how you do it, but in the end, it seems that you always make us believe what you want. It feels like you are a politician on a campaign. I want this manipulation to stop!

> I can easily see why someone would become angry if they feel they are being manipulated. I am not sure I agree with you that I was manipulating you, and I am open to being proven wrong. Still, I want to hear you out first. Do you have some more concrete examples that can help me better understand what you mean?

> Well, I could share several. Pretty much all the recent arguments we had happened that way. I come angry with you, and after a while, I end up agreeing with you. You just say what we want to hear to get away with things. You are manipulating me!

Olga, I am sorry you feel that way. Let me guarantee you that I have no intention of doing that. If you think that I change the way I talk when we are having an argument, I agree with you. I am indeed careful to say things in ways that help people to listen to me. When we are having an argument, it is very important to me that I am more careful with my words so as not to hurt you or anyone else. Does that sound manipulative?

Well, I appreciate you not wanting to hurt me, but you are hurting me with your manipulation.

I'm glad you do appreciate my good intentions at least, because I really want you to understand that I do not change what I want to say; I only change how I say it so that people can understand me better. It is like changing my language and the words I use, but not the content. For example, right now I am disagreeing with you that I am a manipulator. I am not agreeing just to make the argument go away. So, in my mind at least, this is not manipulation, but adaptation. Does that make sense?

It does, but if you do not change what you think, why do we usually end up agreeing after an argument?

Because as we speak the same language and are more careful with words, we probably manage to find the misunderstandings and fix them together. I have no intention to hurt you or manipulate you, at least not on purpose. And as we understand each other better, we usually find that there are few unsolvable disagreements between us.

There you go making me believe you again!

What is the problem with us believing one another? I believed that you thought I was a manipulator and that is pretty tough to hear.

There is no problem with that; it is just that you are always right and that pisses me off!

I am not always right, since I made you believe I was a manipulator. I am actually sorry for that!

Indeed!

> Do you still think I manipulate? Do you think I am manipulating you now?

> Not really, but I need to mull this over a little before I make up my mind.

> Okay! Let me know if I can help. No manipulation, I promise!

In the following sections, we dissect this dialogue to find examples and learnings of transparent advocacy. Transparent advocacy helps us negotiate within a Joint Value Pursuit (JVP) frame, focus on the other party and anticipate communication traps for maximum persuasive impact.

## Advocate for a Joint Value Pursuit

Advocacy is by and large associated with courts, legal battles and opposing sides. Therefore, when it is our turn to talk, we stop asking and learning. It is no surprise then that we end up in a unilateral communication mode and abandon the dialogue pattern. Advocacy within that battle frame leads to bargaining and a distancing of the parties.

### POINT OF INTEREST

**Advocacy vs. Contribution**

"Transparency contribution" is a potential alternative terminology for "transparent advocacy." The meaning of the term "contribution" is better aligned with our Joint Value Pursuit frame and less antagonistic than "advocacy."

Advocacy is meant here as a joint contribution of data, ideas and convictions towards the best negotiation outcome. Thus, it has to include the others as partners and their ideas as building blocks to develop a JVP solution.

### Be Inclusive

Advocating the inclusion of emotions is a complex two-sided topic. On their side, we advocate considering their emotional state. If they are sad or angry, seeing us happy will not help both parties connect. Like a newscaster who does not smile when announcing bad news, we too advocate consistency with our context.

On our side, we can share the emotions behind our speech. For example, we can share how angry or anxious we are about a risky project, despite looking composed. Emotions are a strong indicator of people's intentions so they can help our message to be more credible and humane.

> Wow, Olga, let me just take 10 seconds to say that **I am very surprised and also sorry to hear that you are angry.** This is pretty important, indeed. **I am glad** you made the time to talk to me about it. Tell me more.

Transparent advocacy is inclusive of their ideas and convictions. If they believe that we are closed to persuasion, why should they be any different? Transparent advocacy promotes an open dialogue towards the best possible solution, even if it means being persuaded. That does not mean giving in to any argument, but rather keeping an open posture and sharing our readiness to change our minds if presented with good arguments (legitimacy).

> I can easily see why someone would become angry if they feel they are being manipulated. **I am not sure I agree with you** that I was manipulating you, **and I am open to being proven wrong.** Still, I want to hear you out first. Do you have some more **concrete examples that can help me better understand what you mean?**

Being inclusive about both sides' pros and cons demonstrates openness and commitment to a joint solution. As we acknowledge or agree with their valid ideas, facts or convictions, they are more inclined to reciprocate. Our conclusions become more credible to them, even when we conclude on different interpretations of their ideas, facts or convictions. Being flexible and open, we work together to find the best information from each side and tailor the best outcome.

> Olga, I am sorry you feel that way. Let me guarantee you that I have no intention in doing that. **If you think that I change the way I talk when we are having an argument, I agree with you.** I am indeed careful to say things in ways that help people to listen to me. When we are having an argument, it is very important to me that I am more careful with my words so as not to hurt you or anyone else. **Does that sound manipulative?** (Asking how Olga sees this particular fact connected to the conclusion)

## Avoid Exclusion

Under the battle frame, one side's story has to prevail or exclude the other; unsurprisingly, we end up advocating for exclusion. Conversely, information asymmetry points out that none of our stories are individually complete. By avoiding exclusion, we can bring our resources together and build a joint story with more and better information.

One example is the word "but", which is known to be "the great eraser." "But" or similar adverse terms erase positive preceding phrases and direct attention to the negative message. Adverse terms imply that we are on opposite sides and only one idea will survive, thus inviting positional behavior.

> I like your idea, **but** it is not sustainable in the long term. (Do we really like it or do we just say it to soften the other party up before criticizing them?)

Many people use the word "but" without meaning exclusion. We prefer to use the word "and" instead of "but" as it clearly invites inclusion. "And" would convey sincerity on the compliment while still advocating the need to consider the long-term sustainability risk.

> I like your idea, **and** it is not sustainable in the long term.

How does that sound? A little weird at first, right? Substituting "and" for "but" requires a little more work than just swapping words. Being specific or transparent whenever possible avoids the compliment becoming empty, quickly dismissed and excluded.

> I like your low-cost efficiency idea, **and** it is not sustainable in the long term.

Being specific calls attention to the positive statement while making it sound more sincere. And there are still the questions of why we like it and why it is not sustainable. Do we have any data or is it just our impression? We want to reinforce our statement by transparently sharing its origins:

> I like your low-cost efficiency idea, and **I am afraid** it is not sustainable in the long term.

or

> I like your low-cost efficiency idea, and **I have information that leads me to believe that, unfortunately,** it is not sustainable in the long term.

Finally, to clearly indicate that our advocacy is an attempted contribution, we finish with an open invitation for further learning. By inviting their views, our persuasion increases as they seriously and openly consider our ideas.

> I like your low-cost efficiency idea, and I am afraid it is not sustainable in the long term. **What is your view on its sustainability?**

Questions are an intrinsic part of the transparent advocacy persuasive effort. They deflect immediate or reactive resistance (exclusion) to our suggestions as they invite people to think through before answering. If they cannot find an answer, they become closer to agreeing to our views. As a result, the question increases the chance of our advocacy succeeding.

Another exclusion pitfall in advocacy happens when the other party proposes something seemingly negative. Our impulse is to say no. That, however, equals an early commitment which limits learning and excludes possibilities.

> I would like to sell my company for €10 million.

> But your company is only worth €5 million.

> I don't think so! I believe it is worth €10 million. Do you want it or not?

> No!

> Okay, no deal!

Instead of saying "no" too early, we can say, "Yes, if…," "Yes, and…," or the like. This keeps the dialogue pattern flowing as we share the conditions needed to consider the demand.

> I don't think so! I believe it is worth €10 million. Do you want it or not?

> We can think about it. Here is what I would need to see happen to be able to pay €10 million for your company.

Of course, there are times in which we have to say no. We are just suggesting not rushing to it before exploring possibilities and learning more about them. What do you think?

## Speak to Persuade Them

Many times we prepare our arguments and check if they are persuasive to us. Conversely, we have to frame our advocacy to persuade them. Often, we fail to take into account what is going on in other negotiators' minds. Hopefully, through proactively learning, we would have gathered information to understand how they think and what can be more persuasive to them.

> I am glad you do appreciate my good intentions at least, **because I really want you to understand that I do not change what I want to say, I only change how I say it so that people can understand me better.** It is like changing my language and the words I use, but not the content.

To persuade them, whenever possible we use their particular language, expressions, metaphors and examples. Find out and speak their language so they can better hear: with an economist, speak in terms of effectiveness, charts and numbers; with a lawyer, speak in terms of fairness, principles and standards; with a painter, use colorful and visual metaphors; with a Chinese, speak in Mandarin and not in Mongolian.

> I do not know how you do it, but in the end, it seems like you always make us believe what you want. It feels like you are a **politician on a campaign**. I want this manipulation to stop! (Olga uses the "politician on a campaign" metaphor as she knows Jan is in politics.)

Finally, transparent advocacy **uses legitimacy or examples whenever possible** to back up and explain claims.

> Do you have **some more concrete examples** that can help me better understand what you mean?

or

> I am not always right, **since I made you believe I was a manipulator.** I am actually sorry for that! (Back up the claim with an example that clarifies and makes it concrete.)

## Anticipate Pitfalls

We have the responsibility to anticipate and fix the two ever-present communication pitfalls: perceptions and attributions. One place to start is to anticipate and clarify omissions and generalizations.

> So, in my mind at least, this is not manipulation, but adaptation. Does that make sense?

Another way to anticipate is to introduce what we are about to say. This minimizes erroneous interpretations as our statements are delivered into a prepared context. To further prevent misunderstanding, we can also label what was just said to ensure our desired interpretation. At this point, we can even share our intentions behind the particular statement.

> I am glad you do appreciate my good intentions at least, because I **really want you to understand** that I do not change what I want to say, I only change how I say it so that people can understand me better.

or

> **I have no intention to hurt you** or manipulate you, **at least, not on purpose**.

Our views are based on perceptions and attributions, thus they are but one possible interpretation of reality. Hence, we should express our views as possibilities and perceptions. Even then, we may argue that our perception is, in our belief, the most adequate interpretation unless we are otherwise persuaded. To do so, we can introduce our statements with: "My understanding of the situation is…," "One idea I had…," "What I believe is…," "A possibility is to…, " "If I understand correctly…," etc. To conclude the advocacy, we can return to asking questions. Asking them what they heard us say can minimize or identify attributions early on so we can take the necessary corrective action.

> So, **in my mind at least**, this is not manipulation, but adaptation. Does that make sense?

or

> **Do you still think** I manipulate? Do you think I am manipulating you now?

Transparent advocacy is consistent with the JVP frame and thus treats them as partners in the value pursuit. If we behave consistently, the transparent advocacy techniques above become but reminders to reinforce our intentions. Next, we will cover our key communication skills (ask to learn and lead, proactive learning and transparent advocacy) in a dialogue pattern.

## Ladder of Inference: Communication in Action

Whenever we disagree, instead of becoming positional and dismissive of their views, we are better off suspecting information asymmetry as a cause. The ladder of inference is a simple and systematic way to overcome information asymmetry. It does so by combining proactive listening, asking to learn and lead and transparent advocacy into one persuasive process.

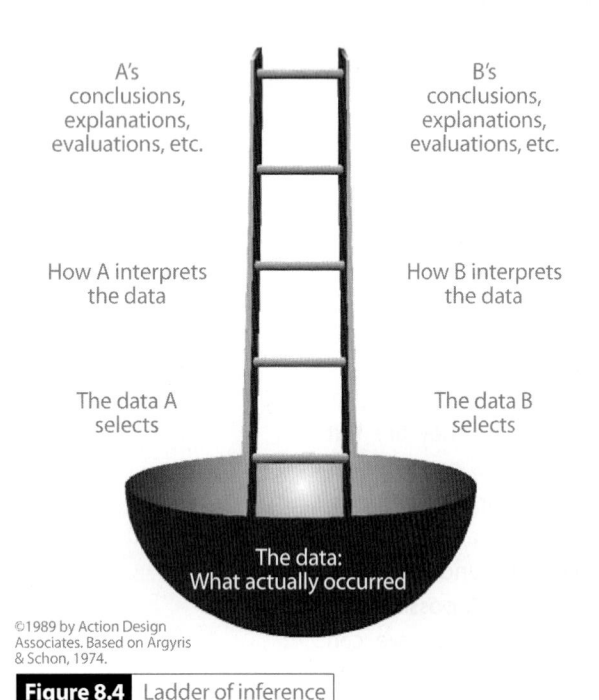

The ladder is a conceptual tool that illustrates how we arrive at conclusions (Figure 8.4). The ground on which the ladder stands represents all available data. The bottom rungs symbolize the sensorially perceived or rationally selected data. The medium rungs represent the interpretation of the data, which then leads to the conclusions (top rungs). Notice that the further away we move from the ground, the further we are from the data and the closer to being afflicted by assumptions.

Often, negotiators communicate at the conclusion level. Now, imagine we are helping a friend paint their house using different ladders. If they need help and say: "Hey, give me a hand over here, will you? Jump over!" Would we? Of course not! It is too risky to jump over. So we will first climb down our ladder, pick it up, walk all the way to their side and climb back up their ladder to meet them at the top. The same steps apply to the communication process which we dissect below:

**Figure 8.4** Ladder of inference

©1989 by Action Design Associates. Based on Argyris & Schön, 1974.

1. **Set up the ladder** – During a disagreement, we first surface our perception or intention to stop the cycle of arguments. Then we can ask a conducting question to invite a new process:

    - "It seems that we have different views on this topic. I would like to better understand how you perceive it so we can better understand one another. Is that okay with you?"
    - "I would like to stop now and try something else. I will be silent for a while and just listen until I understand your point-of-view on this. Do you think that may help us?"

2. **Climb down the ladder** – This means moving from positional disagreement to the rationale and data that support both our conclusions. This is a good time to practice proactive learning.

    - *"Would you mind sharing with me what you see?"*
    - *"What leads you to see things that way?"*
    - *"Perhaps you're seeing a part of the problem that I don't see or seeing it from a different angle. What information or data are you looking at?"*

3. **Get to the bottom of the ladder** – As we understand the big picture, we can ask clarification and confirmation questions. They will serve a dual purpose: to clarify and confirm our understanding; and to show that we listened. Beware of the temptation to counter-argue.

    **Clarification questions:**
    - *"What do you mean when you say...?"*
    - *"Why did you give priority to this information over the other one you also mentioned?"*
    - *"How did you arrive at this conclusion/interpretation?"*

    **Confirmation questions:**
    - *"When you say it is disrespectful, it is because you saw him arriving after you, right?"*
    - *"Is the unequal distribution you mentioned the reason you think the bonus was unfair?"*
    - *"Is it correct to say that you interpreted our absence as lack of concern for you and your colleagues?"*

4. **Getting recognition that we came down the ladder** – When our confirmation questions return positive answers, we can conclude the proactive learning before initiating advocacy. Paraphrase our whole understanding of the message and ask check-in questions. As they hear their own confirmation out loud, they feel heard and ready to reciprocate and listen.

    - *"So this is how you see this problem...Is that correct?"*
    - *"Does it seem that I can now see/understand what you see/believe?"*
    - *"Do you think I have it now?"*
    - *"Do you think I am still missing anything from your point of view?"*

5. **Prepare them to climb up the ladder** – Remember that no one can be forced to learn. After agreeing on our understanding of their views, we ask conducting questions to prepare them to listen to us. If they agree, we have a process commitment against interruptions or diversions.

    - *"Do you mind if I now try to show you what I see and/or believe?"*
    - *"Could I spend some time now showing how I see things?"*
    - *"Would you like to learn how I perceive the situation?"*

Having them realize we made our way down the ladder and preparing them to go up the ladder are important steps. These help move them from advocacy into listening mode. A car going down a highway at 120km/h cannot immediately make a U-turn. Someone set in advocacy mode also needs time to slow down and make the turn and head the other way.

6. **Climb up the ladder** – Once they have agreed to listen, we can explain our perceptions. It helps to start by introducing what will be said or shown. First, we delineate the big picture or context. Then, we share the data and compare the perceived differences in the data selected. Finally, we show how the data was interpreted to arrive at our conclusion.

- "*What I will try to show you now is how I see this as just a mistake and not an intentional deception.*"(Context)
- "*When you said that you were tired, I took it as a hint to leave, instead of to stay and help as you recently clarified.*" (Data comparison + interpretation)
- "*As I heard you talk about money much more than quality, I interpreted it as a choice for the cheaper product.*" (Data comparison + interpretation)

The ladder of inference is supposed to be a template and not to be applied mechanically. Skillful communication early on saves a lot of time, increases understanding and minimizes risk of future conflict. Once done well, the negotiators learn to quickly engage in a dialogue pattern, diagnose assumptions and understand before criticizing.

We conclude the chapter by proposing a win-win alternative dialogue for Paola and her aunt:

> I am so happy that I will have you as a neighbor! I am looking forward to having you around. Please enjoy your honeymoon. I will take care of your place for you.

> Oh, dear auntie! This is so kind of you. I am looking forward to living close to you too. I will come to see you in a week as soon as I return from my honeymoon.

> Before I let you go, is there something specifically that you would like me to do?

> Sure! If you can just check the mail for anything urgent or be available to open the door so that the furniture delivery people can get in the apartment, that will be of tremendous help. Am I imposing?

> Not at all I will be glad to do that. Let me just check by checking the mail you mean opening it?

> If you believe it is urgent, sure!

> Alright! And how about coordinating with these furniture delivery people. How will I know what time they will come?

> I will ask my mom to call them and coordinate with you if that is okay with you?

> Not a problem! One last thing: if there is something else that needs to be done, how would you like to proceed? Can I reach you in an emergency?

> What do you have in mind?

> I do not know. If the bed is not delivered or the couch cannot come up the elevator and the stairs, for example. What should I do? Should I bother you?

> In these cases, I believe you can call my mom as she will know what I would probably prefer.

> Great! Congratulations once again and enjoy your honeymoon.

The conversation above greatly minimizes the risk that the aunt would unwrap the gifts. She now understands what she was asked to do, and to call the mother in case something else came up. Even if she wanted to unwrap the gifts, she could not claim ignorance anymore. We concentrated on the first conversation between the two because the second is always harder to conduct. The idea of good communication is exactly to minimize risks and prevent conflict.

# summary

Communication is the conduit for everything in a negotiation. It is also the element of process. Communication is how, while process is when, something is said or done. The communication goals are effective learning and persuasion; the process goal is to develop an efficient and fair process to maximize value while minimizing risks.

## Information Asymmetry

- Information asymmetry is the biggest enemy of communication.
- It is the gap of information, and subsequently of understanding, between the parties.
- We unconsciously fill in information gaps with assumptions, which create:
  - Perceptions that make us believe we successfully captured and stored information; and
  - Attributions that make us believe we successfully shared what is on our minds.

## Dialogue Pattern: Three-Way Communication

1. Asking questions
   a. Learn information
   b. Lead the process
2. Proactive learning
   a. Ask to listen (conduct, confirm, clarify and check-in)
   b. Acknowledge the feeling
   c. Paraphrase the message.
3. Transparent advocacy
   a. Be inclusive of our emotions, their ideas and the pros and cons of our ideas
   b. Avoid exclusion with the word "but" and by saying "no" too early
   c. Speak to persuade them by using their language and legitimacy
   d. Anticipate pitfalls by introducing what we are about to say and reinforcing it is just our perception

## Ladder of Inference

1. Set up the ladder – Invite a new process
2. Climb down the ladder – Practice proactive learning to gather data
3. Get to the bottom of the ladder – Clarify and confirm understanding to show we listened
4. Getting recognition that we came down the ladder – Ask check-in questions on our understanding
5. Prepare them to climb up the ladder – Ask conducting questions to prepare them to listen
6. Climb up the ladder – Share big picture and data, then how we interpreted and concluded on it

# questions

## Easy
1. Why is information asymmetry the source of (almost) all evil?
2. What are the similarities and differences between perceptions and attributions?
3. What are the similarities and differences between two-way communication and the dialogue pattern?
4. What are the similarities and differences between open and closed questions, and learning and leading questions?
5. What are the similarities and differences between active listening and proactive learning?
6. What is the difference between assertive and transparent advocacy?

## Medium
1. What is the dialogue pattern? How do you put it in place?
2. Why are the communication tools provided here consistent with a value negotiation approach?
3. How do they help promote a Joint Value Pursuit frame?
4. Which three communication moves do you believe are most helpful to build trust?
5. When advocating for a Joint Value Pursuit, what are the three inclusions to insert and two exclusions to avoid in our advocacy?
6. Describe in your own words the Ladder of Inference process. (Max. 8 lines)

## Difficult
1. Identify at least three connections between the major communication steps and the unconditionally constructive behaviors.
2. When I ask a leading question, what relationship messages am I implicitly sending?
3. Based on the communication tools you now understand, what other unconditionally constructive behaviors can you think of (besides the six listed in the previous chapter)?
4. Pick three communication tools from this chapter and analyze their risks. What makes them difficult to use for you?
5. Why is the Ladder of Inference aligned with the dialogue pattern? Are there any differences between them?
6. The curse of knowledge happens when I try to share with someone else something I already know well. How does the curse of knowledge enhance information asymmetry?

# scenarios

## Easy

Are the statements below plagued by perceptions or attributions? Elaborate on the assumption in the person's mind that made them communicate poorly.
- "I'm worried."
- "If you only knew how angry that makes me, you would never say it again."
- "You make me nervous."

## Medium

1. Give two better questions to find out if everything is indeed okay with the other party after the following dialogue. Explain why they are better.

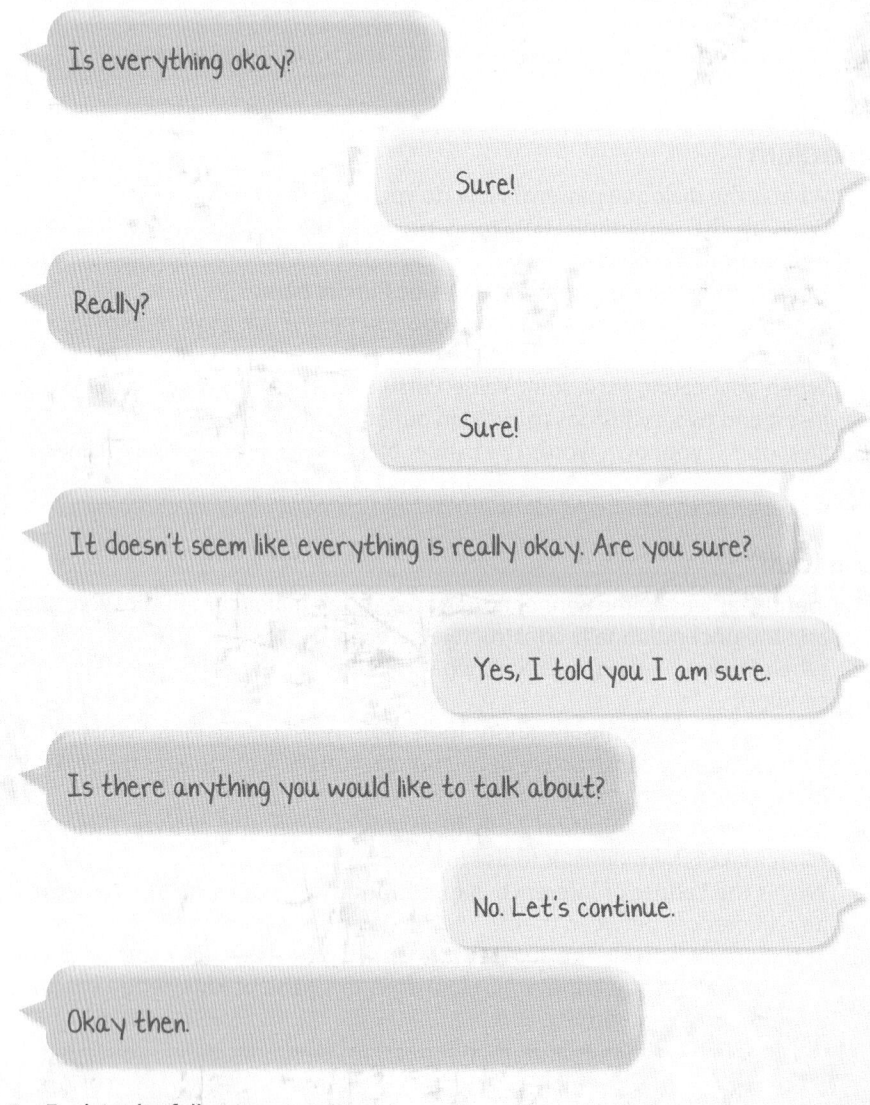

   > Is everything okay?

   > Sure!

   > Really?

   > Sure!

   > It doesn't seem like everything is really okay. Are you sure?

   > Yes, I told you I am sure.

   > Is there anything you would like to talk about?

   > No. Let's continue.

   > Okay then.

2. Explain the following equations.
   - Your explanation + my explanation = mutual understanding
   - Mutual understanding + argument + counter-argument = common solution
   - (Argument + counter argument) - mutual understanding = unilateral or no solution

   Do you agree with them? Why?

## Difficult

1. Specify the perceptions and attributions in Paola's dialogue with her aunt.

> Paola! I am so glad you are back! Have you seen your apartment yet?

> Yes! How could you do this to me?

> Do what? I wanted to show you how happy I am to have you as my neighbor. Knowing how busy you are professionally, I decided to help you out. I organized your place as I promised during your wedding so that everything was ready when you arrived. It took me five days, but you are my favorite niece. I hope you liked it!

> You had no right to do it! I was looking forward to opening my gifts for months now. I had been living in anticipation of this moment as well. How could you do this to me?

> What are you talking about? Do this to you? I told you that I was going to take care of everything while you were gone, didn't I?

> No, you said that you were going to take care of my place, not my gifts.

> But I was trying to help you out! I did not know that this was so important for you. My mom also opened all of my wedding gifts.

> This was not helping out! You had to know that this was not right. You did it on purpose!

2. Pick five segments in the dialogue below and describe the communication tools used.

> Hi, Ritesh, how are you doing?

> Good, William! And you?

> I'm okay, but I have something really important to talk to you about.

> Really? Good or bad?

> Actually, not so good, I am afraid!

> Well, I really want to listen to what you have to say. Is it urgent?

> Sort of. Why do you ask?

> Because I am heading off to a meeting in two minutes. I am assuming that this is not enough time to listen to your story and understand it. I was wondering if I could call you later?

> Well, how long is this meeting?

> It is internal. It should not take more than an hour to an hour and 15 minutes. I could call you right after. Is that okay with you? If you need to discuss this now, I will just need a couple of minutes to let them know I won't be able to make it.

> Actually, that is okay. We have to start doing something today, but one hour is not going to kill us.

> Great! Thanks for your flexibility. What would be the best way to reach you one hour from now?

> You can call my cell phone, as I may be out for lunch. You have my number, right?

> Sure! Will do!

# 09 Powerful Openings: Building a Solid Bridge Quickly

## Learning Objectives:
- How to quickly set the right environment to negotiate
- What small talk is and what it is good for
- How to put together a good opening statement
- What to do if they are not helpful from the start
- How to define a good process in a couple of minutes
- The role of body language and how to use it early

*"It is only the first step that is difficult."*
— Marie De Vichy-Chaconne

Nkiruka found herself in her second meeting with Kingsley, a partner from a company she wanted to join. The first meeting was brief and a little confusing. It was Nkiruka who asked for the second meeting. She prepared extensively for the negotiation, or did she?

> Good morning, Nkiruka! So, how is it going?

> Good morning to you too. Well, you see... I wanted... Okay! I called this meeting so I should start. You are right! Ahh... I have been very busy. I have been clearing my schedule so that we can start working together.

> Excuse me?

> Sorry?

> No, I do not understand where you are going. It seems that your life is very busy right now. Do you really think you are ready for this job?

> I am! I am! I am definitely ready. Well, in all honesty, not right now. As I said, I still have to clear some things first.

> Do you at least know what you want?

> Oh, that I do know. I am very ready to talk about that.

> Okay, so why don't we start again, shall we? Why did you call this meeting?

> I'm sorry! You are right! Let me start again. I called this meeting because I am very excited with the opportunity to work for your company and with you specifically. You asked me last meeting to share with you what I wanted and I worked on that. However, I then found that I still had a few questions that I needed clarification before finalizing my proposal to you.

> Sure, let me know what your questions are and then I would love to hear your initial thoughts on what you are looking for.

First impressions matter! Nkiruka was lucky that Kingsley was open and collaborative. Had she found someone more adversarial in nature, they may have tried to take advantage of her early confusion. Nkiruka was well prepared, but like most negotiators, she gave little if any attention to her opening.

How we start our negotiation defines much of our interaction (relationship and communication) afterwards. For that reason, we need to be more proactive about our opening. Unfortunately, it is common to see negotiators start with small talk and then jump straight into the substance negotiation.

> Hello, Amara. Nice to see you.

> Nice to see you, too, Emilie.

> So how is the family?

> Good, and yours?

> They are okay. So, how much do you want?

> What?

186  PART 3 • NEGOTIATE!

Everyone wants to start a negotiation on the right foot. For a powerful opening, we need to establish strong relationship and communication foundations as fast as possible. To do so, small, early and positive relationship and communication moves can set the negotiation off to a good start. Though each move may be small, if all these align in the same direction, their impact can be significant.

# Relationship

To start building a good relationship as fast as possible, it is useful to consider where we will meet. Should we meet in our office or theirs? The answer should not be based on power, but rather which place supports the negotiation better.

Once the parties meet, much like Nkiruka's situation above, what should we do or say at first? Do we engage in small talk or do we open with something powerful? Actually, we can do either or both. But what if they are not as collaborative as Kingsley? All these are challenges that can influence the early relationship-building effort and are covered below.

## Prepare a Conducive Environment

To help the negotiators connect and communicate more freely, it is important to have a degree of openness and willingness to get closer. Doing or talking about things that are meaningful to the negotiators may surface personal details that make the relationship "click". However, even if these steps are taken, success is not guaranteed. We can at least increase our chances when we quickly promote an environment conducive to trust.

Whenever possible, we prefer to meet instead of interacting over the phone, by email, etc. Meeting face-to-face allows negotiators to see and trust the person, instead of a faceless voice or an email signature. It also helps all parties gather more information about each other and about what is being communicated. So for important or first-time negotiations, we want to put our best effort into meeting the person.

Next, we want to create a relaxed environment where we can express ourselves without fear of misunderstanding or mistakes. In such an environment, power distances and risks are reduced so negotiators can freely and comfortably discuss what they care about. A relaxed environment has a high sense of privacy and security (low risk) or an informal or coordinated feel (low power). Some examples include:

- *"Let's talk about this over lunch at a nice cozy restaurant across the street where we will not be disturbed."*
- *"I already told my secretary that I will be busy and turned off my mobile phone for our meeting. I want to make sure that we really get to know each other better without getting interrupted."*

- "Welcome to my office. I understand that you would like to talk about something important. Would you like me to close the door?"
- "Why don't we remove our ties for a while and discuss this over coffee outside?"

The relaxed environment can also be created halfway through a negotiation. When the negotiation seems stuck on a certain issue, we can call for a break or move elsewhere. Even if for just a while, we leave our official roles and mingle. Many deals are closed when the parties stop to drink, eat, smoke or just relax in a new environment.

An effective environment for relationship-building has them feel that they are with us out of their own choice. Giving them space and control over themselves shows respect and understanding that they will only enter this relationship if they want to. No one likes to feel pushed or pressured into anything and they appreciate having their decision and timing respected. Following are examples of how this space can be conveyed:

> I am not sure if I can come to your event tonight. I can better explain it to you later. Do you mind?

> First, thanks for calling to let me know. I am sad that you will not come! And of course I do not mind. I offered you an invitation, not a demand. If something changes, even if at the last minute, please show up as I still want to see you.

or

> I really like and trust your work. I liked what you showed me and that is why I am sad that I will not be able to invest in your project. I hope you are not too upset.

> Well, I am a little sad, and of course I respect your decision. I wanted to bring you an opportunity, because you are someone I trust. I never meant to put you in a position to have to invest just because of our relationship. Would you mind sharing with me why not? Since your opinion matters a lot to me, I would really like to know if there is something I need to improve.

For all our talk on doing things quickly, relationships have their own timing and are not to be forced. Let's look at the dialogue between a salesperson and a buyer in Table 9.1:

| NEGOTIATION DIALOGUE | DIAGNOSTICS |
| --- | --- |
| *Hi! Thanks for agreeing to see me! I hope this meeting will be a good investment of our time.* | |
| Sure, I was happy to learn about what you do and got curious to learn some more. Do you think that a half hour will be enough for me to learn all I need about your portfolio of services? | Buyer says with a fair amount of interest and expectation |

| NEGOTIATION DIALOGUE | DIAGNOSTICS |
|---|---|
| *Maybe! It depends on how complex your situation is. We can try to find the right services that please you, but if it is just to learn more about our services in general, then a half hour is more than enough. By the way, how is your family doing?* | Seller abruptly redirects the communication negotiation towards the relationship negotiation as he perceives an open door to build trust through the buyer's openness and interest |
| Family? What do you mean? What does my family have to do with this? | Buyer retracts and is now suspicious as well as confused |
| *I just wanted to get to know you a little better before we do business together.* | Seller is already apologetic |
| I am not sure that I have made up my mind about this yet. Why don't we cross that bridge when we get there? Meanwhile, let's keep my family away from this conversation, okay? | Buyer reads that seller thinks that the substance commitment was already made and makes sure to convey otherwise, while also limiting the enthusiasm and openness that were there initially |
| *Okay, then!* | Seller starts to realize that asking about personal things too fast may not have been his best move |

**Table 9.1**
Dialogue between a salesperson and a buyer

Here, the seller may have correctly perceived that the buyer already had some trust about his ability to deliver. When she asked for his advice on process, she demonstrated trusting even the honesty of his intentions. But this was no guarantee that she wanted a closer personal relationship. During the negotiation, we need to gauge and respect each person's timing for building trust.

# Small Talk

With limited relationship or communication impact, small talk is called "small" for a reason: its effect is small! Though small talk should not serve as a core opening strategy, it still has a potentially valuable role in negotiations.

Since most cultures engage in small talk, this can be an opportunity if approached proactively. A targeted small talk can actually produce a positive relationship and communication set-up for the negotiation through three main benefits:

1. Ease the tension and/or anxiety of the parties
   - Are we behaving like people or corporate robots?
2. Develop some level of familiarity and liking between them
   - Do we have related experiences or common acquaintances?
3. Gauge their negotiation attitude to decide on the appropriate opening statement
   - Do they seem to bring a more aggressive or constructive attitude?

Instead of dismissing small talk, we can use it to start building the bridge. We can adopt an open body posture to show that we are relaxed and yet interested in the negotiation (Figure 9.1). A proactive learning stance within an early, respectful dialogue pattern can demonstrate a welcoming attitude. If appropriate, some humor or genuine praise early on can also help diffuse any apprehension. Put together, these behaviors send implicit messages that our goal is to collaborate, not fight.

**Figure 9.1** Positive and negative body language

Positive body language, or open body posture. The person is angled toward the other, relaxed facial expression, with arms uncrossed

Negative body language, or closed body posture. Note the hunched shoulders, the tense facial expression and the crossed arms

Proactive small talk can be directed to topics that allow negotiators to connect as individuals. Topics as simple as similar experiences, people known in common, professional history or hobbies can identify common links among negotiators. The best topics are independent from the transaction and allow negotiators to better know each other. It helps if these topics reveal something in common or admired about the other party. Our goal is to establish some rapport, based on familiarity or liking, to bring the negotiators a little closer together.

To proactively build a JVP frame, we want to seize the earliest available opportunity in the negotiation. During small talk, we can try to proactively share our relationship intentions through our opening statement. Small talk and the behaviors conveyed here give us hints about their relationship intentions: collaborative or positional. We can use that information to adjust our opening statement accordingly.

## The Opening Statement

The opening statement's goal is to establish the desired frame for the relationship negotiation, for example, the JVP frame. The opening statement is usually a sentence or two prepared ahead of time, to the extent of scripting the words. As the first statement we make, we can exercise a fair amount of control over how it is said. In value negotiation, the opening statement tries to promote interdependence as fast as possible. Thus, it contains some interdependence elements: "we" mentality (collaborative roles and sitting side-by-side) and the focus on a common challenge or opportunity.

- I am confident that if we put our heads together, we will be able to better understand one another and sort out this misunderstanding.
- I am glad to have the opportunity for us to discover ways to make our company more productive together.
- I would like us to spend some time understanding what we want and can do together in the hope of finding something that works well for both of us.

However, some opening statements can be less powerful depending on how they are phrased. They may still work but carry a little more risk.

| PROBLEM | OPENING STATEMENT EXAMPLE | THEIR POTENTIAL RESPONSE |
|---|---|---|
| Too general and vague | I am glad to meet you today to see if we can find mutually beneficial solutions to our problem. | Sure! Nice canned statement. You probably say that to everyone… |
| Positional or adversarial | I am here to make sure that I can get a 10% reduction in your price. | Really? Thanks for the advance warning. Over my dead body! |
| Substance-focused | We can make a lot of money if we work together. | We? I can make a lot of money. Why would I need you? |
| Assumption-based | I am sure both of us can benefit from avoiding going to court. | Who says so? I believe you are afraid of going to court. |
| Suspicious | My goal today is to help you make US$1 million! | Yeah, right! And you do this out of the kindness of your heart… |

So when developing an opening statement, towards interdependence, it helps to be specific, relationship-focused, and expressing intentions, not interests or outcomes.

**Table 9.2**

Common problems in opening statements

> Harry, I am here as your friend today to tell you that I really believe we can find ways to finish this project once and for all.

or

> Thank you for coming to this meeting. This is the first time we are bringing together a group of the best people from our companies as one team to find ways for our partnership to become more profitable for us all.

## Share What is at Stake

The relationship negotiation can be particularly difficult in some cases. A belief that a large power difference exists may incite them to behave win-lose. In such case s, a more substance-oriented early move can convince them of the need for a more collaborative relationship. If appropriate and necessary, we can share what we believe is at stake in case of relationship success or failure. These statements usually contain some element of presumed interests (potential success) or alternatives (risk of failure). Two examples:

- **Interests** – "*I believe that if we work together, we can come up with ways to help our companies finalize this project faster and generate an extra €10 million for each of us. Is it worthwhile for us to invest some effort in finding ways to do that?*"
- **Alternatives** – "*We can both find a mutually acceptable solution for this legal dispute or go for a random decision from the courts where either of us could win or lose. Since we are already here, I would much rather spend a few moments seeing if we can do better than going to court. What would you like to do?*"

This technique can be quite risky as it can come across as a mix of relationship and substance. Thus, it should only be used "if appropriate and necessary." The potential satisfaction of the presumed interest (potential success case) can be understood as an early commitment. They may hold us accountable to our promise or concession at the end of the negotiation.

With alternatives (risk of failure case), it may sound like a threat and invite a similar response. A reason to use this opening statement is when our small talk indicates they are coming with an aggressive or arrogant attitude. It has to be more than just win-lose. Actually, more often than not, the better suggestion is to use this as a backup opening statement. In case our first one fails to produce interdependence.

# Communication

Though relationships are important, a process can be even more so. A good relationship and bad communication take us nowhere, but good communication can still lead a bad relationship towards value. Thus, it is important that we try to establish the basis of a good communication process as early as possible.

At the beginning especially, everything we say or do sends a message. How can we make sure that we send the right ones? How can we establish good communication if our body may betray us? Below we see how to answer these questions.

## Negotiating the Four Ps

The communication negotiation defines the process boundaries and direction of the negotiation. If done early on, it can greatly improve the efficiency of the whole negotiation. The four Ps are simple guidelines to negotiate the broader process elements as early and quickly as possible. The four Ps are:

- **Purpose** – What are we trying to accomplish? The purpose is the definition of what the negotiation process is trying to achieve.
    - **Examples:** Get to know each other better, understand if there are possibilities for a deal, explore our interests, come up with solutions to a challenge, attempt to overcome a conflict, close the deal, etc.

- **Product** – The product helps identify when the purpose is fulfilled. It is the material output of the negotiation.
    - **Examples:** A signed contract, a proposal, a memo, a draft text, a list of ideas, a letter of intent, etc.

- **People** – Every deal involves a number of key decision-makers we need to influence. Defining the people means identifying and involving every relevant person in the decision-making process from the beginning.
    - **Examples:** Me, my boss, my department, my husband/wife, my friends, my employer, my priest, my parents, my partner, other departments, my board, etc.

- **Process** – Once we know where we are going (purpose), what we are building (product) and who is involved (people), we can negotiate the best way to get there (process). Process normally includes how and when we will negotiate.
  - **Examples:** Time for the meeting(s), agenda issues and sequence, process rules (regular breaks, brainstorming, no interruptions, etc.).

The four Ps usually come shortly after the opening statement to start modeling the dialogue pattern as soon as possible. Even if less than prepared, we can share our ideas on the four Ps and ask check-in questions: What do you think? How do you feel about that?

In our purpose, we describe our core message. Different from the opening statement, the core message has no relationship goal, but rather a process one. The core message shares our main reason for the meeting to guarantee our process focus and direction. We have to be aware not to share substance interests at this stage, only process ones.

- My main purpose here today is to find a solution for our short-term operational crisis.
- My main goal is to spend as much time as I can until I am sure I understand your reasons.

How do we implement the four Ps? Should we impose ours or accept theirs? The four Ps are supposed to be negotiated within a dialogue pattern. Like a dress rehearsal, the value at risk in negotiating the four Ps is small since only process is at stake. The parties can suggest, listen, advocate, ask and even agree more easily and any mistake can be readily fixed. The four Ps negotiation can create a positive momentum to be carried into the substance negotiation.

Check the four Ps negotiation at a feedback meeting of partner companies after the successful completion of an important project:

If the four Ps negotiation turns out to be tense and difficult, it alerts us to potential relationship or communication problems. In these cases, we need to persist in the four Ps negotiation until we negotiate process rules that address these challenges.

> So, what brings us here together today? (Purpose)

> Well, we would like to see if we could spend some time trying to learn from our recently concluded project. Is that what you had in mind?

> No, I just responded to your meeting invitation, but I believe you have a great idea. Can I ask what you expect to get out of this meeting? (Product)

> If possible, I would like to take away a list of improvements that we can apply on the next project.

> How much detail would you like? (Clarifying product)

> Not much, just general ideas are fine. The details can be sorted out with the technical people later on. Shall we start?

> What do you think about a second list, one in which we actually list some of the things that worked particularly well in this project? (Suggesting an expansion on product)

> I am not sure I understand why we should do this.

> Well, I believe that we should also create some memory of the things that worked well, so that we can ensure that we will repeat them next time instead of trying to reinvent the wheel. Is that something that we may have the interest and time to do? (Arguing for product expansion)

> Sure, sounds like a good idea. Do we need anyone else to do this, though? (People)

> No, I believe all decision-makers in the project are in this room right now. A small question: the invitation said that the meeting was supposed to take one hour, is that right? (Checking on the time process)

> Correct! If we need more time, we can then decide on when to reconvene. Where would you like to start on: the improvements or the successes? (Sequencing the agenda process)

> It doesn't matter to me. I just need to know one thing: are we going to suggest things and they will automatically go in the list, like brainstorming, or do we have to argue and discuss our suggestions? (Checking the rules of the process)

> Good point! What do you prefer?

- If voices and tempers are raised, then take breaks more frequently and set a "no interruption" rule when a party is talking.
- If constant interruptions occur, then set times for each negotiator to express their views without interruptions.
- If they already show positional behavior on process, then agree that demands need to be backed up by legitimacy or be open to other possible options, etc.

Once the environment is right, the relationship set and the process clearly structured, the building of the bridge has started well. Initiating the value conversation should become a seamless transition. The parties can initiate the discussion around the first agenda issue, knowing what is coming and feeling in control.

## On Body Language

Body language as a means of communication is both important and unimportant. Body language is important because it can have a strong communication impact. However, there is a popular belief that to master body language is to have access to the other's deepest secrets. Unfortunately, that popular belief is just a myth and body language is not as magical or as important.

But what is body language after all? Body language includes all messages that our body signals or facial expressions send that convey potential meaning. It includes gestures, expressions, postures, as well as how we look, dress, walk, talk, and even breathe. Body language does not include spoken words or the way words are said (paralinguistic communication includes accent, pace, tone, inflection, etc.).

Body language is important because we communicate a lot through non-verbal ways. The role of body language in communication is considered to be at least 50%. If we then add paralinguistic communication, the combined role can reach beyond 90%. Interpreting body language can enhance understanding, for example, when someone is nervous or upset but does not say it. It can show the emotion behind a message to enhance sincerity or just strengthen the power of something said. Many people, including ourselves, believe in meeting face-to-face to check others' body language before trusting them.

Despite the large role it plays in communication, we still believe that body language is less important when in isolation. Evolution is a case in point since animals mainly communicate through body language. They actually benefit from developed senses to do so, such as dogs' acute sense of smell, cats' sharp night vision or owls' heightened capacity for hearing. We do not have such developed senses and yet we are better communicators than animals. Our developed brains created words to become the tool that allows us to go beyond animals in communicating.

Many negotiators dangerously overestimate the role of body language, as it is also a great source of potential misunderstanding. Relying heavily on body language is actually risky because it is hard:

- **To control** – The body speaks for itself. Despite our intention to control it, we cannot do so 100%. North Asians are famous for hiding their emotions well, but even they cannot do it 100%.
- **To read** – There are literally thousands of messages in body language, from different eye movements to micro-emotions. To make sense of all possible messages is overwhelming, if not distracting, from words and their nuances.
- **To understand** – There is a lot of noise in body language: reflexes, body tics or just the expression of an unconnected emotion. Someone may seem angry and frustrated about something unrelated that happened before our meeting.
- **To interpret** – Different cultures express body language differently. Even within the same city, we may be further apart in the way we express ourselves (consider different generations) than with someone from a different country.
- **To improve** – Being so complex, getting good at reading and controlling body language is an arduous task. It requires years of study and practice to be able to do it well, fast and under tense negotiations.

Most people attempting to detect liars through body language succeed 50% of the time. As a reference, flipping a coin on the same question would produce a similar result. Experts who study and practice for years and work daily on recognizing liars succeed 57% of the time. The best ones go as high as 70%. Improving our success rate by 14–40% may seem like a good time investment at first, but it is hardly our best investment. Especially when there are so many other better things to learn that will help us communicate better.

Though not providing the competitive advantage that many negotiators would expect, body language can still improve our communication. Some recommendations are:

- **Look for consistency** – Look for many signs that point in the same direction or contradict themselves strongly. Literally, do not sweat the small stuff.
- **Different people have different body language** – People especially from different cultures laugh when they are happy, nervous or embarrassed. Instead of judging based on what we would do, explore other potential interpretations for it.
- **Diagnose** – If we pick up a body language message, ask questions about it for confirmation purposes. Perhaps an aggressive demeanor is actually a spillover from a bad meeting earlier in the day. Try to learn more before committing to act.
- **Prepare our own** – Body language is particularly important at the beginning when there is less information to put it into context. Preparing our initial body messages for the negotiation increases our consistency and impact.

An open and relaxed body posture invites a good start. Acting naturally is usually our best strategy. After seeing thousands of people negotiate, the vast majority had a more natural body language and gave away less information than they expected. More often than not, those who try hard to pass as normal are the ones who look awkward. If someone behaves differently, there usually is a good explanation for it. If someone says she is happy yet her face expresses sadness, this is a good opportunity to ask and learn.

That said, for those who want a little more, below is some basic body language advice:

- **Eyes** – We look more at people we like, therefore try to establish comfortable (culturally adapted) eye contact with the other. Beware of staring as it can convey intimidation.
  - In Latin America, it is acceptable to look straight into someone's eyes for quite a while, whereas in Asia, this can be considered rude.

- **Face** – Facial expressions convey the most information, but also the most noise through the multitude of emotions we feel. We hear something good, but our focused expression looks like we just learned that someone passed away. If our facial expressions are not expressing our intentions consistently, proactively disclose the latter:
  - *"I am really excited with your proposal. I know I do not look excited right now, but I was sick and I am still recovering. I hope you understand."*

- **Body alignment** (shoulder placement and distance from each other) – Body alignment gives cues into the negotiators' attitude towards the conversation.
  - Is leaning forward a show of interest or an invasion of personal space?
  - Is leaning backward a way to distance us or to allow them to speak?
  - Does a neutral position display formality or comfort?

- **Arms and hands** – Arms and hands are used to communicate ideas, to offend or to defend. Again, consistency is key. Even wild arm movements can be okay when conveying a wild idea or within certain cultures. A good way to start a negotiation is to have arms uncrossed and hands visible, higher than the edge of the table.
  - Uncrossed arms signal no barriers, confidence and openness.
  - Hands placed on the table communicate nothing to hide, no surprises or tricks.

### POINT OF INTEREST

**To Shake or Not to Shake?**
Some cultures attach significant meaning to handshakes and require decisive and firm handshakes for one to be taken seriously. A soft handshake can be reason enough for distrust. In other cultures, a handshake carries much less meaning and is just a ritual that can be dispensed with at times. Still, in other cultures, a handshake is actually offensive, and bowing is the preferred way of acknowledging an introduction.

- **Rhythm** (breathing, pace and tone of speech) – Mirroring their rhythm has them see similarities between us and appreciate us more. It is also used to lead:
  - If they are anxious, we can breathe slower. This helps calm their heart rate as they naturally start to mimic some of our rhythm.

Most negotiators have no problem doing these things if well prepared. Preparation helps us look relaxed and confident, as well as sincerely open to their ideas. Preparation on the seven elements of negotiation can do more for our body language than most of the specific body language advice above. Merely controlling our body language or monitoring theirs can come across as odd and suspicious; instead prepare well for the negotiation and a positive body language will naturally follow.

# summary

Everyone wants to start a negotiation on the right foot. For a powerful opening, we need to establish strong relationship and communication foundations as fast as possible. To do so, small, early and positive relationship and communication moves can set the negotiation off to a good start. Though each move may be small, if all these align in the same direction, their impact can be significant.

## Relationship

1. Prepare a conducive environment
   a. Prefer to meet face-to-face;
   b. Create an environment without fear of misunderstanding or mistakes;
   c. Give them space and control over themselves; and
   d. Respect their relationship's timing.

2. Small talk
   a. Ease the tension and/or anxiety;
   b. Develop some level of familiarity and liking with them; and
   c. Gauge their negotiation attitude to decide on the appropriate opening statement.

3. The opening statement
   a. It is a relationship statement to build interdependence as fast as possible.
   b. Problems when crafting one are making it too vague, positional, substance-focused, assumption-based and too generous (suspicious).

4. Share what is at stake
   a. Interests
   b. Alternatives

## Communication

1. Negotiating the four Ps
   a. Purpose – Define the scope of our negotiation.
   b. Product – Define the material output of the negotiation.
   c. People – Define the authority of the key decision-makers of our negotiation.
   d. Process – Define the path of our negotiation.

2. On body language
   a. It is both important and unimportant, but non-verbal expression can form 90% of our communication.
   b. It is hard to control, read, understand, interpret and improve.
   c. We should look for consistency, remember that different people have different body language, diagnose what we notice and prepare our own.
   d. The eyes, face, body alignment and arms and hands convey emotions the most.
   e. The best strategy is to be prepared so as to naturally convey a relaxed and confident body language.

# questions

## Easy

1. What can we do to prepare the right environment to negotiate?
2. What are the potential benefits of small talk?
3. When should we consider sharing what is at stake?
4. What are the main features that we should pay attention to with body language?
5. What are the four Ps and how can they help our negotiation?
6. What are the challenges posed by body language? How can we use it effectively to improve our negotiation?

## Medium

1. What are the factors to consider in choosing whether to meet at my office or yours? What are the pros and cons in choosing offices to set the right environment to negotiate?
2. The opening statement is only one or two sentences. Why is it so important to prepare it well? What difference can it really make?
3. What is the importance of asking about the people in the four Ps negotiation? What can go wrong if we don't negotiate it early on?
4. The author says that body language and paralinguistic communication equal 90% of our communication. And yet, he argues that they are less important than words. Do you agree? Why?

## Difficult

1. What is the difference between the purpose and the opening statement?
2. Prepare an opening statement and a core message for your next negotiation role-play. Then describe their elements and analyze why they are good or bad.
3. What are the risks and rewards of an opening statement that is based on substance interests? And on alternatives?
4. Identify if there are any elements of a core message within the following opening statements.
   - "I am confident that if we put our heads together, we will be able to better understand one another and sort out this misunderstanding."
   - "I am glad to have the opportunity for us to discover ways to make our company more productive together."
   - "I would like us to spend some time understanding what we want and can do together in the hope of finding something that works well for both of us."
   - "Harry, I am here as your friend today to tell you that I really believe we can find ways to finish this project once and for all."
   - "Thank you for coming to this meeting. This is the first time we are bringing together a group of the best people from our companies as one team to find ways for our partnership to become more profitable for us all."

# scenarios

## Easy

What are the appropriate products in the four Ps negotiation for the following purposes?
- Get to know each other better.
- Understand if there are possibilities for a deal.
- Explore our interests.
- Come up with solutions to a challenge.
- Attempt to overcome a conflict.
- Close the deal.

## Medium

*This looks like a great deal! Both of us put enormous effort into it. I am glad to hear that you are ready to sign on this. Unfortunately, I will need to run this by my boss before I can do the same. Of course, she may have some final suggestion for changes before we can sign. I am sure you will not mind!*

How do you respond to such a statement within a value negotiation approach?

## Difficult

In your next role-play, negotiate for one to two minutes, while taking notes on the other party's body language. Remember to write down what they did and what you thought of it. Then comment on their body language. Share what you saw and ask their intentions behind it. Ask how they were feeling and compare this with your perception.

# Step 2 - The Value Pursuit

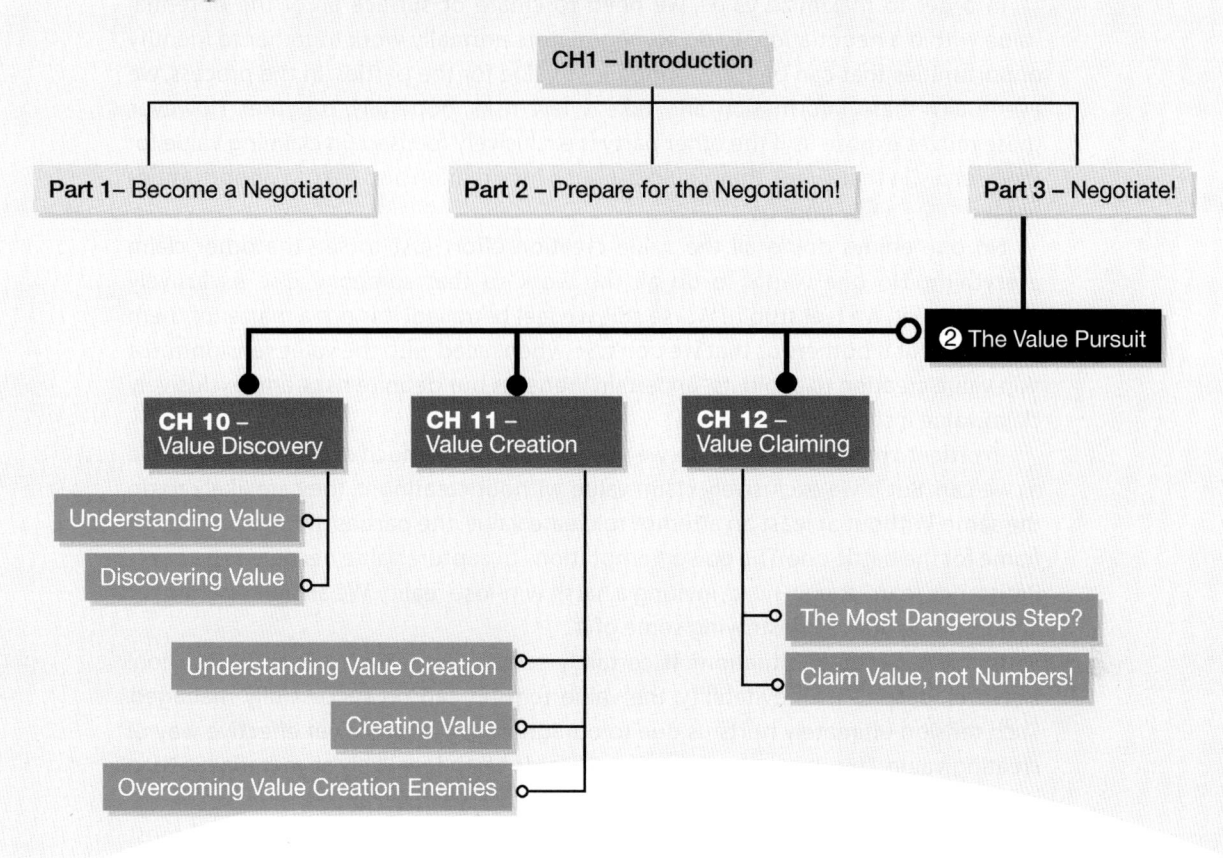

- CH1 – Introduction
  - Part 1– Become a Negotiator!
  - Part 2 – Prepare for the Negotiation!
  - Part 3 – Negotiate!
    - ❷ The Value Pursuit
      - **CH 10 – Value Discovery**
        - Understanding Value
        - Discovering Value
      - **CH 11 – Value Creation**
        - Understanding Value Creation
        - Creating Value
        - Overcoming Value Creation Enemies
      - **CH 12 – Value Claiming**
        - The Most Dangerous Step?
        - Claim Value, not Numbers!

Once the bridge is built, our relationship and communication efforts continue. No concentrated effort is needed anymore, but we need to constantly align our value-pursuit moves with the bridge. To do otherwise is to communicate that we changed our minds and to risk all of our work done so far.

The established JVP frame and dialogue pattern prepare and support our value pursuit. However, it is here where even value negotiators are tempted to take the bridge for granted. As the negotiation starts to address the value at stake, many succumb to their win-lose instincts. Temptations to trade relationship for substance, take advantage of information asymmetry or create power distances return with full force. The bridge is built precisely to minimize these temptations and enable a safer and better value pursuit.

The reason for such temptations resurging is the value tension, one of the most infamous negotiation obstacles. A clash between the value-creation and value-claiming phases of a negotiation, the value tension creates a negotiation paradox:

- If we go all out on our value-creation efforts, we risk our ability to claim value.
- If, however, we go all out on our value-claiming efforts, we have little if any chance to create value.

As a result, bargainers either go all out in one phase (sacrificing the other) or do a half job in both. Either way, no one is truly satisfied. So how does this tension really work?

In order to maximize value, we need to create or surface all of the potential value within a negotiation. To do so, negotiators normally work together to identify opportunities that can be transformed into value for the parties. In the process, we eventually share information and take a few risks, hopefully, together. However, these moves expose us if the other party is exclusively focused on claiming value for themselves. In that event, they could use such information and risks as opportunities to take value away from us.

No one enjoys doing all the value creation effort just to see the other claim everything. No one wants to do all the work so that someone else exclusively profits from it. We feel stupid! Worse still, we feel betrayed! It is not a matter of them profiting, but it bothers us that we don't. So when faced with the value tension, most skip value creation to avoid its "uncertain" benefits but definite risks, and exclusively claim value instead.

In order to maximize our value, we want to capture as much of the available value as we can. But if we exclusively claim value without creating it, they are likely to do the same. Without at least an attempt to create value, the parties give up on the JVP frame for the battle one. The power temptations to capture value become too strong. Resistance rears its ugly head, inviting a harsh win-lose reality. We are left fighting for limited value or even destroying some of it.

Is this a Catch-22 situation? It certainly seems like it with the value tension! However, despite its inevitability, the value tension can be successfully managed. Such tension ultimately hurts us due to our ignorance of a safe yet effective way of creating value. This unawareness makes rewards seem less likely to materialize than risks. Out of fear, we then fall back into the tension described above.

It is no surprise that the value tension is so prevalent. As already discussed, most negotiators are bargainers. Bargaining theories, consistent with the battle frame, devise several ways to claim value, but none to create value. It is natural then that most negotiators know little, if anything at all, about value creation.

On the other hand, a value negotiator is able to create value to optimize rewards, while managing risks. Having created value, we can claim it confident of negotiating our fair share while keeping power temptations at a distance.

As seen above, the value pursuit is a complex and risky phase of negotiation. To better manage, we can separate it into three parts:

1. Value discovery (interests)
2. Value creation (options) and
3. Value claiming (legitimacy)

We break the value-creation phase into two different steps to facilitate our understanding and ability to manage it. Value discovery is intended as an extra step to enhance our chances of managing the value tension. Normally, a good discovery leads to a better creation, which in turn facilitates the claiming exercise. Though not necessarily a linear progression, it does help to follow this order.

Value creation really begins with and includes value discovery then extends itself to the options-generation phase. Thus what we colloquially refer to as value creation would probably be more precisely referred to as value generation. However, for simplicity sake, we chose to use the more colloquial terminology "value creation" when referring to the phase in which options are "created."

Next, we elaborate on the three parts of the value-pursuit phase.

# 10 Value Discovery

## Learning Objectives:
- What value, value discovery and the value of value discovery are
- How to manage value tension
- What the issues are, and why they are important
- How to discover interests
- How to prepare for value creation
- How to manage information to learn their interests, share ours safely and move beyond positions

In this chapter, we focus on two simple tasks: understand what value is and how to discover it. On understanding value, we explain value and its discovery, the benefits of value pursuit and how it manages the value tension. On how to discover value, we take into account that value discovery often starts before the negotiators meet. It starts in the preparation stage and continues during the negotiation. Managing information and positions are also important to successful value discovery.

## Understanding Value

### On Value and its Discovery

As already explained, value discovery is the negotiation step where negotiators focus on finding and understanding each other's interests. Before we can create any value, we need to understand what value means for the parties involved. Even the best idea has no value if it does not satisfy at least one negotiator's interest.

A new mother enters a baby products store and asks a salesperson:

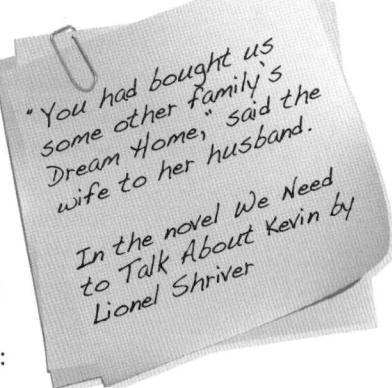

> "You had bought us some other family's Dream Home," said the wife to her husband.
>
> In the novel We Need to Talk About Kevin by Lionel Shriver

> Hi! I am looking for a baby car seat for my three-month old boy. Do you have any?

> Sure, right over here. Let me show you our bestseller.

> Okay! Good.

> Look! This is our most popular baby car seat. It is the cheapest we have. We sell a lot of it every day.

> Thanks, but I am not looking for the cheapest. I want something really good.

> I know! This is very good! It is very cheap.

> Sorry, I am not sure you understand me. This is my first child. I do not want to take any chances. I want the best chair you have.

> This is our best chair. It is the cheapest.

> No! I do not want the cheapest. Money is not a problem. I want the safest you have.

> Oh! Why did you not tell me before? Over here then...

The salesperson was sincerely trying to give the customer what he perceived to be best. The cheapest was the best, not only for him, but also for hundreds of other parents. While most wanted cheap baby seats because they were constrained by other baby-related expenses, this particular mother was not. She wanted safe, not cheap. Cheap had absolutely no value for her; in fact, it probably meant unsafe, the opposite of what she wanted.

Why is value discovery important? The mother almost left in disbelief that she could not find a solution for her interests in that store. Even if the salesperson wanted to help her, a lack of discovery handicapped the value-creation process. Inefficiency and frustration that result from a lack of discovery are responsible for many negotiation failures.

Many other interests may have motivated this unproductive value-discovery process. The salesperson may have behaved the way he did because:

- It was late and he just wanted to close the sale quickly to return home.
- The particular brand he showed would earn him an additional sales commission.
- Not being paid a commission, he did not care much.
- By offering what most people wanted, he would close the sale faster and move on to another client.
- He owned and liked that particular baby seat, thus wanted to sell what he believed was best.
- He assumed she had not much money and was trying to save both their time.

The story above is just one example on some obstacles and the need for the value-discovery process. These obstacles push us into an uncertain and frustrating trial-and-error value pursuit characteristic of positional bargaining. A few common examples are:

1. Our assumptions of their interests make us feel knowledgeable and reduce our ability or willingness to truly learn them.
2. Our eagerness to satisfy our interests prevents us from paying too much attention to theirs.
3. Our limited estimation or preparation has us identify only one or two interests and more likely to behave in a positional manner.

But what is value after all? In sum, **value in negotiations is the negotiators' wants, needs, desires, fears or concerns (interests).** When we say "**I want/need…**," we are also saying "I value…." Value is created when we satisfy interests. In order to create it, we first need to learn and understand what interests negotiators have. Only then can we properly direct our efforts to satisfy them. **Value discovery is the exploration and investigation process to surface as many of the parties' interests as possible.** It starts during the preparation stage and continues into the negotiation process.

## Value Discovery vs. Value Tension

We would like to return to the statement that value in a negotiation is not so much created as it is discovered. The potential value is there to be discovered once the negotiators bring their interests to the table. The value-discovery process does halve the value-creation work. The discovery of multiple interests forces us to look into different directions, which potentially lead to multiple options.

Value discovery stimulates our creativity and focus to efficiently search for and come up with the best possible options. After a successful value discovery, value creation is less challenging than we expect. So value discovery helps value creation, but how does it help us better manage the value tension? Let's look at Sonja and Olivier's story first.

Sonja and Olivier had been partners in a start-up for six months. Sonja was a marketing professional and Olivier had years of IT expertise. One day, Sonja realized they needed to discuss their partnership structure and so began the conversation:

> Dear Olivier, it has been a pleasure working with you so far. Since you came in we made a lot of progress. Thank you for that!

> The pleasure has been mine, Sonja. I actually think that we make a great team. I am very confident that our business is going to be a great success.

> Same here! And that is why I wanted to talk to you today about our partnership. Actually we should have done this long ago, don't you agree?

> You are right! So what do you have in mind?

> Well, since I have been working on this business idea for two-and-a-half years and you came in for the last six months, I thought that it would be fair for us to split our ownership similarly, meaning 5:1 or 83.3% and 16.7%.

> Excuse me?! You mean 83.3% for me, I am assuming. Otherwise, you've got to be kidding me!

> Why? I have been here five times longer than you have, without even taking into account that this business is my idea. I wanted to treat you like an equal on that aspect because I really do not know how to quantify it. But if we were to look at time invested alone, a 5:1 split is more than fair.

> But in your two years you produced very little tangible results. Actually, before I came in you had nothing really.

> What? How dare you say I did nothing? For the two years before I invited you in, I have been networking in the industry and refining the idea. I have been doing an enormous amount of research to define the business concept. I invested two years of opportunity cost into this venture and you are telling me that I did nothing?

> No! I did not say you did nothing. I just said that there was little produced. I am talking output, not input. I believe I was more efficient and productive. So I deserve more.

> More than me?!

> No. Just more than 17%.

> 16.7%! Don't be funny.

> Whatever! 16.7% then.

> What do you think would be fair?

> At least 30% for me.

> But this is almost twice as much!

> I know, but this is what I think is fair ...

Sonja tried to build a bridge with an initial relationship move (using "we" and praise) followed by a process move (purpose of the meeting). However, she then skipped value discovery and went straight into value claiming (the 5:1 split). The conversation became an exchange of accusations and depreciations of each other's contributions. These power moves attempted to claim a bigger ownership share, since it was the only value at stake.

Was Sonja fair in her proposal? We have no clue, since we do not know how it speaks to the interests of the parties. The time-invested argument sounds fair, but the output argument can be equally convincing. So we are left with a positional battle on what is fair. The differing past perceptions make it impossible to find out the truth. So can they still find a solution? Of course they can, but not if they continue to avoid interests. Let's give Sonja and Olivier another chance:

> You are right! So what do you have in mind?

> I would like to find out what actually motivated you to join a start-up in the first place?

> What do you mean?

> Why not go for the big salary of a big IT company instead of coming here?

> Oh, I see! Well, where do I start... I was tired of being just a technical IT guy. I did my MBA to become a manager. Now I do not mind doing IT work within a managerial context, but I do not want to be put in this box forever.

> I didn't know that. I never thought about it. So the MBA was an exit from IT.

> Yeah! So I wanted to join a start-up to make sure that I would get such a position.

> So an IT managerial position is what you were after?

> Not necessarily. I was actually more interested in general management.

> But an IT manager is a general manager as well, isn't it? He does not do IT, just manage people who do, right?

> True! I haven't thought of it that way. Another thing is that I also wanted to own a business. It has always been a dream of mine.

> You never mentioned that before.

> I know! I thought it was obvious. If you join a start-up early on, it is because you want to be the owner of your own business.

> What about being an owner attracted you?

> Well, it is many things. Being my own boss. Controlling my time. Being part of something exciting. Sure, making money is important, but I think that the most important thing for me is that I am recognized for my value. That my output is seen as an important part of making something big happen.

> This is all really important and I am very happy to learn all of this. I want to learn some more and I also would like to share some of my motivations if you want to hear them.

> Sure!

It seems that they are carrying out a good value discovery conversation. Sonja has avoided positional bargaining and learned valuable information from Olivier. She now knows that Olivier would like managerial responsibility, autonomy, flexible hours, shares in the company, and above all, recognition. This will surely help her to craft more and better options later in the process.

A lot of the value tension is due to the temptation to claim value too early. The parties take opposing sides and, like Sonja's first negotiation, doom any attempt to create value before it even begins. Another problem is that value creation is normally poorly or not done at all. In contrast, Sonja conducted a rich value discovery in the second negotiation and enhanced her ability to create value for Olivier and herself.

Value discovery manages the value tension in more ways than one. First, negotiators think about interests, not positions, to focus on what value really is. Second, it builds stronger interdependence and reduces unilateral temptations. Third, it multiplies the number of potential options. Finally, without offers, value claiming cannot happen and we remain flexible and open to maximize learning. All of these steps build a process conducive to and, more importantly, protective of value creation.

For all its benefits, value discovery only facilitates value creation. It does not guarantee it. We could argue that the fight over 83.3% versus 16.7% might return, but it is less likely now. Olivier's 30% position included his interest for control and recognition. Without value discovery, Sonja could not have known of that in the first negotiation. In the second negotiation, Sonja learned these interests and can present options for control and recognition, aside from ownership percentage. If money becomes an issue, she can offer a higher salary or a large options package.

Value discovery also helps in future value claiming. Sonja learned that Olivier is very much focused on the value of his output and thus finds the argument based on output more legitimate. If she finds legitimacy based on output, she can argue for her ownership proposal in ways that will feel fair to Olivier. Based on the kind of legitimacy that speaks to Olivier, she increases her proposal's persuasion and acceptance.

In sum, value discovery prepares us to engage in better value-creation and value-claiming processes. It initiates the value pursuit in ways that help manage the value tension towards maximum value. Next, we explore the different parts of value discovery so that we can prepare and execute it.

# Discovering Value

## Issues

For us to better understand interests, it helps to first understand issues. Issues are the topics under which the negotiators' interests manifest themselves and they want to negotiate over. An agreement on issues is an agreement on which interests we will negotiate. Issues tend to be framed as neutral, while interests are partial. An issue normally contains at least one, if not many, interests. Some examples of issues and interests from the dialogue above:

- "I wanted to talk to you today about our partnership."(Issue)
- "I do not want to be put in this box forever." (Interest)
- "I am more interested in general management."(Interest)
- "I also wanted to own a business." (Interest)
- "Being my own boss. Controlling my time. Being part of something exciting. Sure, making money is important, but I think that the most important thing for me is that I am recognized for my value."(Several interests)

In a negotiation, the conversation about issues is usually introduced with expressions such as: "talk about," "discuss," "hear your ideas on," "cover," "go over," "review," etc. Meanwhile, an interest is usually preceded by the following expressions: "I want/need/fear," "interested in," "very important for me," "what I am looking for," etc.

The number of issues in a negotiation helps in understanding its value-creation potential. Negotiations are often classified as single- or multi-issue. Normally, single-issue negotiations present fewer opportunities for value creation than multi-issue ones. It is simple mathematics: fewer issues mean on average fewer interests, and thus fewer options.

If I find myself in a single-issue negotiation, am I bound to negotiate win-lose? Bargainers accept that as a matter of fact. Indeed, it is harder to create value in single-issue negotiations, but not impossible. Thus, we reject that determinism and try to influence the negotiation towards value. Beneath a single issue, there may be several interests. One recommendation is to frame the single issue as broadly as possible to bring these other interests to the negotiation. After all, value does not come from issues, but from interests.

Issues frame the negotiation scope. If we say we want to discuss salary, we have just framed the scope too narrowly. The negotiation will more or less gravitate around money. Being close to zero-sum, little value creation is possible! However, we can frame it broader to talk about our compensation package. This will bring in different interests: apart from money, vacation days come into the picture. We may discuss a new health insurance plan or reducing travel as our family may be growing. More interests mean more possibilities of finding value for all involved.

Many negotiations are framed as single-issue due to lack of understanding or sophistication from the negotiators. Many ignore the dramatic impact that issue selection and framing have on their value creation or agreement potential. Many times we do not really know what we want. We end up framing our issues too narrowly, sometimes for the sake of being specific or efficient. However, such framing diminishes our negotiation's value potential and drives us into an inefficient positional battle.

Thus, a second recommendation is to add new issues to the negotiation. Who said that a negotiation has to be single-issue? Our client or boss may have passed it on to us as such, but we can change the negotiation boundaries if it makes sense to do so. Few things make more sense in a negotiation than to increase its value potential, so we can find and include topics relevant to our negotiation to create a richer basket of interests.

Returning to salary negotiation, we do not need to accept that our negotiation will stay on salary only. We can negotiate to also include benefits, role, career progression and other aspects that are also valuable to us. For example:

> Good to see you again. We are glad that you are considering our offer. So I am assuming that you would like to talk about salary today, right?

> We can do that! I would also welcome the opportunity to talk about the compensation package as a whole.

> What do you mean? The package is pretty standard.

> That is fine. I just want to make sure we cover it together. I have questions that you may be able to clarify for me. Clarifying the package will help me understand the context of whatever salary figure we discuss.

> Alright! We can do that. I may not have all the answers, but I will do my best.

> Great! Do you mind if I start asking the questions before we talk about salary?

> Not at all! Have you seen the description of our package in our letter to you?

As seen in a previous chapter, the narrow scope can be our common challenge and help build interdependence. Our goal becomes to broaden the scope by expanding the issue either in size (many interests) or number (more issues). Indeed, if we limit ourselves to a single issue and interest, there is little room to maneuver and be creative.

Our third recommendation is to engage in a learning process around the single issue to avoid a positional bargain. If we do not have any additional interests or issues to bring to the table, learning may help. We may find that the other party has other issues or interests that help us move beyond. Last but not least, they may have information, resources or ideas for win-win options to productively address the single issue or interest.

So how would this unfold? Let's look at the negotiation between a salesperson and a potential new customer who sees the product as a commodity:

> Hi, can we talk about the price of your product?

> Sure! We have to talk about it eventually. Can you help me understand what conditions you expect within a price?

> No conditions!

> Sorry, I mean what kind of volume, quality, delivery date, etc.

> Oh, I see. I would expect the standard package in the industry.

> Would you consider a different package if it meant giving you a better price?

> Why not! How much better?

> It all depends on how different the package may be.

> Okay! I may have flexibility on some issues, but not all. What do you have in mind?

In our value discovery effort, we benefit from negotiating the agenda issues at the start. Only then do we go into interests. Some negotiations are more informal, and the parties go straight into interests without an agenda. In both cases, a good value discovery seeks mutual understanding and agreement on the issues.

## Interests

When Fisher, Ury and Patton came up with interest-based negotiation, they put interests at the center of negotiation. Years later, such negotiation has evolved while respecting its roots. Value discovery, and therefore interests, is a cornerstone of our negotiation strategy. Value negotiation, however, recognizes that interests alone do not prevent a win-lose outcome in a power environment. And yet, value negotiation builds from interest-based negotiation to negotiate maximum value within a win-win environment.

Preparing and negotiating interests are some of the best steps negotiators can take to improve their deal. Focus on interests equals focus on value. Our need to find out interests has us proactively ask questions and promote learning within a dialogue pattern. Focus on interests also helps us identify when we may be close to trading between the three negotiations. An interest focus promotes value negotiation behaviors.

To fulfill our goal of satisfying interests and manage the critical moment of talking about value, we consider all parties' interests. To do so, we prepare our interests and conduct our negotiation to maximize value discovery.

## Interests Preparation

Knowing our interests is not easy. Knowing theirs is even harder. And yet we need to know the interest of all parties if we are to be successful. If finding them out is hard enough, keeping the focus on them may be harder. Shagay illustrates this challenge.

When complaining about having missed an administrative deadline with his institution, Mynex, Shagay received the following email:

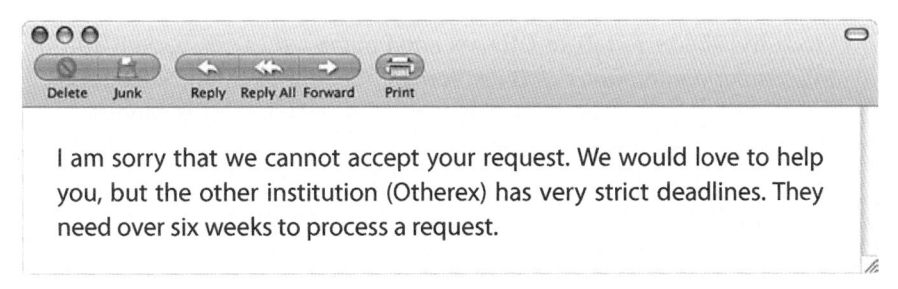

> I am sorry that we cannot accept your request. We would love to help you, but the other institution (Otherex) has very strict deadlines. They need over six weeks to process a request.

After escalating his case to the highest level, Shagay realized there was little Mynex could do. He decided to contact Otherex, which replied to him:

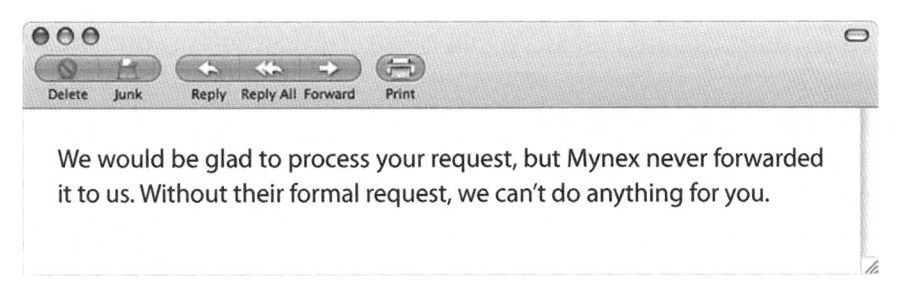

> We would be glad to process your request, but Mynex never forwarded it to us. Without their formal request, we can't do anything for you.

Shagay was fairly angry. He heard from Mynex that it was Otherex's fault, only to learn that Otherex could accommodate his request. He wrote an email to Mynex asking for an explanation with Otherex's message attached. The response came with Otherex on copy:

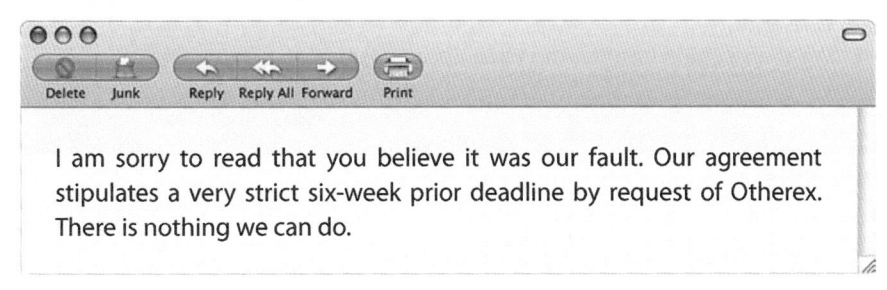

> I am sorry to read that you believe it was our fault. Our agreement stipulates a very strict six-week prior deadline by request of Otherex. There is nothing we can do.

Angry with the situation, Shagay lost track of his interests. Frustrated with Mynex, he lost sight of their interests. By attaching the email from Otherex, Shagay confronted Mynex's version, implicitly calling them a liar. On hindsight, Shagay realized he got Mynex frustrated. They were just following the rules agreed with Otherex, who was now making them look bad. The issue became bigger than Shagay. It became an opportunity to tell Otherex not to play "double standards" anymore.

Instead of the angry email with Otherex's message attached, Shagay could have written:

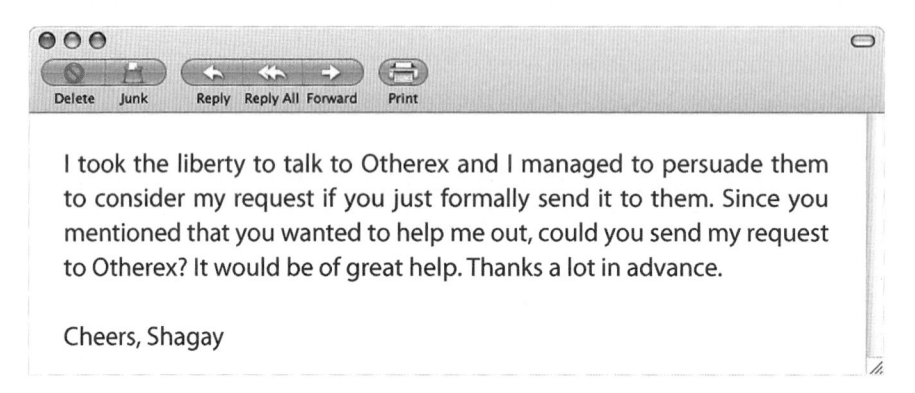

> I took the liberty to talk to Otherex and I managed to persuade them to consider my request if you just formally send it to them. Since you mentioned that you wanted to help me out, could you send my request to Otherex? It would be of great help. Thanks a lot in advance.
>
> Cheers, Shagay

This message taps into Mynex's intention to help, while avoiding a legal-like battle for right or wrong. Allowing Mynex to be seen as the good guy is important as no one wants to be regarded as the bad person. Keeping focused on everyone's interests increases the likelihood of getting our interests satisfied.

## Decide What You Want

Knowing what we want begins by finding out all the parties directly or indirectly involved. Every party is a source of different interests and resources, and can influence the negotiation. Thus, we want to know even the interests of relevant third parties, or else no deal may be struck. Once we know the relevant parties, we then start asking ourselves:

- What do I care about and really want? What do they care about?
- What else could I want? And what about them?

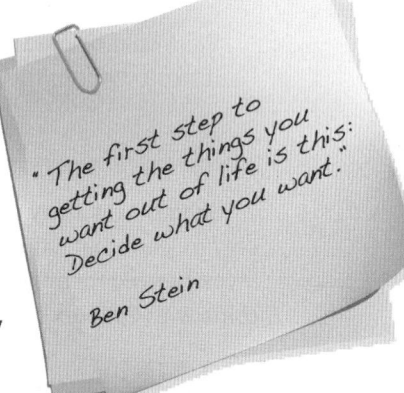

*"The first step to getting the things you want out of life is this: Decide what you want."*

Ben Stein

### POINT OF INTEREST

**Soft Bargainer vs. Value Negotiator**

In the preparation phase, one of the major differences between a soft bargainer and a value negotiator is the amount of interests each puts down. The soft bargainer prepares only a few interests, becoming positional, but ready to concede. Meanwhile, the value negotiator prepares several interests for a value-creation exercise.

Even if the soft bargainer tries to create value, the lack of interests (value creation's raw material) will limit their ability. So they end up in positional bargaining where the only way they can demonstrate flexibility is by giving concessions. The value negotiator can be flexible by finding different interests to satisfy and create or capture the necessary value.

In trying to find out what we want, it helps to think of as many interests as possible. The more the merrier. To discover only one interest is to have a position. To discover merely two to three interests is to have too little raw material for value creation. Imagine if we are given two to three Lego blocks, we will not be able to build much no matter how skillful we are. However, with lots of Lego blocks, we are able to build incredible structures limited only by our creativity and skill.

Discovering many interests may look like we are complicating things, but we are actually giving ourselves possibilities. Having many interests does not force us to pursue them all. Knowing more interests makes us aware of choosing which to negotiate. A good interest discovery brainstorms several interests to give us more flexibility. If they cannot satisfy our interests A or B, maybe they can satisfy C, D, E to bring us similar value.

The same point holds regarding their interests. The more we discover, the more value we can create for them. Knowing and surfacing their interests can make them more eager to get their interests satisfied. That eagerness, if reasonably managed, can lead to their increased willingness to contribute resources to the negotiation's success. This in turn means more resources and commitment to satisfy our interests. Interdependence increases as we see more of each other's interests that our negotiation can satisfy.

Knowing what they want is at best an intelligent guess and normally an assumption exercise. We put ourselves in their shoes, knowing that we will make mistakes as we cannot fully take their perspective. Still, the exercise remains valid and serves as a reminder that we do not really know their interests. These assumptions can make us curious for confirmation and give us focus and context for learning. When they talk, we pay attention to the underlying interests to check them with our preparation.

**What else?**
One of the hardest things about knowing interests is that they are many. Maybe too many! Every negotiation is a moment of flux with new risks and opportunities. Thus, a negotiation can impact the negotiators' lives in many complex ways, even if remotely or indirectly. Awareness over this impact can prepare us for different reactions or strategies.

Working so diligently to discover interests is not easy. More often than not, we develop tunnel vision when thinking about interests. We lean towards the most obvious or seemingly important interests and end up with only one to two in mind. Thus, some structure or discipline can push our imagination further and greatly expand our interest discovery.

There are many models to help think about interests. They normally work as memory joggers or checklists to help us question ourselves and look for interests in new directions. A model also gives us refined assumptions to be adjusted or confirmed during the negotiation. Whatever model we use, we need to keep our particular negotiation in mind to validate the interests we prepare.

As an illustration, we look at the simple and already famous Maslow's hierarchy of needs, illustrated by Figure 10.1. Created by Abraham Maslow, it proposes a general model for understanding basic and higher human needs. Several new levels were subsequently suggested, though most are elaborations on the original five. They are:

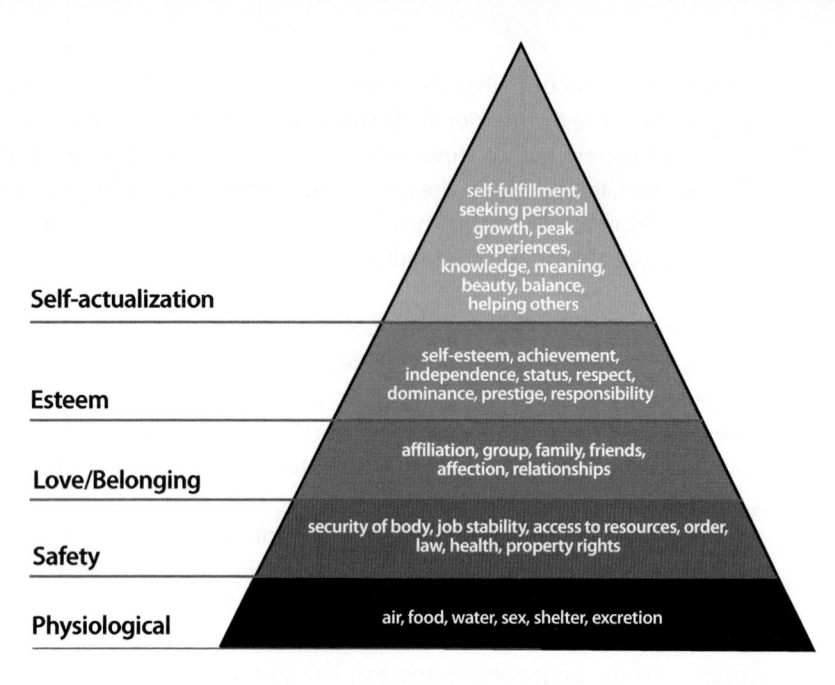

**Figure 10.1** Maslow's hierarchy of needs pyramid

- Self-actualization: self-fulfillment, seeking personal growth, peak experiences, knowledge, meaning, beauty, balance, helping others
- Esteem: self-esteem, achievement, independence, status, respect, dominance, prestige, responsibility
- Love/Belonging: affiliation, group, family, friends, affection, relationships
- Safety: security of body, job stability, access to resources, order, law, health, property rights
- Physiological: air, food, water, sex, shelter, excretion

1. **Physiological** – Oxygen, food, drink, shelter, sex/reproduction, sleep, heat, etc.
2. **Safety** – Protection from elements or others, security, stability, order, law, etc.
3. **Love/Belonging** – Affiliation, group, family, affection, relationships, etc.
4. **Esteem** – Self-esteem, achievement, independence, status, dominance, prestige, responsibility, etc.
5. **Self-Actualization** – Realizing personal potential, self-fulfillment, seeking personal growth and peak experiences. Some sub-categories:
   a. Cognitive – Knowledge, meaning, etc.
   b. Aesthetic – Beauty, design, balance, form, etc.
   c. Transcendence – Helping others grow and realize their potential.

Giving the five levels a hierarchical order has been criticized by many who believe needs have an ever-changing or no hierarchy. Others criticize its lack of cultural sensitivity. The hierarchy is less important than the knowledge of the different interests someone possibly has in a negotiation. Maslow's hierarchy, however, can help identify potential interest priorities or raise flags about potential misunderstandings as we learn their reactions. For example, if someone is afraid for their life (physiological), it is hard to care about their job (safety). If their job is threatened (safety), they may not bother with bonus targets (self-actualization).

As said before, many interests get lost in the negotiation tunnel vision, which favors short-term substance interests. We usually see negotiations as immediate transactions with a focus on what we will get at the end of this deal. To help expand on that list, we can purposefully ask ourselves:

- Is that a short-, medium- or long-term interest?
- Is that a substance, relationship or communication interest?

Thinking in the short, medium and long term reminds us to look at the consequences of our actions and decisions. More money today may mean less money tomorrow. The time dimension prevents us from making bad decisions, rewarding bad behavior or forgetting to reward good behavior. For example, if someone threatens us, one instinctive response is to give in to stop the threat. We just rewarded bad behavior! In doing so, we solve the short-term problem, but create a long-term one. We have indirectly taught them to threaten us in the future whenever they want to obtain something from us easily.

It is okay to trade one short-term interest for a long-term one if we are aware of the trade-offs of our choice. It is however very risky to trade a relationship interest for a substance one (trading between the three negotiations). Hence, it is helpful to discover interests on these three negotiations to avoid trading them by mistake. Table 10.1 illustrates them:

| Relationship Interests | Substance Interests | Communication Interests |
|---|---|---|
| Appreciation | Money | Efficient and effective messages |
| Affiliation | Payment terms | Topics to discuss (issues) |
| Authority | Discounts or increases | Order or sequence of issues (agenda) |
| Status | Delivery date | Time allocated to meeting or issues |
| Role | Duration of contract | Purpose of the meeting |
| Acceptance | Commission | Desired product |
| Respect | Quality | Decision-makers to bring/involve |
| Emotional involvement | Volume | Rules of engagement (frequency of breaks, etc.) |
| Empathy | Unit cost | Who starts talking? |
| Rationality | Profit margin | How to make the first offer |
| Sincerity | Level of satisfaction | When to offer |
| Inclusiveness or belonging | Benefits | Meeting location |
| Be heard and understood | Guarantees | What information is confidential? |
| Be consulted or communicated | Right of first refusal | Information management |
| Reputation | Fair outcome | Proactive and transparent process leadership |
| Reliability | Incentives and penalties | Dialogue pattern |
| Effort | Promotion | Choice of law, forum and dispute resolution mechanism |
| Concern | Career plan | Learn (diagnosis and data) |
| Honesty | Training opportunities | Make well-informed decisions |
| Love | Stability | Fair process |
| Trust | Upside potential | Conditions for termination of the contract |
| Interdependence | Pension | etc. |
| Truthfulness | Resources | |
| Fairness | Constraints | |
| etc. | etc. | |

**Table 10.1**
Example of relationship, substance and communication interests

As already discussed, substance interests relate to value; relationship interests to behaviors and emotions; and communication interests to when and how to negotiate. Some communication and relationship interests are linked: the way we communicate impacts our relationship and the way we behave also sends them a message.

For example, many relationships fail not because of poor intentions, but because relationship interests were not discovered or communicated. In the rare event when relationship expectations are shared, it is usually with vague terms: "I want respect" or "I want to feel like I am part of the team." Consequently, different ideas develop on what a good relationship is and lead negotiators into misunderstandings:

> But you told me you wanted me to take more initiative in this relationship!

> True, but not that much initiative, and not in these particular cases either. Right now, I want you to just follow what I asked you to do.

> Well, so you do not really want me to take any initiative, do you?

> No! I do want your initiative, but not towards this particular case.

> I don't get it.

**What for?**
Many times interests are thought of superficially or vaguely. And if so, how can we satisfy them? We do not need interests to be too specific, otherwise we fall into the opposite trap of becoming positional. However, we need to have a good understanding of what interests really are. For that, we need to be clearer about them and thus we can ask:

- How do we measure or recognize such interests?
- Is this one interest or a bundle of interests?
- Can this interest mean something else to them?
- Why do I want/fear this? What purpose will it fulfill?

How do we measure the satisfaction of an interest so that we can create appropriate options to satisfy it? Many daily negotiations are about money. Still, money comes in different forms (we are not referring to different currencies). Money can be given as rebate or incentive, payment or penalty, expense or investment, cost or marginal profit, net or gross, and structured as debt or equity. Money can mean that they value our work or that they exploit us like a commodity. And these are just a few examples.

In an investment, we expect future money in return, while with an expense we may expect a tax rebate. An investment structured as debt gives us a smaller risk, on average, than an equity structure. A payment is much more pleasant to fulfill than a penalty with its negative connotations. So when talking money, we could be talking about various aspects: money today or tomorrow, more or less risk, emotionally charged or not.

All of this means that money is a bundle of or repository for many other interests. Money can be productively negotiated if that multiplicity is taken into account. The worst way to negotiate on money is to flatly consider it just a fixed number in a linear progression. This approach empties money of all its meaning and additional interests. It limits the negotiation scope while transforming money into a positional zero-sum issue.

One common example of poor value discovery: angel investors investing money in start-up companies in exchange for shares (direct equity investment). However, it is impossible to accurately assess a company without proven value or revenues. Most valuation models do not apply for lack of data. Thus, calculating the risk, the expected return and the fair share price is futile. Often, a start-up's value is as close to fiction as one can get. And yet both investors and entrepreneurs have to agree on a certain share value.

Being so uncertain, when investors and entrepreneurs agree on the company value, one party is making a bad deal: either the investors overvalued the company and overpaid; or the entrepreneurs undervalued it and sold cheap. Both sides just do not have enough data or knowledge. For lack of information, negotiations over the share price are normally hard positional bargains or soft, friendly money handovers.

The equity model endangers many angel investors' interests, which usually are largest possible returns at minimum risks. Smooth relationship, efficient process and fair outcome are other interests commonly in jeopardy. Buying a company we do not know the worth of is surely risky. When trying to define the share price early in the life of the start-up, an angel investor risks all of the above.

Based on these interests, entrepreneurs and angel investors came up with a convertible loan note option. It supposedly minimizes the investment risk while increasing returns in the short and long term. It postpones pricing shares to when enough company history and data enable an objective calculation of the company's value. It reduces positional bargaining and helps the parties close a fair deal. However, the note requires paying today but only knowing the share price one to two years later.

Despite the clear advantages, many angel investors fear the convertible loan note over the direct equity investment. When asked why, most are unsure. They do not know what their interests really are. When further questioned, we find that many do not understand the note and prefer to stick with what they know. Some fear it to be too complicated and partial to the entrepreneur, especially if proposed by the latter.

If we understand these fears or interests of the angel investor, we can explain how our option (convertible loan note) better serves them. We can simplify it. We can show the pros and cons to both sides so they see the advantages, but more importantly, the balance. In sum, we need to consider all parties and surface all potential interests, including the underlying ones behind vague statements.

## Preparing Interests for Value Creation

Once all interests are on the table, we have the necessary value-creation ingredients: the bridge is built and the value discovered. Organizing the ingredients beforehand facilitates the cooking if it turns out to be more complicated than expected. The organization of interests for value-creation purposes is fairly simple: prioritize and categorize.

Prioritizing, or ranking interests, involves going beyond the definition of the interest to its relationship with other interests. Prioritizing starts by unbundling or unlinking interests, as we saw with the money example above. Then it becomes a simple, though not easy, matter of putting them in relative order. We can allocate points (100) among interests to keep track when they are too many and measure relative weights.

### POINT OF INTEREST

**Prioritizing & Choice**

Remember, the value negotiation approach intends to give us choices and the ability to pursue maximum value. There may be times where we may choose not to bother or invest the time or resources necessary to get it. It is our perfectly legitimate choice to value time or effort over another desirable outcome. However, we cannot then blame our shortcoming as a negotiation limitation, but rather take personal responsibility for such a choice.

For example, job stability, money and vacation are three priorities. A closer look gives their relative importance: job stability (70), money (25) and vacation (5). A risk-taker may have a similar priority but a completely different split: job stability (40), money (35) and vacation (25).

Prioritizing assists value creation in many ways. First, it keeps us focused on what brings more value and away from distracting interests. Second, it helps early identification of resource constraints, artificial limits or narrow scopes, if any. Third, it helps early identification of worst-case scenarios and potential conflict points. If both parties want more money today, it is likely they will enter into conflict; it would be easier if at least one wanted more money tomorrow instead of today.

Categorization bundles similar objects or ideas for ease of handling and thus should serve a purpose. Earlier, we categorized interests by nature (substance, relationship or communication) or time horizon (short, medium or long term). The purposes are to help us find more interests, resist trading between negotiations and avoid rewarding bad behavior.

However, Roger Fisher once said: "I can classify snakes with more or less than one meter or being or not poisonous. When I am in a jungle, I want to identify the poisonous one to know when to run." The most valuable purpose of interest discovery is value creation. The simplest interest categorization for value creation is by affinity:

- **Common** – Also called "shared," "mutual" or "joint" interests; happens when the negotiators want to do something together or good for all.
- **Different** – Happens when one negotiator wants something that the other does not want or care about.
- **Opposing** – Also called "conflicting"; happens when the negotiators want the same thing or incompatible things.

This categorization helps to create value because it already separates interests based on their ability to generate options. Though most people believe that common interests are the best for value creation, Lax and Sebenius argue differently: common interests bring the parties together, but different interests are a potentially richer value source. After all, if we want something that they do not care about, it is easier for them to give it to us.

## During the Negotiation

Once prepared, we want to make sure that interests are at the heart of our negotiation. We want to satisfy all of our interests, which usually involve finding ways to satisfy theirs as well. This exercise though is often hampered by the fear of saying too much and the assumption of knowing too much. These two impact negotiations as we share less information or make positional statements.

### Information Disclosure Tension

The information disclosure tension represents the clash between the rewards of sharing interests versus the risks of doing it poorly. Do it poorly and we risk saying too much. Say too much and they may take advantage of us or at least believe they can. However, not sharing interests places our value-creation efforts in peril. What do we do then?

Actually the question is not so much about what we do, but rather how we do it. Is sharing interests really worth it though? The rewards of this are many, especially if done early in the substance negotiation. For example:

- **Communication** – Improves efficiency by giving the right focus to the negotiation (i.e., what is value for me?) and avoids wasting time with other issues.
- **Relationship** – Improves trust as it communicates openness and having nothing to hide. Openness works as a proactive invitation to collaborate.
- **Substance** – Improves value creation since knowledge of more interests allows better option generation.

The risk is quite well known: we say too much and give away information that gives them power over us. We come across as weak and invite a power dynamic. Unfortunately, this risk frightens many negotiators away from a candid interest exchange and they cannot enjoy the rewards above.

It would be great if we could enjoy these rewards, without fearing the risks. The good news is that we can. We just need to manage the risk by carefully conducting this part of the negotiation. Some suggested steps are:

- **Don't share; exchange!** – Instead of monologues on unilateral interests, we can share one interest and then invite them to share one as well (dialogue pattern).
- **Be proactive** – If no one starts the interests-exchange process, we risk falling into a positional approach. As process leaders, we are responsible and better prepared to start it.

- **Start safe** – Start small and slow and as they reciprocate, move faster. The safer interests are usually common or obvious, positively and generally phrased.
- **Focus on value, not power** – Probably the most important step. Avoid even implicit statements on alternatives; they invite power and move us away from value.

The above is highly recommended when there is a sincere fear of a power distance and unclear interdependence. In these situations, the interests-exchange process is riskier and requires a more conservative approach. On the other hand, if the negotiation has a solid bridge, the exchange of interests can be relaxed. Below we cover the more common questions that arise from the suggested interests-exchange steps.

Sometimes a one-by-one exchange is too rigid, so can we do two-by-two or more? We have flexibility here, and just need to be careful with the increased risks. The more we share without their reciprocation, the more they may believe they have power over us. The dialogue pattern and interdependence is reduced. We risk sharing too much without having something in return, inviting power temptations into the negotiation.

What if they do not reciprocate? In this case, since we only shared one or two interests, we can stop and minimize our exposure. The whole point of one-by-one is to promote a dialogue pattern and interdependence to minimize the interests-exchange risk. They may not understand what we are doing and an explanation of our process may open them up (process transparency). Alternatively, they may be reluctant to share their interests for fear of saying too much. If this happens, we should show the benefits of our interests-exchange process and our positive intentions (intention transparency).

Can we start the interests-exchange process with a question? Certainly. Questions are a powerful negotiation tool and they will work just fine in a good negotiation environment. However, interest-seeking questions like "So what do you want?" can still invite the positional answer "A 20% discount!" Hence, in positional situations, we should lead by example and share an interest to show exactly what we want to do. We may go as far as to explain the difference between a position and an interest. This way, we minimize the risk of entering positional bargaining due to a misunderstanding.

## POINT OF INTEREST

**Information Disclosure Tension vs. Intention & Process Transparency**

We need to be careful with our substance interests to avoid power temptations over value. However, for relationship or communication interests, transparency is the safest move.

With substance interests, we want to carefully exchange them to keep the power balance and the value focus. But with relationship and communication interests, sharing our intentions and process interests (transparent advocacy) are powerful ways to build trust and lead proactively.

Why spend time on exchanging obvious interests? Because of assumptions. What is obvious for us may not necessarily be obvious for them. Exchanging the obvious confirms or dismisses assumptions, facts and expectations in a common knowledge base (Table 10.2). When the obvious matches their expectation, we show that we speak the truth and can be trusted. The obvious is also a safe, baby step that gives them an easy opportunity to reciprocate.

| NEGOTIATION DIALOGUE | DIAGNOSTICS |
|---|---|
| I want to share something obvious that is important to voice out: I want to explore if I have something if value for you. What do you think? | Sharing an obvious interest after announcing it to give it a purpose. |
| *Sure! You are a salesperson, what else could you want? (Ironically) So please go ahead.* | *Sharing that she is ready to listen further, indicating potential interest in buying.* |
| Good, I do not want you to see me as a pretender. I want to add that I pride myself in only selling if we find real value for you within my portfolio of offerings. Does that make sense to you? | Sharing another interest which is less obvious, still positive, general and hopefully common. |
| *It does. You may have something for me. You may not. Let's see.* | *Sharing that she has some needs and is hopeful to find a valuable option within the portfolio.* |
| Good to hear. I normally start by asking a few questions to find out more about your business and your interests. Does that work for you as a process? | Introducing a process option to learn more about her interests. |
| *Sure. Ask whatever you want.* | |

**Table 10.2**
Exchanging the obvious

Should we talk about our most important interests first? Or avoid them? Neither one. Professor Dierickx explains in his classroom that the amount of information, not importance, is relevant for sequencing issues or interests. Normally, obvious interests have the most information available. So if the most important interest is an obvious one, we can start with it. Obvious interests are the least likely to give something away. Common interests are good for all parties, therefore working together rather than fighting is the likelier route.

Why positively and generally phrased, and what does this look like? An example: "I would like to do business with you!" It starts with possibilities (positive) instead of risks or problems, without giving too much away (general). If they respond: "This is good to hear" or "Okay, how can I help you?" they are at least interested in learning more. To start with negative interests can raise resistance that potentially kills the negotiation. To start too specific may give away too much too soon or come across as being positional.

How do alternatives appear in our interest exchange? Even if indirectly, we may reveal alternatives when talking about interests: "I want to talk to you" versus "I need to talk to you." While it is safe for us to use the first interest statement, the second conveys more than just our interest. It communicates that if we do not talk, something bad may happen to us. It is thus important to weed out any information about alternatives when exchanging interests. Instead of "If there is no deal tomorrow, I lose lots of money," I can say "Time is an interest of mine."

But what if we have good alternatives? Can we mention them? Yes, we can, but it is probably not advisable to do so early on. It is easier to see how sharing a bad alternative works against us. However, any talk about alternatives brings power into the conversation. Even if subtly and softly, alternative statements given early on damage the still fragile relationship or invite a power response. For example:

> Before we continue, in the spirit of full disclosure, I thought it is fair for you to know that I am talking to your largest competitor too.

> No worries, because we are also talking to all of your biggest competitors. Since there is a shortage of our commodity in the market, we will only sell to whoever pays the most. Still, thanks for sharing this with me.

No matter how we dress up our alternative, it is usually perceived as a power move. As such, it likely generates similar or defensive reactions. So should we never mention our alternatives? Should we not have any? No, even in a value negotiation, alternatives are important to have as insurance policies. The choices of having, disclosing or using our alternatives are very different ones. Our concern is that their potential negative power impact is particularly damaging early in the negotiation. Alternatives shared early damage our interest exchange, focus the negotiation on power, not value, and promote a win-lose dynamic.

In sum, exchanging interests early in the substance negotiation is often a positive move if done correctly. Meanwhile, sharing good or bad alternatives early on is more often than not a risky move.

### Every Position is Made of Interests

Interests, unlike options, do not provide solutions. An interest too closely linked to a particular solution is a commitment to a single option, and therefore a position. When only one option is presented to satisfy an interest, it also becomes a position. When the option to satisfy an interest cannot be legitimately explained, once again we have a position.

In value negotiations, our incentive is to focus on and clarify interests (value), not positions (power). Positions limit both relationship and substance value,

> "Money was never a big motivation for me, except as a way to keep score. The real excitement is playing the game."
>
> Donald Trump

while interests enable options more valuable than either position alone. Despite the strong evidence supporting a focus on interests, most negotiations still end up being positional. Thus, to surface the negotiation value, we need to know how to move away from positions towards interests.

Luckily, every position is made of interests, if not many then at least one. When we ask for money, we want buying power, recognition of work done, assurance against risks, etc. Thus, moving from positions to interests is mainly an exercise of surfacing the interests underlying a position. We anticipate part of this exercise when we prepare on interests. Interest preparation helps us to avoid being positional ourselves and to model the desired behavior (interest focus). Preparing their interests allows us to better recognize and surface them from their potential positions during the negotiation.

However, during our interest exchange, they may be set on positions and stuck in a win-lose mentality. Saying: "I read in this excellent negotiation book to clarify interests, not positions. You are being positional, so I believe…" is probably not going to work. So what can we do?

First, mirroring our approach to minimize the information disclosure tension, we proactively lead the interest exchange to preempt positional bargaining. Proactively sharing some of our interests can model the desired behavior from them. If we are not ready to share our interests, how can we expect them to be? However, if they start with a position, there are many ways to move them into interests. A few examples are:

1. Ask to probe for the underlying interests ("**Why? Why not? What for?**"). Sometimes, they just share their position because that is what they are used to. If we ask further, they may come forward with additional information, usually leading to interests.

> I want a 20% discount!

> Why?

> Because I do.

> I understand, but why 20% and not 19% or 21%?

> It is none of your business.

> Why is it so important for you to have a 20% discount? What if I can't give it?

> I need 20% because that was our budget reduction but our targets did not change.

> So you need to respect your smaller budget but deliver like last year, is that right?

> Yes!

2. **Explain** why we are asking if they refuse to enter the interest exchange. This explanation transparently elaborates on our process and intentions. We explain why they should not fear disclosing interests and the process we are trying to follow.

> I want a 20% discount!

> Why?

> It is none of your business. I just want my 20% discount.

> I cannot give you a 20% discount. But if you give me some more information, I will be glad to work with you to find a way to help you save 20%. Is that okay?

> Sure. I do not care how I save 20%.

3. **Reframe** positions as clues to their interests. Instead of repeating positions, surface the interests we believe are behind their position. Then either test our understanding or expand our discussion to find more interests.

> I want a 20% discount!

> I am hearing you say that you want more money now. Is that correct?

> Yes! Not tomorrow, now!

> Okay, what if there are other ways to help you get more money today that dos not involve a discount. Would that work for you as well?

> Why not! What do you have in mind?

4. **Confirm** our understanding of their interests by asking for feedback and allowing them to critique it. This allows them to feel in control especially in adversarial dynamics.

> I want a 20% discount!

>> If I am not mistaken, you would like to get this same quality product for a cheaper price, is that correct?

> I just do not want to pay more than 80% of this price.

>> Good to know. I offered you this product because you asked for it directly. I have another very similar product. It is exactly the price you want and its differences are hopefully not relevant to you. Would you like to hear about it?

> Okay, but please be fast!

5. **Test** possible options. Different from confirming understanding, this technique puts a concrete idea on the table, and then similarly asks for a critique.

> I want a 20% discount!

>> Would it be okay then if we increased your order by 40%? This could allow me to give you a 20% discount.

> I cannot order 40% more. It's too much! I can at best ask for 25% more products.

>> With 25% more volume, I can give 10% as my unit cost will go down accordingly.

> But 10% is not enough!

>> I understand, but we are making progress, aren't we?

> Indeed!

The techniques above will get you at least some interests on the table in the vast majority of cases. If these techniques do not seem to help, the obstacle may be in the relationship or communication negotiations. There may be a lack of trust or interdependence, or a process misunderstanding. They may still not understand what we are trying to do or why it is better for them.

Value discovery is an important value negotiation step to keep our negotiation focused on interests and thus on value. How well we discover value will greatly impact the final success of our negotiation. At the end of the day, it is for this reason that we bother to negotiate at all. Thus, we could advocate that value discovery is the most important negotiation step of all.

# summary

Value in negotiation is the negotiators' wants, needs, desires, fears or concerns (interests). Value discovery is the exploration and investigation process to surface as many of the parties' interests as possible. Value discovery is the negotiation step where negotiators focus on finding and understanding each other's interests. Value discovery helps manage the value tension and prepares us to engage in better value-creation and value-claiming processes.

Value discovery obstacles arise from:
- Our assumptions of their interests.
- Our eagerness to satisfy our interests.
- Our limited estimation or preparation.

## Issues

1. Issues tend to be framed as neutral, while interests are partial.
2. Negotiations can be single- or multi-issue.
3. Single-issue negotiations have less room to maneuver and be creative.
4. To apply a value negotiation approach to a single-issue negotiation, we can broaden the scope by expanding the issue in:
    - Size (many underlying interests) or
    - Number (more issues)

## Interests

1. Interests preparation
    a. Decide what you want
        i. Find out all the parties directly or indirectly involved.
        ii. Think of as many interests as possible.
            1. Use an interest model (e.g. Maslow: Physiological, Safety, Love Belonging, Esteem, Self-Actualization)
            2. Think short-, medium- and long-term
            3. Think substance, relationship or communication
        iii. Interests are often thought of superficially or vaguely (e.g. money).

    b. Prepare for value creation
        i. Prioritize
        ii. Categorize (Common, Different and Opposing).

2. During the negotiation
    a. Information disclosure tension
        i. Don't share; exchange! (dialogue pattern).
        ii. Be proactive.
        iii. Start safe.
        iv. Focus on value (interests), not power (alternatives).

    b. Every position is made of interests
        i. Ask to probe for the underlying interests.
        ii. Explain why we are asking.
        iii. Reframe positions as clues to their interests.
        iv. Confirm our understanding of their interests.
        v. Test possible options.

# questions

## Easy
1. What is value?
2. What is value discovery?
3. Why is value discovery important to a negotiation?
4. How do issues impact a negotiation?
5. What is a position? How do we identify it?
6. What is the information disclosure tension?

## Medium
1. What is the value tension? How does value discovery help manage it?
2. What are the differences between value, interests and issues?
3. What are the major value-discovery tasks? Which ones are used in preparing interests for value creation?
4. What are the risks and rewards of talking about interests during the negotiation? How do we manage such risks?
5. What are six ways to focus the negotiation on interests, not positions?

## Difficult
1. What can we do if we find ourselves in a single-issue negotiation?
2. If someone says: "I want you to trust me!", what are the different interests you believe they may have?
3. Is transparency an unconditionally constructive behavior on substance, relationship and communication aspects of the negotiation?
4. How are interests exchanged in your culture? What is the impact of initiating an interests exchange? How can it be improved?
5. What should we do if the other party shares their alternatives early on?

# scenarios

## Easy

Professor Cialdini in his classic negotiation book *Influence,* shared an experiment run in a used car sales shop. Half the salespeople would only be able to ask questions for the first 15 minutes of their conversations with potential clients. They were told that this experiment would run for three months. As expected, the half that was imposed with the restriction complained loudly, but to no avail. Interestingly though, by the end of the first month, they had outperformed the other half by a significant percentage. Before the end of the three-month period, all salespeople were engaging in the questioning exercise even without being forced to do so.

1. Why?
2. What six to eight questions would you ask in a similar situation?

## Medium

Come up with three follow-up statements or questions for each of the positional statements below. Explain why you believe your suggestions will help move the conversation from positions to interests.

1. "I want this done now!"
2. "Sorry! This is the only way we can do it."
3. "Take it or leave it!"

## Difficult

*With substance interests, we want to carefully exchange them to keep the power balance and the value focus. But with relationship and communication interests, sharing our intentions and process interests (transparent advocacy) are powerful ways to build trust and lead proactively.*

1. Do you agree or disagree with the statement above?
2. Why? Support with examples.

# 11 Value Creation

## Learning Objectives:
- What value creation and value claiming are
- Does value creation really create value?
- How to focus on and create value
- How I can create better options
- What the enemies of value creation are
- How I can overcome these enemies

After building the bridge and discovering value, negotiators are in the coveted position to create value. Every time a negotiation creates value, it challenges the positional bargaining determinism and zero-sum mentality. Value creation is the biggest asset against a win-lose defeatist view of negotiations and towards positive change.

However, value creation is not easy. It takes lots of good decisions, effort and discipline to get us to where we can create value. Interdependence, trust, dialogue pattern, three-way communication, value discovery and more were all done to bring us exactly to this point. Unfortunately, many negotiators who arrive at a value-creation moment underestimate or waste its potential. This chapter gives ideas to optimize value creation and to avoid obstacles and traps that reduce the negotiation's value.

## Understanding Value Creation

### What is Value Creation?

Consistent with Lavoisier's statement, value creation transforms available resources into options that better satisfy the parties' interests. Value is not created out of thin air, but rather from the resources negotiators bring to the table. Resources are added, allocated, assembled, tailored and transformed to increase their value to the parties.

*"In nature, nothing is created, nothing is destroyed, everything is transformed."*

*Lavoisier*

Good value discovery invites to the table the raw material necessary to create value. Negotiators only bring resources if they need to satisfy the other's interests to see their own satisfied (interdependence). Otherwise, why bring anything at all, if we can just take what is theirs without any negative consequences to us? Making our resources available to satisfy their interests encourages and entitles us to ask for reciprocation.

Creativity, though necessary to create options towards the best solution, is not as critical as we would expect. After a successful value discovery, value creation can be a simple matter of combining resources. Value is created through new (and potentially unlikely) combinations of the negotiation's unique context, parties, interests and resources.

Any option with the potential to satisfy an interest can create value. Yet not every agreement (committed option) creates value. Win-lose options, for example, only take value from one party to give to another. Value creation happens when an option increases the value available in the negotiation. Conversely, value claiming happens when an option increases value to one at the other's expense.

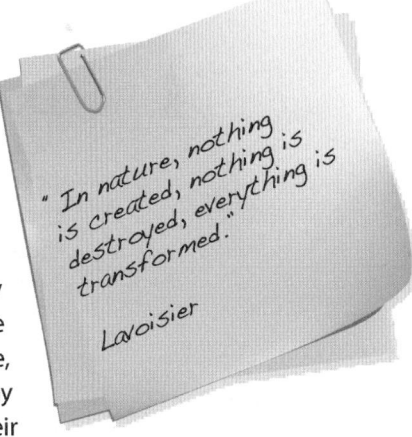

If a negotiation has 100 value units, after value creation it has, for example, 150 value units to distribute. However, if we believe we can get 50 out of 100 units, but then get 65 of 100, we claimed value well. In this case, no value was created as the negotiation started and ended with the same 100 value units. Therefore, ending a negotiation with more units does not imply value creation, but may only be good value claiming. Claiming more value from them does add value to us, but it does not create value for the negotiation.

## POINT OF INTEREST

**Value Creation vs. Compromise**

Many people mix value creation and compromise. The wrong assumption that any deal is automatically good means for many people that even a compromise creates value. Indeed, compromises can add value to the parties above their BATNAs. This does not mean that value was created, just claimed.

Value creation is the expansion of the available value. Compromise accepts the available value, instead of attempting to increase it. A value-claiming move (compromise) halves the available value (50/50) to guarantee having at least a deal.

Compromise is probably the biggest evidence that a negotiation created no value. A 50/50 split often means that no value was created on top of the original. Value creation allows for at least a 51/50 split or better.

Value creation is an option-generation process to increase the perceived or real value of the negotiation. This increased value results from manipulation of resources into options that better satisfy the parties' interests. Such increase can happen through:

1. An increase in the amount of resources available; or
2. A more efficient use, combination or allocation of available resources.

## Does Value Creation Create Real Value?

We could argue that value creation just makes available the negotiation's original potential, but does not really create value. Consequently, its potential is either there or not to begin with. However, this assumes that a negotiation has value independently from the negotiators, taking on a life of its own. That, as seen before, is just not possible!

The negotiators' decisions and moves impact the negotiation and its value potential. For example, a negotiator concentrating on a single issue reduces the negotiation scope and thus its potential. However, if the other party manages to introduce new issues into the negotiation, its value potential increases proportionally (Figure 11.1). Different issues bring different value potentials that expand the Pareto frontier of the negotiation (from PFA to PFB or PFC).

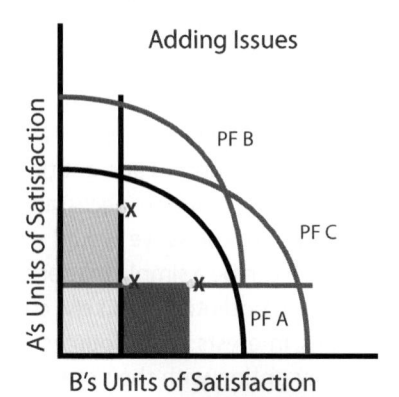

The negotiation is nothing apart from what we make of it.

**Figure 11.1** Many issues = Pareto frontier expansion

Unfortunately, value potential is not equal to value availability. Real life presents many obstacles which make it hard to render the potential value fully available. Information asymmetry, poor communication, assumptions, power distances, conflicts or positions make the potential value harder to see or make available. Value negotiation aims to handle most real-life challenges so value discovery and creation can take place.

Value discovery's goal is to surface interests to maximize the value potential of a negotiation. Value creation's goal is to generate options to transform that potential into reality. The value-creation effort seeks to increase the value potential (interests) plus the value availability (options). With an increased potential and availability, we now have more value than before our value -discovery and -creation efforts. The right value-creation steps can indeed create value.

# Creating Value

To achieve the goal of choosing the best option, we first have to create many options. That in turn requires the surfacing of many interests. Interest categorization builds a detailed map of what value means to the parties. This map allows us to tailor our option generation to efficiently use resources and accurately satisfy interests. As a result, we increase satisfaction at a lower cost, which means we increase value.

With many options, we do not expect one to be the best, but rather a combination of them. Unfortunately, this greatly increases complexity as we now have to consider individual options and all their different permutations. This potentially overwhelming complexity can tempt negotiators to oversimplify them to positions or to commit early. Since the best solution is more likely a combination of options rather than one option, value negotiators focus on packages.

## Be the Tailor! Make Options Suit Interests

The best dress and suit are normally tailored to make us look our best, while minimizing wastage. Tailor-made dresses or suits are much preferred to ready-made ones. Similarly, value negotiation outcomes create more value at a lower risk, as options are tailored to better fit interests. The similarity though does not extend itself to the longer lead time the tailor needs over ready-made clothing. Value negotiations, as opposed to bargaining, may actually save time by avoiding misunderstandings, conflicts and other risks.

The interest categorization done during value discovery highlights the similarities and differences between the various interests. That knowledge helps us to quickly find the best techniques to generate tailored options (Table 11.1).

| INTERESTS | OPTIONS | TECHNIQUES |
|---|---|---|
| Common, shared or joint | Mutual gains | • Economies of scale or scope<br>• Dovetailing<br>• Expand the pie |
| Different | Trades | • Non-specific compensation<br>• Logrolling<br>• Cost cutting |
| Conflicting or opposing | Contingent clauses | • Conditional exchanges<br>• Bridging |

**Table 11.1** Interest categorization

## Mutual Gains

Also called "joint gains," a mutual-gains option brings similar value to both parties even if not at the same amount. Initiating the option generation with mutual-gains options is a good strategic move for several reasons. Mutual-gains options move the parties closer to the Pareto frontier together (Figure 11.2).

Mutual-gains options have their logic captured in the equation: High value for A + high value for B = value creation for A & B.

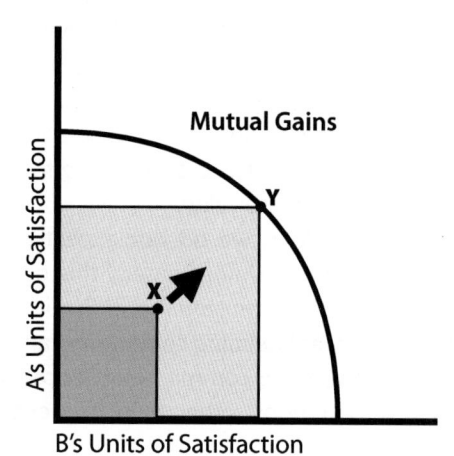

**Figure 11.2** Mutual gains and Pareto improvement

Mutual-gains options are normally built in three main ways:

1. **Economies of scale or scope** – If the parties share similar skills and resources, they can join forces or resources to increase volume.
    a. Economies of scale – Reduce cost as the bigger volume helps pay for the fixed costs and reduces the cost of each unit produced.
    b. Economies of scope – Increase profit as the bigger volume helps reach more customers and sell more with the same investment.

2. **Dovetailing** – Combine different skills and resources to create something neither could do alone.

3. **Expand the pie** – Adding skills or resources by the negotiators or third parties.

Imagine the hypothetical dialogue between representatives of two large competing companies (where they are careful not to talk about prices) (Table 11.2):

| NEGOTIATION DIALOGUE | DIAGNOSTICS |
|---|---|
| I have problems getting my products to the remote areas of the country. My transportation costs are too high for the proportionally small demand. Do you have a similar issue? | Sharing a potentially common interest to lead the value discovery then seeking theirs (dialogue pattern) |
| *Actually I do.* | *Confirming the interest is common* |
| Would you consider a joint transportation agreement so that our combined volume could help us reach more customers? | Proposing a mutual-gains option based on economies of scope |
| *This sounds like a great idea.* | *Indicating potential* |
| I am glad to hear that. Do you have any other concerns? | Inviting further option generation |
| *Quite a few, I fear. Our top priority is to reduce or eliminate our products' potential negative health impacts no matter how small. We are investing heavily in research.* | *Welcoming the question and introducing a new potentially common interest as well as a resource* |
| Interesting to know that because we are doing the same. Though it is not a very straightforward topic, don't you agree? | Reciprocating the information (rewarding good behavior) and diagnosing for more |
| *Indeed, not easy at all. It is our largest research project right now and we still feel that we are not as close as we wanted to be. As a responsible company, we want to be even prouder of our flagship product. Would you consider some information exchange on this topic?* | *Proposing a mutual-gains option based on economies of scale* |
| I was about to propose the same. I even thought of formalizing a collaboration on this topic. | Proposing another mutual-gains option based on economies of scale |
| *Something to consider. Actually if we start to work on this together, we may be able to present a united front to the government to ask for some extra resources.* | *Keeping options open and proposing a new mutual-gains option based on expanding the pie* |
| I had not thought about that. This is a great idea! | Excited with learning of new resource |
| *I am glad you like it. I think that we would only be able to do that though if we show that we have been working together for a while, so this may be a second step.* | *Explaining further the option to clarify expectations and avoid early commitment* |
| Something to aspire to! | Agreeing to hold on commitment |
| *But meanwhile, we have the government proposing some heavy taxes on us due to health concerns of our products.* | *Introducing another potential common concern or interest* |
| I am aware of that. We are preparing a heavy marketing campaign to educate consumers about the real health concerns and our ongoing efforts to minimize them further. | Sharing resources available to satisfy this interest |
| *This is good to hear, since you are very good at this. We, on the other hand, were working hard on conducting the most stringent tests to separate truth from myth.* | *Reciprocating (rewarding good behavior) with information on their resources* |

**11 • VALUE CREATION**

| NEGOTIATION DIALOGUE | DIAGNOSTICS |
|---|---|
| Would you mind sharing the data so that we can strengthen our campaign further? We are basing it on more scientific data to really show the validity of our claims. It seems that your work can really fit in our campaign. | Proposing a mutual-gains option based on dovetailing |
| *I believe it is okay. I will need to check on that though.* | *Positive without early commitment* |
| Sure! What else could we talk about? Would you like to elaborate on some of the ideas we just had? | Process leadership transparency: continue option generation or make options more specific? |

**Table 11.2**
Avoiding talk of prices

While expanding the pie adds resources to the negotiation, economies of scale or scope and dovetailing mainly increase the available resources' efficiency. Expanding the pie happens when at least one of the negotiators expands the negotiation issues, interests or parties. New issues, interests or parties normally carry new and additional resources. Even external parties who carry a common interest can bring new resources to the table.

Economies of scope or scale as well as dovetailing happen if the parties have a good understanding of each other's resources and skills. It then becomes easier to generate options that invite a collaborative effort towards more value.

## POINT OF INTEREST

**Mutual-Gains Options vs. Other Options**

Initiating option generation with mutual-gains options is a smart strategic move. Yet not all options will or need to have mutual gains.

Still, process transparency can help lead clearly: "I assume that not all options will be good for both of us. Still I wanted to start with some so as to show you my commitment to understand and work towards your interests as well as mine."

## Trades

In trades, much like in mutual-gains options, all parties gain. Unlike mutual-gains options, trades tap into different interests to provide different value to the parties. Trades are probably the most common value-creation move: I give you Z in exchange for Y. The parties move through different paths towards the Pareto frontier (Figure 11.3).

Most people seek common goals or interests for their relationship benefits and, as seen above, mutual gains. However, if we are both interested in money, we may fight over it. Alternatively, if we want a salary and they want to make money from hiring us, then we have a deal. Though similar at first, the interests are different. The salary is low-risk money without much upside. Meanwhile, hiring our labor is high-risk money since they pay us a salary even in a downturn, but have a potential high upside when things go well.

**Figure 11.3** Trades and Pareto improvements

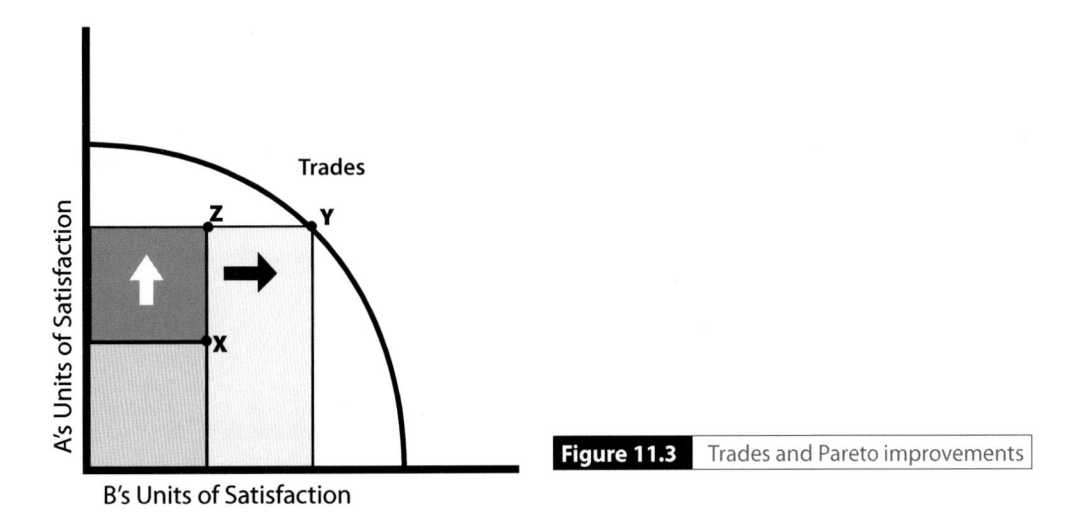

Differences in interests hide an even larger value potential than similarities. As we saw in dovetailing, differences in skills or resources can generate valuable options. Differences in rewards, risks or time preferences have a similar potential. Different forecasts of uncertain events are valuable, but better explored through contingent options. The different preferences that are best explored by trades are:

- **Reward** – We want something from them that they value less than what they want from us.
  - When we buy a product, we usually value it more than the money we pay.
- **Risk** – We want to run a risk or not to, while they feel the opposite. Some people are risk averse, while others are risk-takers.
  - We pay the insurance company to take risks from our hands.
- **Time** – We want something now or in the future while they want the reverse.
  - When we invest, we forego money today for more money tomorrow.

Once we understand what the negotiators' preferences are, we can start putting potential trades together. From the pattern above, trades normally follow a two-step logic:

$$\frac{\begin{array}{l}\text{High value for A – low or no cost for B = value creation for A}\\ +\;\text{High value for B – low or no cost for A = value creation for B}\end{array}}{\text{Value creation for A \& B}}$$

This equation normally happens in three main ways:

1. **Logrolling** (priority trade) – We give low-priority to get higher-priority value.
2. **Non-specific compensation** – We compensate them to get what we want.
3. **Cost cutting** – We reduce their costs to give us what we want.

The salary negotiation in a small company can illustrate many of the concepts above (Table 11.3):

| NEGOTIATION DIALOGUE | DIAGNOSTICS |
|---|---|
| Hi boss! I came here to ask you for a raise. | Sharing a process interest and introducing a substance interest (probably different = raise) |
| *Why do you think you deserve one? Can't you wait until the end of the year when we make these decisions?* | *Time preference (raise today vs. end of the year)* |
| I didn't say that I deserve it just yet. Something came up and I sincerely need a raise. Are you in principle against it? | |
| *Not in principle. I just do not see why I should do it now. I am glad to give you a raise three months from now.* | *Time preference (raise today vs. in three months)* |
| Thank you! Unfortunately, time is of the essence for me and I would appreciate a raise by my next paycheck. | |
| *It seems that you are having some financial issues. I am glad to try to help and I do not want to set a negative precedent of early raises. What if I lend you money today?* | *Risk preference (precedent) + Reward preference (raise $ > loan $) + Time preference ($ today vs. $ tomorrow)* |
| Thanks for the idea! Mine unfortunately are longer-term issues, so a loan would not help much. I do not want to create a problem for you; I only want to solve mine. Could I ask what could motivate you to give me a raise now? | |
| *Since you asked, we need someone to cover our operations on Saturdays as soon as possible. This would mean extra work and pay which I could easily justify. Interested?* | *Logrolling money for extra work + Cost cutting extra work to avoid precedent setting* |
| Potentially! I am doing a part-time MBA on Saturday and Sunday mornings. When do you need me in on Saturday? | Time preference (Saturday afternoon vs. whole day expectation) |
| *You can arrive around 12:30pm on Saturdays so that you can continue with your course. Would that help?* | *Cost cutting (Saturday time reduced to afternoons only)* |
| Sure! | |
| *Could you actually help on Sundays as well?* | *Logrolling (more work and money)* |
| If I do Sundays, then I will not have a lot of rest time or time to do my MBA homework and I fear flunking the tests. | Reward (rest vs. money) + Risk preference (flunk tests vs. money) |
| *I can give you Mondays off if you do Sundays as well. It is just for a couple of months until we find someone else. However, the Sunday additional compensation will be made as a one-time payment, since it is temporary.* | *Non-specific compensation (Monday + $ vs. Sunday) + Risk preference (raise risk > one-time payment risk)* |
| That is fair! So Sunday afternoons only, right? | |
| *Actually, while you are here during the weekend, I do not mind if you do your MBA homework. I just need someone I trust here to answer calls. It is usually quite quiet.* | *Cost cutting (study time while at work) and assuming a reward preference* |
| Works for me. Should we next talk about the raise? | Leading the process transparently |

**Table 11.3** A salary negotiation

When dealing with multi-issue trades, keeping track of all possible trades can be quite confusing. The increased number of possibilities can make us feel unsure of the quality of our decisions as if comparing apples and oranges. Additional techniques can simplify the handling of multi-issue trades:

- **Even swaps** – Converting all options to a single currency helps compare them.
  - How many apples is an orange worth to me?
  - How much would I pay for extra vacation days, a better working environment, more flexible hours, a new location, etc.?
- **Points** – Giving points to each option to clarify the negotiators' preferences and trade accordingly.
  - If we all had 100 points, how would we allocate them to the different options on the table?
  - If we gave more points to option A and they to B, we get A and they get B.
- **Bundles** – Bundling several options into packages of similar value to facilitate choosing or even allowing the flip of a coin.
  - We are equally glad to do A+B, B+C or A+D+E. What do you prefer?
  - If we can do A instead of B, I am open to the choices you gave.

The multi-issue techniques are just ways to organize these more complex trades. They do not solve the difficult trade-off questions that frequently arise in these situations. Thus they make the decisions simpler, but not necessarily easier.

# Contingencies

Contingent options normally create value out of opposing or conflicting interests which seem unsolvable at first. Many of these interests originate from different forecasts of uncertain events. As a result, the parties cannot agree on what the future holds. Instead of fighting over the unknown, contingent options manage uncertainty through conditional scenarios.

### POINT OF INTEREST

**Difference in Risk Preference vs. Forecast of Uncertain Events**

Different forecasts of uncertain events have us disagree on the odds of a future event: we expect an 80% chance of rain and they see 50%.

Difference in risk preference assumes we agree on the likelihood of rain (60%), but feel and behave differently towards it. We may find 60% too risky and not leave the house without an umbrella. Meanwhile, they think 60% is okay and may leave without it or even lend us theirs.

Contingent options are a special category of trades. They are conditional time-deferred trades. If we deliver our part, then they also deliver theirs. However, if we do not deliver, then their fears materialize but not the risks as no trade happens.

Contingent options are normally based on an If-Then logic better explained below:

IF A delivers, THEN B also delivers = reward maximization for A & B
or IF A doesn't deliver, THEN B doesn't deliver either = risk minimization for A & B

Value creation for A & B

Contingent options deliver different value to the negotiators at different times as they create value out of disagreements. They can motivate a professional to work harder and better towards targets to earn a bonus. They also allow us to progress with a deal independently of our different views about the future. Instead of stopping the negotiation opportunity, a conditional agreement isolates the uncertainty and progresses with the other issues (Figure 11.4). The isolated uncertainty is resolved in due time when new data or future events clarify the original disagreement.

Contingent options reduce risks as they normally allocate these to whoever is better prepared to handle them. Consequently they minimize lying, overconfidence or information asymmetry when making the potential liar or overconfident party responsible for the risk. For example, if a contractor promises on-time delivery, the customer does not know if they are lying or overconfident. The contractor has better control over and information on the delivery risk to minimize it for the customer.

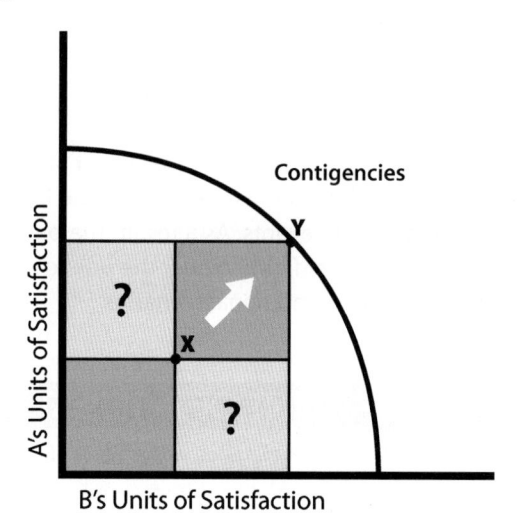

**Figure 11.4** Contingencies and Pareto improvements

Consistently, a contingent option could be a penalty for delay or payment performed upon delivery. This is value for the customer. The customer now does not need to ask for a discount ahead of time to account for the delay risk. Not having to give a discount is also value for the contractor, if they indeed deliver on time.

Contingent options are normally structured through:

1. **Conditional exchanges** – If one party delivers, then the other will as well.
2. **Bridging** – A new innovative option to satisfy opposing interests is developed.

Let's see how the IT department of a big company manages the negotiation with their supplier:

| NEGOTIATION DIALOGUE | DIAGNOSTICS |
|---|---|
| I am calling because I am frustrated with your product X10. | Interests |
| *I am sorry to hear that. What can we do for you?* | *Apologizing for the frustration + call for options* |
| I would like you to replace or fix it ASAP. My whole system relies on it. You promised me reliability and it now breaks down almost every week. I cannot continue like this. | Option generation + more interests |
| *Sure, we will fix it for you.* | *Commitment* |
| Great! When can you do it? | Clarifying commitment |
| *We can take it on Friday night and fix it over the weekend. You do not need it over the weekend, right?* | *Suggesting a time option + checking interest assumption* |
| Right. Friday evening is okay. So when do you bring it back? | Commitment + clarification |
| *By Monday early morning to install it for you. Is that okay?* | *Suggesting a time option* |
| Fine! But what if you are not ready by 6am on Monday? | Sharing a new interest |
| *Don't worry! We will be there guaranteed!* | *Dismissing interest* |
| Guaranteed? | Suspicion of overconfidence or lie |
| *Yes, 100% guaranteed.* | *Overconfidence or lie (100% guarantee is impossible)* |
| If you are sure to deliver on time while I run huge delay risks, then you can waive your fees if you are late, right? | Conditional exchange (delay risk vs. fee waiver) |
| *No sir, we cannot do that.* | *Double-checking statement* |
| But aren't you 100% certain to be on time? If you are, then no waiving of fees is necessary. Why would this not work? | Confirming fairness of proposed contingent option |
| *Well sir, it is almost 100%, not 100% exactly.* | *Clarifying or adjusting overconfidence or lie as risk is transferred back* |
| So what do we do in the rare event that the delivery is late? | Learning question inviting options |
| *I will leave a substitute product with you when I pick yours up. This way, even if we are late, you will have your system running. Would that work for you?* | *Bridging — innovative solution to minimize delay risk (similar to time-deferred cost cutting)* |
| That could work. I only do not want disruption. If my system works, I can wait a little to have my product fixed. | Confirming interests to be satisfied |
| *Will do!* | *Commitment* |

**Table 11.4**
Contingent options in a dialogue

Many negotiators shy away from contingent options due to fear, ignorance or misunderstanding. As they protect against a risk, if it does not materialize, a party may feel as if they overpaid. On hindsight, it is always easy to forget the value of a guarantee or an insurance after the risk does not occur.

Indeed, a contingent option can be quite risky as it may exchange value at different times: we do our part today expecting them to do theirs later. Since it requires future compliance, there are risks of a party trying to play the system. The perceived power difference from the time lag of deliverables generates temptation for the party responsible to deliver later. Contingent options are different from trades, because they have to manage that temptation through a careful structure.

The way a contingent option is structured can minimize the risks of it going poorly. Contingent options are safer when created within a longer-term relationship or at least where there is guaranteed continuing interaction. The expectation of a continuing interaction can work as an incentive for the parties to comply. If they do not expect future interaction, the incentive to unilaterally take one's deliverable and "run away" may be strong. Thus, enforceability or the power to guarantee their compliance if the right conditions take place is paramount.

Finally, transparent conditions based on objective criteria give us certainty over our successful delivery or dissipate the future uncertainty. Transparency prevents disagreement at a later date over the interpretation of the conditions for the trade to take place. Thus, instead of a bonus for overperformance (subjective), we want a bonus for performance above 100% of our target (objective). Bear in mind that the conditions to achieve our target should be, as much as possible, within our control. Otherwise, we may become victims of manipulation as they are tempted to boycott our delivery.

## Value Comes in Packages

Value creation's biggest ally is a good value discovery and a great number of issues, interests and resources. Its biggest enemy is early commitment, the eagerness to reach a deal fast or to quickly reject a bad option. Early commitment can be motivated by time constraint, assuming the best possible outcome, not entertaining bad options, etc. They all reduce learning and thus the negotiation's value potential. Even in learning conversations, our brain's limited processing power tempts us to commit early to reduce complexity. However, it is this complexity that generates value when managed well.

A commitment is considered early when it happens before a thorough conversation on interests, options and legitimacy. Early commitment prevents learning and knowing if we are making the best possible decision or even just a good one.

Packages are the best way to efficiently manage the options-generation complexity. Packages reduce or simplify the number of ideas discussed. They help negotiators think about options as a system that needs to be balanced to succeed. Packages prevent negotiators from committing early as they can only commit once the package is finalized. Finally, they prevent closed positions and remind us to unbundle them, since packages are metaphorically meant to be opened.

In packages, options have no individual value if not consistent with the whole. Thus, value negotiators rarely say "no" to an option; instead they share conditions they need satisfied to accept it. This is an example of the use of a package approach. An option may seem bad at first, but within a package it could become acceptable or good as the following example shown:

> Could you work for all 365 days of this year?

> I don't know! Tell me more. Under what conditions?

> You could work from home during the weekends.

> Understood. What are you willing to give in return? 365 days a year is a lot!

> I would pay you US$0.75 million for the year.

> Sounds good for now! I need to understand more before I can finally commit to the idea. Do you mind if I ask you a few more questions?

> Ask all you want.

Initially, the request seems absurd, with "no" the only acceptable answer. But if we do not keep the conversation open, we would never find out what they are willing to give in return. They, or even we, may generate options that make it possible, reasonable or even attractive. Meanwhile, we show openness and flexibility while retaining our right to commit or not to after learning what we need to decide.

A package approach to option generation keeps the conversation open and flexible, while avoiding early commitment. It manages the temptation to value claim, which can invite early commitment and interrupt value creation. The package approach also manages the fear around value-creation complexity to continue generating options. It does so by helping negotiators know when and how to commit, and to avoid doing it early.

## Options: A Double-Edged Sword?

We have linked value discovery with interests, value creation with options and value-claiming with legitimacy. However, real negotiations are not so clean cut. Though interests and legitimacy mostly stay within value discovery and value claiming respectively, options are not exclusively limited to value creation (Table 11.5). Options also lead to value claiming. A proposal normally gives value creation ideas together with a suggested value split.

**Table 11.5**
Options in value creation and value-claiming

| Value Creation | | | Value-Claiming |
|---|---|---|---|
| Interests | OK → Options (Structure) CAREFUL → Options (Numbers) ← OK | | Legitimacy |

This dual purpose of options creates confusion for many negotiators who sincerely attempt to create value. Some of their options may unintentionally be perceived as and invite value-claiming behaviors. Even the smallest perception of value claiming can move us away from value creation. For example (Table 11.6):

| NEGOTIATION DIALOGUE | DIAGNOSTICS |
| --- | --- |
| I believe that our joint project can be a huge success. | Positive opening statement |
| I couldn't agree more! It has lots of potential. How would you like to structure it? | Positive reciprocation |
| I believe that today we can put a team together from both our companies to start the project as soon as possible. | Giving options to structure the deal |
| Great idea! What else? | Inviting new options to structure the project, not to define details |
| Well, in discussing the team, I believe that the CFO of our joint venture should be a talented lady from our company. | Getting detailed in the option generation without a structure in place |
| Why is that? We are a finance-oriented organization. I am sure we will have more capable choices inside our company for the CFO position. | Reacts to what is perceived as a value-claiming move (CFO = control over money?) and tries to claim in return |
| Do you mean more capable or more loyal to you? | Gets suspicious and sarcastic |
| What are you suggesting? You were the one rushing to secure the CFO position, not me. | Blames the other for starting the power struggle/value claim |
| I did not mean to grab anything! I just gave a suggestion, since I have someone who would be perfect as CFO. | Argues innocence as generated options for the sincere good of the partnership |
| Really? It surely did not come across this way! | Suspicious of value-claiming intention |
| Well, you also seem awfully interested in this position for your company and I find this very suspicious. | Blames the intention of the other as a resistance to feeling pushed |

**Table 11.6**

Moving away from value creation

We concentrate first on generating structural options to create the architecture of the deal. Structural options do not have any numbers or details that claim value or invite claiming behaviours. In this case, it may have helped to define the roles and profiles being sought (structure) and then search both companies for the ideal candidates (specific). Numbers or details present in specific options surface our intended value split. Thus, specific options invite early value-claiming and positional commitments.

If value claiming comes early, we can always return to value creation however hard it may seem. Still, it is easier to maximize value creation before claiming it. To return to value creation after claiming attempts is usually less effective. We may create value but with too many claiming ideas in mind, our creativity and openness are now hampered.

# Build Value-Creation Momentum

The sequencing of negotiation issues has an impact on our ability to create value. It can assist in generating positive value-creation momentum and hold value claiming back. Good sequencing focuses negotiators on value and avoids positional bargaining by pushing zero-sum discussions to the end of the process.

If we had children and were to amicably negotiate our divorce, how should we sequence our issues? We want to do it so that we maximize the value momentum of our negotiation. Let's concentrate on two issues that are bound to come up in such situations: custody of the children and visitation rights. Custody of the children debates which parent will live with the children. Visitation rights define days, times and conditions when the children visit the non-custodial parent. What would be the right sequence?

If we are like the vast majority of people, we would think of discussing custody first based on **dependence**. Visitation rights seem to depend on custody and thus cannot be discussed without the knowledge of the custody outcome. On second thought, do we really need to discuss custody to devise a potentially fair visitation rights structure? Not really! Custody may be more important, but the importance of an issue is irrelevant to sequencing. Visitation does not depend on custody though it may seem so at first.

Let's also imagine what would happen if parent A won the custody battle? What would be his or her incentives? Be fair in the subsequent visitation rights discussion or minimize losing time with the children? The most likely scenario is that during the custody battle, the parties will be positional.

## POINT OF INTEREST

**Gain vs. Loss Frame**

Framing also impacts sequencing. Starting with custody risks having them feel like the winner. This feeling of gain inhibits incentives to be fair on the rest.

If they won everything they wanted, every new issue to discuss is a loss over their initial gain. The visitation rights conversation becomes a discussion over how many days they will give away. It becomes something painful and to resist at all costs.

However, to discuss visitation rights first makes custody be about "how many more days I will spend with my children." This gives a feeling of added gain, which normally is less aggressive than resisting pain.

Even parents who may not want their children living with them will fiercely negotiate. For one thing, they need to prove they are good parents and that they love their children. Then they want to ensure some control over being with their children.

So custody first seems to be a dangerous sequencing choice. But why would we choose to discuss visitation rights before custody? Two reasons mainly: **veil of ignorance** and **value-creation potential**. First, if the parties do not know who will gain custody, each one may fear losing it. Ignorance and fear give both parents a strong incentive to negotiate a fair package. Each one wants to be prepared and happy with the visitation rights if they lose custody.

Second, custody has three potential outcomes (father, mother or joint), while visitation rights has an infinite number of potential outcomes. The higher number of potential outcomes demonstrates a better ability to tailor the options to the parties' interests and realities. That in turn grants the visitation rights issue a higher value-creation potential. In fact, custody is zero-sum since custody for one parent means no custody for the other. This all-or-nothing outcome is a fertile ground for win-lose tactics.

Sequencing to build value momentum prioritizes issues with higher value-creation potential. Next, we check which issues provide a veil of ignorance over others. Then, we organize them from a loss to a gain frame. Finally, dependence fine-tunes sequencing.

## To Close or Not to Close — Is That the Question?

Of course, at some point we close the negotiation. Not only that, we do it as efficiently as possible. We just do not want to waste value while doing so. Thus the question is not whether or not to close a negotiation, but whether or not to do this during value creation.

We are physically unable to negotiate several issues simultaneously because we can only speak about one thing at a time. Most people then negotiate sequentially, discussing one issue after another. This in turn leads most negotiators to advance until exhausting or closing an issue before moving to the next. Is that the correct way to do it? What are the consequences? Do we close an issue or not before moving on to the next?

To discuss and close one issue before the next creates separate silos and a fragmented process. Dealing with issues sequentially reduces our commitment quality as we are unaware of the interests and options in issues that follow. It also obstructs package deals, since putting separate pieces together is different from building a cohesive system. The separate pieces may be incoherent and the final deal increasingly difficult to achieve as we advance. Even multi-issue win-win negotiations may look like the process below (Table 11.7):

| Issue A | Issue B | Issue C | Issue D | Issue E |
| --- | --- | --- | --- | --- |
| Interests A | Interests B | Interests C | Interests D | Interests E |
| Options A | Options B | Options C | Options D | Options E |
| Legitimacy A | Legitimacy B | Legitimacy C | Legitimacy D | Legitimacy E |
| Commitment A | Commitment B | Commitment C | Commitment D | Commitment E |

**Table 11.7** Multi-issue sequential negotiations

Under multi-issue complexity, negotiators normally crave to secure what was achieved and feel that the negotiation is progressing. The first mistake is to lock an option in too soon as it leads to early commitment. This reduces value-creation flexibility as the number of elements open for negotiation diminishes with each commitment. The second mistake is to measure progress as a move from Issue A to E. This process impacts the negotiators' openness to create value: a fight over Issue A may reduce openness and trust for Issue B.

The eagerness to reduce complexity and stay within an issue undermines a negotiation's value potential. Closing on an issue too soon sets it aside from creating value. To avoid this mistake and enhance value creation, many try to keep everything open until the very end. Then again, doing so increases complexity and uncertainty that can stifle value creation. Thus, the answer is neither close nor not close!

So how do we satisfy the process interests of securing and measuring progress while keeping value creation alive? Our answer is to commit tentatively. We **tentatively close each issue until all are negotiated and closed as a package**. Until then, commitments are open for Pareto improvements, i.e., improving it for at least one party without making anyone else worse off. The fundamental condition to reopen a tentative commitment is its value-creation intention. A tentative commitment can be established in the following way:

> It seems that we have somewhat agreed on how to satisfy this issue. Pending learning of new opportunities to improve it at least for one of us without making anyone else worse off, let's assume that this issue is tentatively settled for now so that we can move on to the next topic. What do you think?

Tentative commitments give parties a feeling of security through stable agreements that can only be reopened for improvement. They also deliver a better sense of progress to move from A to B without limiting value creation. Tentative commitments keep all possibilities open for Pareto improvements until the very end, hence providing maximum flexibility. If new value opportunities arise on issues already discussed, we are still free to reopen them for improvement.

Tentative commitments free us from negotiating issues sequentially by not exclusively measuring progress from A to E. As humans, we are surely bound to discuss issues sequentially, but tentative commitments allow for simultaneous progress on some elements. With the goal of building tentative commitments, we can now progress from interests to commitment like in Table 11.8 below:

| Issue A | Issue B | Issue C | Issue D | Issue E |
|---|---|---|---|---|
| Interests |||||
| Structural options |||||
| Structural legitimacy |||||
| Specific options | Specific options | Specific options | Specific options | Specific options |
| Legitimacy | Legitimacy | Legitimacy | Legitimacy | Legitimacy |
| Tentative commitment | Tentative commitment | Tentative commitment | Tentative commitment | Tentative commitment |
| Final package commitment |||||

**Table 11.8**
Multi-issue simultaneous and sequential negotiations

Interests can be discussed at a package level by joining all of them in one conversation. Structural options and their legitimacy can be similarly handled. These elements benefit most from an interconnected understanding of the whole. Once the deal is generally structured, sequentially negotiating specific options towards tentative commitments becomes much less dangerous. The awareness of the whole enhances the tentative commitments' quality and prepares them for the final package.

In sum, value negotiators tailor options to interests to create the best possible value package. Options are tailored through mutual gains, trades or contingencies. Packages reduce complexity to increase value creation by limiting the claiming side of options, sequencing for value and making commitments tentatively.

# Overcoming Value-Creation Enemies

Besides complexity, value creation has many more "enemies," internal and external to the negotiation. These enemies include everything that pushes us into bargaining and obstructs value creation. They first have us bypass, ignore or quit value creation and then force us directly into value claiming.

The internal enemies are already well known to us: power distance, trading between negotiations and information asymmetry. The external enemies were already briefly introduced when we discussed relationships in Chapter 7: resource constraint, artificial limits and narrow scope. Below we explore how they work and how to manage them.

## Internal Enemies

Internal enemies are inherent to the negotiation structure. They are not externally imposed and impact any negotiation independently of the context. They tempt negotiators to ignore value creation and focus on value claiming too soon.

### Power Distance

Power distance is an internal value-creation enemy because it has negotiators view one another as obstacles to value (Figure 11.5). Negotiators who intentionally or unintentionally focus on power normally do not even think about value creation. When looking at the negotiation pie, their automatic questions are: "Will I be able to get the bigger share? How can I get the bigger share?"

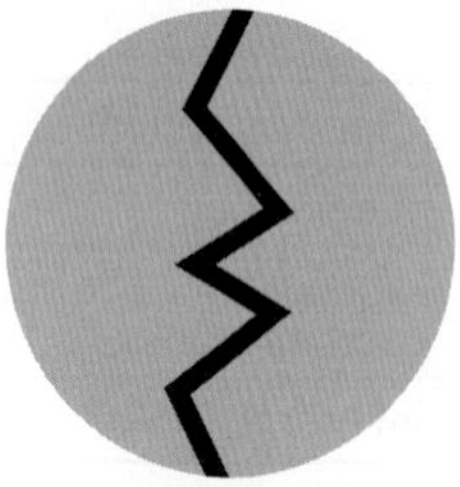

**Figure 11.5** Splitting the "pie"

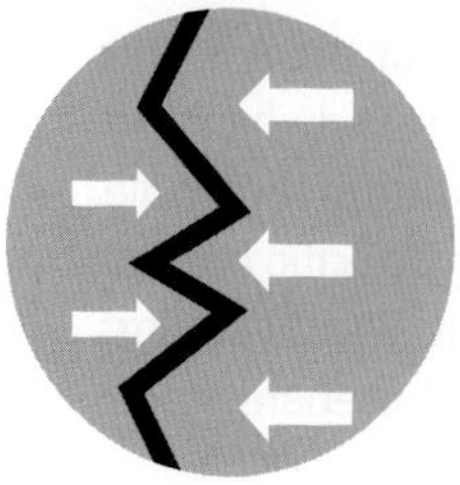

Power distance makes this question even easier to answer. The stronger side has no incentive to ask another question, while the weaker side has an easy but negative answer. The resulting confidence or fear drives negotiators to apply maximum power or resistance to claim value (Figure 11.6). In the end, the outcome is predictable yet poor in value.

Most negotiators never give a second thought to the validity of the questions above. Though the idea of value claiming is indeed inherent to negotiation, these two questions are not. Even if they were, they should not take precedence over value-creation questions, but rather follow them. To minimize the power distance impact in value creation, it **helps to first maximize value creation, not value claiming!**

**Figure 11.6** Power escalation and resistance

We focus on value creation by calling their attention first to the outer line of the pie. The new common challenge becomes to overcome the external value-creation limitations together (Figure 11.7). Our power distance becomes irrelevant as we are not confronting one another. If they have more power, it actually helps as we will both be pushing in the same direction: value creation. The first question then becomes: "How might we make more together?" Only after successful value creation, then we ask: "How can I get my fair share to satisfy my interests?"

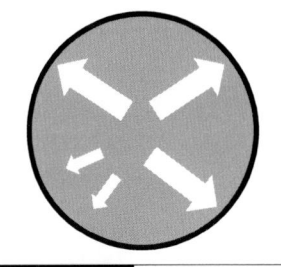

**Figure 11.7** Jointly overcoming external value-creation limitations

## Trading Between Negotiations

Trading between negotiations is an internal value-creation enemy because it uses concessions to try to build relationships and value. Concessions give something of value in exchange for nothing. In concessions, we hope to build relationships by pleasing the other side to move a negotiation forward, normally at a substantive and unilateral cost. The concession logic is we give them something, they like us more, resulting in a better relationship. In time, such a relationship is expected to yield substantive returns for us. However, concessions have no guarantee of value reciprocation and often yield nothing.

On the other hand, a concession actually hides its intention to get value in return. The relationship becomes just a tool to get value. Thus, a concession may even worsen the relationship if its hidden agenda is uncovered. All told, concessions are risky trades between substance and relationship which often lose both. Concessions are also another form of early commitment and thus detract from value creation.

### POINT OF INTEREST

**Concessions vs. Gifts**

Concessions are unilateral, but are not intended as such. As a soft bargainer's tool, future reciprocation is silently expected. They are not given altruistically or to denote friendship. Instead, it is an attempt to invest on the relationship with the expectation to receive future value.

Gifts are different from concessions when given to express true friendship or gratitude. A gift is intended to be a unilateral value move. A gift given with the expectation of reciprocation is no true gift, but rather a disguised concession of an expected trade.

Giving something away for free encourages bad behaviors. It implicitly says: "expect things from me in exchange for nothing" or "whatever I give you has no value." Negotiators get used to concessions, but instead of appreciating the giver, they get angry if they stop getting it. Thus, concessions generate a vicious cycle of unilateral value expectation that can worsen relationships.

**Reactive concessions**, which negotiators make when under pressure, **are the worst** of them all. They send a strong and dangerous additional message: if they apply more pressure, we will eventually concede more. Thus, their incentive to constantly apply pressure increases dramatically.

Instead of concessions, we prefer trades. Trades help negotiators think in a dialogue pattern: "If I am going to ask for something, I should be ready to give something in return." A concession can be easily transformed into a time-deferred trade with clearer expectations: "I will give something to you today in exchange for something for me tomorrow."

Trades build a healthier, transparent and value-creating negotiation. They make negotiators think harder about creating value, instead of getting comfortable with being selfish. They also clarify the relationship pattern and promote good behaviors. Both relationship and substance improve as they are managed autonomously.

## Information Asymmetry

Information asymmetry is an internal value-creation enemy because it generates assumptions that create a false sense of certainty. This false certainty focuses negotiators on an idea as if it were the best or only solution. There is no straighter path for positional bargaining to reduce value creation than a thorough belief in only one option. Think about a Brazilian and an Argentinean being asked: "Who is the best soccer player ever?" They will passionately debate over Pelé and Maradona and probably never agree.

Evolutionary reasons result in us being perceived by peers as more powerful the more adamantly we support a position. Therefore, questions, doubts or ideas lacking certainty are not status-enhancing for most people. An Argentinean who declares: "Maybe Pelé was better than Maradona" may be at risk of having his nationality stripped away. Naturally, when generating options, negotiators fear criticism or judgments, and looking stupid, foolish, unreasonable or weak. Add the fear of revealing too much and we understand why negotiators typically put very few options on the table.

Information asymmetry will have negotiators jumping to conclusions and vehemently supporting them without full awareness of their ignorance. Consequently, negotiators may accept the first good option they hear without attempting to expand further. It may sound good enough already, so why bother to learn more? Others quickly criticize or reject what does not work for them. These examples of early commitment block learning about potential additional value.

How can we minimize the negative impact information asymmetry has on value creation? By **separating generation from evaluation**. It suspends judgment and early commitment, freeing negotiators to think, generate and elaborate on options without fears or risks. One famous example is the brainstorming process which aims to generate the widest possible range of ideas. In brainstorming, even crazy ideas are invited to stimulate other, more pragmatic ones. No judgment is allowed, negative or positive. Only after exhaustive option generation can negotiators stop to evaluate and decide on their preferred options.

Processes such as brainstorming need to be clearly introduced to preserve the separation between generation and evaluation: "For the next 10–15 minutes, we could share ideas on how to satisfy the interests we uncovered so far. I believe it would be best if we did not justify or explain our ideas just yet. What do you think? Should we add anything?" Otherwise, it is hard to control parties from criticizing what they consider bad or appreciating what works for them. Any subtle expressions are already an early commitment.

Other processes besides brainstorming can spark creativity with less potential risk. One example is to ask for a higher number of potential solutions: "What could be some other ways to get a similar outcome?" Other examples are asking hypothetical questions or proposing different scenarios for criticism:

- If we were in a long-term relationship, what else could we do?
- If we had upper management support, how would we go forward?
- Without this problem, what possibilities would open up?
- If we try to convince them for the fourth time, what would we be risking?

## External Enemies

External value-creation enemies are imposed from the outside and thus not inherent to the negotiation (Figure 11.8). Thus, theoretically not all negotiations have external value-creation enemies. Though in reality, few negotiations will lack at least one external enemy. External value-creation enemies resist negotiators' attempts to create value until they resign themselves to value-claiming only.

External enemies are ideal targets for the opening statement to create a new value-oriented focus (JVP frame). Much like internal value-creation enemies, negotiators are often not even aware of the external ones. Normally, an invitation to collaborate to address the external value-creation enemy is enough to raise such awareness.

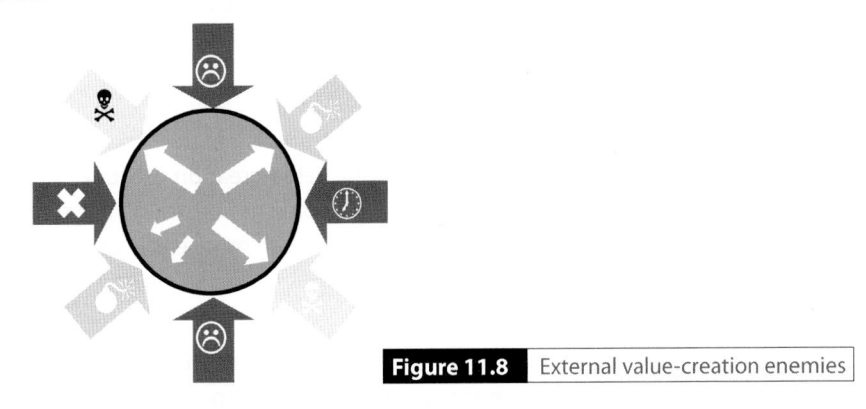

**Figure 11.8** External value-creation enemies

### Resource Constraints

Resource constraints are an external value-creation enemy because they **limit the number of options we can implement**. Like having only one color, we are much more limited in our creative expression than with several colors. Resource constraints do not strictly block negotiators from generating options, but rather their potential implementation. However, this foresight generates negative assumptions of impossibility that drag creativity down.

Resource constraints can be absolute or relative:

- **Absolute** – There is no more of a desired resource available in the world.
- **Relative** – There seems to be no more of a desired resource available to the negotiators, but there is no absolute scarcity of it.

The distinction between absolute and relative resource constraint is relevant as they require different approaches. First, absolute resource constraints are much less frequent than relative ones, which is good news. Few things overcome an absolute resource constraint: save on the resource, find substitutes or change the process to one that requires different resource inputs. It usually takes a lot of effort and ingenuity to overcome an absolute resource constraint. Just look at the amount of money and research going into alternative energy sources in anticipation of an eventual oil shortage.

Relative resource constraints may seem absolute at first, though it may be for lack of broader search or exploration. Using the oil example again, many companies start to drill overseas, in arctic or sandy regions, horizontally, etc. Resource constraints are mostly a scarcity from the normal source. The three ways to handle an absolute resource constraint also help relative constraints, though they will operate on a smaller scale as the situation is usually less dire. Some alternative ways to handle relative resource constraints are:

- Offer more (money, volume, etc.) to get preferential sourcing
- Wait for the resource to become abundant again
- Create agreements for future supply
- Use existing resources in more creative or efficient ways
    - Relative reduction of constraint
- Expand search to other areas
    - Seek different budgets or different markets to source from
- Add new issues or parties, or unbundle them
    - These can bring in new resources

If we realize that a resource constraint is relative, imagination and hope are our only limitations. With the right value-creation attitude, we may make the resource available again or even overcome its constraint. The reason to fight over limited value goes away and the parties can more easily reach an agreement.

## Artificial Limits

Artificial limits are an external value-creation enemy as they **reduce the number of options we can generate or implement**. An artificial limit is a human-made one, such as a law, policy, rule, tradition, habit, assumption, agreement, etc. These are human decisions that artificially make the feasible unfeasible. They not only stop negotiators from implementing an option, but also from generating ideas for lack of information or access.

Though apparently similar, artificial limits differ from relative resource constraints. An artificial limit may have the resource sitting in the room next door, but forbidden to us. Imagine an empty first-class seat at an airplane first class. The resource is there, but we cannot use it if we do not pay for it.

Time, for example, can be a relative resource constraint or an artificial limit. If we are late to catch a plane, it has left and we are unable to catch it anymore. It is physically unavailable. No matter the reasons, the airline cannot give you more time to catch that plane. However, if we are late submitting an application, the office and the people are still there. They may not accept it for other reasons.

Artificial limits normally exist for a reason, such as seeking to protect or advance an interest. This underlying interest opens two main ways to negotiate artificial limits:

- Learn the interest they want to satisfy; and
- Learn how applicable that reason is to our particular situation.

Since artificial limits increase information asymmetry, it all starts with learning before we can generate valid options. After learning, we tailor options to satisfy the underlying interests behind the artificial limit and our interests. We can either suggest or invite them to generate options to respect their interests while also advancing ours. At the very least, these invitations or suggestions surface additional information on what can or cannot be done.

Artificial limits are routinely negotiated through Pareto improvements to get what we want while not making them worse off. An example of this is in Table 11.9:

| NEGOTIATION DIALOGUE | DIAGNOSTICS |
|---|---|
| So your monthly salary will be 100K Rupiah. | Specific option |
| *Is that what others in my team make?* | *Seeking to learn more* |
| Not really. Why? | Curious about the question |
| *I just wanted to know if I would be paid similarly to them. Can you help me understand why I would make less?* | *Sharing an interest in fairness and asking for legitimacy* |
| Well, what can I say, it is our company policy. | Artificial limit |
| *What is the policy exactly?* | *Asking to learn* |
| Sorry?! Oh, the policy is... The policy requires that new hires receive a lower salary for six months until they prove themselves and their fit with the team. | Surprised that the artificial limit was not enough to move on. Sharing the policy details |
| *What I am hearing is that the company wants to treat their internal people fairly by only paying newcomers a similar salary if they prove their performance. Is that right?* | *Seeking clarification on the perceived underlying interest (fairness & performance)* |
| Never thought of it. It is just our policy. But now that you put it that way, I would say that this is about right. I believe that this is how people feel internally. | Confirming that the assumption was probably correct |
| *I want to respect your policy and your interest in treating people fairly. Since we already agreed that I bring more experience than the average new hire, I just do not believe that this policy is fair to me. How could we adjust the policy to my particular case?* | *Expressing respect for their interest behind the limit. Inviting them to think about options while arguing that the case is not applicable to him. Arguing that the same interest applies to him* |
| I agree with you that you are more experienced, but I don't know what we could do. I have never done it before. If it were up to me, I would be glad to pay you more. | Agreeing with the non-applicability but going back to the inevitability of the limit. Trying to show empathy |
| *I am glad to see that you agree that I deserve more and still I respect that you want to follow your policy. I thought of an exam or another way for me to prove my ability more quickly. This would allow us to show that I am a different case and thus that the policy is not applicable to me. Maybe if we could have a few team members test my knowledge to see if I am up to their expectations?* | *Insisting on respecting the policy's and his interests. Generating options tailored to respect what he learned from the policy's interests while advancing his own (Pareto improvement)* |
| That could be done... I am not sure. Let me check with a couple of people and come back to you. | Checking commitment before making a mistake. Changing a limit alone is risky (see next part on narrow scope) |

**Table 11.9**

Negotiating artificial limits through Pareto improvements

While the resource constraint normally afflicts all negotiators, artificial limits may favor one party. This can instill a power distance if we are not careful when moving around the limit. If to overcome the artificial limit we call it unreasonable, they may perceive it as an attack. And if they feel attached to or identify with the artificial limit, they can become protective of it. We undermine the "we" mentality over an "us vs. them" relationship. Instead, we can claim its inappropriateness, while expressing respect for its rationale.

Being man-made, artificial limits can always be negotiated no matter how intractable or absolute they may seem. There may be high costs in time and effort to tailor options around a policy, but probably less for a precedent. At the very least, we can choose to continue creating value or not depending on our required investment and expected return.

## Narrow Scope

A narrow scope is an external value-creation enemy because it **limits the number of options we can generate, commit to or implement**. When negotiators come with a self- or externally-imposed, narrow mandate, value creation habitually gives way to positional bargaining. So not only do we not think of many options, we also restrain from committing to them for lack of preparation or mandate. To commit to options suggested by them beyond our mandate is a great risk.

When faced with a narrow scope, negotiators will fear or avoid going beyond it for lack of authority or preparation. This limits the view of the negotiation possibilities and reduces information exchange and understanding. Many value-creation attempts fail precisely because of a narrow scope on the other side of the table. How can we manage their narrow scope towards value creation?

The narrow scope may be self-imposed, if the negotiator comes with a positional assumption of the negotiation. Bringing new issues and interests while persuading them of the value to do so can expand the scope. However, when the narrow scope is an externally-imposed narrow mandate, the challenge is more complicated, though still manageable.

Figure 11.9 represents the value the parties can create in a negotiation. It separates them in "pies" related to their original scopes. The first (Scope) is consistent with the negotiator's original mandate. Most options within that pie can be accepted and committed to as the negotiator will feel safe, entitled and prepared to do so.

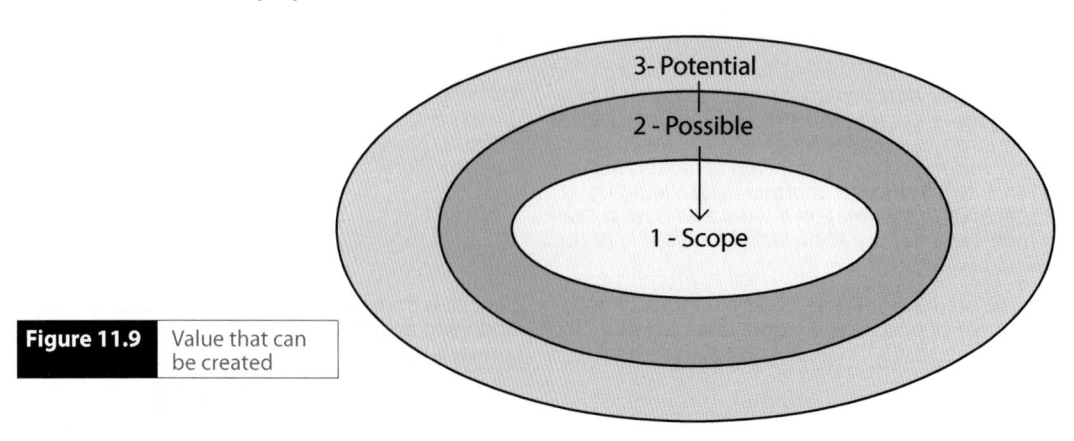

**Figure 11.9** Value that can be created

As negotiators create more value, they eventually go beyond their scope to enter the realm of what could be possible. Their successful information exchange and value focus has allowed option generation beyond the originally expected scope. These options clearly add value while still being directly relevant to the scope. Some negotiators that are afraid of hierarchy or mistakes may resist. Many, however, will go along if they see the benefits. But then we have another problem.

Even if negotiators generate options of possible value, how can they guarantee that their agreement will hold inside their organizations? If they had a narrow mandate and went beyond it, they cannot guarantee anything. They may have a good relationship with or a good understanding of their boss's or client's interests. They may feel comfortable to argue internally for the added value of the possible options. But they cannot guarantee that their agreement will be accepted and implemented as they do not have the final authority.

In this case, we can help them continue with the option-generation exercise by reducing the commitment pressure. We can do this in two ways. First, we try as much as possible to tailor options to guarantee the fulfilment of the scope. Notice that at times it can be hard to independently satisfy narrow scopes without entering into positional bargaining. Despite our best efforts within the scope, we may still need the value within the possible options.

Then, we commit to a process to take a deal based on the possible options that need internal approval. If time allows, we can offer to give them time to renegotiate their mandate internally. These processes give negotiators time to prepare and internally negotiate whatever is needed to agree on the new ideas. If nothing works, we can always commit to the best possible deal within the scope.

If conducted well, many negotiators will at least entertain the conversation about possible options. However, in the Potential pie, most will feel that the negotiation has gone too far. Potential options are those that potentially generate value to the parties but are normally far removed from the original scope. An example of how all three pies relate to the two competing companies' conversation above:

- **Scope** – Research information exchange
- **Possible** – A more formal collaboration agreement involving exchange of personnel and equipment
- **Potential** – Initiate merger talks about parts of their businesses

And yet when potential options are discussed, it is because the negotiators probably created a uniquely successful negotiation environment: one where they can find value while most others cannot. As risky as it is to commit to these options, to throw them away would also be irresponsible. After all, negotiators are value investigators with the responsibility to bring value to their organizations at the lowest risk.

We frame potential options as early opportunities for further investigation. Otherwise, fear of the unknown can freeze us. The risk of making a serious mistake and committing our organization or client to something unrealistic can create serious problems. Again, we commit to a tentative process of escalating the ideas to our superiors. Then we see if it is worth the time to study, prepare and negotiate them further. Finally, when faced with a narrow scope, we commit to the substance within the scope, but only to a process beyond the scope.

In sum, value creation helps us generate options to maximize the potential and available value in a negotiation. To create value, we tailor options into the best possible package that will also help us to manage complexity. We finally look out for the value-creation enemies that push us directly into value claiming and early commitments. With these steps, we will have done our best to maximize the available value and are ready to claim.

# summary

Value creation transforms resources into options to better satisfy our interests. Value is created from the resources negotiators bring to the table. Value creation happens through:

1. An increase in the amount of resources available; or
2. A more efficient use, combination or allocation of available resources.

Any option with the potential to satisfy an interest can create value. Value creation is different from value claiming in that it increases the value available, but not the value secured by each negotiator. The value-creation effort seeks to increase the value potential (interests) plus the value availability (options).

## Creating Value

1. Tailoring options to interests
   a. Mutual gains (originate from Common, shared or joint interests)
      i. Economies of scale or scope – The more we do, the more we get
      ii. Dovetailing – Combining complementarities
      iii. Expand the pie – Adding new resources

   b. Trades (originate from Different interests such as reward, risk and time preferences)
      i. Non-specific compensation – Paying for what we want
      ii. Logrolling – Trade low- for high-priority value
      iii. Cost cutting – Reducing their cost

   c. Multi-issue trades (a subsection of Trades)
      i. Even swaps – Converting all options to a single currency
      ii. Points – Giving points to each option to clarify preferences
      iii. Bundles – Bundling options into packages of similar value

   d. Contingent clauses (originate from Conflicting or opposing interests)
      i. Conditional exchanges – If A, then B
      ii. Bridging – Innovative solution (creativity)

2. Value in packages
   a. Limit the claiming side of options (structural vs. specific options)
   b. Sequencing (value creation potential, veil of ignorance, gain/loss frame & dependence)
   c. Making commitments tentatively

## Overcoming Value-Creation Enemies

1. Internal value-creation enemies (intrinsic to every negotiation)
   a. Power distance – Focus on value creation first, then value-claiming
   b. Trading between negotiations – Prefer trades over concessions
   c. Information asymmetry – Separate generation from evaluation of options

2. External value-creation enemies (specific to particular negotiations)
   a. Resource constraint – Absolute or relative resource limitation
   b. Artificial limits – Human-made limitation
   c. Narrow scope – Negotiation-specific limitation (scope, possible and potential)

# questions

## Easy

1. What is value creation and value claiming?
2. How do we focus on and create value?
3. What are mutual gains, trades and contingencies?
4. What is the difference between economies of scale, economies of scope and dovetailing?
5. What are the enemies of value creation?
6. What are the differences between relative resource constraints and artificial limits?

## Medium

1. Does value creation really create value?
2. What is the difference between internal and external enemies?
3. Why is complexity damaging for value creation?
4. Choose three value-creation enemies and give at least one solution for each.
5. What are three things to do to manage complexity in value creation?
6. What is the worst external value-creation enemy? Why?

## Difficult

1. Please explain the following statement: "Concessions are the soft bargainer's negotiation tool of choice."
2. In a salary negotiation, what should we discuss first: salary or benefits? Why?
3. Are concessions in general negative? Why? Why are reactive concessions worse?
4. Do trades need to be of equal value to inspire a dialogue pattern? Why?
5. What is the problem with the following questions: "Will I be able to get the bigger share? How can I get the bigger share?"
6. If after agreeing on a tentative commitment, the other party decides to come back to it suggesting an option that makes you worse off. What should you do? If they ask why you want a commitment to be tentative, how should you respond?

# scenarios

## Easy

After reading the text below on insurance, determine whether it is a trade or a contingent option and explain why:

*In a car insurance contract, we may pay instalments all our life and never need it. Still, that contract gave us the peace of mind we needed and minimized the cash-flow risk of fixing the car if something big happened. That is value for us. Of course, the value for them is making more money than the risk they believe (and exhaustively calculate) to run. Insurance companies are better prepared financially to pay in one go what could bankrupt an individual. They can take that risk. Most individuals cannot.*

## Medium

Figure 11.10 shows what may happen with the Pareto frontier when we add new resources to the negotiation. We basically push the potential of the negotiation forward and thus the Pareto frontier as well. Do you agree or disagree with this statement and figure? Do more resources push the Pareto frontier forward or just help us to reach the frontier? (Consider the discussion between potential versus available value).

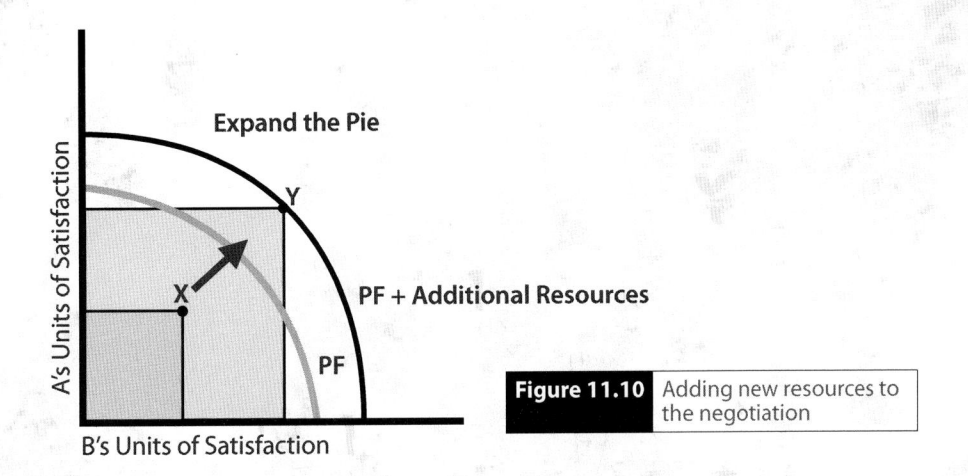

**Figure 11.10** Adding new resources to the negotiation

## Difficult

A. When we share an interest or put an option on the table first, we are leading the process by example.
   1. Aren't we making a concession even if proactively? Why?
   2. What could we say or do to minimize the risk?
   3. Should we never make concessions?
   4. When could concessions be least risky?

B. Some negotiation experts suggest proposing many mini-packages or making multiple offers simultaneously in multi-issue negotiations. Do you agree? Why?

# 12 Value Claiming

**Learning Objectives:**
- What value claiming is
- How value claiming is different from bargaining
- What some famous bargaining concepts and risks are
- What the role of meaning and focal points is
- How I can use legitimacy to claim value, not numbers
- How do we open; with whom, when and where?

Value claiming happens when the parties negotiate how much of the existing or created value they will take. As mentioned in the previous chapter, value claiming happens when an option increases value to one party at the other's expense. It is also called the "distributive phase", since it is when the parties distribute the value among themselves.

To claim value well, we need to understand its inherent risks and how to best manage them. These risks are a consequence of value claiming's proximity to bargaining. We look at elements of bargaining theory that supposedly help but often actually hinder value claiming. It is only by resisting bargaining that we can claim maximum value at minimum risk. Finally, we recommend the value negotiation approach to value claiming.

## The Most Dangerous Step?

After winning his lawsuit against Inson, an insurance company, Magnus decided to negotiate. Both sides knew that appeals could delay payments by another 10–12 months. Since Magnus wished to be paid faster, he invited them to negotiate.

- Thanks for inviting us to negotiate! We are ready to offer you 50% of your claim just to get this behind us.
- *50%?! This is absurd! It is insulting. I won the lawsuit; you can't offer me 50%.*
- Well, this is our offer. Do you like it or not?
- *Of course not!*
- So what is your counter offer?
- *90% and not one cent less.*
- You've got to be kidding me! I thought that you were ready to negotiate. With this kind of number, it is better to just go to court.
- *If this is what you want to do, just remember that I will win at the end of the day.*
- That is what you think! Even if you win, we can make your life miserable until then.
- *Am I supposed to get scared?*
- Okay then, 60% and not one cent more.
- *That was funny! I thought I heard you say 60%, when I said 90%.*
- Come on! Do you even want a deal? I made an effort here. The ball is in your court now.
- *Okay, okay! I am ready to go to 85%, but just to solve this fast.*
- No, you don't get it. 85% is impossible. Let me just say it plain and simple so even you can understand: it is NOT going to happen!
- *You asked me to move and I moved, and now you are complaining. Maybe I should go back to 90% then.*
- You can't be serious. You can't do that! You know what? I am not going to stay here if you are going to play games with me.
- *Games! I am playing games?! You were the one who lost the lawsuit and you come here and offer me 50%.*

265

- 60% now! And remember that you were the one who begged us to come to the table to negotiate. So we are doing you a favor here. To show once again that we are willing to help, I would exceptionally offer 65%.
- Seriously, you should become a comedian. If you were not such a sad individual, you would be making me laugh until tomorrow.
- I demand you to retract what you just said. That is unacceptable! Do you want to make a deal or not?
- Okay then. So that we can both go home I can offer you 82%.
- Excuse me?!
- 82%. Any problem?...

---

With exchanges of threats and positions marking the broken and aggressive communication, the result is a damaged and antagonistic relationship. It is no surprise the negotiation above did not go well. The parties may still reach a deal, most likely a compromise of sorts, yet the negotiation may also break off any minute now. Welcome to the value claiming phase.

As we approach value claiming, it feels like the end of our journey is in sight. Most of the work has been done. The driving is almost over. And yet, most car accidents happen within a few blocks of people's homes. While the accident rate is constant per mile, statistically speaking we drive more often, and thus more miles, close to home. So, it is no surprise that we will have more accidents in absolute terms, where we drive most often.

Negotiators are similar to drivers in this aspect. When claiming, we are closest to a deal and it is easy to underestimate the dangers of the value-claiming moment. Having done all the hard work to build a bridge, discover and generate value, what could possibly go wrong now? Simple as it is, the answer does not make dealing with it any easier: value claiming resembles bargaining too closely. Most of us spend most of our negotiation time bargaining and thus value claiming.

In fact, bargaining is all about value claiming. The absence of a bridge and a value-creation process limit bargaining to value claiming. Bargaining already starts with rigid, specific options or positions to claim maximum value. These positions are normally extreme and far apart, thus do not allow for a deal at this stage. Instead, the trading of concessions begins and leads to a compromise or, in the worst case, a walk away. Bargaining, more so than negotiation, is one big value-claiming process.

The danger of value claiming lies in its resemblance to bargaining. Since most negotiators know some bargaining theory, they struggle to resist both the temptation and their bargaining conditioning. Associating value claiming and bargaining inevitably leads to a win-lose negotiation. After all, aren't both processes about taking value away from the other side? Fortunately, the answer is "No"!

Luckily, the dialogue above is but one way to claim value. Not all value claiming is bargaining. Bargaining is a famous value-claiming process but a poor one at that because it is filled with win-lose risks. Still, when claiming, most negotiators feel that they are in a fight for value, because that is what most end up doing.

Even win-win negotiators frequently fail to avoid bargaining while claiming value. Indeed, we could argue that value claiming is the most difficult part of a negotiation. For these reasons, it is vital to identify and then counter bargaining risks and temptations while value claiming. There are other, better ways to claim value.

# Is It All About Numbers?

Bargaining theories have concepts to help claim value, i.e., bargaining concepts. Though some concepts help us think about value claiming, they are less helpful in practice.

Bargaining concepts try to reveal the negotiation parameters and boundaries from all sides of the table. Such parameters supposedly help negotiators delineate the perfect outcome, as if out of a mathematical optimization exercise. This exercise in turn allegedly gives negotiators a clear target to pursue. The boundaries apparently allow negotiators to know where to use maximum power and thus claim the most value.

> **POINT OF INTEREST**
>
> **Price vs. Value**
> *"Price is what you pay. Value is what you get." Warren Buffett*
> Giving the above quote a different spin: price is a singular number, while value is the satisfaction of different interests. Thus price is positional and singular, whereas value creates an idea of a package coherent with our value-creation approach. Even if you go into bargaining, thinking about reservation value instead of reservation price helps to keep the value focus.

Bargaining concepts are somewhat helpful in win-lose instances, when power separates the winner from the loser. But even then, they have significant limits. Bargaining concepts fail to impact the outcome much or are difficult to define. In addition, since negotiations do not need to be win-lose, bargaining concepts become even less useful. Bargaining's adoption of a win-lose stance and increase in power may not increase value, but risks.

Though not really effective in most instances, it helps to know what concepts bargainers pay attention to. These reference points reveal what bargainers want or expect from the negotiation. Knowing their focus, we can better understand the value they expect. Then we can better influence them, as we compare their expectations with win-win processes and their superior outcomes.

## Reservation and Aspiration Prices

Most bargainers who prepare for a negotiation think about their worst and best desired outcomes. Thus, two main bargaining references are the reservation and aspiration prices.

The reservation price is a negotiator's indifference price or walk-away point. If offered, it makes us equally likely to close the deal or walk away. As it is just one value unit away from us leaving, it is important to know where this point lies.

If the reservation price is our walk-away point, is it the same as the BATNA? No. Our reservation price may be higher, equal to or lower than our BATNA. For example, someone offers an "insulting" price that creates a terrible precedent. We walk away since the offer was below our reservation price though we may have no alternatives (BATNA = zero). Conversely, we may accept an offer lower than our BATNA as transition costs make it worse-off to walk away.

Many negotiators ask: "How can I figure out their reservation price?" Knowledge of their reservation price enables us to make the lowest acceptable offer to claim maximum value with minimum risk. Many bargainers use mathematical models to predict the other's reservation price. Fortunately or unfortunately, these are rarely successful.

Asking questions or making extreme offers can reveal someone's reservation price, though at a cost. When asked, few share their reservation price to avoid being at a disadvantage. The reason is simple: If we share the least we are willing to accept, what is their incentive to pay us more? Extreme offers surface the reservation price but resistance emerges to prevent the offer from going any further. It risks coming across as a power move, damage the relationship and the negotiation.

The aspiration price is a realistic expectation of the best possible outcome. Though it creates positive thinking and a vision of success, it is often seen as a stretch and unrealistic goal. Our aspiration price should always be equal to or beyond what we want. This, however, may at times mean that we want everything, leaving them with nothing. Is having them accept nothing a realistic scenario? If not, how little can they accept? Without value creation, the zero-sum becomes reality and knowing exactly how little they would accept is indeed a difficult task. Consequently, aspiration prices are seen as hard to estimate or reach instead of being a goal to realistically work towards.

## Zone of Possible Agreement

The Zone of Possible Agreement (ZOPA) is an important concept for negotiation, but even more so for bargaining. In bargaining, ZOPA represents the distance between the parties' reservation prices (Figure 12.1). It is the difference between the maximum one wants to pay minus the minimum the other is willing to accept. For example:

| | |
|---|---|
| Buyer's reservation price | = $100 |
| - Seller's reservation price | = – $80 |
| ZOPA | = $20 |

A ZOPA of $20 indicates room for a deal and the amount up for value claiming. So if we close the deal at $90, it means that each of us claims $10. If however we close at $100, then the seller claims the entire $20 available.

This distance is important for bargainers to anticipate limits and maximize value claiming with minimum risk. If they know the ZOPA, they know how much to push us without forcing us to walk away. If they know our reservation value, they can offer us the minimum acceptable to claim more value. However, the ZOPA could be reversed:

| Buyer's reservation price | = $80 |
|---|---|
| - Seller's reservation price | = – $100 |
| ZOPA | = – $20 |

In this case, the ZOPA of -$20 means there is no ZOPA and thus no room for a deal independently of value-claiming abilities. As the minimum acceptable exceeds the highest willingness to pay, no matching possibility exists and thus no deal can be made.

Bargainers who anticipate no ZOPA avoid entering a futile negotiation exercise. This, however, leads to a fatalist view of negotiations where they have a life of their own, independent from the parties. Bargainers would then think of ZOPA in a rigid way: there either is a ZOPA or not. Of course, we can understand such an assumption since bargainers negotiate through positions that are supposed to be immovable.

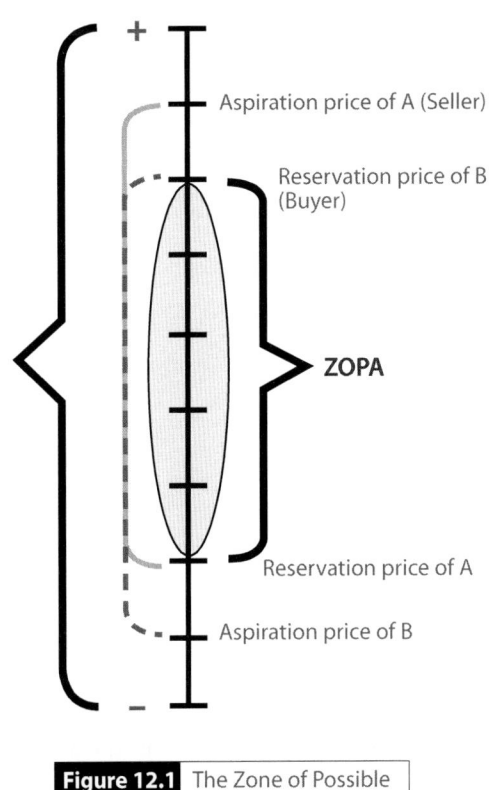

**Figure 12.1** The Zone of Possible Agreement

## POINT OF INTEREST

**ZOPA vs. Zhopa**

The Russian word "zhopa" is phonetically similar to ZOPA and can create serious confusion. "Zhopa" has two meanings in Russian:

1. Butt, buttocks, behind
2. Bad, disastrous
   - It was bad at first, and then became full zhopa. [Complete disaster]
   - It's just plain zhopa. [Describing situation]
   - Life is like a zebra: white stripe, black stripe, white stripe, black stripe, and then zhopa.

It is rather difficult for Russians to associate ZOPA with the Zone of Possible Agreement. So be careful when suggesting to expand the ZOPA in Russia.

How do we really know the ZOPA before the negotiation? We don't. There are no good or easy ways to really know their reservation price. The estimation of the ZOPA before and even during the negotiation is usually a guesstimate. The ZOPA can only be accurately calculated if reservation prices are shared, which no one wants to do.

However, in any win-win approach, the ZOPA is not assumed to be fixed. Both the ZOPA and the reservation price can be influenced. If we discover and generate extra value, they may pay more (or charge less) to get it. In the process, we change the reservation price and indirectly the ZOPA.

The ZOPA can expand, but it can also shrink. After receiving a better offer than our reservation price, we may still ask for more if someone treated us poorly. The increase on our reservation price due to bad relationship, for example, can reduce the ZOPA.

For value negotiation, the ZOPA represents the value up for claiming. It is a dynamic concept that changes based on the parties' negotiation moves. The idea of "no ZOPA" is one that a value negotiator will always challenge. Within a bargaining context, clearly no extra value is created and the ZOPA does not improve. However, with good value moves, a negotiator may create a ZOPA where initially none existed.

## Opening Offer and the Negotiation Dance

Higher reservation or aspiration prices have little if any impact on claiming more value. What actually impacts value claiming is the opening offer. The opening offer is the first specific option a party offers, normally with numbers, to the other. It rewards ambition by helping the party that opened to claim more value. Thus, the higher our opening offer, the more we are likely to claim.

The opening offer premium comes from anchoring. Anchoring happens when a negotiator shares a number and the other cannot correctly discount away from it. The anchoring power comes from how we, human beings, imperfectly make decisions. Once on the table, we have difficulty correcting or ignoring even an unreasonable number.

In negotiation, anchoring mostly happens during the opening offer. Once we are anchored, we are at risk of offering even more than what is reasonable. The first to share a number has the advantage of anchoring the other.

An example of anchoring is a negotiator making a $1 million opening offer, knowing that $500K is a reasonable price. The counter-party may have initially found $400K–500K to be reasonable, but after anchoring, starts to believe that any possible deal will now be $500K or higher. The negotiator influenced the counter-party towards a higher offer by anchoring the opening offer.

In bargaining, after the opening offer is put on the table, there is normally a counter offer. The opening offer ($200K) and the counter offer ($60K) are normally the most extreme claiming moves. The parties go back and forth with offers and counter offers as if they were in a dance. Every time a party makes a new offer, the other makes a concession and shaves some value off their previous offer. In bargaining theory, this exchange of offers and concessions is called the "negotiation dance" (Figure 12.2).

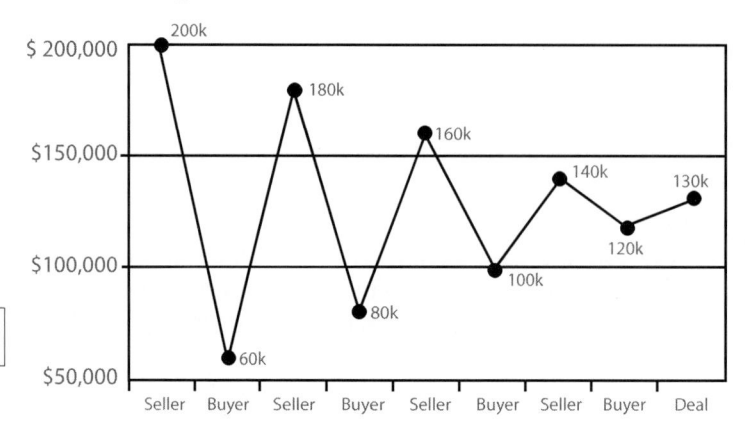

**Figure 12.2** The negotiation dance

Because this dance relies on concessions, bargaining experts recommend the "noble art of losing face" or preparing to retreat. This means preparing a justification for each concession, which requires us to anticipate the moves they will make. Though this preparation allows us to be flexible, it also has us think in terms of giving value away.

In addition, the negotiation dance demonstrates how portraying difficult behaviors can work in bargaining. To claim more value, bargainers have incentives to lie, be rigid and positional, manipulate, etc. Below are some additional examples:

**Negotiation dance #2** – (Figure 12.3) The buyer makes smaller concessions than the seller, however the seller is reducing the concession size with every move. Who is signaling more that their limit is approaching?

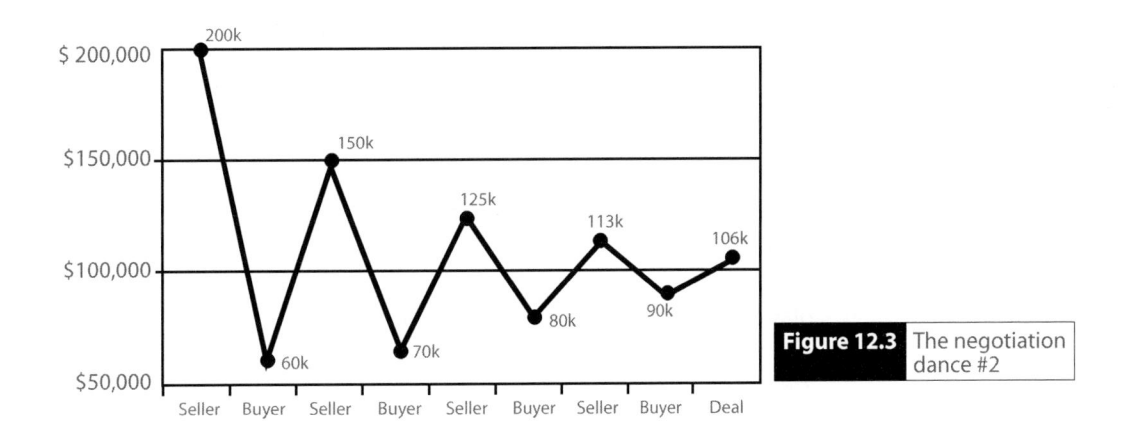

**Figure 12.3** The negotiation dance #2

**Negotiation dance #3** – (Figure 12.4) The buyer is being very positional and not moving from the $60K offer. Meanwhile, the seller is coming down quite rapidly.

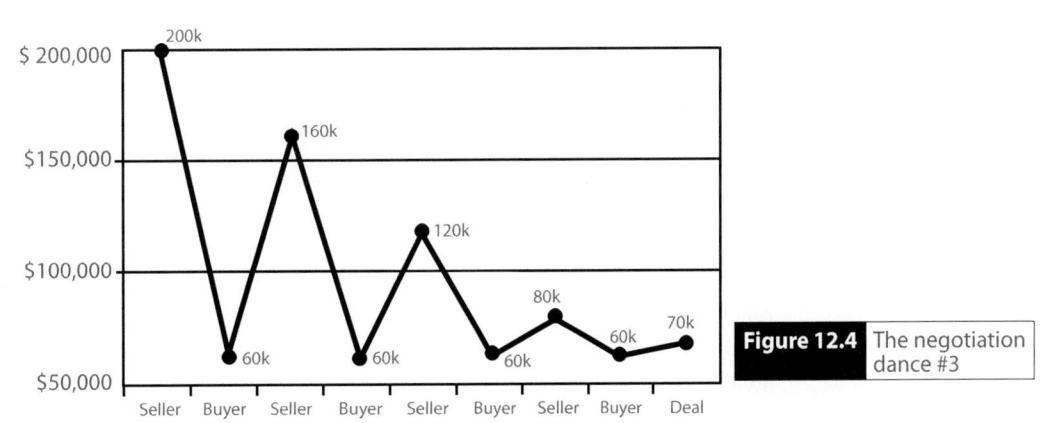

**Figure 12.4** The negotiation dance #3

**Negotiation dance #4** – (Figure 12.5) Both buyer and seller are being very positional and no one knows if the other will ever concede anything. Both seem to be waiting for the other one to crack. What if no one does?

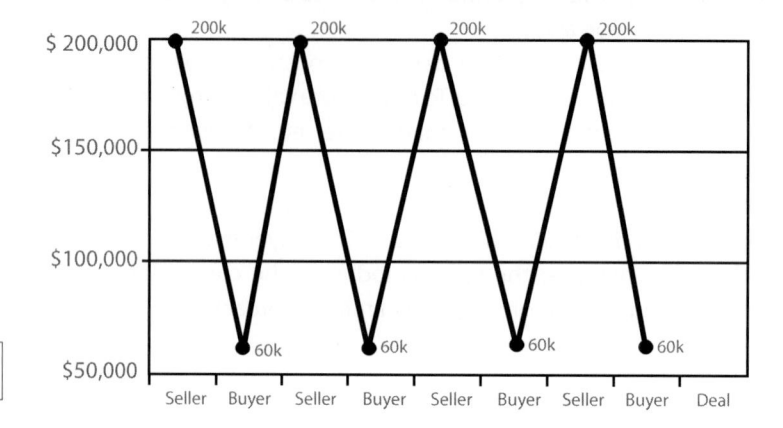

**Figure 12.5** The negotiation dance #4

We could ask at the end of all these dances: who is winning? And no one would be able to answer for sure. Additionally, every time we move in the negotiation dance, we send a negative message. The offer we just moved away from was not firm; thus who can tell if our new offer is? The practice of retreating through concessions weakens previous and future offers leading to a potential overall loss of credibility. Thus, the negotiation dance is a dangerous game to play and seemingly the main way to bargain.

These dances, the reservation and aspiration prices, opening offer and ZOPA are all about numbers. If negotiation, or bargaining for that matter, were indeed just about numbers, why not let computers deal with them? After all, they have much better processing power and accuracy. However, we do not leave value claiming to computers, because it is not just about numbers. A number alone means nothing. Negotiations are about what people want. When we forget that, we are left bargaining on numbers with their respective risks.

## Value-Claiming Risks

After centuries of bargaining, centuries of experience and literature were collected. Lots of bargaining tactics were devised to manipulate one side so that the other can get what they want. Why discuss bargaining tricks here? Because they can be used against us.

Do these tricks work? Certainly. Distilled after centuries of practice, bargainers have a collective knowledge of tricks that can work really well. Worse, we may not even be aware of them working. Worse still, they may work even if we are aware or expect them.

However, bargaining tricks come with a price. One is the invitation of resistance; another is the advantage it gives to the party that is better versed in them. In sum, while we can use tricks, they generate more risks than we need to run. When adopting them, we discard the JVP frame for a lower value win-lose battle frame. Fortunately, there are better ways to claim value than through bargaining tricks. For now, we will explore the more common tricks so we can be prepared when bargainers attempt them on us.

These bargaining tricks play into a win-lose mentality, basic flaws or short-cuts in our decision-making. Bargainers, hard and soft, exploit the shortcomings in our thinking to force us into a decision that is in their best interest, not ours. These shortcomings fall into three categories:

- Win-lose fallacies
- Decision-making biases (flaws)
- Judgmental heuristics (short-cuts)

Bargaining tricks have another perverse effect: they can backfire. They are a double-edged sword that can hurt all parties and thus another reason to beware of bargaining.

## Win-Lose Fallacies

A win-lose perception is the value-claiming shortcoming mentioned the most in this book. Certain value-claiming moves or assumptions generate either a zero-sum mentality or put negotiators into direct competition. These fallacies misdirect the negotiators' focus towards bargaining and motivate poor value-claiming behavior.

**Zero-sum mentality** – Motivated by the negotiators' assumptions of limited resources; can enhance the assumption that the pie is fixed and negative impacts of information asymmetry.
- **Mythical fixed pie** fools us into believing that the negotiation is zero-sum. Value creation becomes impossible. The only value source is seen to be claiming.
  - *There is nothing to be done here! It is all about price.*
- **Information asymmetry** creates the illusion of having all the information and overconfidence when claiming. It reduces learning and thus value creation.
  - *I know exactly what I am doing. I have tried everything already.*

**Direct competition** – Motivated by the negotiators' competitive drives.
- **Irrational escalation** has negotiators work hard to avoid losing. They invest resources in an ever-increasing fight, where the value goal is all but forgotten, often failing to recognize sunk costs.
- **Winner's curse** has negotiators want to win so badly that they do whatever it takes. They may win but then spend more than they won.
- **Comparative gains** instill jealousy over the other's gains even in an environment of abundance. Negotiators claim competitively just to have more than the other.
- **Reactive devaluation** has a party undervalue an offer just because it came from the counter-party. The negotiator fears a trick and thus keeps bargaining for more. The same offer would have been accepted if made by a neutral party.

# Decision-Making Biases

Decision-making or cognitive biases occur when information is presented in ways that fool or prevent us from thinking straight. As if our brains were short-circuited, biases blindside us into making bad decisions and consequently bad value-claiming moves. Anchoring, already mentioned above, is such a bias. Others include:

- **Framing** is like a painting frame, a movie soundtrack or lighting in a show. It highlights or subdues a particular message to change its meaning. E.g.:
    - **Losses vs. gains** – People are more likely to do something or take risks to avert a loss rather than to accumulate new gains.
    - **Short vs. long horizons** – Tendency to prefer good things in the short term and bad things in the long term.
    - **Small vs. big steps** – People are more likely to make a series of small concessions than a big one even if they add up to the same value.

- **Sunk costs** are costs that once incurred, cannot be recovered. They have us believe that additional investment will save our previous poor one.
    - *I know it's a bad movie, but I will watch it anyhow as I already bought the ticket.*

- **Overconfidence**, like an exaggerated optimism, has us overestimate our abilities (or theirs) to deliver on unrealistic or overly risky tasks.
    - *Committing to a narrow deadline, a tight budget or an overly strict diet.*

- **Availability bias** makes recent, emotional or extreme information play a bigger role in our memory than other equally valid but less vivid data.
    - *Since a plane I took almost crash landed once, I became afraid of flying though I know there are many more car than plane fatalities.*

- **Knowledge curse** has us assume that the meaning in our heads is the same as theirs. It misleads us into assuming we understood them and reduces our learning.
    - *Say no more! I know exactly what you are thinking.*

Framing can catch us unaware due to our limited processing power. If we identify a frame that goes against our interests, our awareness is already half the answer to neutralizing it. However, since we can frame a single situation in a number of ways, it is hard to be alert to all possible framings at all times especially since many frames we use stem from deeply imbedded cultural values.

Decision-making biases do lead us to poor value-claiming decisions. So it is reasonable to ask why we have them. Why do most human beings seem to be hardwired with them? Are they just flaws in our blueprint or do they serve a better purpose? Indeed, there are two main hypotheses on biases: first, they are just a human imperfection as we were not created to process so much information; second, they are adaptive mechanisms helpful for the survival of the species.

How can these biases mislead us and yet be an evolutionary survival mechanism? Actually, they are probably good for humans as a group, but not as good for the individual in isolation. Evolution cares for the survival of the species, not for its members. In other words, while these biases may work on average, every now and then they will push us onto making mistakes.

As an example, overconfidence is what encourages entrepreneurs to face, and a few to beat, incredibly adverse odds (an 50% failure rate). They create new companies that fuel our economy as needed for the survival of our society and species. If everyone feared these odds, no one would ever become an entrepreneur. If that happened, our society would wither and our species, as we know it, would risk disappearing. While the success achieved can be outstanding, the evolutionary bill equals 50% of entrepreneurs failing due to our collective overconfidence.

## Judgmental Heuristics

Professor Cialdini, in his book *Influence*, describes six ways to influence people. Each one exploits what he calls "judgmental heuristics" or "decision short-cuts."

Decision short-cuts are different from decision-making biases in that they are not flaws, but just short-cuts. As short-cuts, they facilitate and speed up our hundreds of daily decisions. Like intuition, they clue us into decisions without too much exploration or thinking. They help individuals make many good decisions, while decision-making biases often lead us into poor ones. Unfortunately, as short-cuts, they are still prone to mistakes and vulnerable to exploitation.

Most of these short-cuts seem to be the result of centuries of social evolution and are likely common to nearly all cultures. Many are already used extensively and consciously by salespeople, marketers, negotiators and other professionals in roles of influence.

- **Reciprocation** is the sense of obligation to pay back someone who did something for us. The basis of most social interactions, positive reciprocation can be a pillar of successful win-win negotiations. However, reciprocation is geared towards the gesture, not the amount. Its poor sense of proportion may have us reciprocate in larger amounts than what we were given.
  - *When you have given nothing, ask for nothing. (Albanian proverb)*

- **Social proof** has people believe that something is good or important just because of the number of people who adopt or pay attention to it.
  - *A full restaurant is probably a good restaurant.*

- **Consistency** is an inherent desire of human beings for things to come together and make sense. It represents the power of a promise and the dislike of a surprise.
  - *You said you were going to help me and now you are backing off.*

- **Liking** causes us to be more persuaded by the people we like as if it were the same as trust. However, who we like most can make mistakes or be less knowledgeable.
  - *I do not believe him, but since you are also saying it I will think about it.*

- **Authority** leads people to be persuaded based on someone's stature. Experts are often accorded automatic credibility, even when their success rate is doubtful or when talking about issues unrelated to their expertise.
  - *Five out of seven dentists use Toothex dental paste.*

- **Scarcity** creates the fear of resource limitations and a sense of urgency. Scarcity has people react on impulse and fear then hurry into a decision.
  - *"Today only — Super Sale — 50% discount on everything!"*

The above are just samples of the different value-claiming risks, which are often used as bargaining tricks. We do not need to memorize them all, just develop a sense for what they are or look like. To even entertain the risks above is to accept and invite them into our negotiation. Instead, we want to invite a value negotiation process to protect us from them. Good value claiming moves the negotiation in a completely different direction.

# Claim Value, not Numbers!

It is hard to ignore how bargaining terms and tricks reduce value claiming to numbers only. And yet numbers can mean a variety of things: fair, reasonable, appropriate or just the opposite. A number is just the output of an equation and it depends on the underlying rationale for its validity.

Because of our positional inclinations, we may limit our negotiation and our claiming to numbers. However, a number alone means nothing. Yet as humans, we attach meaning to everything we come in contact with. We attribute meaning to numbers which then represent things such as value, fairness or respect. Since we want and perceive different things, the same number may carry different meanings for each negotiator.

Let's explain: $10,000 can be a lot of money or not enough, depending on the situation, people or intention. Selling a product for $10,000 could be seen as fair or unfair, depending on the country we are in. The price may not change, but its meaning and thus the perception of fairness might. It is this perception that ultimately determines the value claimed and if the price will be accepted.

Numbers alone only give us positions, but little in terms of value or meaning. To have real value, a number needs to mean something for us. Thus to be persuasive and value-focused, we should not limit ourselves to numbers. While we might negotiate numbers, we are really negotiating reasons and meanings, and thus value.

## A Journey for Meaning

As we negotiate, we seek numbers or solutions that have a common and acceptable meaning to all parties. An important meaning most negotiators seek is legitimacy, which includes fairness. It is much easier to agree to a value-claiming proposal if the negotiators perceive it to be legitimate. Thus legitimate ideas, concepts, standards or arguments are likely to convey common meaning and become powerful focal points. These focal points can influence the value distribution to which negotiators will converge and agree.

# Focal Points

Focal points are numbers or ideas that people find obvious or natural. As a result, focal points have attractive and staying power. Negotiators converge to even implicit or unstated numbers or standards, unaware of their reasons for doing so. Imagine the focal point as a natural or obvious meeting point in a negotiation space. The easier the parties identify one, the easier it is for them to agree.

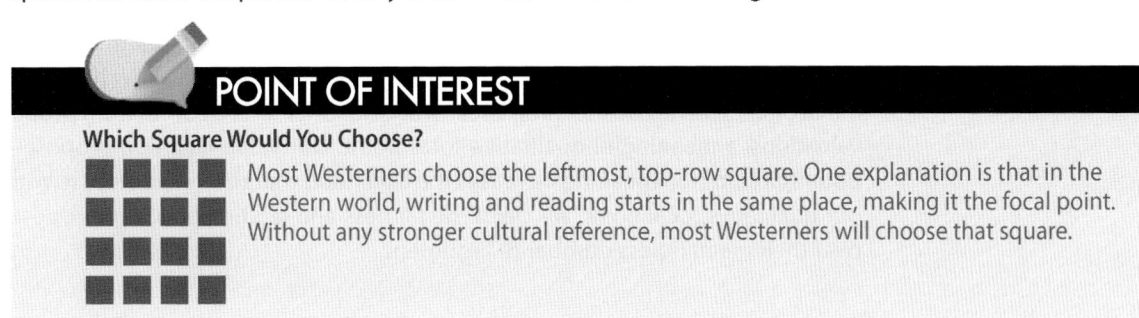

> **POINT OF INTEREST**
>
> **Which Square Would You Choose?**
>
> Most Westerners choose the leftmost, top-row square. One explanation is that in the Western world, writing and reading starts in the same place, making it the focal point. Without any stronger cultural reference, most Westerners will choose that square.

Since what is obvious or natural changes from person to person, focal points are not absolute concepts. They are cultural conventions internalized by negotiators, which then determine the meaning and power behind a specific focal point. Focal points can be very helpful if qualitative (standards), but are less so if exclusively quantitative (numbers).

## Quantitative Focal Points

Quantitative focal points are mainly numbers or quantitative conventions, and mostly associated with bargaining. For example, focal points impact concessions. Any negotiation dance generally moves in multiples of 1, 5 or 10 instead of 3, 4 or 7. A move from 100 to 103 instead of 105 would raise many questions. As the next focal point, a move straight to 105 would be expected and natural. Notice while a move to 105 may be less suspicious it is not necessarily logical or better for the negotiator.

These focal points also create an indirect anchoring effect as they explore the negotiator's own bargaining frames. The numbers or references work as anchors and become obvious, natural and almost unavoidable under the eyes of the negotiators. If they offer 100 and we 50, where are we likely to end up? Most people would answer 75! The focal point power has negotiators unconsciously move towards 75 as if it were the inevitable solution. However, both 100 and 50 can be arbitrary, potentially making 75 an unfair outcome.

## Qualitative Focal Points

Qualitative focal points however are extremely important to identify common ground between negotiators. As seen above, the number 75 alone is void of meaning and merely an anchor. However, 75 is the result of splitting the difference of the offers equally. As such, the parties may see themselves as equals and want to treat each other as such. Seeking the qualitative focal point behind the number surfaces the legitimacy used.

Legitimacy, or what is fair, right or appropriate in any given situation, can be a qualitative focal point. As a cultural construct, legitimacy gives numbers meaning and a reason to agree to them. Though 75 can be fair to most negotiators, some may disagree that a 50/50 split is fair for their particular situation. They may have brought more value to the table and desire a different outcome. Here, the legitimacy is not shared. The focal point cannot converge the parties to agree on how to distribute the value.

Negotiators can set the number 75 aside to focus on finding common qualitative focal points. If they argue a split in half is fair, we can show how their initial offer of 50 has no meaning. Meanwhile our offer of 100 comes from proper valuations, a meaningful qualitative focal point. Our value-claiming proposal's potential common meaning increases the likelihood that they will accept it. With our qualitative focal point, we claim the fairness and legitimacy of our proposal over their meaningless number or argument.

## This Little Thing Called "Fairness"

Several books have been written on fairness and we cannot possibly expect to exhaust the topic here. Still, we can cover the essential about fairness for value-claiming purposes in negotiation. For that, we use two very simple definitions of fairness for negotiation:

- An **outcome** is fair if negotiators believe now and later they got the value they deserved.
- A **process** is fair if negotiators believe they were properly involved and the right steps to distribute value were taken.

### Fair Process

Interestingly enough, people care more about a fair process. Of course, no one likes a bad outcome, yet most can live with it if they believe it came out of a fair process. Thus, a fair process can persuade negotiators about the fairness of the outcome, accepting that a bad outcome for them individually is still the right one for the negotiation.

But a fair process can do more than that. One day, Antonis decided to teach his two children a lesson in fairness. He bought one big slice of chocolate cake. He called his two children, put the cake on the table and said:

> If you can agree on how to split this cake, it is yours; otherwise, I will eat it alone. I will come back in a few minutes to hear your decision. I want no fights!

Dimitris and Nikolaos quickly started their negotiation:

> I am bigger, so I should get the bigger part.

> But you always get the bigger part. It is my turn now!

> I always get the bigger part, because I am bigger.

> That is not fair!

> Oh, yes it is. And if you do not like it, remember who protects you at school from your class bullies.

> That has nothing to do with this cake.

> Of course it has, you owe me.

> No! I like chocolate cake more than you do, so I should get more.

> Who said so! I also like it a lot.

> If you do not agree to give me more, I will tell Daddy that we did not have an agreement.

> If you do that, I will beat you up after he leaves!

Luckily, Antonis returns right on time and, as he expected, finds no decision. As the boys are about to start blaming each other, the father says:

> Dimitris will cut the cake into two pieces, but Nikolaos will choose first.

Dimitris stared at his father for a short while. He then stared at his younger brother. You could almost hear his brain spinning furiously. Then, without any warning, he disappeared into his room. Before Nikolaos got too excited that he would eat it all, Dimitris returned with a ruler. He approached the slice of cake and, with the aid of the ruler, cut it in half with surgical precision. The two portions came out identical in size.

Dimitris did not have a change of heart and decided to act fair. Neither did he read a negotiation book to understand that a fair process would increase his chances of closing the deal. His father created a procedure (i.e., I cut, you choose) that incentivized him to behave in a fair manner. There are several mathematical models to help negotiators perform fair divisions. Mostly complicated and dry, they may not properly take emotional value into account. In more controlled situations, however, they can be very useful.

More accessible to non-mathematical gurus are contingency options, which create similar incentives for negotiators to behave fairly. One benefit of fair procedures is that they take away the need for trust as they usually increase the cost of bad behavior. Fair procedures make people put forward their best behavior based on self-interest. Examples include when we agree to pay only on delivery, or when we require a guarantee for a default or a deposit to secure an opportunity.

Value negotiation sets, from the beginning, the basis for a fair value-claiming process. The JVP frame and the "we" mentality have negotiators treat each other as partners, instead of enemies. The dialogue pattern focuses on diagnostics and learning. Meanwhile, the process-leadership transparency enhances inclusiveness, consultation, shared control and coordination (as opposed to subordination).

Processes are believed to be fair if people perceive they were consulted and heard. If they had a reasonable chance to influence the final outcome, they may even accept unfavorable ones. Courts rely on fair processes to ensure peace and social cohesion. Not all court decisions are fair, but most are still accepted as part of a fair process. Still, a fair process that ends with a fair outcome is even better.

### Fair Outcome

When claiming value, we are normally trying to persuade others to give us what we want. Fairness is an important persuasion tool to claim value. In value claiming, we need to identify good and fair reasons why we deserve the value we want. Then we can explain the fairness of our proposal. If they believe it is fair, they are likely to agree even if it is not the best outcome for them.

The challenge is that for any given negotiation, there are several focal points of fairness. Our job is to find at least one persuasive to both sides, i.e., that has joint meaning. It is sad to see how often negotiators forget that and enter into a fruitless "fairness" debate:

> $100 is fair!
>
> No! $50 is fair!
>
> NO! $100 is fair!
>
> NO! $50 IS FAIR!
>
> NO! $100 IS FAIR!
>
> NO! $50 IS FAIR!

As if there were only one possible fair focal point in a negotiation. Many different outcomes may be fair in any given situation. Fairness can even change for the same person at different times. Since there are so many fairness focal points, where do we start looking? Fairness focal points can normally be considered:

- **Internally** – Resources, benefits, contribution, needs, seniority, principles, etc.
- **Externally** – Precedent, history, law, market/benchmark, social norms and values, best practices, expert opinions, culture, etc.

As it quickly becomes apparent, the different fairness focal points will at times conflict. For example, we may believe that fairness is to apply the same rule to everyone. However, they may believe that if someone is in a particularly different situation, it is fair to allow an exception. Some other examples of conflicting fairness focal points when deciding to allocate value (Table 12.12):

| | | |
|---|---|---|
| People only deserve what they work for. (Meritocracy) | vs. | Everyone deserves certain opportunities in life. (Socialism) |
| I contributed a lot for this firm to get where we are today. (Past contribution) | vs. | You were compensated for that, but now it is about who brings in more money. (Current contribution) |
| I picked it first, thus I deserve it. (First come, first serve) | vs. | I am older, thus I deserve it. (Seniority) |
| The group's well-being takes priority over the individual's. (Collectivism) | vs. | Everyone is free to do as they please. (Liberalism) |

**Table 12.1** Examples of conflicting fairness focal points

It seems that there is no universal fairness focal point applicable to all people at the same time. Fairness is culture- and situation-specific, and there is a plurality of fair reasons to behave one way or another. If we strongly disagree over a value-claiming proposal, there is no reward in fighting over it and becoming positional. A better strategy is to seek a different fairness focal point that provides common meaning to all parties.

Harder though is when a person changes their view of fairness in the short term due to a particular situation. These changes are normally caused by distortion factors:

- **Emotions** – Like Boulware learned the hard way, it is not the proposal, but our emotions towards its authors that may color our perception of fairness.
- **Relationship** – We may see a proposal as unfair if made by a long-term partner, but as fair if made by someone in a short-term transaction with us.
- **Perception of risk/power** – Negotiators with an abundance of time or alternatives may see as fair to ask for what they themselves would consider unfair otherwise.
- **Magnitude** – What we may consider fair in a small deal, may come across as unfair in a bigger one, such as a tip of 15% in a restaurant vs. in an M&A deal.

### POINT OF INTEREST

**Different Fairness or Distortion Factor?**
Differences in culture as in ethics, religion, gender, social group, age, profession or even nationality can mean differences in meaning and thus in fairness focal points. Culture is not a distortion factor as it does not cause a short-term change on an otherwise stable perception of fairness.

Some negotiators may be emotionally trapped into believing that even if their demand is unfair, they still deserve it. Others are intentionally positional about fairness, as they believe that a certain focal point can bring or exert power. In any event, distortion factors increase the risk of being positional about fairness and, with good or bad intentions, transform the negotiation into a win-lose game.

Before we move on to legitimacy, let's remind ourselves that fairness is just one kind of legitimate qualitative focal point. Certainly the most important and complex one, but it is definitely not the only legitimate one. So fairness is but one way to persuade people to distribute value in a certain way. Next, we look at the even broader concept of legitimacy.

## Legitimacy: An Even Broader Concept

Legitimacy is the basis for any argument made to persuade the other side that an option is more acceptable or less acceptable. It highlights qualitative focal points to support or reject an option as the fair, right or appropriate thing to do. Legitimacy is the most effective method of persuasion as it creates the least resistance. In fact, legitimacy alone is the best value-claiming strategy against bargaining tricks.

Legitimacy, being based on fairness, standards or focal points, is not about being naïve or nice. It persuades negotiators and their constituents, while preventing them from bargaining with non-legitimate or purely quantitative focal points. Its promotion of persuasion, instead of coercion, helps craft sustainable agreements while enhancing the working relationship.

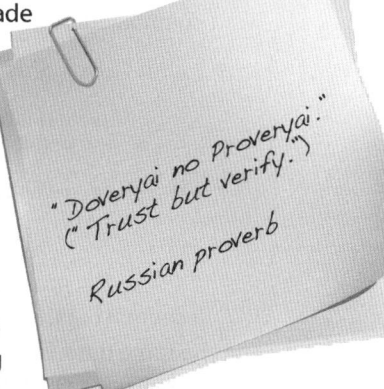

*"Doveryaï no Proveryaï."*
*("Trust but verify.")*

*Russian proverb*

### POINT OF INTEREST

**Because!**

In an experiment, social psychologist Ellen Langer had people trying to cut the copier line asking: "Excuse me, I have five pages. May I use the copier because I am in a rush?" 94% of people agreed. As expected, when they asked: "Excuse me, I have five pages. May I use the copier?" only 60% agreed to a request without reasons. Interestingly, when they asked: "Excuse me, I have five pages. May I use the copier because I need to make some copies?" 93% agreed to their obvious request.

Sometimes, the term "because", even without additional information, increases persuasiveness. It shows reason over coercion. When children say: "Because!" to their parents they demonstrate an intuitive understanding of that effect.

How does legitimacy work? Legitimacy is at the heart of the unconditionally constructive behavior of persuasion. One of the ways to bring legitimacy is relying on objective criteria generated externally and neutrally, legitimacy invites reason. Rationality helps us avoid fallacies, biases and short-cuts that otherwise trick us into bad decisions. Let's look into that a little more:

## Point/Counter-point

- *What happens if someone offers us a seemingly normal pen for £500,000?*
- Well, I would say this is crazy!
- *Exactly, but what are we calling crazy: the price or the person?*
- The person who fixed the price, I imagine, as a pen cannot be crazy.
- *True! And seeing as how that person probably will not enjoy being called "crazy," why would we say something to damage our relationship with them?*
- Most likely to show that the price is inappropriate and should go down.
- *Correct! This demonstrates the bargaining tension: if we want a lower price, we should criticize it, but doing so also criticizes them.*
- But if we don't do that, how can we bring the price down?
- *Many negotiators fall on the other side of the negotiation tension trap: they do not criticize the price to prevent damaging the relationship, but in doing so, they feel less empowered to bring the price down and end up paying more.*
- So, criticizing and not criticizing are both wrong?
- *Yes! We do not have to choose between criticizing or not, as bargaining suggests. Seeking legitimacy allows us to find out if the price is based on objective, external and neutral criteria.*
- That's it?
- *Pretty much! We may find out, for example, that the pen is worth £500,000 because it belonged to James Joyce, given to him by his former secret lover, with a cap encrusted with certified diamonds.*
- But I may not want to buy such an expensive pen from a writer I do not know.
- *Of course, but it has now become a matter of interest, not fairness. And we no longer think that the seller is crazy, which makes it easier to say no and still cater to a positive relationship.*
- Say I want the pen. I still want to pay less.
- *We can, for example, ask other specialists for new estimates. Their reports can show the price was not biased or mistaken, and still suggest a lower price.*
- But honestly, sometimes people just lie. Why not just call it as it is?
- *Because we cannot be sure that is the case, and we may damage the relationship or ignore the real substance value.*
- So this means that people can lie to us and give us a crazy price?
- *Well, they can, but to no avail. By insisting on objective, external and neutral criteria, at some point, they will give an explanation or change their offer. If we do not like it, we do not need to accept it. We can keep asking further or offer another number based on legitimate standards to persuade them instead. They will soon realize we are not so easy to fool.*

This is not to say that rationalization and legitimacy are perfect, because they are not. They too can lead us to mistakes, though significantly fewer than bargaining tricks will. As humans, we need to make sense of the world around us. First we tried religion, and then we "evolved" to explain the world through science and rationality. However, rationalization, or platonicity, can cause us to overestimate our abilities and theories to grasp the real world.

### POINT OF INTEREST

**Emotional Legitimacy?**

In a conversation where personal relationship and people's feelings are the main topics, then an emotional reason can be entirely legitimate even if subjective, internal and not neutral. After all, what we are seeking is common meaning, an acceptable reason (or emotion) that justifies claiming value or behaving in a certain way. Caution should be given to inter-trading negotiations, i.e., mixing relationship and substance.

Platonicity can develop the Ludic fallacy, when we start to mistake our mental maps and theories for reality. We then risk underestimating the complexity, volatility and unpredictability of reality, which no theory can fully grasp because:

- No one will ever know all the information.
- No one will ever know all data variations, inter-relations and impact.
- No one will ever know all future events that could fall outside our theories (which are built upon past events).

Despite these loopholes, the fact still remains that we live in the age of science and reason. Nowadays, people want cause-effect explanations and to see to believe, otherwise they are not persuaded. Rational explanations are convincing as people feel the need to rationally understand their experiences, let alone their decisions. If we legitimize our options, we satisfy their rationalization need and increase our chances to persuade them.

## Preparing Legitimacy for Value Claiming

Many negotiators think and use legitimacy during value claiming, but think of only one objective rationale. If their focal point lacks common meaning, they risk becoming positional (our argument vs. theirs). We do better when we develop a range of fairness focal points instead of having only one "right" answer. Preparation can be of great help:

1. **Prepare many focal points and standards.** A creative and comprehensive list is likely to have at least one common qualitative focal point. Otherwise, several standards pointing towards the same option can also be very convincing.
2. **Prioritize legitimacy for options.** Support options (ours and theirs) with our researched legitimate standards and prioritize them from most to least favorable for each side. What new options does our legitimacy research raise for us or them?
    a. **Quantify their value.** Each qualitative focal point supports an option. We want to know the option value before arguing legitimately for or against it.
    b. **Use the reciprocity test.** To verify if our researched focal points have common meaning and are persuasive to them, we put ourselves in their shoes. Would we still find them to be fair?
    c. **Think of their constituents.** Prepare objective, neutral and external focal points common to their constituents, so they also agree to our options.

This preparation enhances proactive learning about standards they apply or believe in and thus will be receptive to.

## Negotiating Legitimacy for Value Claiming

When negotiating specific options and value claiming, legitimacy is our best ally. It helps avoid bargaining risks, while increasing the persuasiveness of our preferred options. A few ways in which legitimacy can help us do a better job of value claiming are:

1. **Frame value claiming as a joint pursuit for legitimacy.** Consistent with the JVP frame, invite a search for common focal points, standards, arguments or processes to legitimately distribute value (Table 12.2).

| Instead of asking for a number; | Ask for ways to get to the right, fair or appropriate number(s). |
|---|---|
| ✘ "How much do you want?" | ✓ "What is a good way for us to find the fair number?" |
| ✘ "How much can you pay?" | ✓ "Considering workload, how much does each of us deserve?" |
| ✘ "What is your best price?" | ✓ "How can we reduce price while preserving your profit?" |

**Table 12.2**
Search for common focal points, standards, arguments or processes

2. **Transparently share own reasoning (Label our moves).** To maintain process leadership, we share our legitimacy whenever proposing an offer. We set the right tone and encourage positive reciprocation.
   a. "Let me share with you how I came to this number."
   b. "Based on the inflationary increase of the last three years, we are only now adjusting our prices by the same amount of 10%."
   c. "Since we have never done anything like this before, I suggest we start with a prototype to prove the concept first."

3. **Diagnose their legitimacy.** When faced with their offers, even if positional, avoid counter-offering, and instead diagnose uncompromisingly.
   a. "Where does this number (or company policy or confidentiality) come from?"
   b. "Do you mind sharing with me how you came up with this proposal?"
   c. "Why would it be fair for us to split the value this way?"
   d. "Why would you accept this if you were me?"

4. **Be open to persuasion and show it.** If we do not change our minds even if confronted with better legitimacy, why should they? We need to model the behavior and show that persuasion is a two-way street.
   a. "If you prove what you just said, your offer is probably more appropriate in this case."
   b. "If you have any better reason to act differently, I will be more than glad to look into it."
   c. "Here are the three things that I need to see before I can view your proposal as fair."

5. **Do not yield to power, only to legitimacy.** If we give in under pressure or manipulation, we reward bad behavior. We have to be firm and clarify that we will only negotiate based on legitimacy and value, not pressure or power.
   a. "Unless you give a fair reason why I should give you a discount, I am not ready to do it."
   b. "I will only pay you more if you help me see the extra value that I will get from it."
   c. "I am sure you believe that your proposal is fair, but I can only accept it if I can see the fairness behind it, which I still don't."

While discussing their new partnership, Samuel and Leila came to the topic of ownership (Table 12.3):

| NEGOTIATION DIALOGUE | DIAGNOSTICS |
|---|---|
| Samuel, I would like to find a fair way to split the equity in our company based on our contributions. I did some research and found a valuation model that is specific for start-up companies. | Frame value-claiming as a joint pursuit for legitimacy (fair process) |
| *I am not sure. This sounds too formal and strict. Too business-like. I would rather have us split the company based on how we feel about it. Say 50/50.* | *Subjectively offering 50/50 (possible anchoring or emotion distortion factor?)* |
| Why 50/50? | Diagnose their legitimacy |
| *I believe it is fair. You don't?* | *Vague answer + pressure* |
| It is not that I do not think 50/50 could be fair, I just do not understand it. I want to say that we will only agree to something that makes sense to you and to me. Could you help me understand? | Insisting on legitimacy, not yielding to pressure |
| *Well, my son who has an MBA told me that 50/50 was fair.* | *Authority short-cut* |
| What were the reasons he gave to justify 50/50 as fair in our case? | Insisting on legitimacy |
| *Since we are partners, we should split all equally. And even if your model is objective, I am not sure it is fair.* | *Partners = 50/50 focal point + Challenging legitimacy* |
| What do you mean? | Showing openness to persuasion and diagnosing |
| *I understand that this business is your idea and that you are investing 100% of your time in it as opposed to my 50%.* | *Reciprocating with openness about data and perceptions* |
| True, and it is your technical expertise that is making this possible. So what bothers you? | Rewarding good behavior |
| *Well, I am sure that your model will give you more of the company's ownership.* | *Focusing on the final result (manipulation?)* |
| And do you think that this is unfair? | Bringing it back to legitimacy |
| *Not really, but I fear losing control and 50/50 gives me control.* | *Sharing a new interest* |
| What do you want control for? | Seeking to clarify the interest |
| *Our products have my name, so I have to protect my reputation.* | *Sharing yet another interest* |
| Why do you think that we won't protect your name and reputation? | Diagnosing for legitimacy |
| *Let's face it: you are a businesswoman and I am a scientist. I care about quality; you about the bottom line. This is what makes us a good team, but I fear that you may choose money over quality.* | *Sharing the origin of his need for control* |
| So, if I hear you well, you want to protect your name and reputation through control of our product quality. | Proactive listening: summarizing/paraphrasing |
| *Right!* | |

| NEGOTIATION DIALOGUE | DIAGNOSTICS |
|---|---|
| I agree that quality is fundamental and the main foundation of our business. If I betray quality, our clients and the money leave. Even as a businessperson, I see quality as key to making money. | Agreeing on a focal point; sharing its common meaning |
| *I see! You see, for me all businesspeople care about is money.* | Sharing a perception |
| This is somewhat true! But we make money by having and sticking to a clear strategy. Our strategy is to make us better than our competitors through our higher quality. | Linking that to the focal point and creating additional common meaning |
| *That makes sense to me and I can now see how we are more aligned than I initially thought.* | Agreeing to the qualitative focal point |
| So would you consider using my model? | Linking that to the intended fair process |
| *We can give it a try, but I still would like to have some control.* | Accepting the legitimacy and insisting on the control interest |
| If the model suggests an ownership structure where you have less shares, we can try to give you control over major quality decisions. We could look into a veto power for particular cases. | Tailoring an option to give desired control, without giving other ownership advantages |
| *That could work. Can you give me some time to think?* | |

**Table 12.3**
Negotiating legitimacy for value claiming

How did Leila move away from the less-than-legitimate 50/50 proposal from Samuel? She kept her focus firmly but flexibly on using legitimacy to evaluate options. The focus on legitimacy allowed them to negotiate the substance without damaging the relationship, thus improving both. The negotiation moves showed respect for each other as partners in a legitimate pursuit for value. They also prevented Leila from accepting the content of Samuel's offers until persuasive reasons or relevant information was provided.

# Claiming Value Through Reason, Not Numbers

A good negotiation outcome is where value claiming takes place based on legitimacy. During the potentially critical moment of an opening offer or counter offer, we seek and use objective, external and neutral criteria. To exercise legitimacy in value claiming, we have to consistently frame it, model it, diagnose it, be open to it and yield only to it. Thus, the use of legitimacy during the opening offer and counter offer can greatly impact value claiming.

## Opening Offer

When? Who? How? The opening offer is frequently regarded as the most important moment of bargaining. While relatively less important in value negotiation, it is still a moment where much can go right or wrong. Below are some opening-offer best practices from a value negotiation approach.

## Who Opens?

The main risk of letting the other side open is giving away the process leadership. If they open, they can put a number on the table (position) and employ bargaining tricks such as anchoring. On the other hand, though less likely in practice, they may open with a good proposal for us. The risk of letting them open into bargaining is generally high.

However, if we open, we lead the process towards a value-claiming dynamic based on legitimacy and reason, not numbers. Some will say that additionally we can anchor them; however, we prefer not to recommend this way of thinking.

## When to Open?

Process leadership alone (or even anchoring) should not make our decision to open a constant. If we are well prepared in terms of legitimacy and specific options, we can open. If we are going to open, let's remember to do it after most interests and general options have been discussed. Otherwise, we may invite value claiming too early into our negotiation and jeopardize the value-creation process.

However, if we have done little or no research on legitimacy, we may let them open. Another case is if we believe that they have a much stronger willingness to pay than our best legitimate option. And yet, in letting them open, we risk their trying to anchor us.

## Where to Open?

There are basically two risks of opening: undershooting or overshooting. If we come with too low a value (undershooting), they may accept it and we leave claimable value behind. If we come with too high a value (overshooting), they may think we are not serious and walk away, or know that we are bluffing and try hard to bargain us down.

Our recommendation is to open as high in value for us as we possibly can within our researched legitimacy (Figure 12.6). This protects us from both overshooting and undershooting, while maximizing our potential to claim value.

**Figure 12.6** Making an opening offer

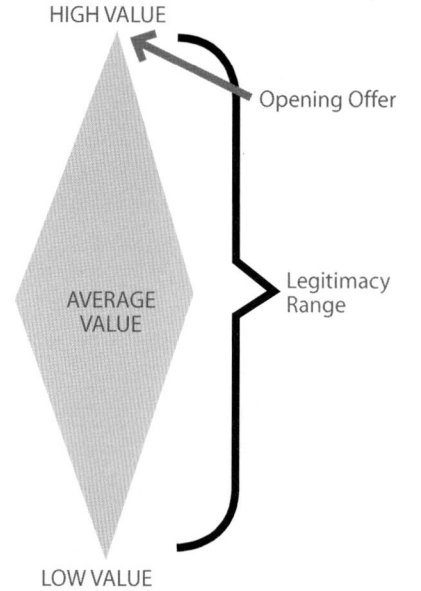

If they find the value too high, we can always back it up with legitimacy to prove its reasonableness. If the value turns out to be too low, at least we did the best we could with minimum risk.

They may always be able to pay more, but as seen before, we can never really know their reservation price. We actually may not want to know it! If the highest possible legitimate value for us still undershoots, there is probably nothing more we could have done. How would we possibly know their willingness to pay without risking the relationship in the process? Plus, their higher willingness to pay does not mean we should take it all, just what is legitimate.

Some question if the highest legitimate value can be too aggressive. It can. In some instances, the highest legitimate value can sound as an aggressive value-claiming move. If afraid of such risk, **we recommend being reasonable, not average**. Many negotiators mistake average for reasonable.

Average is one focal point, but seldom the most legitimate. Instead of reasonable, an average offer may be seen as a bargaining weakness.

Imagine making a generous offer in the middle of the legitimacy range to a bargainer. Instead of gratitude, trust or a quick commitment, they may respond with a counter offer. Should they respond differently? If they see such a good opening offer, why should they trust that it is already a reasonable offer? What prevents them from thinking that a little haggling could get them even more? Why should they not even try to get some more?

The risk of opening below the highest legitimate value is that they may still try to bargain us down. It is much harder to go up in value after our initial offer. By asking for less than the highest legitimate value, we limit our value potential and advocate against ourselves. What if they perceive more value from our offer than we could anticipate? Information asymmetry may be preventing us from fully appreciating the value they are getting.

If they find our value too high, we risk overshooting. Sharing legitimacy minimizes the overshooting risk as it explains the rationale behind our offer. If they still complain that our offer is too high, then we can show our openness to persuasion and better legitimacy. After all, we want the highest legitimate value, not the highest value.

Finally, the opening offer has an undeniable anchoring power, but that should not be the reason why we open high. We open high not to anchor but to get the best deal within reason. This different attitude is vital to show that we are not trying to take advantage of them. Though we do not advocate against ourselves, we are open to persuasion,

## How to Open?

If we share an offer, they may react to it with another number, potentially initiating a bargaining exchange. Even if we legitimize it later, their minds may already be focused on how to bring our value down. They are less likely to listen to our reasoning. Our offer may have surprised them and they could already be committed to bringing it down.

Hence, our recommendation is to **share the legitimacy before the specific option or offer**. In doing so, they are curious to learn the number and more likely to listen to our reasoning. This listening increases the likelihood that they will see merit or meaning in our legitimacy. It also prepares them to rationally anticipate the offer our legitimacy supports and minimizes its negative emotional impact. Finally, it invites reciprocation to share legitimacy if they are to counteroffer, keeping the focus on value and meaning.

## Opening Counteroffer

Two scenarios may occur if they open first: their offer is bad; or it seems to be good. In both instances, we highlight the importance of legitimacy.

If they open with a seemingly bad offer, they may be anchoring us. Bargaining theory will say that the best response is to counter-anchor, i.e., put another extreme number down that favors us. Unfortunately, to counter-anchor does not prevent us from being anchored; it just anchors them as well. We all end up in an anchoring race.

Counter-anchoring has limited positive impact and moves us away from value negotiation. Instead of accepting their anchor or counter-anchor, we want to reduce its impact on us. We need to keep our process leadership and refocus the conversation to qualitative focal points. To do that, we diagnose their offer's legitimacy and ask: "Where does that number come from?"

The diagnostic question leads the value claiming to set numbers aside and explore the reasoning behind them. The renewed focus on meaning has negotiators discuss the rationale, not the outcome. In doing so, the search for legitimacy also sets the anchoring aside and minimizes its impact on us.

What about an offer made to us that seems really good? The bargaining temptation here is to close on it fast before they realize what a stupid move they made. But how many people whom we negotiate with are really stupid? If their offer seems really good, we should still diagnose their legitimacy and ask: "Where does this number come from?"

We can then expect one of three answers:

- Good – They really value what we have for reasons unknown to us;
- Medium – They have conditions before they can pay the offered price; or
- Bad – The offer has hidden tricks or conditions that are very bad for us.

In any event, we are now prepared to argue and agree only to a legitimate offer. Next, we revisit the hypothetical negotiation between Magnus and Inson, the insurance company, but before the judge has awarded any decision on the dispute (Table 12.4):

| NEGOTIATION DIALOGUE | DIAGNOSTICS |
|---|---|
| To finish this fast for both of us, I offer you 50% of the value of the lawsuit. | Opening offer (an attempt to anchor?) |
| Can you help me understand why 50%? | Diagnosing their legitimacy |
| 50% is fair considering you have nothing right now. | Threatening with alternatives |
| 50% could be fair, I just would like to know why 50 and not 51 or 49 for example. I just need to first understand where this number comes from. | Ignoring alternatives threat and insisting on a joint pursuit for legitimacy |
| Well, do you have a better number? What is your counteroffer then? | Inviting bargaining |
| Actually, I do have some ideas and I would like to run them by you first if you do not mind. | Rejecting the bargaining and transparently suggesting a process based on legitimacy |
| No. Go ahead. | |
| Based on similar past cases, the odds of winning the lawsuit are 88%. So one way to consider this is to multiply the total lawsuit amount (kr4 million) times its odds of success. | Sharing own reasoning transparently—notice that Magnus had other legitimate standards but chose to open with the one that gave him the highest legitimate value |
| So your counteroffer is kr3,520,000? | Trying to focus only on the quantitative |
| No! If I win, then you will also have to pay for your lawyer and mine. The cost of my lawyer so far is kr250,000. With a similar success rate of 88%, this sums up to kr3,740,000. | Adding additional legitimacy that improves value claiming and again being transparent about his reasoning |
| But what if I disagree with your success odds? | Challenging legitimacy |

| NEGOTIATION DIALOGUE | DIAGNOSTICS |
|---|---|
| Fair question. Do you? | Showing openness to persuasion as they stay on a joint pursuit for legitimacy |
| *I do. I believe your odds of success are at best 72%.* | *Putting forward another number* |
| Do you have data on how you arrived at this number? | Insisting once again on legitimacy |
| *My lawyer actually showed us a compilation of previous decisions in similar cases which shows that only 72% of cases gave the decision to your side.* | *Sharing the potential legitimacy behind his number* |
| So it seems that both of us agree that a good assessment of my chances of winning the case could be a good calculator of the final deal between us. This is good! I believe we made some progress. | Highlighting the qualitative focal point or legitimate standard that seems to have been accepted by both. Though no numbers yet, a fair process has been agreed upon |
| *So it seems. Indeed.* | *Confirming and committing* |
| I will be glad to look into your lawyer's estimates. I would like to learn why they have more than a 15% difference between them. If however they seem to be more appropriate than my lawyer's estimate, I will be glad to consider your number to calculate the final deal. | Showing openness to persuasion again |
| *Really?* | *Positively surprised at potentially persuading Magnus* |
| Sure! After all, what I want is to find with you a fair deal. Of course I want money, and as much as possible, but I also want it to be fair. Let me just be clear that in the same way that I am willing to go to 72% if it turns out to be the fair number, I am expecting you to go to 88% if my lawyer's estimate turns out to be correct. | Reinforcing the joint legitimacy pursuit frame as well as the joint commitment to accept the outcome of the fair process |
| *That's reasonable. But how are we actually going to figure this out?* | *Committing, but bringing up the differences between legitimacies* |
| We could share the cost of a third lawyer or expert for a quick decision on this. Do you have any other ideas? | Sharing yet another option that legitimately settles the difference |
| *No, your idea sounds good to me. So I will just run this internally and come back to you.* | *Accepting the option* |
| There is actually one more thing as I want no surprises afterwards. Though the lawsuit is for kr4 million, this was almost 12 months ago. The judge is likely to award some adjustment of the price and they usually use the inflation rate for cases like this. Since the inflation has been 4.3% for the last year, we need to add that to the final value. | Adding another legitimate standard to claim more value and increase the value of the option |
| *Do you have that already calculated so that I can see the final number if your estimates are correct?* | *Committed to legitimacy as well* |
| It would sum up to kr3,900,820. | Not rejecting numbers once they come in the right legitimate context |
| *Is there anything else? If not, I will come back to you with an answer soon.* | *Open to exploring more options and legitimacy and committing to a process* |

**Table 12.4**
Arguing and agreeing only to a legitimate offer

Can we only move based on legitimacy? Not really! Legitimacy maximizes value-claiming rewards, while minimizing its risks. However, if after much legitimacy discussion, the distance between our values is very small, we can choose to compromise. To avoid a potentially long negotiation over little, a simple solution may be better than the best fair solution. Just beware of doing this too early in the process or as a reaction to their bad behavior. If we decide to compromise, ensure it does not create a bad precedent.

## It is About Value, Not Power

Hiroshi was transferred to Singapore. After a few months, he wanted to bring his wife and recently-born baby to live with him in Singapore. However, she offered strong resistance. When asked why, she said:

> Of course, I would like to be with you and have our family be together even if away from our homeland Japan. However, our baby is very young and I am afraid of taking him abroad especially at such an early age. I trust Japan's medical system to take care of our baby if we need to!

> Thanks! I now think I understand better your resistance to go to Singapore.

Hiroshi learned of his wife's interests over their baby's safety and health, but also of staying with him. He then did some research and met with her to continue the conversation.

> Hi, I did some research and found out that Singapore has a lower infant mortality rate than Japan (4/1000 vs. 5/1000). I believe it reflects the quality of the health and medical care for infants in Singapore as similar to ours in Japan. Does that help you feel more secure about going to Singapore with me for a while?

> Actually, that makes me feel a lot more comfortable. Thank you!

Hiroshi could have fallen into a bargaining trap and fought over moving to Singapore. He could have used a bargaining trick to fool or threaten his wife into making the trip. However, any of these could lead to a deteriorated relationship and an unsustainable commitment, especially if she learned the truth.

Often at the value-claiming phase, we develop tunnel vision. We only see the end goal, the deal in front of us. It is hard not to believe that if we just push a little bit harder, they may yield. However, what prevents them from thinking the same? The result is just more resistance.

> **POINT OF INTEREST**
>
> **Shadow of the Law**
> When lawyers negotiate, many times it is hard to avoid two strong legitimate focal points:
> a. What the law would say or
> b. What would a judge decide if the case went to court.
> Thus when negotiating legal cases, it is said that negotiators are under the shadow of the law.

This tunnel vision and "us vs. them" mentality creep up slowly and are hard to perceive until late in the negotiation. They can make us forget our real objective: value!

Hiroshi first focused on his wife's interests. While he could have come up with many legitimate reasons why he believed Singapore to be a good place for kids, instead he went straight into what mattered and was persuasive to his wife. It was not about making her travel to Singapore (position), but in jointly finding a fair solution to the interests at stake.

What if there were no arguments to prove that the Singaporean and Japanese health systems were of similar quality? It would be tempting to bargain or use tricks. A better approach is to remember that **we can always go back to interests and options**. If the interests were to be with his family and provide the best care to his son, he could have:

- Negotiated for her to come for a few months per year
- Paid for a Japanese-speaking maid (qualified as a nurse) to take care of their baby
- Signed up for the best possible health insurance in Singapore
- Promised to fly them back to Japan if there ever were an emergency
- Negotiated with his boss to be transferred back to Japan (if all else fails)

Many arrive at value claiming believing that it is time to focus on numbers or positions, and that learning and value creation are over. This could not be further from the truth. Value claiming does open windows to learning and value creation alike. When numbers come to the table, they often reveal additional interests. Positions or unsolvable differences beg for more interests and options as they show the lack of enough value for all.

# summary

Value claiming happens when the parties negotiate how much of the existing or created value each of them will take.

## Bargaining

Bargaining is one big value-claiming process. The absence of a bridge and a value-creation process limit bargaining to value-claiming.
1. Bargaining moves
    a. Reservation and aspiration prices
    b. Zone of Possible Agreement (ZOPA)
    c. Opening offer and anchoring
    d. Negotiation dance
2. Bargaining tricks
    a. Win-lose fallacy – Generates either a zero-sum or a competitive mentality.
    b. Decision-making biases – Data presented that induce us into bad decisions.
    c. Judgmental heuristics – These short-cuts make us vulnerable to exploitation.

## Value Negotiation

1. Focal points – Qualitative (standards) or quantitative (numbers).
2. Fairness – Fair process and fair outcome
    a. Internally – Resources, benefits, contribution, needs, seniority, etc.
    b. Externally – Precedent, history, law, market/benchmark, social norms, etc.
    c. Distortion factors
        - Emotions
        - Relationship
        - Perception of risk/power
        - Magnitude
3. Prepare legitimacy
    a. Prepare many focal points and standards.
    b. Prioritize legitimacy for options.
    c. Quantify their value.
    d. Use the reciprocity test.
    e. Think of their constituents.
4. Negotiate legitimacy
    a. Frame value claiming as a joint pursuit for legitimacy.
    b. Transparently share own reasoning (label our moves).
    c. Diagnose their legitimacy.
    d. Be open to persuasion and show it.
    e. Do not yield to power, only to legitimacy.
5. Opening offer
    a. Who opens? – If we are prepared with legitimacy, we do.
    b. When to open? – After value creation.
    c. Where to open? – As high as legitimately possible.
    d. How to open? – Legitimacy, then the number.
6. Opening counteroffer – Where does this number come from?
7. We can always go back to interests and options

# questions

## Easy
1. Define value claiming. How is it different from value creation?
2. What are the differences between the reservation and aspiration prices, the ZOPA and the opening offer?
3. What are the differences between win-lose fallacies, decision-making biases and judgmental heuristics?
4. What is the difference between a quantitative and a qualitative focal point? Give two examples.
5. What is the difference between a fair outcome and a fair process? Give two examples.
6. Describe in your own words the key points of making an opening offer.

## Medium
1. Bargaining is a value-claiming process more so than a negotiation process. Why?
2. How are the reservation and aspiration prices, the ZOPA and the opening offer potentially helpful in a negotiation?
3. What are the differences between the win-lose fallacies "mythical fixed pie" and "comparative gains"? What about between "mythical fixed pie" and "scarcity"?
4. Could information asymmetry lead to "winner's curse," "irrational escalation," "comparative gains" and "reactive devaluation"? How?
5. What are the main steps for preparing and negotiating legitimacy?
6. How do you respond to the question: "How much do you want to pay?"

## Difficult
1. Many people who learn about value negotiation want to polish up on legitimacy first, and more than the other elements. Why?
2. When bargaining or exchanging numbers, does it make a difference if we are negotiating in dollars and cents or if we are discussing percentages? Why?
3. When bidding for a contract, most financial calculations indicated that the bid should be $100,000. However, a negotiator bid $100,001. Why?
4. If we use the test of reciprocity in a negotiation and ask: "Would you do this if you were me?," what should we expect as an answer? Why? What would be a better question along the lines of reciprocity?
5. If the other party's legitimacy is more persuasive, but the outcome does not carry enough value for us, what could we do?
6. The other party makes an offer that is very good for us but we then realize that it may be bad for them. Why does something like that happen in the first place? What could we do?

# scenarios

## Easy

1. *Bargaining concepts try to reveal the negotiation parameters and boundaries from all sides of the table. Such parameters supposedly help negotiators delineate the perfect outcome, as if out of a mathematical optimization exercise. This exercise in turn allegedly gives negotiators a clear target to pursue. The boundaries apparently allow negotiators to know where to use maximum power and thus claim the most value.*

   Do you agree with this? Why?

2. *We want the highest legitimate value, not the highest value.*

   Do you agree with the statement? Why? What is the difference between the two?

## Medium

1. Here are a student's notes from a negotiation class:
   *In the negotiation:*
   1. *Obtain information about their reservation price.*
   2. *Manage our opponents' belief about our own reservation price.*
   3. *Identify the most likely candidates for a negotiated agreement.*
   4. *Find ways to dig in and resist concessions.*
   5. *Make it easier for our opponent to concede.*
   6. *Important side note: negotiation is first about 'give', then about 'take.'"*

   What are the risks with the advice above? What are the potential rewards? Prepare a similar list with value negotiation recommendations and compare the two.

2. Identify and describe all qualitative focal points within the arguments below:

> I am bigger, so I should get the bigger part.

> But you always get the bigger part. It is my turn now!

> I always get the bigger part, because I am bigger.

> That is not fair!

> Oh yes it is. And if you do not like it, remember who protects you at school from your class bullies.

> That has nothing to with this cake.

> Of course it has, you owe me.

> No! I like chocolate cake more than you, so I should get more.

> Who said so! I also like it a lot.

> If you do not agree to give me more, I will tell Daddy that we did not have an agreement.

> If you do that, I will beat you up after he leaves!

**Diffficult**

> Thanks for inviting us to negotiate! We are ready to offer you 50% of your claim just to get this past behind us.

> 50%?! This is absurd! It is insulting. I won the lawsuit; you can't offer me 50%.

> Well, this is our offer. Do you like it or not?

> Of course not!

> So what is your counter offer?

> 90% and not one cent less!

> You've got to be kidding me! I thought that you were ready to negotiate. With this kind of number, it is better to just go to court.

> If this is what you want to do, just remember that I will win at the end of the day.

> That is what you think! And even if you win, we can make your life miserable until then.

> Am I supposed to get scared?

> Okay then, 60% and not one cent more.

> That was funny! I thought I heard you say 60%, when I said 90%.

> Come on! Do you even want a deal? I made an effort here. The ball is in your court now.

> Okay, okay! I am ready to go to 85%, but just to solve this fast.

> No, you don't get it. 85% is impossible. Let me just say it plain and simple so even you can understand: it is NOT going to happen!

> You asked me to move and I moved, and now you are complaining. Maybe I should go back to 90% then.

> You can't be serious. You can't do that! You know what? I am not going to stay here if you are going to play games with me.

> Games! I am playing games?! You were the one who lost the lawsuit and you come here and offer me 50%.

> 60% now! And remember that you were the one who begged us to come to the table to negotiate. So we are doing you a favor here. To show once again that we are willing to help, I would exceptionally offer 65%.

> Seriously, you should become a comedian. If you were not such a sad individual, you would be making me laugh until tomorrow.

> I demand you to retract what you just said. That is unacceptable! Do you want to make a deal or not?

> Okay then. So that we can both go home I can offer you 82%.

> Excuse me?!

> 82%. Any problem?...

1. Using the concepts learned in this chapter, diagnose the different lines of the dialogue.

2. Then choose two moments in which you would have tried to lead the dialogue into a value negotiation process and give two examples on how you would do it.

# Step 3 - Make the Best Possible Decision

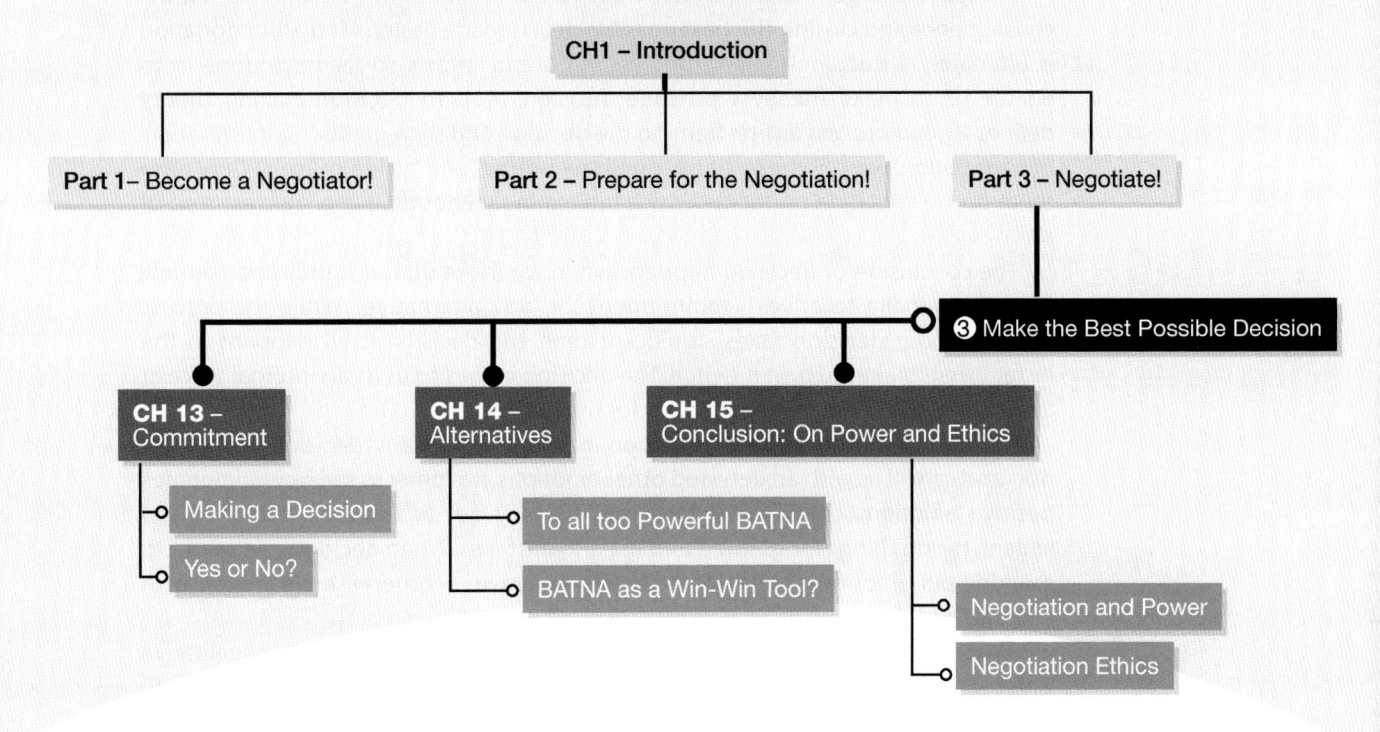

- **CH1 – Introduction**
  - Part 1 – Become a Negotiator!
  - Part 2 – Prepare for the Negotiation!
  - Part 3 – Negotiate!
    - ❸ **Make the Best Possible Decision**
      - **CH 13 – Commitment**
        - Making a Decision
        - Yes or No?
      - **CH 14 – Alternatives**
        - To all too Powerful BATNA
        - BATNA as a Win-Win Tool?
      - **CH 15 – Conclusion: On Power and Ethics**
        - Negotiation and Power
        - Negotiation Ethics

So we finally arrive at the moment of truth. When a seemingly magical "yes" or "no" rewards or punishes all our negotiation efforts. Exhilarating or frustrating as it is, there is nothing magical about arriving at or making the best possible decision.

Making the best possible decision is the final step. As the conclusion of the whole negotiation effort, it can be an extremely difficult step. If anything has gone wrong, it is here where it invariably waits to be handled by us. If the other side is unsatisfied, it is here where they err on the side of "no" rather than "yes". If they had proceeded too quickly, it is here where they slow down. If we had been too demanding, it is here where they make their last stand.

In general, negotiators focus too much on the final outcome. They rush through the negotiation as if building a house by just throwing pieces of wood and nails together. Neither a house nor a negotiation can be built like that. We need a clear plan, a systematic process and hard work.

One of bargaining's biggest mistakes is to skip straight to this phase of the process. By rushing to a "yes" (commitment) or "no" (alternative) decision, a good decision-making process is prevented from taking place. The use of power in its many forms forces us to decide without proper or sufficient information. Most bargainers mistakenly believe that power only comes through the element of alternatives.

When negotiators make a commitment or try to push for one too early, they ignore risks and rewards along the way. The likely result is either resistance or closing a deal of low value. When moving too fast, we cannot be sure if we are on the same wavelength or are keeping up with one another.

Instead, we should seek a better path where commitment becomes a natural consequence and closing the best possible deal is made easier. After all, negotiation is ultimately a decision-making process. All of our efforts so far have gone in to enable us to make the best possible decision. Modern decision-making theory defines a good process as first framing the decision and then gathering information. In negotiation, we call these steps "build the bridge" and "value pursuit". Only after them do we conclude or decide, which interestingly enough is the shortest step of all.

The conclusion or decision happens when we make up our minds and commit, even if internally, to a "yes" (commitment) or "no" (alternative). While the process leading to our decision takes significant time, the decision itself happens in the instant that it takes to turn a switch. The decision comes to us as an internal voice at an unknown moment and sometimes for unclear reasons.

Despite all the quantitative decision-making models, any decision still carries risks and can fill us with anxiety and other emotions. It's funny to see how sometimes positive emotions could taint it as well. We may get too excited and then too lenient, taking things for granted and making mistakes. When deciding, we ought to examine our emotional state — positive or negative — otherwise we are left with bad decisions.

A good negotiation process handles both the quantitative and qualitative aspects of our decision. Considering how difficult this is, it would be great if it all ended here. However, it does not! After we decide to commit or walk away, we have to face the aftermath: future (re)negotiations and relationships, the implementation of the deal, etc. Other parties are impacted by our decision and thus we have to take them into account when deciding.

In the subsequent chapters, we will explore the elements of commitment and alternatives: the "yes" and the "no" of our decisions. Besides this, we delve into the concepts of negotiation power and ethics, without any ambition to exhaust them.

# 13 Commitments

## Learning Objectives:
- What the BOpoT is
- What are the rational and emotional sides to commitment
- The role of intuition and other decision-making systems in commitment
- How regret impacts our choices
- How to say yes and get what we want
- How to say no positively
- How to overcome a last-minute "no" or an impasse

A successful negotiation process anticipates and deals with many of the complicated commitment variables. A commitment happens when the parties respond to the "best option on the table" (BOpoT). In an instant, a "mental click" has the parties decide to say yes or no to the BOpoT. A good bridge and value pursuit may give the impression that commitment comes about easily and quickly, but this is rarely the case.

The element of commitment is fairly complex. The conclusion of a process greatly depends on the success of our previous efforts. It also relies heavily on being better than alternatives, over which we may have very little control. Thus, many assume that commitment is just a simple step, with everything already done and little else to be said other than yes or no. Yet, the element of commitment is much richer than that.

We have already discussed quite a bit about commitments: we criticized concessions for being unilateral commitments; we advised to commit early on process, but late on substance; we identified early commitment as the enemy of learning and value creation. Still, there is much more to commitment than meets the eye.

Commitments contain several different perspectives. They have rational and emotional components. We can say yes or no to them, but so can the other party. People may avoid commitment and create an impasse. Next, we explore these variables to successfully manage them.

## Making a Decision

The element of commitment is being extensively researched by behavioural economists, psychologists and other decision-making experts. They have been making significant contributions to better understand and rationalize the commitment element within negotiations.

However, commitment is not all about rationalization. Besides being a rational process, commitments are greatly influenced by emotions. For example, nowadays a lot of attention is given to understanding the impact of regret in making decisions.

Legend goes that Professor Howard Raiffa, the pioneer of decision-analysis methods in negotiations, was once offered a job to move to a new university.

His students quickly approached him to ask which models, curves, and graphs he would use to decide whether to move. This complex decision impacted his wife's job, his children's schools and his future career, among other variables. When prompted by his students, Professor Raiffa is claimed to have said: "This decision is an important one. This one I will decide here!" And while saying that, he smiled and pointed to his heart.

## The Rational Side

Many rational models can be used to determine our commitment. They provide tools to help us better understand our variables and make a sound decision. The value negotiation process is, in many ways, a major decision made jointly which can still benefit from the models below. The main ones are: intuition, rules and decision weights.

### Intuition

Intuition, different from instinct, is claimed to be based on reasoning at an unconscious level. It is also known to operate faster than our conscious mind. Intuition has us gather, process and analyze information to make decisions, though we might be unaware of it.

> "The very essence of instinct is that it's followed independently of reason."
> 
> Charles Darwin

Intuition is an almost instantaneous decision-making process that can lead to different outcomes despite the similar context. For example, my intuition is telling me to choose Answer A over Answer B, though I am not rationally sure why. Students who have been through multiple-choice exams enough times know that when in doubt we should go with our initial hunch. How many times have we changed our answer against our intuition, only to regret it later!

Despite the debate on whether humans truly possess instincts, we cannot deny the colloquial use of the term. Without getting too technical, an instinct is a hardwired evolutionary behavior that has an animal always decide and thus behave in a certain way when given a certain key stimulus. For example, if I am hungry (stimulus), my instinct will be to stop doing anything besides searching for food (behavior).

Malcolm Gladwell's bestseller *Blink* made public the potential role of intuition as a smart decision maker. Intuition is said to be most effective when processing an abundance of information and variables. Our intuition works best when we gather all relevant information and put our mind into something else or simply sleep on it. It is as if we are adding the processing power of our unconscious mind (hard disk) to help process something too big for our conscious mind (RAM). Then, we go with our gut and choose the preferred course of action, seemingly without thinking about it.

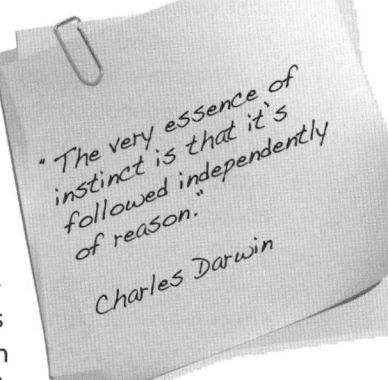

Actually, spending time to weigh pros and cons with many variables can lead to a loss of perspective or the bigger picture. As a result, it produces worse results than using intuition because we have bounded rationality, i.e., a limited conscious capacity to process data. Hence, more rational methods outperform intuition when only a few variables are relevant. For example, weighing pros and cons resulted in better decisions when there were only four variables. However, at 12 variables, intuition outperformed them.

Despite the advantages of speed and processing large amounts of data, intuition can be unreliable. Intuitive decisions are actually plagued by emotions, laziness, lack of focus, fatigue, etc. Even experts sometimes trust their "experience" and bypass their own processes to arrive at biased or incorrect decisions. The "noise within" may get to the best of us and prevent our intuition from working properly. The worst of it is that we may not know in advance when our intuition is wrong, so adding a few guidelines can help us be more disciplined.

## Rules

As seen in the previous chapter, rules are at the heart of decision short-cuts. They help us decide on our daily matters quickly and often successfully. Originating from experience or simplified advice, rules avoid complex decision-making, which we usually have little time for anyway. Especially for negotiations, we feel more in control with rules than intuition, as rules allow for further explanation of why a decision was made.

However, there is no guarantee that rules are correct. Rules as decision short-cuts may oversimplify the situation and ignore valuable information. Rules normally have an all-or-nothing cut-off point. As a result, following them rigidly hinders us from seeing the nuances or adapting to the differences in each negotiation.

And yet, rules are everywhere and extremely helpful. This book was written with two such rules set by the publisher: "Sentences should have a maximum of 20 words and paragraphs, up to 100 words." Some examples of rules applying to negotiations are:

- In bargaining
  - Round numbers beg to be negotiated, usually by counter-offer round numbers. Odd numbers sound harder, firmer, less negotiable.
  - Always say 'no' to their first offer!
  - When negotiating your salary, you can aim for a 20–30% increase

- In value negotiation
  - Only close a deal which is better than your BATNA.
  - Satisfy interests, not positions.
  - When negotiating your salary, aim for the highest legitimate number.

Of course, some rules are better than others. Always saying no to the first offer is typical bargaining advice that curtails learning. A better rule would be to ask: "Where does this number come from?" However, the rule: "Only close a deal which is better than your BATNA" promotes best possible results. Much of legitimacy, for example, is based on which rules resonate as fair, right or appropriate with the different negotiators.

Besides allowing decisions to be made fast and with little effort, rules also generate consistency and consequently, a sense of fairness. However, as most people know, using a rule without considering other variables can lead to unfair decisions. That is why most rules have exceptions to afford some flexibility. If a rule is part of a coherent system of rules, then the lack of flexibility partially disappears as other rules compensate for the rigidity of the first. The Negotiation Balanced Scorecard presented in Chapter 3 is such an example: satisfy interest, improve the working relationship, etc.

Is a system of rules the answer to the shortcomings of a single rule? It is certainly an improvement, but still not the answer. Imagine that our boss asks us to close the deal if:

1. We get the deal with this client to keep a solid relationship;
2. Sell at least 10,000 units;
3. At no more than a 10% discount on price;
4. For delivery no earlier than the next month; and
5. Only offering a national warranty.

**Table 13.1** BOpoT versus BATNA in a system of rules

| BOpoT | BATNA |
|---|---|
| ☑ We close the deal with this client | ☒ *Walk away to another client* |
| ☑ Sell 10,000 units | ☑ Sell 15,000 units |
| ☑ At 10% price discount | ☑ At listed price (no discount) |
| ☑ For delivery next month | ☑ For delivery in 2 months |
| ☒ And international warranty | ☑ And only national warranty |

What should we do now? Do we close the deal or walk away? While the BOpoT fulfills almost all requirements, the BATNA seems to be much better overall. We see that rules, and even a system of them, still have their shortcomings. Many rules, if not part of a coherent system, can generate conflict. In such cases, it may be hard to settle which rules take precedence over others. This is one problem that decision weights try to address.

## Decision Weights

Whenever there are several variables, intuition seems to be a good way to decide. Intuition deals with the limitations of our conscious mind (bounded rationality) by internalizing the decision-making into the unconscious. However, if such a decision repeats itself numerous times, intuition may prove to be volatile. In this case, the negotiator may benefit from a more reliable decision-making process. Unlike intuition, decision weights manage our bounded rationality by externalizing and rationalizing our thought process as much as possible.

Decision weights have the advantage of being consistent and at least match the top expert across several decisions. Also called "bootstrapping", decision weights generate the different criteria and their relevance based on the experience or advice of experts. It then creates a decision template to consistently replicate the decision-making process. The template increases the individual's accuracy and reduces "noise" in commitments.

Decision weights work by allocating weights (relevance) to the different variables. Imagine the deal discussed above, but now we ask about the relevance of each issue. Our boss may share based on her experience or the opinion of an internal expert that:

|  | Relevance |
|---|---|
| 1. We get the deal with this client to keep a solid relationship;, | 30% |
| 2. Sell at least 10,000 units; | 25% |
| 3. At no more than a 10% discount on price; | 30% |
| 4. For delivery no earlier than the next month; and | 10% |
| 5. Only offering a national warranty. | 5% |

**BOpoT**
- ☑ We close the deal with this client
- ☑ Sell 10,000 units
- ☑ At 10% price discount
- ☑ For delivery next month
- ☒ And international warranty

**BATNA**
- ☒ Walk away to another client
- ☑ Sell 15,000 units
- ☑ At listed price (no discount)
- ☑ For delivery in 2 months
- ☑ And only national warranty

**Table 13.2**
BOpoT versus BATNA using decision weights

Now we know that the BOpoT is pretty good since the advantages of closing with this client outweighs the undesirable international warranty. However, we still do not know if it is better than our BATNA. We do not know how much better selling 15,000 units at list price is to selling 10,000 units at a 10% discount. It could be marginally better or enough to walk away.

We need to go back and ask our boss: How do I compare each category? We can create a common currency to compare the different categories and give each category 100 points (Table 13.3):

| BOpoT | Points | Remarks | BATNA | Points | Remarks |
|---|---|---|---|---|---|
| Closing this client | 100 |  | Walking away | 0 | (least preferred) |
| 10K units | 0 | (unacceptable if less) | 15K units | 50 | (max 20K = 100) |
| 10% discount | 0 | (unacceptable if less) | List price | 100 |  |
| Delivery next month | 50 |  | Delivery in 2 months | 100 |  |
| International warranty | 0 | (acceptable but bad) | National warranty | 50 | (no warranty = 100) |

Then we multiply the points with the percentages and sum the result for each option (weighted average). In this case, the BATNA proves to be much better than the BOpoT and we have the numbers to make a reliable and defensible decision (Table 13.4).

**Table 13.3**
Comparing each category (1)

| BOpoT | Points | Rel | Pts x Rel | BATNA | Pts | Rel | Pts x Rel |
|---|---|---|---|---|---|---|---|
| Closing this client | 100 | 30% | 30 | Walking away | 0 | 30% | 0 |
| 10K units | 0 | 25% | 0 | 15K units | 50 | 25% | 12.5 |
| 10% discount | 0 | 30% | 0 | List price | 100 | 30% | 30 |
| Delivery next month | 50 | 10% | 5 | Delivery in 2 months | 100 | 10% | 10 |
| Regional warranty | 0 | 5% | 0 | National warranty | 50 | 5% | 2.5 |
| **Total** |  |  | **35pts** | **Total** |  |  | **55pts** |

What are the problems with decision weights? One problem is its complexity and the time and effort consumed. Another problem is the illusion of mathematical perfection. Since the allocation of percentages and 100 points is subjective, so will the final decision. In addition, we may weigh factors

**Table 13.3**
Comparing each category (2)

wrongly, independent of their importance. When we rent an apartment, we may overemphasize size over noise because we focus on more available or articulated factors.

The practical advantage of decision weights is its process. The exercise of defining the relevant variables and their value vis-à-vis one another greatly improves understanding. This debate gives the parties a better sense of each other's priorities, even if mathematically inexact. The final output does not need to be the final decision, but an indication or approximation of what it could be.

On the substance, especially for repetitive decisions, a manager can deliver consistent mandates for similar negotiations. Not only will the mandate be more elaborate, but the discussion will also better prepare the negotiators to understand the trade-offs and limits. If the percentages or points are incorrect, we can systematically collect and examine feedback to improve the system in two ways: recalibrate numbers for accuracy or identify new variables as new options are negotiated (payment) terms for our example above.

## POINT OF INTEREST

### Decision Weights vs. Decision Trees

As a decision weights system, decision trees help choose between competing courses of action with sequential implications by balancing risks and rewards.

Decision trees use a tree-like graph to plot the different solutions and subsequent decisions to an original question. Then we estimate their cost, revenue and success probability. Finally, we calculate the value of each course of action to find which one has the greater payoff.

Below is an example of a decision tree structure:

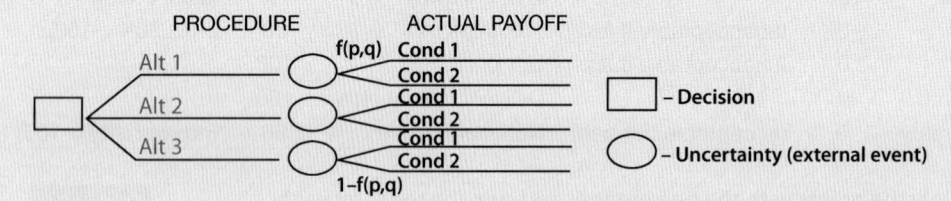

```
             PROCEDURE          ACTUAL PAYOFF
                           f(p,q)  Cond 1
                Alt 1              Cond 2
                                   Cond 1
        ◻       Alt 2              Cond 2            ◻ – Decision
                Alt 3              Cond 1
                                   Cond 2            ◯ – Uncertainty (external event)
                           1–f(p,q)
```

http://home.comcast.net/~dshartley3/PSYCHALG/DECTREE2.jpg  http://www.time-management-guide/image/decision-tree.gif (on September 14, 2009)

## The Emotional Side

Intuition, rules and decision weights are how most people make decisions. But to better predict or understand parties' commitments, we need to account for an emotional side. In negotiations, it is not rare to find a party committing to a course of action that makes little rational sense. Every day, negotiators around the world walk away from value-adding deals out of anger, fear or distrust of the other party. One of the emotions most connected and impactful to our commitments is regret.

Regret is what we feel when our commitment turns out to be worse than another option or our BATNA: "I regret choosing this hotel! I wish I had chosen the other one. It surely could not be as bad!" It is important to differentiate regret from disappointment. Disappointment is what we feel when our outcome is worse than what we hoped for: "I am disappointed. I thought this hotel would be better from the pictures I saw on the website."

Regret also comes in two ways: omission or commission regret. Omission regret happens when we fail to take action and then regret it. Commission regret happens when we do take action and then regret it. Which of the three situations below feels worst?

1. To make an investment and not profit from it. (Disappointment)
2. To make an investment and then change to another one, only to find out that your original investment gave a return of 100%. (Commission regret)
3. To receive a tip to invest but fail to do so, then learn that the investment gave a return of 100%. (Omission regret)

If you are like most people, you would have said that No. 2 feels worst. Commission regret feels worst in the short term because we feel as if we lost something within our control. We got it right but gave it away. Since we generally perceive that life does not give us many opportunities, to lose the few we have feels really bad. The fact that we could not possibly know that we got it right in the first place does not seem to count, emotionally at least.

As for disappointment and omission regret, we cannot expect to know or be in control of all possible choices. We need to accept that as humans, we will make mistakes. It is just natural that we evolved to handle omission regret and disappointment better. Otherwise, we would live in constant frustration since a better choice can always be around the corner.

Funnily enough though, in the long run, No. 3 (omission regret) seems to feel worse. This is probably because of the near infinite possibilities any situation can develop over time. Consequently, it is always possible to find an alternative long-term scenario much better than our current one had we simply chosen differently back then.

Pragmatically, regret can impact implementation of the deal or our long-term relationship. More importantly, it can influence our decision to commit as we anticipate how our commitment may affect our future. We may experience anticipatory regret (fear of regretting our choice) and avoid committing. Many people feel this when they are about to buy something expensive. We wonder if it will be worth the price as opposed to buying something cheaper or just not buy and save the money. Regret in its many forms can create inertia and prevent people from committing to the BOpoT. We may find negotiators not committing under uncertainty, fearing anticipatory commission regret. In this case, reducing uncertainty and giving assurances of success may persuade them to commit Others may prefer not to commit as they are less concerned about omission regret in the short term. Enabling them to see negative long-term effects of their omission may spring some into action.

Our present commitments are also made based on our memory of past ones. So besides anticipatory regret, we also have post-decision regret (what we feel after making a decision worse than our BATNA or other unselected options). The more choices we have, the more common it is to encounter post-decision regret. Too many choices make it likelier that the unselected options or BATNA had attributes that we now want.

We are always looking for the perfect choice and whatever we choose will never seem perfect. How often do we take a long time to examine a restaurant menu? Knowledge of all the delicious dishes we will be unable to try can be cruel indeed. So when presenting options, we want to present a number of them, but not too many at any given time. We also want to make options somewhat similar so that the other party does not feel he is missing out something by choosing one of them.

The emotional side of commitments may be the reason why many restaurants offer dessert sampler dishes with several desserts in small portions. We do not have to commit to a choice and can still have it all. After all, no commitment, no regret! But then, no pain, no gain! Decisions, decisions and more decisions…

# Yes or No?

When the BOpoT is put together, we may say yes or no to it. When we say yes, we often create new responsibilities and obligations on ourselves. When we say no, we risk closing the door on future relationships and value possibilities. In sum, our decisions may develop unintended negative consequences. Though we cannot anticipate or control all of these, we can at least minimize their impact.

When the BOpoT is put together, they may say yes or no to it. When they say yes, we celebrate. But they may say no or not say anything and create an impasse. When they say no, what is preventing them from saying yes? When they just do not say anything, what can we do to enhance their chance of saying yes?

Saying yes or no does not happen in isolation nor is it the end of the commitment negotiation; it is the beginning. The negotiation must go on.

## Saying Yes!

If the BOpoT is legitimate and better than our alternatives while satisfying our interests well, saying yes seems to be the only thing left to do. Indeed, in doing so we close a good outcome and satisfy our Negotiation Balanced Scorecard (NBS).

> "The devil lies in the details."
> Popular saying

However, saying yes is frequently just the beginning of the relationship. After the excitement of closing a deal, we are left with the responsibility of delivering on it. Implementation is the real test of a commitment's sustainability. To prevent unpleasant surprises at this stage, we ought to say yes only around a well-planned commitment. While making our commitment clear, sufficient and operational helps, this is just a start.

To prevent saying yes in ignorance, Gordon and Ertel suggest we anticipate the future implementation of the deal before committing. It is common for negotiators to get emotionally committed to the success of a negotiation and lose sight of the bigger picture. Many develop tunnel vision and may forget why they engaged in the negotiation to begin with. Thus, as we come to the final stage of our negotiation process, we should take a step back and regain perspective. We want to ensure that the commitment we craft is not only sustainable, but also enables the best possible implementation. It helps if we:

- **Remember the bigger picture**
  - **Treat the deal as a means to an end** – The negotiation, and the deal, is usually just a step in a bigger relationship or project. What do we really need out of this negotiation? How will it help our relationship/project? How else can it contribute?
  - **Run past the finish line** – Once we sign a deal, we often feel like our job is done and we can relax. This, however, can hurt the momentum. It is important to remain focused and involved, even if at a distance, to ensure at least a steady transition.

- **Confront reality**
  - **Avoid overcommitment** – Overcommitment usually leads to resentment. In addition, overcommitment often means poor implementation when the parties face their inability or unwillingness to deliver as promised.
  - **Air our nightmares** – If we do this, the other party may have preventive solutions. If we don't, we transfer the risk to those who implement. If or when our nightmares come true, it may be too late to solve them.

- **Facilitate implementation**
  - **Consult broadly** – We want to ensure that all relevant parties were consulted before we commit. Not only can we benefit from their resources, but we also ensure their buy-in when implementing the deal.
  - **Make history** – Every deal discusses and validates principles for the parties' relationship. Thus, commitment is an opportunity to set precedents to help make better decisions or easily solve conflicts during implementation.

In early 2009, the soccer world was the setting for an interesting commitment example. Adriano, the player known as "the Emperor" in Italy, went to Brazil and held a press conference. There he announced he would stop playing indefinitely, claiming to be depressed and having lost the joy to play. Responding to such a dramatic situation, his soccer club FC Internazionale Milano (Inter Milan) cancelled the contract without any financial consequences to Adriano. It included waiving a €10 million transfer fee if Adriano were to leave for another club. Inter Milan said yes to Adriano.

Interestingly, three weeks after his press conference and shortly after the contract cancellation, Adriano said he wanted to join Flamengo FC. He did so a few weeks later without any transfer fees being paid. Adriano helped Flamengo win the 2008 Brazilian national championship and was one of its top scorers. Inter Milan, received nothing.

Did the negotiators from Inter Milan not anticipate that possibility? We do not know, but are left wondering. In thinking about Inter Milan's response, we could imagine a partial cancellation of the contract where the transfer clause would remain valid for a few months. New options could have been raised allowing Inter Milan to be equally responsive to Adriano's needs, while protecting their interests amounting to millions of euros. Alternatively, Inter Milan could have said no.

# Saying No!

Saying no is, for many people, one of the most difficult steps in a negotiation. Our willingness to come across as collaborative, and thus flexible and helpful, can create a fear of saying no. This, however, may lead to a mix of relationship and substance. We say yes, not because we agree on the value proposition of the BOpoT, but to please the other side. In the process, we end up doing more than we needed to or what we did not want to begin with. We then resent ourselves for not being more assertive when necessary.

Can we say no yet keep a positive tone in our negotiation? Indeed, we can. Professor Ury described it very well with his concept of the Positive No, which is basically a "no" sandwiched between two "yeses." He actually summarizes it as: Yes! No! Yes?

Let's explain this a little more:

1. **Yes!** – First, we understand the positive reasons why we want or have to say no. These reasons ground us on something positive and give us confidence to say no.
   - By saying no to more work, I say yes to more family time, a healthier lifestyle and my hobbies.

2. **No!** – Second, we say no and explain our positive reasons to help the other party accept or at least respect our answer. It shows we are not being negative or prejudiced against them, but rather, are protecting a positive interest of ours.
   - "I thought long and hard about your request to work on Saturdays, and unfortunately I will have to decline (saying no). I hope you understand that I want to dedicate time to my family and the extra work would prevent me from doing this (protecting our positive interest)."

3. **Yes?** – Finally, if we want to keep the negotiation open, we can demonstrate our willingness to work together. We can suggest new options to satisfy their interests (that underlie the request we just rejected), while respecting ours.
   - "However, if you only want to manage the extra workload as you said before, I can train my assistant, who has some time, to handle the easier cases (suggesting a new option). We both know that those make up 20% of the total but only need standard answers. What do you think? Any other ideas?"

While working through the Positive No, there are a few other things we can do. We may acknowledge the impact of our no on them to demonstrate that we care. We do not need to come up with all the new options when in the Yes? phase, but rather invite them to think of some. Finally, if they manage to persuade us that their request takes priority over ours, we can always change our answer. Similarly, if they bring a new option to satisfy our interests, we might say yes to their initial request.

> I understand you need family time. What if I give you days off to compensate you for your work on Saturdays? You can spend more time with your kids during their long summer school vacation or take the occasional trip with your wife to spend more time with her as well. Does it help?

Does it? No? Then say it. But say it positively.

# Getting Them to Yes

Of course, almost everyone wants to know how to get the other side to say yes. It is no surprise that the bestselling negotiation book is named *Getting to Yes*. In addition, this whole book is about getting people to say yes to us through a value-focused, win-win approach. Then what is the reason for this particular section? Here, we limit the scope to when we believe we have done everything right, but just at the commitment phase they say no.

At this point they may appear to be unreasonable. All seems in place, yet at the very last minute they say no. Why could this be? One common problem is that we often believe that everything is alright without fully understanding how they see it. Our assumptions once again blind us from success. Despite a productive negotiation process and a positive relationship, the BOpoT may not look that great to them. If we have already expressed our best legitimate arguments and they are still saying no, maybe we should stop and look a little deeper.

First, we want to understand why they are saying no. Otherwise, how can we know where they stand? How can we understand the path towards making them say yes instead? Imagine looking for someone who is lost in a dark room. We want to help them find the exit. Instead of wandering around aimlessly, we may as well call them out. Once they answer, we have a better idea of where they are. We can quickly meet them, before we take them to the exit. The same goes for negotiations, where the exit is their saying yes.

How do we do this? One good way is to understand their Currently Perceived Choice (CPC), which is **how they see their choice and its consequences**. If it turns out that their no makes sense at least for them, we have to either change their choice (BOpoT x BATNA) or how they see it. This is often achieved by improving the BOpoT relative to the BATNA, thus creating a new choice called the "Yesable Future Choice" (YFC). It helps if the YFC only requires a yes to set things in motion. Lots of acronyms!

## Their Currently Perceived Choice (CPC)

Let's make the acronyms become more concrete and useful concepts. We start with their Currently Perceived Choice (CPC). It helps to diagnose their no in the following way:

1. **Zero in on the decision-maker** – Usually the negotiator in front of us. It is important to single out a person in a group, such as the person who is most influential or opposed to our proposal.
2. **Understand how they see our BOpoT** – We may believe we are proposing something great, but it could have been framed or interpreted negatively. Beware of the temptation to look at the BOpoT as we see it, instead of how they see it.
3. **Surface their perceived consequences for both yes and no** – Write down what they believe will happen if they say yes or no. If they do not explicitly say this, we can include what we expect. Indicate if these are positives or negatives.

Imagine a hypothetical situation where George W. Bush wanted to invade Iraq, yet wished to come across as having given Saddam Hussein a chance. In this scenario, he really wants Saddam to say no so that he can invade. Bush comes to us, his negotiation expert, and asks what would be Saddam's likely answer to the demand: "You have 48 hours to surrender or we will invade Iraq!" We come up with the CPC:

| Decision-maker: Saddam Hussein<br>Question he (probably) understood: "Should I give in to my biggest enemy or fight to the end?" ||
|---|---|
| If I say YES, then… | If I say NO, then… |
| + I may save my country from foreign invasion (though I do not really believe that)<br>+ I may save my life, but go to prison for life<br>− I come across as a weak leader<br>− I may be tried in a (biased) court and sentenced to death<br>− My family may die<br>− I lose everything I have<br>− They may still invade<br>− Iraq as a nation may collapse without my leadership<br>− My biggest enemy wins!<br>… etc. | + I look strong to my people and my country<br>+ We may be able to resist or even win since we learned from the previous war<br>+ Other countries may join us to support our cause<br>+ They may be bluffing as they are already involved in other costly wars<br>+ I may have more time to run or move my family, money and others<br>+ I may become a martyr<br>− I may die and still bring great suffering to my country<br>… etc. |

**Table 13.5** What Saddam Hussein's CPC may be

By looking at the above CPC, we go back confidently to Mr. Bush to say that Saddam will likely reject the demand. The answer is normally no when the negatives to saying yes or the positives to saying no are more numerous or relevant. The consequences may not be real, but their perception is because that is what they are basing their decision on.

The question they understood can take many forms but is always from their perspective. It helps to use the term "I" and their own words in phrasing it. We are putting ourselves into their shoes to learn more about them. This may be the most difficult step in the CPC exercise, especially if we find ourselves in an emotional conflict. In real life, we may ask: "What did you hear me say/offer? What are the problems you see with saying yes to it? How does saying no help you out?"

## Their Yesable Future Choice (YFC)

With a good understanding of their CPC, we can try to change their no into a yes. We can work on a Yesable Future Choice (YFC) for them, one where they are more likely to say yes. The CPC example above reveals two separate yet important pieces of information:

- The negative consequences to a yes reflect their unmet interests; while
- The positive consequences to a no reflect their alternatives perceived strength.

These are two areas to improve on for crafting a new YFC. We can then ask ourselves:

- What other options can we put forward that still satisfy our interests while satisfying more of theirs?
- Are there any other ways to make our BOpoT better than their BATNA?
- Are there ways to worsen their BATNA or at least their perception of it?

> **POINT OF INTEREST**
>
> **Yesable vs. Target Future Choice**
> Professor Roger Fisher calls this the Target Future Choice (1), and then adds making it a yesable proposition (2), while also adding a success speech (3). All these moves are designed to help make our BOpoT or their choice easier to say yes to. We decided to bundle these three tools as one system: the Yesable Future Choice. The renaming serves to better reveal its purpose: make the future choice easier to say yes to, thus "yesable".

Once we have brainstormed new options, we choose the best ones and check their potential validity. We can run a CPC process on them to check the other side's potential perceived consequences to a yes or no answer.

Our new and improved BOpoT may be the best future choice, but it is still not a **yesable proposition**. A YFC presents a new BOpoT where a yes answer suffices. There is no need for caveats or elaborations, since saying yes is enough to get the wheels in motion. This means the YFC has to be simultaneously realistic and operational. This makes it easier for the other party to decide as they know exactly what they are agreeing to. It also helps them as they save time and effort from not worrying about the details.

Let's think about the situation where someone was to ask: "Do you want to join me in the kitchen to cook dinner?" We may want to eat but not to cook, thus end up saying no to it. However, if they asked us: "Do you want dinner? I am about to finish cooking. Do you mind setting the table and preparing our drinks?" We still have to do our part, but everything seems to be ready for us. It probably feels a lot easier to say yes here.

Last but not least, especially when we negotiate with a person who represents someone else, we need to think about their success speech. No one likes to walk away a loser, especially when they have to account to others and fear additional negative consequences. A **success speech** is a positive story that they will share to their constituents when asked to explain or sell the deal. If they see a BOpoT that makes them look good to their constituents when explaining, they are more likely to say yes to it.

Could Bush have proposed a YFC to Saddam? This is possible if Bush's main interests were to remove Saddam from power, bring democracy to Iraq, combat terrorism and minimize the risk of Weapons of Mass Destruction (WMD). First, a private setting should be chosen to avoid public posturing. Bush could then have offered the following YFC to Saddam:

> You have 48 hours to initiate a new election process to take place in the next six months under UN supervision. Meanwhile, you will hand over to the UN all of your WMD in Iraq or wherever else you may have transported them, to ensure that they do not fall into the hands of terrorists. Then you will step down from power and we will allow you to request voluntary asylum in another Arab country. In exchange, we will ensure that we will not invade Iraq and we will not bother you in your asylum. The UN will ensure that your country and army will not be weakened during this transition so that Iraqi citizens are safe.

To make it explicit that this is a yesable proposition, he could add:

> If you say "yes," we will send you a team with all the expertise necessary to help you organize the elections. We will also make sure that the WMD will be given to the UN to be properly disposed of. We will invest a proportionate amount in training and equipping the Iraqi army to assist the UN in combating terrorism in the region. We already have a friendly Arab nation that is willing to grant you asylum. If at any time you return to Iraq or meddle in Iraqi affairs, this deal is considered void. We will then seek you out and invade Iraq without further notice.

He could also provide a success speech for Saddam to read to the Iraqis:

> Dear Iraqis, I am glad to have been the president that you loved so much. I am glad to have stood strong in the face of so many challenges and be the one who is moving us into the 21$^{st}$ century. With new elections and a new democratic government, we will become a regional example of political progress. This will bring us strong allies that will allow us to reduce our spending on weapons so that we can invest more in education and in new and modern infrastructure for our country's development. A modern country is a prosperous country. A prosperous country is a strong country. And when Iraq decides on their future president in the upcoming elections within the next six months, I will step down together with my people. I will move on, victorious like Iraq!

Saddam might still not agree to this. However, it seems a much better deal than for him to leave Iraq regarded as a coward and put on trial with his family, facing the death penalty. Hypothetical as it is, this example is bound to be controversial. Yet the lesson it illustrates is the way we can apply the YFC to our negotiations, where the stakes are almost always lower.

# Overcoming an Impasse

Sometimes, negotiators simply do not decide. Maybe they have the luxury of time or are building a strong alternative on the side. Maybe they are paralyzed with fear or just dislike the BOpoT, but have no idea how to move forward. Maybe we have asked them to make a tough decision and they are merely procrastinating. Whichever way it is, we have an impasse, which for practical purposes is usually the same as a no. However, an impasse can be worse than a no when it prevents us from knowing if we can or should move on to our BATNA.

A value negotiation approach helps negotiators facilitate their choices as often as possible. After all, no one likes to make difficult choices. Yet some negotiations come down to exactly that, where stalling occurs for the reasons listed above. As Professor Watkins mentions, negotiators only make hard choices when they lack a better BATNA and when doing nothing is not an option. We cannot expect them to act if they believe that doing nothing and buying time costs them less than deciding.

It then becomes our responsibility to eliminate "doing nothing" as an option. Our ultimate goal is to build momentum in the direction of positive value. If a no is verbalized, we could use the CPC to build the YFC and break the impasse. However, if nothing is said even after our proactive learning attempts, we may need to either shape their perceptions of time-related costs or introduce action-forcing events. We elaborate on these below.

- **Shape perceptions of time-related costs** – Negotiators feel time pressure when a delay either reduces important resources or prevents them moving on to other important opportunities. We can shape their perception by convincing them that:
  - We have time (no diminishing resources or opportunities).
  - We will walk away before our time is over (thus having time to act on something else).
  - Their own delay costs are not as low as they might think.

- **Introduce action-forcing events** – These are external or internal events that increase delay costs and motivate negotiators to act. We can generate them by:
  - Increasing the chances that important options or resources will be lost.
  - Setting deadlines.

NOTE: These moves are not risk-free as they invite conversations about walking away, BATNAs and differences between both sides (including power differences). That is why we discuss them here, close to the end of this book. These are last-resort strategies, after we have tried more value-positive avenues. Still, the above can be introduced in ways that are more value-focused, such as deadlines.

# A Deadline Story

Deadlines can be good but also tricky. Though they create a process goal and a motivation for negotiators to focus, deadlines are not set in stone. As a result, negotiators can fail to meet them and be left with either a process breakdown or meaningless targets. Due to these risks, we have to be careful since setting deadlines goes beyond merely picking a date in the future.

On February 1, 2008, Microsoft announced an unsolicited bid for Yahoo at a price of US$31 per share (62% premium over Yahoo's stock price). Many market analysts commented on how attractive the offer was and that Yahoo should take it. Still, less than two weeks later, Yahoo claimed it was "substantially undervalue[d]" and rejected the offer. For the next three months, Yahoo kept Microsoft's bid on the table. Meanwhile, it separately engaged News Corp, AOL, MySpace.com and even Google over potential collaborations or mergers. On March 18, after several negative quarterly results, Yahoo released an optimistic revenue forecast.

Microsoft was clearly dealing with an impasse. Without a deadline, Yahoo could claim that the offer remained open while going to the market to improve its BATNA. Yahoo indeed sought external partners as well as to reinvent itself for new growth. Once it had a better BATNA (internal or external), it could return to Microsoft with a demand to increase the offer price. Microsoft could not sit idly by and watch this happen.

So on April 5, Microsoft issued a three-week deadline to Yahoo after which the bid would expire. The deadline passed without a word, and a week later, Microsoft raised the offer to US$33/share. Yahoo demanded a minimum offer of US$37/share. Microsoft immediately withdrew its offer just to see its own share price drop 6% in one day.

The timing of a deadline can greatly impact the odds of whether it will be respected. While Microsoft initially failed to set any deadline, it then swung to the other extreme by setting one that was too short. But how do we know the deadline was too short?

A week after Microsoft withdrew its offer, billionaire investor Carl Icahn bought over 50 million shares of Yahoo. He began a proxy fight against Yahoo's board of directors for being irresponsible to shareholders by rejecting Microsoft's deal. Icahn ultimately joined Yahoo's board and ousted the CEO by year's end. By then, Yahoo's stock had plummeted to US$15/share and it seemed stuck in a downward trend.

Until October 2009, Yahoo seemed to lack a better BATNA and doing nothing was not an option as its stock price kept plunging. A hypothetical Microsoft offer at this stage would have a much higher chance of being successful. Should Microsoft then have set a deadline of six months to wait for the tide to turn? No! But a three-week deadline seemed overly optimistic, since Microsoft was not proactively helping Yahoo overcome the impasse.

When setting a deadline, especially for a multi-faceted player such as a listed company, we need to consider both operational decision-making challenges and negotiation risks:

- Operational decision-making challenges
    - Internal decision-making process
        - Do they have a large number of people involved and consultative decision-making processes?
    - Issue complexity and information availability
        - Is this a highly complex issue or one with little information that requires research and time to appreciate?
    - Management attention
        - What is their management availability to decide at this time?

- **Negotiation risks**
  - **Potential internal resistance**
    - Are there many or powerful people against us or our options?
    - Did we build the deadline together?
  - **Potentially unintended power messages**
    - Could the length of our deadline send a message that we are either trying to bully or are desperate to close?
  - **Deadline credibility**
    - Do they regard the deadline and its consequences seriously?
    - Do we? How will we behave if they do not comply with it?

Yahoo quickly reacted to Microsoft's original bid (less than two weeks), thus the decision-making process seemed lean. However, the speed of the rejection indicates potential internal resistance too, maybe from the CEO but also further widespread within Yahoo. A closer look at Yahoo's culture and pride in being the "anti-Microsoft" for years potentially reinforces such resistance. Setting the three-week deadline could be seen as a power move to put pressure on Yahoo. Finally, Yahoo did not seem to have seriously regarded Microsoft's deadline. Rightly so, since after the deadline Microsoft not only failed to withdraw the bid, but went on to increase the offer.

Thus, it seems that Microsoft's three-week deadline was indeed tight, considering all the obstacles that it and Yahoo would have to overcome before committing. In theory, the more ignorant we are about these issues, the longer we should set our deadline. In real life, however, neither our ignorance nor the existence of several obstacles means that we can just sit idly. As seen above, we should try to overcome the impasse by facilitating the decision.

- **Breaking impasse actions**
  - **Time-related costs perceptions**
    - Do they believe that a delay benefits them?
    - Do we believe the same thing? Are we doing something to change it?
  - **Action-forcing events**
    - Who or what could help them decide?
    - What can or are we doing to influence them to move out of the impasse faster?

For example, inviting Icahn or other activist investors in early to move and pressure Yahoo could have sped up the change in leadership and raised the momentum towards the offer. Asking Yahoo how much time it needed to respond and commit to the offer would limit how much shopping around for a BATNA it could do. This process would also increase the chances that the deadline be seen and set as a collaborative move, not a power one. Internal messages could even be sent within Yahoo that Microsoft was serious about working together.

Microsoft seemed to feel pressured by time and short of alternatives. Yahoo looked to be their only option and it appeared to be using time against Microsoft. In these situations, we want to set a shorter deadline but, as seen above, the risks can be high. A long deadline hurts Microsoft's interests and gives Yahoo time to find a BATNA.

How could Microsoft set a deadline without revealing desperation or weakening their negotiation ability? Instead of saying: "I desperately need to close in three weeks!" Microsoft could initiate the conversation as having interest in a timely and efficient process: "Among other interests, we would rather get a deal on this sooner than later. How do you feel about that?" This would convey that time is important without showing desperation or weakness.

If the other side resists this interest, we have an early warning: they may intentionally delay or create an impasse to put pressure on us. Below are a few suggestions on how to handle it:

- "I hope you understand that the longer the deadline I give you, the worse the situation can get for me. So I am going to give myself a deadline to wait for you until X day and if I do not hear from you, I will then feel free to pursue this with someone else. Make no mistake, I started this negotiation with you because I did and still do believe that you are potentially my best partner for this initiative, and I sincerely hope that we will still be able to do this together. I just cannot put myself in a situation of weakness because of time. Do you have any concerns with the timing I am giving myself?"

- "I know I cannot ask you to go faster just because I would like to. Still, my reality is that if we do not find a solution fast, I will have to look for something else. I am glad to invest as much time and effort as is necessary to make this work for both of us, and I need to understand if you are ready to do the same. Is there anything I can do to help you decide faster?"

- "I would still like to set a deadline for us to reach a conclusion as fast as possible. Do you have any timing in mind? Remember to ask "Where does this number come from?" and to negotiate the number if it does not work for us. I would also like to ask that we commit the time to reviewing this proposal instead of spending time looking around for other competing possibilities. We have to be honest that we will feel free to pull our proposal out if we learn that you are talking to others or shopping our proposal around. Of course, if you decide to reject our offer and then go somewhere else, we will fully respect your decision."

What was previously a win-lose weapon for them, i.e., put us out of time and under pressure to concede, now becomes a joint interest in moving together faster. The window of opportunity has been combined: the faster it closes for us, the better it closes for them as well.

If they set an unrealistic deadline, be curious. This may just be an artificial limit. If the deadline puts us under undue pressure, we have the right to negotiate on it. If they create improper expectations on their side, we have the responsibility to clarify and negotiate more realistic ones. Deadlines are supposed to create positive momentum and expectations. It is our right to negotiate deadlines whenever they are being used as a power move.

## What if They Never Wanted a Deal?

What if Yahoo never really wanted to sell? Could that explain some of their behavior? Maybe, but then why would they make a US$37 per share counter offer? This counter-offer could have been a serious move or just a deterrent price (an offer we are almost sure the other side will reject). If it was a deterrent price, then we can infer that Yahoo never really wanted to sell. At this stage, we can only conclude that finding a negotiator's true intentions is a difficult task.

Why would someone negotiate if they have no intention of settling at all? There are many possible reasons. Some people may merely be posturing for reputation's sake as several politicians do. Others may just want to demonstrate that they listen and are open. A few do it because they have to show their constituents that they went through the process. Finally, some may negotiate with us simply to buy themselves time or build alternatives to improve their situation somewhere else. What all of these people have in common is that they had already made up their mind against a deal with us.

If Yahoo indeed wanted no deal, it could still have negotiated with Microsoft for three hypothetical reasons. First, the CEO might have been against any deal with Microsoft, but he had to show his shareholders he was at least considering it. Second, by engaging with Microsoft, Yahoo kept its share price higher for a few months, thus buying itself time to develop internal growth solutions. Finally, with the Microsoft deal alive, Google (a preferred Yahoo partner) would have the urgency to do something to prevent it.

Hypotheticals aside, how can we know if the negotiator in front of us sincerely wants a deal? The answer is that we cannot know for sure. However, if any suspicion arises, before rushing to assumptions, we recommend looking at the "totality of conduct". This means looking not at one or two moves, but at their whole behavior before reaching a conclusion. Some questions to pay closer attention to are:

- **Purpose – Why are they here in the first place?**
    - It is easy to assume that what we are offering is a good deal, much like how Microsoft and many market analysts saw the transaction as a shoo-in. But could one or more of the reasons to negotiate for no deal be relevant to Yahoo?

- **Substance – Did they make an absurd offer?**
    - Yahoo made a US$37/share counter offer, which was a little over 10% of Microsoft's last offer of US$33/share. It did push Microsoft off the table, but was it deterrent pricing, a bargaining tactic or just differing value expectations?

- **Communication – Are they complicating normally simple process steps?**
    - Yahoo did not comply with the deadline, but there are several potential reasons for that, including never agreeing to do so in the first place.

- **Relationship – Do they seem hostile or apathetic overall?**
    - Though Yahoo was not friendly, at no point did they seem more aggressive or indifferent than the usual bargainer trying to get a better deal for himself.

Again, this is not an easy conclusion to reach. Hopefully though, it will become easier when we are directly involved, using our intuition plus further data to better inform us. What we can conclude, if we find ourselves in this situation, is that there is no value negotiation taking place. Even in the Yahoo case above, many of their behaviors resembled bargaining. Bargaining helps camouflage not actually wanting a deal since it uses similar behaviors as tactics to get a better deal.

If they consistently reject our invitations to a value negotiation process, this forms powerful data. If they still reject it despite the superior value we show, they probably never wanted a deal to begin with. We can then surface our assumption, share the data we believe supports it and ask them to clarify. Depending on their response, we can then decide if it is still worthwhile to continue negotiating.

As we can see, commitment is a very rich element. It is the final line to be crossed, which contains and thus reveals a lot of pressure, temptations and ultimately truth. Thread it with care, but rejoice because the end is near.

# summary

Commitment happens when a party responds to the "best option on the table" (BOpoT).

## Making a Decision

1. The rational side
   a. Intuition – Unconscious-level reasoning
   b. Rules – Simplified summary advice that acts as decision short-cuts
   c. Decision Weights – Externalize and rationalize our thought process

2. The emotional side
   a. Regret – Feeling we choose an option worse than another choice
      i. Omission – When we regret failing to take action
      ii. Commission – When we regret having taken action
      iii. Anticipatory – Fear of regretting our choice
      iv. Post-decision regret – The normal regret after the regretful choice

   b. Disappointment – Feeling we choose an option worse than expected

## Yes or No?

1. Saying yes
   a. Remember the bigger picture
   b. Confront reality
   c. Facilitate implementation

2. Saying no
   a. Yes! – Understand our interests to say no.
   b. No! – Say no and legitimize.
   c. Yes? – Suggest new options to satisfy their interests.

3. Getting them to yes
   a. Their Currently Perceived Choice (CPC)
      i. Zero in on the decision-maker
      ii. Understand how they see our BOpoT
      iii. Surface their perceived consequences for both yes and no

   b. Their Yesable Future Choice (YFC)
      i. Create a new Target Future Choice
      ii. Make it a yesable proposition
      iii. Prepare their success speech

   c. Overcoming an impasse
      i. A deadline story
         - Operational decision-making challenges (decision-making process, complexity and availability, management time)
         - Negotiation risks (internal resistance, power messages, credibility)

      ii. What if they never wanted a deal?
         - Purpose – Why are they here in the first place?
         - Substance – Did they make an absurd offer?
         - Communication – Are there unreasonable complications?
         - Relationship – Do they seem hostile or apathetic overall?

# questions

## Easy

1. What does the BOpoT mean? What is its relationship with the BATNA?
2. What are the problems with concessions?
3. Why should we commit early on process, but late on substance?
4. How does early commitment impact value creation?
5. If you were a manager, which decision-making style would you require from your employees when negotiating? Why?
6. What is regret and disappointment? What is the difference between omission regret and commission regret?

## Medium

1. What is the difference between intuition and instinct? Why is this difference important?
2. Give three examples of rules that you use in (i) your daily decision-making and in (ii) negotiations.
3. When and why is commission regret worse as a feeling than omission regret? When and why is omission regret worse?
4. How does anticipatory regret impact our commitments? How can we manage it?
5. This chapter covers how we can say yes, how we can say no and how we can change their no to yes. Why did we not cover *their* saying yes (i.e., when they agree)?
6. What is the difference between the other side saying no and an impasse?

## Difficult

1. "Close a deal if it is better than my alternative." Is this statement a rule? Why? Does it share the same disadvantages that rules have? Why?
2. If we do not know the process behind intuition, why are we calling it rational decision-making? Could it be irrational?
3. If you regret a previous decision, how do you think you will decide next time?
4. When saying yes, we could also categorize the three main tasks as Remembering the Past, Focusing on the Present and Preparing for the Future. Explain the connections between them.
5. How do you overcome an impasse? What are the risks?
6. How do you set a deadline when you have little time and no alternatives, while the other side has plenty of both?

# scenarios

## Easy

1. What are the pros and cons of deciding through:
   - Intuition
   - Rules
   - Decision weights?

Compare the methods and advise when using one is better than the other.

## Medium

1. Review either a recent negotiation or a current negotiation you are handling and prepare a decision-weights template for it.
2. How do you say no in a positive way when your boss asks you to do something unethical? Describe such a scenario, followed by the best response.

## Difficult

1. For years, the UN has been asking Iran to stop uranium-enrichment research and yet they have always said no. Imagine that you have been appointed the UN's new envoy; prepare a CPC and then a new YFC to persuade Iran to say yes.

# 14 Alternatives

## Learning Objectives:
- Why it is important to have alternatives
- What to do when they mention their BATNA
- How to reduce the negative power of their BATNA
- How to best use our BATNA
- Which is better: a threat or a warning?
- How to use time as an alternative
- How to use the BATNA as a win-win tool

This chapter explores a very important, and yet dangerous, element: alternatives. Misunderstood or mishandled, alternatives invite win-lose moves and can undo much of our value negotiation effort. However, they are also an important part of a value negotiator's toolkit, just one that comes with a tag: "Handle with care!"

Why do we have to handle alternatives with care? Because, maybe more than any other negotiation element alone, alternatives are very powerful. Maybe too powerful. Maybe too blunt. Maybe too notorious. Maybe too easy to use. Definitely too tempting. And yet, for any action there is a reaction. For any move to an alternative, we will face resistance. And if we manage to overcome such resistance, we would likely have done it in a win-lose way. In sum, the power of alternatives tempts us away from our value-focus into a power struggle.

More than just wanting to be value-focused, we need to learn how to effectively negotiate alternatives from a value negotiation perspective. Only then will we be able to avoid polluting our negotiation with one of the most common win-lose power moves.

We need to once and for all understand if or why we need to have alternatives. What does "Handle with care!" really mean? How do we manage a negotiation when they bring their alternatives in? How do we manage our alternatives? Do we share them? If so, what is the best way to do it? And when? As alternatives are usually linked to power, can we still keep the win-win spirit as we bring them forward?

## The All-Too-Powerful BATNA

Many a salesperson complains that they have to give discounts to buyers to close deals. Due to the need of many listed companies to demonstrate quarterly results, they establish quarterly sales quotas for their salespeople. Quite often, a day or two before the quota deadline arrives, savvy buyers call these alespeople and ask:

> So, how is it going?

> Not too bad. Why?

> I don't know. Just thought that I could use some of your products soon.

> Really? What do you have in mind?

> Quite a few things if the price is right. I know your quota deadline is in two days. So how much of a discount can I get if I buy a decent volume right now?

We have clients that have offered discounts in the order of 90%. When asked why they give out such large discounts, we hear:

- "What can I do? We are told that we have to close deals!"
- "We cannot walk away from deals in our company. It will look as if we failed."
- "I was below my quota and I had to close the deal."
- "My performance is measured by revenue, not profit. So if I sell a little more even if at a loss to the company, I still make my quota and my bonus."
- "If I let go of this opportunity, what else can I do?"
- "If I do not give them the discount, my competitor probably will."

As we diagnose the statements above, they all have in common the sense of a lack of alternatives or that the buyer's alternatives are stronger. Alternatives are the emergency exits, the safety net in a trapeze show, the insurance policies in our drawers. It almost goes without saying that having alternatives is important. As we said earlier, having alternatives is also dangerous; however, it is even more dangerous not to have them.

Alternatives bring an element of choice that prevents us from being hostages in our own negotiations. Alternatives give us the freedom and the ability to walk away if the BOpoT or the negotiation's value potential is low. Whether to have alternatives is not the difficult question, because the answer is to have them. The challenge with alternatives is to know how to successfully manage and use them.

The paradox with alternatives is that most people are quick to talk about, but reluctant to prepare, them. We should do just the opposite: be quick to prepare and reluctant to talk about them. In other words, we should always work to have alternatives, but only use our BATNA as a strategy of last resort.

When preparing alternatives, instead of assuming all will go well, we need to consider the consequences of no deal being reached. This will give us an idea of the parties' alternatives and their potential BATNAs. It is important to consider both the hypothetical and concrete alternatives available to all parties. This will allow us to understand what we actually have and what has to be worked on. Then, we can improve on our alternatives or build more of them. This effort makes sense whenever an alternative seems like a good investment: attractive returns at a reasonable cost of time, money, etc.

Expanding our knowledge about alternatives improves our ability to manage our BATNA and theirs. It also allows us to increase our alternatives and probably improve our BATNA in the process. An improved BATNA raises our ability to choose to either walk away or work towards a better outcome. We may improve alternatives to the point that they satisfy all of our interests and find that negotiation becomes unnecessary.

Assuming that we go into the negotiation, we may face the following challenges: the other side displays a powerful, and maybe even an internal, BATNA. Meanwhile, we are left with the challenge of appropriately managing our BATNA.

## Handling Their BATNA

To "handle their BATNA" means to productively manage the negotiation whenever they mention their BATNA. By "productively manage", we mean to keep the value-focus even when faced with a strong power move like their BATNA. It also means to avoid reciprocating with our BATNA. A value negotiator negotiates away from the power struggle of a win-lose dynamic both inside and around the negotiation.

### Inside the Negotiation

When they mention their BATNA in a negotiation, there are mainly two potential interpretations: first, it is a threat; or second, they are sincerely worried that our BOpoT is low. We either improve our BOpoT value or their perception, or they may have to walk away. Neither scenario seems pleasant at first, but both can be productively handled.

The first challenge is that we may not know if it is a threat or a genuine concern. Consider the statement: "I hope you understand that I have another offer 15% better than yours."

Is this a threat or the expression of a genuine concern? Hard to tell. It depends on their body language, context, intention, relationship, etc. If said early in the negotiation, it is likely to be a threat. But it could simply be from an inexperienced negotiator or one that is in a hurry. We are left to guess, hope or assume between them. In other words, it depends on many variables and we are likely to conclude wrongly sometimes.

Two main mistakes can stem from our assumptions: first, we react in kind and threaten them with our BATNA; or second, we panic and make concessions to improve the BOpoT. Our reaction depends on our perception of how strong our own BATNA is. The win-lose dynamic of these two reactions would be heightened if we then add that their statement of a better offer might not be true.

If we are unable to independently verify this, we want to avoid mistakenly assuming it is a lie, threat or genuine concern. Instead, we can see this as an opportunity to learn how to pursue value. Behind the apparent risk of them walking away, their statement is ultimately an invitation to improve the BOpoT. If they are willing to work with us (and it is our task to ensure that they are), this can be a good moment in the negotiation. With our JVP stance, we can avoid both aggressive reactions and concessions at the same time.

When they share their alternatives, irrespective of the truthfulness or underlying reasons, our strategy remains the same. Faced with a BATNA statement, we should **reality test their statement**; then **redirect the conversation towards value**.

Reality testing is making sure that all parties have a clear understanding of the alternatives, their details and consequences. Reality testing is learning the true impact of the BATNA statement to the negotiation. Often, negotiators will try to commoditize what we are offering, which may give them an inflated belief of the value of their alternatives. They may overestimate the quality of the alternatives, their reliability, the switching cost or even misunderstand their true nature. Reality testing helps negotiators deal with reality instead of wasting time or money on a distorted version of it.

A reality-testing dialogue could then flow like in Table 14.1:

| NEGOTIATION DIALOGUE | DIAGNOSTICS |
|---|---|
| I hope you understand that I have another offer 15% better than yours. | Statement on alternatives (threat, genuine concern, lie or truth?) |
| It sounds like a big difference. To make sure I really understand it, could you share what you think allows them to ask for 15% less? | Acknowledging that it has to be addressed and seeking to better understand it (reality testing) |
| Well, their product is similar to yours, but I think that the product is just cheaper or they want this deal more than you do. | Commoditizing our offering and sharing either a bluff or a concern |
| It is possible! As far as I understand from my main competitors and I am assuming that one of them made you the offer, for them to be able to offer you 15% less, they would not be able to offer you the same product. | Acknowledging the possibility without commitment. Sharing our estimation of their BATNA based on our previous research (reality testing) |
| Indeed, not 100% the same; you are from different companies after all, but their product will work just as well. | Insisting on the BATNA as a better choice without giving much data |
| If I am to make any moves based on your other offer, I need to understand a little more about it. Do you mind explaining how their product, being different, will work as well? | Insisting on more detailed assessment of BATNA (reality testing) |
| Well, to some extent I do. You know, for confidentiality's sake. | Trying to legitimize not sharing data |
| Since you could share its value, I believe that it is consistent to help us understand a little more about it. Without any other information, I cannot change my offer. But if I learn more, I may be able to change ours accordingly. After all, I really want to make sure this deal is good for both of us. | Not calling their reason a threat or bluff. Starting to suspect it is not genuine concern due to resistance to share data. Insisting on data for learning and transparently leading the process for joint value (reality testing) |
| Okay! They are not offering some of the extra services… | Finally sharing further details and thus bringing reality to the negotiation |

**Table 14.1**
A reality-testing dialogue

From the dialogue above, we see that **estimating their BATNA** during preparation can be quite helpful. First, it reduces the surprise element and our potentially negative reaction. Second, it helps us to spot or even estimate how much of a bluff or how far off from reality they may be. Finally, if they resist our reality testing, we can share our suspicion. This can help us see if it is not us who needs reality testing; or stimulate a more specific conversation while sharing that we may know more than they think.

The dialogue above indicates that when an alternative is shared out of a genuine concern, they will often collaborate to improve the BOpoT. On the other hand, if it is a bluff or threat, they are more likely to resist sharing information because they may be lying, exaggerating or keeping us in the dark on purpose. Without trying to corner them, we should insist on reality testing towards value, instead of accepting a power play.

Once our reality testing has clarified the differences between our BOpoT and their BATNA, we can redirect the conversation towards value. If they lean towards their BATNA, we need to relearn interests and tailor better options to increase our BOpoT's value. If our BOpoT is already better, but they do not see this, we need to legitimize its added value.

To avoid offering concessions and unilaterally rewarding their BATNA statement, we can frame the value pursuit as a collaborative exercise. If we improve the BOpoT for them, they should be ready to do the same for us.

Table 14.2 shows how the dialogue in Table 14.1 can be redirected towards value:

| NEGOTIATION DIALOGUE | DIAGNOSTICS |
|---|---|
| *Okay! They are not offering some of the extra services.* | *Difference between BATNA and BOpoT* |
| Thanks for sharing that. This is very helpful. Do you mind if I then ask which ones specifically? | Rewarding good behavior (sharing data) + learning further |
| *The worldwide guarantee and full maintenance service.* | *Detailed differences between BATNA and BOpoT* |
| And is that okay for you? | Enquiring if interests are satisfied |
| *Well, it does make the package cheaper.* | *Confirming that one interest is satisfied* |
| Am I hearing correctly that price is more important? I thought reliability was key and that millions were at stake if something failed. That is why I offered you our most robust package, which is of course more expensive. | Clarify understanding over interests (reliability vs. price) + explaining the rationale behind the BOpoT offered |
| *Price is always important. But so is reliability. They asked for 15% less and told me their product is as reliable as yours.* | *Confused about interests priorities + BATNA (are they equally reliable?)* |
| Of course, price is important and please let us know if at any time you believe our price to be unfair. On the issue of reliability, did they give you any data that proves their point? | Acknowledge interests and checking for potential perception of unfair pricing + legitimacy on reliability |
| *No. You are not telling me that they are not good as well.* | *Afraid of BATNA-bashing* |
| I would not dare to say they are not good. In terms of reliability, I do believe they are not as good as we are. If you have a few minutes, I have some data on clients who have returned or switched from our main competitors to us. Their main reason is exactly reliability. | Being specific on the advantage of the BOpoT over BATNA + presenting legitimacy to clarify perception of added value |
| *I did not know that. Do you have comparative reliability data?* | *Asking for more legitimacy* |
| Unfortunately not. We only have the numbers our clients give us and the amount they lost through lack of reliability. We also have data on how reliable our offerings are. | Sharing legitimacy that is available |
| *I would love to see those.* | *Engaged in a value conversation* |
| Here they are. | Sharing data (legitimacy) |

| NEGOTIATION DIALOGUE | DIAGNOSTICS |
|---|---|
| This is very helpful, thanks! | Appreciative as it facilitates decision |
| I am glad you like it. | Rewarding good behavior |
| But I still would like to have your package cheaper. | Insisting on lower price (win-lose temptation?) |
| Alright. I have a few ideas to make our package cheaper with minimal reliability impact. I also have ideas on how you can help reduce our delivery price. Would that help? | Making this an opportunity to revisit and re-tailor options to better suit both sides' interests (reliability + lower price and profitability) |
| That would be great actually. What do you have in mind?... | Inviting new options |

**Table 14.2** Redirecting towards value

While reality testing and redirecting into value productively manages their BATNA, at times these will not be enough. Eventually, even after our best value efforts, we may find out that our BOpoT is still worse than their BATNA. What do we do then?

If we are seriously committed to a value negotiation approach, we need to help them make their best possible decision. To do otherwise is to send a very negative message that our value negotiation effort was just a set-up. Helping them make the best possible decision, however, does not mean giving up. If their BATNA seems to be better than our BOpoT, we can still try to close the deal. Can we further understand their interests, come up with better options or have stronger legitimate reasons? Why or how could our BOpoT still be their best choice?

But if after our best efforts, our BOpoT is indeed worse than their BATNA, there is little we can do. It would make little sense for them to close a deal with us. As much as it hurts to have them walk away after all our efforts, we need to understand and accept it. Acknowledging their right to walk away can strengthen the future of the relationship and weaken potential threats. This acknowledgment affirms our commitment to the win-win message. It also shows them that we will not panic and make concessions, thus deflating potential threats.

## Around the Negotiation

Just before closing the deal, Ghassan asked Tali for a 25% discount. Tali worked hard to improve the deal without reducing her margin, but Ghassan rejected all her ideas and insisted on the discount. She then legitimized her price, which Ghassan acknowledged to be fair, but he continued to insist on his position. When this failed, Ghassan hung up the phone without telling Tali if he would close the deal. A couple of hours later, Alon (Tali's boss) called her saying that he finally gave Ghassan a 20% discount and "successfully" closed the deal for her. Tali was mortified.

### POINT OF INTEREST

**Internal vs. External BATNA**

An external BATNA is an alternative that a party can pursue if they walk away from the negotiation, i.e., they seek resources external to the negotiation.

An internal BATNA is an alternative where a party walks away from the negotiation as it is intended. It happens in multi-party negotiations, or when decisions are shared by more than one person on each side. An internal BATNA is a BATNA to the individual negotiator, but not to the organizations or all parties.

For example, if A, B, C and D are negotiating, A's internal BATNA may be to deal with B and C, but not D. A is still walking away from a deal with all parties to commit to an alternative resource arrangement inside the negotiation. Another example is when someone goes over someone else's head to get a decision.

Tali managed Ghassan's BATNA inside the negotiation, but failed to understand the moves around the negotiation. Alternatives, for example, invite outside factors linked to our negotiation that can greatly impact its outcome. Hence, we have to be aware of and proactively manage moves around the negotiation. Lax and Sebenius call these "moves away from the [negotiation] table," which form a major part of their 3D negotiation system.

If the other side has a threatening BATNA, we cannot just try to handle it once it is brought inside the negotiation. It may already be a case of too little too late. We need to also look and manage around the negotiation. For example, whenever legitimate (right, appropriate or fair), we can try to reduce the power of their BATNA. Doing so lessens their ability to threaten or engage us in a win-lose battle, while encouraging them to focus on value.

Six months later, the original project ended and Ghassan wanted a new project. He called Tali once again and they negotiated their new project extensively. Table 14.3 shows the lead-up to the closing of their negotiation:

| NEGOTIATION DIALOGUE | DIAGNOSTICS |
| --- | --- |
| *Since you like our proposal, when do you want us to start?* | *Clarifying commitment* |
| Actually, before we go forward, I want a 20% discount. | Bad behavior (concession) was rewarded before, thus trying it again |
| *Can I understand why?* | *Thinking: "Not again!" but focused on learning* |
| Well, I just want a discount. | Positional |
| *I will be glad to see if we can do something with the project to have it cost you 20% less, if this is what you are interested in.* | *Suggesting tailoring new options to accommodate new interests* |
| No, don't touch the project. I like the project as it is. It took us two months to define it. I just want a price that is 20% lower. | Expressing strong interest in the project as it is and new price position |
| *I am afraid we cannot do this. Are you saying that our price is unfair?* | *Resisting giving in to position + checking pricing legitimacy perception* |
| No! Not unfair, just high. | Not legitimizing claim (positional?) |
| *Well, it is a high-value project. If we understand correctly, you will both save and make money with it. We actually have good reasons to believe that we are pricing ourselves quite fairly. Would you like me to share it with you?* | *Reinforcing how the option satisfies their interests and suggesting legitimacy be further clarified* |
| No! That is not the point here. If you are not willing to give me the discount, maybe I should call my friend Alon, your boss, instead of wasting my time with you. You told me previously there was nothing that could be done about the price, yet he gave me 20% off. | Threatening Tali with his internal alternative + challenging her authority |
| *I remember. That is why before we started talking I prepared him on our progress. He fully supports this price. But if you still want to talk to him, I will be glad to transfer you. Would you like me to do it?* | *Sharing how she worked around the table to reduce the power of his internal BATNA (thus showing no fear)* |
| No! There is no need to bother him now. I can always talk to him later. I need to think about all the data you gave me. | Seeing his BATNA deflated, tries to save face and move on |

| NEGOTIATION DIALOGUE | DIAGNOSTICS |
|---|---|
| Sure. Should I expect an answer shortly? I have to start reserving resources if we are to start your project soon. | Clarifying commitment process |
| I will try to call you within a couple of days. If I don't, call me back. | Committing to a process and creating a safeguard |
| Okay! Will do. | |

**Table 14.3**
Lead-up to closing of negotiation

Ghassan called the next day to close the deal without further asking for a discount. Tali had reduced the power of Ghassan's BATNA by preparing her boss, making it useless for Ghassan to go over her head. As seen here, moves away from the table can be crucial. In this case, it meant reducing the power of their BATNA, but it could mean several different moves: establishing a new precedent (legitimacy), building a better BATNA (alternative), finding an intermediary to connect the parties (relationship), etc.

Note: Like every move to an alternative, despite our best win-win intentions, our efforts to reduce their BATNA's power can be seen as win-lose. Thus, we prefer to avoid unilateral power moves, since they risk ruining the relationship if identified or misinterpreted.

## Using Our BATNA

Ubiratan's company had to move offices within three months. His boss asked him to find a new office space and negotiate the lease contract. However, Ubiratan faced two particular challenges. First, they were in a "hot" market, where prices increased as fast as available office rental space disappeared. Second and worse, his boss had already pre-selected a space and shared their three-month deadline to the potential landlady, Linda.

And that is how Ubiratan's negotiation started. With him trying to talk with Linda who was consistently on vacations, sick, in meetings, etc. The only time he spoke to her, she briefly said that she wanted double the rent they were now paying. Now this amount was, by Ubiratan's research, too much even for the market standards. However, he never got a chance to share that with Linda.

### Around the Negotiation

As the end of the contract was only six weeks away, Ubiratan realized he had no alternatives. He then decided to change strategies. He started to search for other places while negotiating an option to stay at their current location for another three months. Though the search didn't lead to a better place, the extension option was accepted. Two weeks before their rental contract was about to expire, Linda called Ubiratan to talk (Table 14.4).

| NEGOTIATION DIALOGUE | DIAGNOSTICS |
|---|---|
| I am sorry I was not available before. | Genuine or a lie? We may never know |
| *No problem, I understand you are a busy person.* | *Realizes raising a doubt will not help and shows understanding* |
| Indeed. Thanks for your understanding. So what do you think of our place? | Seeks level of interest |
| *We like it a lot, as my boss mentioned to you before.* | *Expresses interest as it does not weaken his position* |
| So are you ready to sign the rental agreement? | Rushing to commitment |
| *We are not sure about a few terms and conditions, including but not limited to the price.* | *Raising new interests* |
| What do you mean? | Confusion or threat? |
| *From my research of the market, the price you are asking for is higher by over 30%. Is there a reason for that?* | *Shares research on price to legitimize interest discussion process* |
| Well, as far as I understand you do not have much of a choice. Your boss told me that you have exactly two weeks to move and our place will be available then. I guess with the specific requirements you have, you do not have a lot of choices in this market. | Implicit threat with her BATNA, but explicitly testing the weakness of Ubiratan's BATNA |
| *You are right that we do not have many other choices yet and yours is a good one for us. Unfortunately, the price is still high. Actually, in terms of the deadline to move, I should tell you that we have an option to extend our current contract if we need more time to find the right place for the right price. I hope your place will be the one for us and I will not need to exercise my option.* | *Discloses his BATNA to dismiss her power move and pressure on him + expresses his main interests (right place and right price) + continued interest to work with her* |
| What do you mean an option? You are not moving? | Confused, surprised or angry? |
| *I never said that. I would love to move in two weeks and get this done already. However, it is very important for me and my company that we do not rush into a bad deal. We are committed to getting the right place for the right price.* | *Clarifies main interests (right place and right price) + continued interest to work with her* |
| Are you saying that I should not increase my price? | Challenges his request's legitimacy |
| *We agree that you need to increase the price over your previous tenant. It is the state of the market and we cannot help it. We just do not think it should be so much.* | *Acknowledges legitimacy to increase, but not the amount. Clarifies it is not a matter of "if", but "how much"* |
| Well, what do you have in mind? | Unaware of best next process move? |
| *The average price per square foot in this area for the last few months is 30% lower and we believe that would be a fair price. I will be glad to show you my research if you would like to double-check it.* | *Opening counteroffer backed by legitimacy + sharing data as transparent collaborative move after the best solution* |
| No! (Pause) Actually yes, do give it to me. I need to show it to some people internally before I decide anything. | Remembering that she needs to run the decision by others before commitment |
| *Of course. Should we talk about some of the other conditions?...* | *Leading the process to other interests* |

Though a few other terms and conditions were not as flexible, Linda accepted the 30% lower rent. Ubiratan also found that paying the rent a few days earlier made a big difference to Linda and little for them. The company moved within two weeks and the current landlord did not charge for the option in the end.

**Table 14.4**
Using BATNA around the negotiation

When Ubiratan realized he had no alternatives then worked to produce some, he engaged in moves away from the table. As a consequence, he increased his choices and reduced Linda's power over him. **Knowing and improving on our alternatives** prepares the negotiation for a win-win process. It potentially reduces the power distance, gives us confidence not to close just any deal or give in to a power struggle. The result is we can take more risks and work harder towards a win-win, value-rich deal.

What if we only have bad alternatives and cannot improve them because we lack time or other resources? At least we now know that we need to negotiate carefully since not reaching a deal can be costly to us. It makes us work harder on value creation and to be even more careful in value claiming.

## Inside the Negotiation

Ubiratan also disclosed his BATNA to Linda after she threatened him about having no choice. Indeed, disclosing our alternatives can be a risky move especially early in the negotiation. However in this case, not only was it late in the process, but Ubiratan was also suspicious of Linda's intentions. Her threat to him confirmed her win-lose attitude. Throughout the process, she kept on putting time pressure on him to accept a bad option (high rent). She operated under the assumption of Ubiratan's lack of or weak BATNA, which she eventually voiced to him. Ubiratan then decided to share his BATNA.

Did he disclose this at the right time? Actually there is no right time, but there are times when it is more appropriate to do it. For example, when they dismiss our BATNA and continue insisting that we accept a bad option late in the negotiation. So it was an appropriate moment for Ubiratan to correct Linda's assumption about his BATNA.

But could he have mentioned or used his BATNA earlier? Certainly, it is always a choice of risk and reward. We just need to keep in mind that the sooner we reveal our BATNA, the more risks we run: the more we may damage the relationship; the less value we may discover and create; the more likely we are to trigger win-lose resistance. Such resistance could take the form of fear and thus defending their position, or anger and then counter-attacking ours.

Besides timing, it is also notable that Ubiratan did not share all details of his BATNA (option for three months only). Instead, he mentioned: "…we have an option to extend our current contract if we need more time to find the right place for the right price."

This management of information is important to avoid creating a ceiling and reducing our value possibilities. By revealing our BATNA details, we create a clear reference mark for them to beat. And though it can force them over a certain limit, it demotivates them from going further. If we say that we have an alternative offer of 50 million yen, they have no reason to offer us more than 50,000,001 yen. Instead, saying that we have an offer higher than theirs opens possibilities beyond this figure.

Ubiratan also reinforced his interests to continue the collaborative exercise with Linda by saying: "I hope your place will be the one for us and I will not need to exercise my option."

He did so to limit the alternative from coming across as a threat, thus protecting the relationship. Mentioning alternatives suggests our intention to walk away from the relationship. Of course, this has a negative impact as it surfaces our belief that the relationship is unimportant or not our focus. And though people know this may be the case at times, it is still a hard message to hear for most.

## Walking Away from the Negotiation

What if Linda had returned with an ultimatum: double the rent or nothing? The question then is whether Ubiratan should walk away. That then begs the questions: when and how should he do it?

Our belief is that walking away is a strategy of last resort, since coming back afterwards can be very risky. In this case, before walking away, Ubiratan could try to diagnose the reasons for Linda's positional ultimatum. He could find out it was a bluff or that Linda did have another potential tenant willing to pay double the rent. He could then reality-test. He could discover if she truly needed more value or just had to appear strong before her team. He could try to tailor new options or find stronger legitimacy to persuade her. In sum, there are many things that he could have done even if she issued him an ultimatum.

However, there are surely times when we have to walk away. After we exhaust our value-creation ideas or if they insist on something below our bottom line (or BATNA), we may walk away. If we decide to do so, there are a few things that can help us do it well.

First, we are responsible for the success of our own negotiation. If they are bluffing or testing our limits, they may overdo it and push us too far. They may then have a hard time calling us back into the negotiation without losing face. It is difficult to imagine them saying after we walk away: "Please come back! I was just pushing you to learn your limits. Now that I know them, I am willing to negotiate with you more flexibly."

We cannot let them spoil our negotiation because of their wrong tactics or mistakes. Thus, it is important that we help the negotiation succeed as much as possible despite their errors. To do so, we can:

1. **Open the door** – If we are close to walking away, instead of storming out and surprising them, we can warn them of this if nothing changes.
    - "I would love to see if there is a way for us to improve this proposal together. However, if this is indeed your best proposal (BOpoT), then I am afraid that it makes little sense for me to agree to it considering that I have other better offers."
    - "If you continue to insist on this proposal, which I have already mentioned does not work for me, you will be forcing me to walk away. I would prefer to still work with you to improve it, but if I see that you are not willing to, you will leave me no choice."

2. **Leave an open door** – As we walk away, we leave them with our best possible option. If appropriate, we disclose the details of our BATNA to back up our BOpoT.
    - "Before I go, I would like to leave with you the best possible proposal I can give. I know you said it does not work for you, but if something changes on your end and you can agree to this (or something very similar), do let me know."

- "Since I have another offer of 50 million yen, if you find out that you can do better than that, please contact me so that we can continue this conversation."

3. **Invite them through the door** – We do not want to restrict our ability to go to our BATNA, while giving them a reasonable time to rethink.
    - "I can wait until 2 pm tomorrow to talk to my alternative so you have some time to review my BOpoT internally. If your team likes it, please call me before 2 pm."
    - "I will start talking to my alternative later today, but if something changes on your end that makes my BOpoT acceptable, feel free to call me until tomorrow morning when I can still stop my talks with them."

Second, it helps to walk away from the proposal, not from the person or the negotiation. This is particularly true if they were collaborative, but unfortunately the substance negotiation failed to generate more value than our BATNA. Here, we can legitimize our decision to walk away purely on substance grounds. Thus, we separate the substance from the relationship, while preserving and appreciating the latter. This facilitates their return as it minimizes losing face and keeps future possibilities open. An example would be.

> I really appreciate all the effort we put into this together. It seems there is nothing else we can do to make this deal better. Unfortunately, it is still significantly below my BATNA on the points I mentioned. I hope you understand that I have to make the best decision for my organization. It was a pleasure working with you and I would like to be able to come to you next time a new opportunity arises.

## Threat vs. Warning

When we open the door to walk away, we can come across as either delivering a threat or a warning. A threat is a message that a negotiator is willing to engage in an act of coercion against the other. A warning is a signaling of danger ahead. In a negotiation, both threat and warning aim to influence behavior with potentially negative consequences from ignoring our words.

In bargaining theories, the general advice is to make our threat credible so it effectively influences behavior. We, however, prefer warnings to threats as warnings are more credible and more positive to the relationship. Warnings are much more matter-of-fact and less of a power move. Warnings such as "I have to walk away if the price is not right for me" can be used to protect an interest. It depersonalizes the act of walking away from negative intentions.

Below are some recommendations for effective warning statements in negotiations. We illustrate them with an example of retreating (walking away) from an attempted interest exchange in a conversation:

1. **Specify the negative behavior we want to influence** – "For the last few minutes, I have been sharing information with you, but have gotten nothing in return."

2. **Clarify why it creates danger ahead** – "I am afraid that your behavior puts me at a disadvantage while indicating that you have no collaborative intentions."

3. **Legitimize how their behavior makes the danger imminent** – "I do not see a reason to collaborate with someone who is not willing to reciprocate. If I continue to get no information from you, I will be left with no choice but to protect myself."

4. **Leave exact details of danger unsaid** – "To protect myself, I may be forced to start withholding information as well." (Don't commit to behave in ways that limit our choices until we are ready to act.)

5. **Show them an easy way to avoid or retreat from the danger** – "If however you start sharing information with me, I will be glad to start reciprocating your effort."

**NOTE: Keep the danger ahead realistic** – We do not threaten to force information out of them, for example, since we do not know if we can. Otherwise our warning becomes a threat, which may sound like a bluff and be less credible. Bluffing about walking away can be quite risky. First, they may call our bluff. Second, if we do walk away, but then need to return we will have dramatically reduced our credibility.

## The Time Alternative

When making the best possible decision, many negotiators simplify it to a "go or no go" situation. Between committing to the BOpoT and walking away to our BATNA, we already have a handful. And yet, sometimes, neither BOpoT nor BATNA look attractive. In negotiations, the decision should usually include a "maybe go" element, which relates to committing in the future.

### POINT OF INTEREST

**Seller's vs. Buyer's BATNA**

Buyers normally have alternatives, i.e., other sellers. However, sellers usually see themselves as NOT having any alternatives. Though less obvious, this is a misperception.

Sellers of unique, value-added offerings or limited capacity have other buyers as alternatives. Now, most sellers are probably not in this category. But for them, there is still the element of time.

Time is a seller's most precious commodity. Time spent with a bad buyer is time NOT spent with a better one. Instead of exhausting time and other resources with a win-lose client, sellers can seek and be rewarded with win-win ones.

In bargaining, normally the choice is go or no go, because the strategies close the door on a later commitment. Aggressive or manipulative power games do not lend themselves to a willingness to deal again in the future. But a value negotiation approach strengthens the relationship so the parties may walk away today to return tomorrow.

Time is an important factor in negotiations, since it works as an alternative to closing a deal today. With more time, we can develop or improve our alternatives. With more time, we feel less desperate to close a bad deal today. Alu was an INSEAD MBA student looking for jobs during a market downturn. After much effort, she finally secured one interview. Unfortunately, at the very first meeting, her interviewer asked if she had any other offers. Not wanting to look weak or desperate, but also not wanting to lie, she replied: "Not yet. Though I am not worried since I have time. I invested a lot on my MBA and I am committed to finding the right job and compensation package. I hope this job is the one."

By revealing that she had time, Alu communicated that her lack of concrete alternatives was no weakness. She then took advantage to redirect the conversation towards value by introducing her interests of the right job and compensation package. Having time is like having a strong alternative as possibilities remain open; the pressure to commit is thus reduced. But Alu's interviewer did not stop there. After a couple of other questions, he dropped the following one on her: "Alu, your CV is very impressive and I like you a lot. I trust that we will be able to offer you a position. Could you stop talking to other companies until our interview process ends?"

Now, Alu had no job interviews scheduled, but was negotiating with some companies to be interviewed. Two of these looked to be quite promising. To stop talking to them now would be to throw away potential alternatives, while putting her under significant time pressure. If she received no offer at the end of this process, she would have lost precious time. That fear could make her feel more desperate, want to move faster and make mistakes. To negotiate at her best, she could not accept his request:

> Do I understand correctly that you are offering me something guaranteed?

> No, I cannot guarantee you anything at this point. I am just saying that I have a good feeling about this interview.

> Thanks, I also have a good feeling about our interview. Do you mind if I first ask if you are interviewing other candidates?

> Of course we are. We are in recruiting season and looking for the best. Why do you ask?

> I have to confess that I have a hard time agreeing to not talk to other companies, especially when you will continue to talk to other candidates.

> What are you saying?

> I am trying to say that I do not understand your request very well. Why would it be fair for you to talk to others, while I cannot do the same? I believe that you cannot expect me to stop talking to others without your doing the same or making me an offer.

> **I just want to ensure that you will be here when we hopefully make you an offer.**

> I appreciate your concern and share your hope. I will love an offer from you. Could I suggest something?

> **Sure! What do you have in mind?**

> Instead of not talking with other companies, I can warn you if something is about to happen so that we try to conclude our process faster.

> **I believe this could work.**

> Good! This way we guarantee that I will be here if you decide to extend me an offer. However, if you decide to hire someone else, I will not have to start from zero again somewhere else.

Alu rejected the request of closing the door to her potential alternatives. She legitimized it by demonstrating the lack of reciprocity or balance as the interviewer was unwilling to forego his alternatives or time. She then generated a new process option to satisfy the interviewer's interest over her availability in case of an offer. This afforded her time to negotiate without having to rush into a deal. In the second round of interviews, the same interviewer surprised her by asking:

> What if I were to make you an offer now? How much would you want?

> **That would be great. Are you making me an offer?**

> Not yet. But if I offered you a job right now, how much would make you say yes? I need an answer now. What will it be?

At this point, Alu was being interviewed by other companies, though they had not talked numbers yet. Once again, Alu found herself under time pressure. In pressing for early commitment, the interviewer was taking away her time to enter into new interviews, get other offers or even just think. He could have been betting on her fear of not getting other offers or ignorance over future offers. There was pressure on Alu to ask for something potentially lower but guaranteed. Alu replied: "I am very excited about your potential offer. As I shared with you, I am now interviewing with a couple of other companies. Before I commit to anything and forego these opportunities, I need to feel comfortable to not regret my decision later. So I can say yes today if you make me an offer I cannot refuse! An offer that is…"

Alu transparently shared the consequences of a commitment and demonstrated how unfair it would be for her to just let go of the value potential from the other interviews. She also indicated her interest to make a good decision and close a good deal. She then proposed the option of "an offer I cannot refuse" as a potentially agreeable BOpoT. She went on to define a very favorable option, which she believed to be superior to the value potential of her alternative interviews.

## BATNA as a Win-Win Tool?

As we already mentioned, despite alternatives playing a bigger role in win-lose negotiations, they are still an important value negotiation element. The key contributions of alternatives to a win-win dynamic lie in the choices they provide and a recourse from being pressured into a win-lose dynamic. Still, as we have been seeing, using alternatives in a win-win way is difficult, which makes us wonder if it can be done at all.

Much of what we did before was to help keep alternatives away and refocus on value. When it is time for us to exercise our choice, we try to do so in the spirit of the Positive No. But our alternatives provide a few different uses that also deserve mention.

In many cultures, we find jobs through networking with friends and acquaintances. At times, we can put them in an awkward situation. They may feel pressured to do us a favor even at great personal effort or cost to them. In these cases, we may want to put them at ease and, funnily enough, sharing our BATNA may do just that. When Inna was looking for a job, she naturally turned to her former mentor Stanimir. Stanimir held an important position in a large yet fast-growing company. Inna prepared two statements:

- I do not want you to feel pressured to give me a job just to be a good friend or because you may think I need one. I have other ongoing projects and as much as I would love to work with and learn from you, if this is not the right time, maybe it will be in the near future."

### POINT OF INTEREST

**Non-Negotiables vs. Alternatives**

Negotiators are often tempted to quickly reveal non-negotiables for efficiency's sake. If I say early on "We need at least $100K" and they reply "Sorry, we can't do that!" we may feel as if we saved a lot of time from being wasted.

But how can we tell if they merely failed to see value that justified paying $100K? What if they were ignorant of our value possibilities?

Non-negotiables are negative interests framed as alternative threats. Not only do we scare them into resistance, we may cap our upside too.

Thus, we recommend sharing non-negotiables after everyone sees enough value in the deal. Only then do we include risks and limitations. To do so before this is to create barriers that the parties may not know or want to overcome.

- "Though I would love to work at your company and particularly with you, if there is nothing there for me right now, please tell me. I believe you would like to know that I actually have a couple of other offers, so no matter what happens, I will be okay. I already appreciate your considering my request for a job."

In unique cases, revealing the alternatives can improve the relationship. One such case seems to be hostage negotiations, which most people will hopefully never be involved in. In other situations, just getting rid of alternatives altogether can be quite powerful, like in the expression "burning the boats."

Famous hostage negotiator Dominick Misino shares that his alternative in a hostage negotiation is police intervention. He also reveals his joint interest with the hostage taker of getting the latter out alive. Without feeding false illusions that he will help the hostage taker escape, Misino uses the alternative as an external enemy. Actually, both hostage taker and negotiator sincerely want to avoid the alternative, which makes sharing it a genuine effort to find a better solution.

History exemplifies the power of burning the boats to strengthen relationships and commitment. In 1519, when Spanish conquistador Hernan Cortes arrived in what is Mexico today, he ordered all boats to be sunk. Both Alexander the Great and Julius Caesar are attributed to have used similar strategies. Hernan Cortes not only reduced, but literally eliminated everyone's alternatives, including his own. In making retreat impossible, he forced everyone to focus on working together and doing their best to succeed. Though many argue over his later tactics, Hernan Cortes' campaign was a military success.

This can be a risky strategy. Had Hernan Cortes sunk all ships but his own, mutiny may have resulted instead of unity. If he sunk only his ship, the others may have abandoned him. When burning the boats, our assumptions of their "boats" and of our ability to "burn" them must be correct. Otherwise, we may find

> Since we both do not want to go to court, how about we focus on getting the best solution to our problem?

> Who said I do not want to go to court? You may not want to because you have no case. I, on the other hand, am more than ready to take you to court.

ourselves caught out:

To minimize this move's risk, all parties have to be willing to burn the boats at the same time. We do not want to burn our boat, only to find out that they did not burn theirs. If we try to burn their boat first, they may stop us and burn ours instead. Hernan Cortes, Julius Caesar and Alexander the Great pulled this off because they had a large power difference over their armies. Most negotiators will not have such a power difference and need to be extra careful when attempting this move.

In this chapter, we explored the role of alternatives and the BATNA in a negotiation. We saw how to handle their BATNA both inside and around the negotiation. We also learned to manage our own BATNA inside, around and when walking away from a negotiation. We saw the difference between a threat and a warning, as well as how to use alternatives in a win-win way.

# summary

Alternatives are an important part of a value negotiator's toolkit, just one that comes with a tag: "Handle with care!" Their power can tempt us away from our value-focus. Thus we should be quick to prepare and reluctant to talk about them.

## The All Too Powerful BATNA

1. Handling their BATNA - We want to productively manage the negotiation if they mention their BATNA
   a. Inside the negotiation
      i. Estimate their BATNA
      ii. Reality test their statement
      iii. Redirect the conversation towards value
   b. Around the negotiation (moves that are away from the negotiation table)
      i. Reduce the power of their BATNA

2. Using our BATNA
   a. Around the negotiation
      i. Knowing and improving on our alternatives
      ii. Be careful if we have bad alternatives and cannot improve them
   b. Inside the negotiation
      i. When they dismiss our BATNA or insist we accept a bad option
      ii. We disclose our BATNA, but not all of its details
      iii. We reinforce our interests to continue the collaborative exercise
   c. Walking away from the negotiation
      i. Open the door – Warn them we may leave if nothing changes
      ii. Leave an open door – Leave them with our BOpoT
      ii. Invite them through the door – Give them a fair, but limited, time to rethink
   d. Threat vs. Warning
      i. Specify the negative behavior we want to influence
      ii. Clarify why it creates danger ahead
      iii. Legitimize how their behavior makes the danger imminent
      iv. Leave exact details of danger unsaid
      v. Show them an easy way to avoid or retreat from the danger
      vi. Keep the danger ahead realistic
   e. The Time Alternative
      i. Time is a possibility for future alternatives, but it can also be shortened to apply pressure

## BATNA Can Be Used as a Win-Win Tool

1. To avoid putting relationship under the pressure to do us a favor
2. To create a common challenge or opportunity (external enemy)

# questions

## Easy

1. Why are alternatives good and bad for negotiation at the same time?
2. When should we think about, have or build our BATNA?
3. What are the two main potential reasons for the other side to mention their BATNA in a negotiation?
4. What are negotiators' likely reactions when the counter-party purposefully reveals their BATNA as a power move?
5. What is the difference between handling their BATNA inside and around the negotiation?
6. How can we tell if the BATNA they disclosed is a lie, a threat or a genuine concern?

## Medium

1. What is the suggested two-step approach to handle their BATNA inside the negotiation?
2. What is the advice to handle it around the negotiation?
3. How do we redirect the conversation towards value?
4. What are some of the relevant steps to use our BATNA inside the negotiation?
5. If we prepare and find out that we have some great potential alternatives before entering the negotiation, what do we do?
6. What do we do if we only have bad alternatives and cannot improve them due to lack of time or other resources?
7. What are the similarities and differences between having time and having a BATNA in a negotiation?

## Difficult

1. What do we do if after our best efforts in handling their BATNA, it is still better than our BOpoT for them?
2. Why would acknowledging their right to walk away strengthen our win-win message? How do we do it? Give an example.
3. What are the differences between an internal BATNA and handling their BATNA inside the negotiation?
4. Give three examples of how to reduce the power of their BATNA.
   a. What are the potential negative consequences?
   b. How can we manage such negative consequences?
5. When should we disclose our BATNA early? Why? How do we do it? Give an example.
6. What are the problems with the following statement: "If you continue to withhold information, I will have to walk away." How can you improve on it? Give an example.

# scenarios

## Easy

1. To reality-test, we are supposed to test their reality. This means first, telling them what is really going to happen. Second, asking them what they think is going to happen. Third, challenging their views and correcting them where necessary. And finally, offering a new option that is more realistic than the one they mentioned.

   Do you agree with the statement above? Why?

2. When Hernan Cortes sunk all boats, he used the BATNA in a win-win way. Explain how this was a win-win move and the risks involved in it. How would such a move look like in a negotiation of yours? Give an example.

## Medium

An external BATNA is an alternative that a party can pursue if they walk away from the negotiation, i.e., they seek resources external to the negotiation.

An internal BATNA is an alternative where a party walks away from the negotiation as it is intended. It happens in multi-party negotiations, or when decisions are shared by more than one person on each side. An internal BATNA is a BATNA to the individual negotiator, but not to the organizations or all parties.

What are the similarities and differences in terms of impact that the internal and external BATNAs have? How do we handle the internal BATNA?

## Difficult

Diagnose the dialogues below:
1. The Last Minute Discount Request Dialogue

| NEGOTIATION DIALOGUE | DIAGNOSTICS |
|---|---|
| This all looks great! So can I have a 20% discount? | |
| I am glad that you like our offering. Can you help me understand how did you come up with 20%? | |
| I just think that our brand name in your client list is worth something. It is definitely worth something to your competitors. | |
| I agree. Your brand name in our client list is good for us. | |
| So will you give me the 20% discount? | |
| Do you sell your brand name to people's client lists? | |
| Of course not! | |
| I assumed as much. Wouldn't we get to use your name in our client list if we deliver the work to you anyhow? | |
| Well, yes. But I still believe that I deserve a 20% discount. | |

| NEGOTIATION DIALOGUE | DIAGNOSTICS |
|---|---|
| *Why would that be fair?* | |
| I am not saying it is fair, I just want a 20% discount. | |
| *It seems that you are interested in a reduced price. Maybe you have a budget. If this is the case, I will be glad to work with you to reduce our offering to fit it.* | |
| I have no budget. I just want my 20% discount! | |
| *Alright. I am glad to see what you can do for us in return for the 20% discount. Is there something you have in mind?* | |
| No! Are you telling me that you will not give me the 20% discount? | |
| *If we do not find any other value for my company, I do not see a reason to do so. I believe that we are already offering you a very good service for a fair price. I will be glad to reduce the price if the total value for us is kept at least the same.* | |
| But I may go to one of your competitors. | |
| *Indeed you may. It is actually a right of yours to do so if it makes sense to you. But I would prefer to lose one customer, even an important one like you, than to reduce my price for no fair reason.* | |
| You know what, that is fine. Thanks for your time. I will think about it and come back to you tomorrow on this one. | |
| *Okay! And if you have any ideas to improve this package for you without making it worse for us, please let me know.* | |
| Okay. | |

2. The Early Conditional Job Offer Dialogue

| NEGOTIATION DIALOGUE | DIAGNOSTICS |
|---|---|
| *Am I understanding correctly that you are offering me something guaranteed?* | |
| No, I cannot guarantee you anything at this point. I am just saying that I have a good feeling about this interview. | |
| *Thanks, I also have a good feeling about our interview. Do you mind if I first ask if you are interviewing other candidates?* | |
| Of course we are. We are in recruiting season and looking for the best. Why do you ask? | |
| *I have to confess that I have a hard time agreeing to not talk to other companies, especially when you will continue to talk to other candidates.* | |
| What are you saying? | |

| NEGOTIATION DIALOGUE | DIAGNOSTICS |
|---|---|
| I am trying to say that I do not understand your request very well. Why would it be fair for you to talk to others, while I cannot do the same? I believe that you cannot expect me to stop talking to others without your doing the same or making me an offer. | |
| I just want to ensure that you will be here when we hopefully make you an offer. | |
| I appreciate your concern and share your hope. I will love an offer from you. Could I suggest something else instead? | |
| Sure! What do you have in mind? | |
| Instead of committing to stop talking with other companies, I can warn you if something is about to happen so that we try to conclude the process faster. | |
| I believe this could work. | |
| Good! This way we guarantee that I will be here if you decide to extend me an offer. However, if you decide to hire someone else, I will not have to start from zero again somewhere else. | |

# 15 Conclusion: On Power and Ethics

## Learning Objectives:
- What real negotiation power is
- The four main negotiation power levers and obstacles
- How to use power in a value negotiation way
- The five main ethical tensions
- What bounded ethicality is
- How value negotiation encourages ethical behavior

In this concluding chapter, we link all the previous chapters. It was not by chance that we finished Chapter 14 with the topic of alternatives. As we saw there, the power of alternatives tempts us away from our value-focus into a power struggle. Our power struggle generates many types of resistance, which in turn often invites unethical behaviors such as lies, tricks, deceptions, threats, etc.

Once power moves and unethical behaviors are exchanged between parties, the "gloves are off". Fair play is gone. Rules do not matter anymore and the conflict possibilities become free of limits or impediments. "All is fair in love and war" exemplifies the popular excuse that the end now justifies the means.

However, in value negotiation, we try to avoid both "love" and "war." We do not negotiate to love or be loved (except in unique situations) and, in the process, become soft bargainers. The other extreme of wanting only to win transforms us into hard bargainers engaged in a war-like bargaining process. What we do want in our negotiations is value; not to win, not love, not war, not even power.

Power is a means to an end since most people do not seek power for its sake. Most people seek power to protect or secure interests. Power is what bargainers mistakenly seek to guarantee value. On the other hand, ethics can be an end in itself, even though behaving ethically can also satisfy other interests such as feeling good, generating better relationships, etc. In attempting to maximize value, we consider that most people would prefer to behave ethically when given the choice.

As ethics and power become entangled, they influence every point in a negotiation. This makes them a perfect combination to revisit the key concepts in value negotiation. We look into power in negotiations and invite looking beyond alternatives. We want value negotiators to be able to create and claim value from every available negotiation element. Finally, we look into ethics in negotiations and suggest how to handle some common ethical dilemmas.

> "It is not the strongest of the species that survives, nor the most intelligent that survives. It is the one that is the most adaptable to change."
> — Charles Darwin

# Negotiation and Power

Ms. Kim's landlord asked her to vacate the apartment for his personal use. As she started to look around, she faced a very tight market with few and expensive options. After much time and effort, she found an apartment that was smaller, more expensive and of lower quality. However, it suited her and she was without alternatives. She made an offer with a guarantee deposit check of S$12,000 (equivalent to two months' rent) to her real estate agent. Once her agent handed the offer and check to the new landlord, the deposit became non-refundable.

But what surprised Ms. Kim was returning home to a message on her answering machine which said: "Ms. Kim, this is your landlord. I hope you have not yet committed to move. I have just been transferred to Hong Kong for work and I would love to have you stay at my place for another year. Please call me!"

Ms. Kim really wanted to stay. She quickly called and was ecstatic to learn she could stay for at least another year. But soon her excitement turned into concern as she thought of her S$12,000 deposit. She then mentioned that she would be unable to stay if she could not get her deposit back. Her landlord wished her luck and asked to be kept informed.

When she called her agent, he still had her offer and check. She could cancel the transaction without any penalty so she asked him to do so. However, minutes later, her agent called back confessing his mistake of handing the offer and check to the other agent. Ms. Kim was in complete disbelief. Was he lying? Did he really give the check? After her request to cancel, did he rush to guarantee his commission on the non-refundable deposit? She did not know the truth and would probably never find out.

Worst-case assumptions rushed through her mind as her blood boiled in rage. Upon talking to the agent, he insisted there was nothing more he could do. The offer and check were delivered and that constituted a formal offer. When she asked for the contact information of the other agent, he refused to disclose this saying it was not good practice. Ms. Kim felt powerless to change the situation.

When she found herself screaming at her agent and with a massive headache, she decided to hang up the phone and think. As she saw it, there were three main choices open to her: first, move to avoid losing the S$12,000; second, negotiate for the return of her check; third, find a creative arrangement to stay at her current apartment. She decided to pursue all of them.

She first called a lawyer friend, who advised her to cancel her check. Doing so could increase Ms. Kim's power as their alternative of cashing the check without her consent was taken away. However, such cancellation put her at risk of being embroiled in a potentially costly and time-consuming legal battle. Moreover, Ms. Kim was likely to lose since she had little proof that her requested cancellation was timely. On the other hand, the other side might simply give up and move on. She felt uncertain about the outcome and decided against cancelling the check for now.

Then, Ms. Kim called her landlord. He declared he really wanted to see her stay at his place since she was such a good tenant, and that he could try to help her. After some conversation, the landlord agreed to **waive rent for the next month**.

He could do so because his employer was paying for his own rental next month, and in any case, it would take him at least one month to find a new tenant. After a little more negotiation, Ms. Kim secured an additional two months' stay without any rent increase. The difference was smaller than the fee for a real estate agent to find the landlord a new tenant.

On further discussion, she found out that, for personal reasons, he would return for a few weeks and stay at a hotel. Since that coincided with her vacation trip, Ms. Kim offered the apartment for his stay. Though incredulous at first, the landlord loved the idea and **waived her rent for that month as well**.

There remained the issue of how much the rent would eventually be. The neighboring apartment was going for S$6,000 a month. Since Ms. Kim would pay S$6,000 a month for the other apartment, the landlord agreed to match that offer (an increase from the current S$3,800). Not only was the raise substantial, he knew Ms. Kim would take good care of his property. In the past, he had terrible experiences with tenants who paid more but damaged his apartment. He ran more losses in repairs than gains in rent.

At the end, Ms. Kim had negotiated two free months plus two months without any increase in rent. Considering there was now no need to pay moving costs, she had negotiated savings of over S$12,000 while staying at her preferred place. She gladly agreed to this arrangement.

Staying for Ms. Kim did not mean giving up recovering her check. She felt that it was unfair to lose her deposit since she had asked to cancel the offer in time. After two weeks of arguing with the agents, she managed to get the contact number of the property owner. Interestingly, the check had not been cashed yet. She called him and said:

> Hi, Mr. Chang. This is Ms. Kim. Your agent probably mentioned me.

> Yes. I was aware you were going to call. How can I help you?

> I am calling to see if there is something that can be done about the deposit.

> What do you mean?

> You may or may not know that I made the offer thinking I had to leave my current apartment, which I love. Once I returned home, I found out that my landlord's plans had changed and that I could stay. I called my agent as fast as I could to cancel the whole transaction and he said it was okay. Shortly after, it seemed that the check was handed to your agent. I am not sure what happened.

> I think I see what you are saying. I also do not want a tenant who does not want to be there. But why should I return you the money if it is non-refundable?

> I understand that once you receive my check, it is non-refundable. I just believe there was a misunderstanding in our case. I would be glad to explain the situation in more detail if you want to hear it. I also understand that your apartment has not been taken off the market thus no harm was done, which if I am not mistaken is the reason for the deposit being non-refundable. In such a hot market, you can quickly get another tenant and for a slightly higher rent.

> True. But what if I don't get anyone?

> If you do not get anyone to move in by the same date I would have, then I will be glad to pay you a pro-rata rent for any additional day that your apartment is off the market. Would that work for you?

> Do I keep the check until then as a guarantee and then return you the balance, if any?

> Since you have held onto it until now without cashing it, I believe it is safe to trust you to keep it as a guarantee.

> Okay, I will keep you posted.

> Thanks!

As Ms. Kim expected, within 10 days, Mr. Chang received an offer of S$6,300 a month for a lease starting earlier than hers. He returned her check in full.

# Power in Negotiation vs. Negotiation Power

Ms. Kim was advised to use her power or alternative of cancelling her check early on. She debated internally whether to do it. There was only a small window of opportunity before the other party could cash her check. However, Ms. Kim found cancellation to be a move that was too strong, too adversarial and too soon. She thought that using her power would send the wrong message and legitimize their doing the same. The most likely result would be a power struggle with an uncertain outcome.

Ms. Kim chose not to use power in the negotiation, but rather to use her negotiation power. Resisting her anger, she believed she could succeed and was persistent in finding solutions or at least new possibilities. She thought carefully about her initial move, its implicit message and the impact on her potential success. Ms. Kim chose to reason first, since she could always go to court if things did not work out. She looked at her possibilities, weighted their chances and strategized to improve them. She approached all counter-parties with a win-win attitude. Her choices led to valuable opportunities that carried low risks and people willing to deal reasonably with her.

> *"You cannot simultaneously prevent and prepare for war."*
> Albert Einstein

# Power in Negotiation

Normally, negotiators seek power. Thus, we often find those with a good BATNA feeling all-powerful, while those without one feeling weak. Power, seen this way, is a direct consequence of the quality of one's BATNA. As a result, BATNAs are widely and promptly used in bargaining. Indeed, they are powerful tools in win-lose negotiations. With a better BATNA, we can apply stronger pressure on them to give us what we want in our negotiation — we are using power.

However, the power of the BATNA does not necessarily translate into value or success. Damaging the relationship is but one of the risks to using our BATNA in a negotiation. Some communication problems that follow the raising of resistance are information availability, learning and diagnosing being reduced. Another risk of bringing power into our negotiations is sending a message that this is a battle where everything goes, and inviting the other party to use their power to the fullest.

Neil Strauss in his novel *The Game* demonstrates how Pick-Up Artists (PUAs) operate. Masters of seduction, PUAs are also seen as excellent persuaders within the realm delineated by the laws of attraction. Here, metaphors such as "conquer" or "pedestal" surface the intrinsic power dynamic. PUAs strive to become (or at least project to be) the alpha male to get the woman they desire. It is notable that the alpha male is defined by his relationship of power over others.

One common PUA tool is the "neg," a backhanded compliment to put a woman down without her directly noticing it. Not a direct or cruel insult, the neg is sometimes funny; it ultimately directs attention to a woman's flaws. Some examples are:

- "Your lips look nice, but there is something funny about them. I am not sure why."

- "I like your dress. My grandmother always says that she loves this color."
- "A pretty face like you should pay more attention to her hair style."

A good neg communicates a lack of interest and the ability or willingness to seek another woman (BATNA). This simultaneously intrigues the woman and makes her feel insecure or less powerful. The man who has negged a woman needs to be ready with a smart comment for when she negs back (escalation). He is also never supposed to tell her that she is being negged (no transparency). The book narrates how Strauss became a successful PUA, using the neg and other techniques to win over many women.

The book goes on to describe how Strauss realized he cared little for most of these women. He grew increasingly focused on becoming the best. This power pursuit became more important and sidetracked him from the original aim of a PUA: women. He comprehends how the techniques that helped him "close" a new woman every night were preventing him from being with the woman he really wanted.

In other words, when Strauss had more power (technique) or a short-term concern, his win-lose attitude produced good results. However, as soon as value (love) replaced power as his goal, he realized the power attitude or techniques did not work as well. On the contrary, at every attempt, he further risked losing the woman he wanted.

Similarly, Robert Greene in his famous book *48 Laws of Power* describes stories of historical personalities using power. Interestingly, many winners in one story were also the losers in another story that was under a different power law. Their use of power led some to success, but invited their enemies to seek another power source against them. As the stories show, the power struggle and subsequent damage can go from dismal to fatal. The constant concern and maintenance of the power distance led to paranoia, escalating costs and terrible outcomes.

Notice how both books were at the time among the top 300 and 500 Amazon.com bestsellers respectively. This shows how most negotiators (persuaders, seducers, etc.) seek power to achieve their goals. And while power in negotiations can yield results, its win-lose approach carries significant risks as discussed throughout this book.

Having said this, there are times that we take risks and use our power in negotiations. But we only do so after we have tried most other avenues and reduced the risks from using our power.

## Negotiation Power

What is the difference between power in negotiations and negotiation power? Power in negotiations is our use of power to force or manipulate others into giving in. Negotiation power is our ability to persuade. We go on to explain further.

**Negotiation power is our ability to get the value we want in a negotiation.** Persuasion or bringing power into a negotiation are some ways to do so. Every negotiator actually has several abilities to get value, and our Negotiation Balanced Scorecard (NBS) helps us to keep them balanced and focused. For example, since behaving ethically has value to many, how far should we go to get more money?

A broader definition of negotiation power expands our choices to maximize rewards with minimum risk. It protects us from developing tunnel vision about power, while reminding us that negotiation has several roads to success.

Power in negotiations is a relative concept; the bigger the difference, the more powerful one party is. The concept is contextual, so one side may possess significant power as a monopoly, but be without power in another situation. On the other hand, negotiation power is closer to negotiation ability. It is closer to an absolute concept as it depends less on the context. This lack of relativity means that if any party has a high negotiation power, all parties can benefit from finding better deals.

Ms. Kim was rather powerless in terms of the BATNA. While the agents knowingly tried to take advantage of this, she did not respond in kind. First, she refocused on her interests and on value. Then she sought out things that would increase her ability to get what she wanted. A quick look at her negotiations shows the use of different power sources at each stage:

- **Relationship and communication** – For example, after trying to reason with her agent, Ms. Kim changed the process and sought her own landlord. Relying on their prior relationship, she worked closely with him to find opportunities that most people would miss.
- **Interests and options** – Once Ms. Kim found out the landlord wanted her to stay, she focused on this and other interests to generate and tailor options that made both of them better off.
- **Alternatives** – She also thought of alternatives such as going to court, cancelling the check or just moving, but decided to not act on these for now.
- **Legitimacy and commitment** – She insisted on the legitimacy of her claim with the real estate agents, and managed to renegotiate their commitment from returning the check to getting the owner's contact details.
- **Interests and options again** – She persuaded the owner through a combination of value discovery, generation and claiming that made both of them better off. She negotiated to minimize risk (no losses), while creating value for him (doing the right thing, finding a more willing tenant, securing a higher rent) and ultimately for her as well.

At the end, she got a deal better than she could have ever expected even though she did not have good alternatives. She was able to do so because she sought to maximize her negotiation power by looking at the different power sources available.

Insisting on some preferred power sources at the wrong time or with the wrong person could actually backfire. The win-lose use of alternatives (BATNA to gain power in negotiation), relationship (manipulation) and legitimacy (I am right!) carries risks.

- **Alternatives** – Ms. Kim had little power over the real estate agents since they had her check. She could cancel it but risked frustrating the owner. She chose not to jeopardize the relationship with the owner to keep that avenue open for the future.
- **Relationship** – Her personal relationship with all parties, including her landlord, was distant, therefore she had little grounds for manipulation. Trying this would not only be ineffective, but would frustrate the counterparties.

- **Legitimacy** – Insisting that the check was refundable could have engaged the owner in a debate over right and wrong or what happened in the past. Ms. Kim had little to gain from this move, since in the owner's eyes he was right.

There were many decisions to be made and it seems that Ms. Kim made many right ones. Was it all skill? Not necessarily; there was a certain amount of luck in the agents not depositing her check and the owner's willingness to talk. But those were calculated risks, which she minimized by not pushing the counter-parties to behave in negative ways.

Was there any method to her ways? Indeed there was. This method can help anyone to maximize negotiation power within a win-win context. Negotiation power is actually built by making four choices and acting on them (Table 15.1).

**Table 15.1**

Increasing negotiation power through choices

| We Choose | Not |
| --- | --- |
| Empowering assumptions | Crippling assumptions |
| Negotiable boundaries | Physical limitations |
| Active leverage | Passive acceptance |
| Negotiation preparation | Negotiation improvisation |

Next, we elaborate on these four building blocks of negotiation power.

## Assumptions

As we mentioned at the beginning of this book, we can be our worst enemy. Crippling assumptions reduce our ability to think and act towards success. Under them, even the proper use of value negotiation techniques delivers much less impact. On the other hand, empowering assumptions can help us reach our full negotiation potential.

Crippling assumptions are our premises or beliefs that **negatively** frame the way we think and act. For example, we can try to create value even if we still hold deep beliefs that negotiations are win-lose affairs. However, with these assumptions we are less likely to try as hard and may give up at the first difficulty. Why keep looking if we know there is nothing there anyway? Our value-creation technique may be flawless, but there are no supporting assumptions to positively leverage it.

At the other end, empowering assumptions are our premises or beliefs that **positively** frame the way we think and act. For example, if we believe value creation is possible in negotiation, we are more likely to prepare and try harder to find value, seeing opportunities that others with less effort would have overlooked. Professor Seligman, in his book *Authentic Happiness*, demonstrates how positive-thinking people work harder and better than depressed ones. We want to have as many empowering assumptions supporting our negotiation efforts as we can.

In Table 15.2, an example of a crippling assumption, its empowering version and the conclusion are given for each negotiation element:

| Element | Crippling | Empowering | Conclusion |
|---|---|---|---|
| Relationship | My counter-party is my enemy. | My counter-party is my potential ally. | We can work together to find the best possible solutions for us. |
| Communication | They are insane/unreasonable/stupid. | Their logic and reasons are just very different from mine. | If I communicate well (listen and speak), I may understand and persuade them. |
| Communication | There is no use in talking to them. | We only know the outcome of the negotiation after it is done. | Careful communication may find out what we cannot anticipate. |
| Interests | This is a zero-sum negotiation. | This may be a positive-sum negotiation. | Value creation is probable and will depend on my efforts. |
| Interests | Negotiations are all about numbers and value. | Negotiation is about numbers, value, people, relationships, process, etc. | There are several power sources so I need to find and develop mine. |
| Options | There is only one right answer. | There are usually several good answers. | We can focus on interests, not positions, to create several options. |
| Legitimacy | Rules are rules. | Rules are made by people for a reason. | Mine can be a fair request if it does not conflict with the interests protected by the rule. |
| Commitment | Whoever has more power wins. | Whoever has more power may still not get what they want. | Thus I should not focus on power (not necessarily use my BATNA). |
| Commitment | Power is my ability to coerce, pressure or manipulate them into giving me what I want. | Power is my ability to get what I want. | Thus I should focus on value. |
| Alternatives | Power is absolute. | Power is relative, can change hands and be based on facts or perceptions. | If I am more powerful, I need to be careful and have a backup plan. If I am less powerful, I can work hard to change this situation. |
| Alternatives | An alternative is power in negotiations. | An alternative is a safety net and negotiation power goes beyond the BATNA. | Let me try value creation first. |

**Table 15.2**
Crippling and empowering assumptions

How do crippling assumptions impact us? They inspire overconfidence or certainty (if I have power, there is no way I can lose) which shuts us from learning. At the other extreme, crippling assumptions create a sense of rigidity or helplessness (if I have no power, there is nothing I can do) which stops us from acting to influence the outcome.

For example, if we find them incoherent, unreasonable or stupid, we accept we can do little to change them. That belief saps our confidence and we feel powerless to persuade them. In the end, we are the ones who lose out.

More often than not, their apparent incoherence or unreasonableness hides a different logic that we fail to understand. Such an assumption makes us more likely to listen and probe, think laterally and finally understand them. This understanding brings us one step closer to finding a solution that works for all parties.

Empowering assumptions inspire a sense of responsibility and possibility. They also create a healthy dose of doubt and attention necessary for positive negotiations.

## Boundaries

Roger Fisher tells a story of when his doctor said that he would probably not outlive his wife. After such a blunt statement, Roger asked the doctor why, and he answered:

> First, you are a man and men's average life expectancy is lower than women's.

> Well, there is nothing I can do about that is there?

> No, but the second [reason] is because you smoke and she doesn't.

> Oh! Hard as it is, I can do something about that. Thank you! (He left the doctor's office to work on quitting this habit)

*"God grant me the serenity to accept the things I cannot change, the courage to change the things that I can, and the wisdom to know the difference."*
— Reinhold Niebuhr

The doctor gave Roger the "wisdom" to focus on what he could change; now it was up to Roger to muster the courage (empowering assumption) to quit smoking. As Roger did not have to waste his time on something he could not change, he increased his chances of successfully negotiating change. Most of us, however, do not have "negotiation doctors" around to tell us where to focus. Alas, we have to develop our own wisdom.

One of the first and maybe biggest questions in negotiation we seldom ask ourselves consciously: "Is this negotiable?" And even before we try to negotiate, our minds subtly yet quickly seek an answer, which can be wrong in two main ways:

1. We assume we can negotiate, when we can't.
2. We assume we cannot negotiate, when we can.

Our tendency is to assume from our experiences or others' that a situation or issue is non-negotiable. This is a crippling assumption for two reasons. First, others or ourselves may have lacked the negotiation abilities to succeed then. Second, assuming that something is non-negotiable based on past experiences is to assume that situations or people do not change. In sum, what is not negotiable yesterday may be negotiable today as the elements in the equation may have changed.

We believe that the negotiation process includes the exercise of learning if a situation is negotiable. To learn whether a situation is negotiable is "the wisdom to know the difference" as Niebuhr quoted above. And to gain such wisdom, we have to start by engaging them in a conversation to find the boundaries. Well, isn't this a negotiation already?

We may end up learning that the situation is indeed non-negotiable. However, the costs of learning are normally low if correctly managed. Most people, if asked using the value negotiation approach, will not resent a request for information even if their answer is "no". On the other hand, unexpected negotiation possibilities may reward our learning conversation.

If a negotiation is important, we would like to recommend this: **assume first that we can negotiate**. We see this as an empowering assumption, though it will be wrong at times. However, we believe that the rewards more than outweigh the costs of acting under this assumption.

Besides, assuming the situation is negotiable empowers us as it puts the responsibility for success in our hands. For this responsibility to become empowerment and action, we need to visualize what success could be. Without all the information and to set our minds in the right direction, it helps to ask ourselves:

- What is the best outcome we could dream of if there were no limits?
- What would it take for us to negotiate it?
  - Communication – What could we possibly say?
  - Relationship – Who could possibly want it?
  - Interests – What could they possibly want?
  - Options – What options could possibly satisfy us and them?
  - Legitimacy – Why would they possibly accept it?
  - Alternatives – Where else could we go to get what we want?
  - Commitment – How can we possibly help them say "yes"?

After a single-issue negotiation exercise, we asked if an outcome 200% better than the best class result was possible. The MBA participants were almost unanimous in denying its possibility. However, within seven minutes of asking these questions, the whole class became convinced of its feasibility because they themselves came up with 8–10 different ways to achieve it. Some ideas were certainly better than others, but what mattered was that several could be (and were) successfully applied.

How do these questions help us? After asking them, many quickly come up with ambitious goals and practical ideas for success. These questions make us think about possibilities instead of limitations. They momentarily suspend disbelief to challenge our assumption of non-negotiability. Even if as an exercise, posing and accepting an ambitious goal can peak our curiosity. This challenge releases our creative minds for answers.

Ms. Kim assumed she could negotiate her check back, though Mr. Chang apparently had nothing to gain from that. It seemed a non-negotiable at first and indeed Mr. Chang may not have budged. But she could only be certain after she tried, which she did until she got her money back. If instead Ms. Kim believed she could not change his mind, she would not have worked so hard to contact him. Consequently, she would never discover his willingness to return her check.

What if the costs or risks attached to the learning conversation are too high? Of course, things are different then and we may err on the side of caution and avoid negotiation. If my colleague was fired for asking our boss for a raise, then I may avoid doing that until the market gets better.

As an example, Ms. Kim should not sign a lawsuit waiver to test if she could negotiate the return of her check. The cost of letting go of her BATNA may be too high. However, she could still try to negotiate the waiver itself as it hindered value creation. Is this an artificial limit, a tactic to extract concessions or a narrow scope?

We will never know the real answer until we test it through negotiation. To just speculate is to give room to assumptions that could cripple our ability to succeed. Believing we can change the risks and opportunities around us empowers us to negotiate with better results.

## Setting the Stage (Leverage)

We may see something we can change, but do nothing about it. This is termed "passive acceptance". An example would be seeing a huge wave coming our way, but just waiting or hoping for it to go away. We could however take cover, run away or, better still, buy a surfboard. In these cases, we are actively leveraging ourselves to improve our chances before the situation occurs. We call this "setting the stage".

As already discussed, power distance is one of the biggest obstacles to value negotiation. In a battle, most armies prefer to occupy the higher ground with their backs to the sun. This is an attempt to increase the power distance between the parties. We would like to approach setting the stage from a value negotiation perspective. We set the stage to either limit or prevent them from increasing the power distance, increasing our ability to conduct a successful value negotiation. We do not want to reduce their choices, but rather to increase or maintain ours.

Imagine if in the Battle of Thermopylae, the 300 Spartans simply confronted the Persian army in an open field. A quick massacre would result and change history forever. Instead, they carefully chose the battle ground to reduce their power distance with the Persians. The narrow and difficult-to-circumvent passage forced the Persians to line up and attack only a few at a time. The Persians still had much higher numbers, diverse weaponry and other resources, which led them to victory. However, the battle was better leveled as the Spartans set a proper stage before the encounter.

How can a battle help us understand power in a win-win negotiation? While negotiations differ from actual battles, a positive negotiator recognizes that negotiations can turn sour. To set the stage is to make preparatory arrangements to avoid entering a negotiation critically unbalanced or having already lost. When done well, we clear our process path of obstacles, traps or temptations that prevent us from pursuing value. If they have the higher ground, we climb the hill before we negotiate. If we have the higher ground, we descend before the negotiation starts (while keeping our ability to return).

Similar to "moves away from the table", setting the stage is already part of our negotiation process. It is unique as it takes place before or between, but not during, meetings with the counter-party. To help set the stage we can ask ourselves:

### Relationship
- Who can we talk to or negotiate with before this negotiation?
- Who can we bring into this negotiation?

**Communication**
- What time or place to meet will help create the right atmosphere?
- What messages can we send before we meet to facilitate our negotiation?

**Interests**
- Can we guarantee or at least protect access over resources we need?
- How can we learn their interests ahead of time?

**Options**
- What steps can we take to make options that do not currently exist viable?
- How can we test or check feasibility of our key options in advance?

**Legitimacy**
- What different frames of fairness have they used or accepted in the past?
- Which evidence do we need to produce to enhance our case?

**Commitment**
- How can we put in place a process that facilitates value negotiation?
- How can we buy ourselves more time if we need to?

**Alternatives**
- How can we improve our BATNA so that leaving is a realistic choice?
- How can we worsen their BATNA if they threaten to use it?

Of course, asking these questions is a way to prepare and focus us into action, not an end in itself. To learn that a situation can be changed yet not act on it is similar to passive acceptance. It is a choice we have, but it should come with the knowledge that we are not maximizing our negotiation power.

Many salespeople face procurement departments that force them into bidding or reverse auction processes. This is a clear move from the department to increase their power distance even before the negotiation "starts." We say "starts," because of course the negotiation actually began the moment the department crafted the bidding process and invited the salespeople (critical moment #1 – initiating the interaction). It is already ongoing when the salesperson accepts to join the bidding process (critical moment #2 – defining the process).

Naturally, these processes give more power to the department at the expense of the salesperson. Many salespeople enter these bids because they feel they have no choice. However, every negotiator always has a choice. Setting the stage here could include several moves such as:

1. Create an early relationship with the client to become a preferred vendor to:
    a. Deliver enough value that a bidding process becomes unnecessary and too expensive
    b. Learn their interests better than the competition
    c. Share our business logic and understanding on the topic of our expertise to help them develop their requirements
    d. Co-develop options for their needs that no one else can

2. Suggest (and prove) there is a negotiation process that is better for all (including the procurement person, whose interests may differ from their company's).
3. Negotiate inside our company for:
   a. The ability to walk away from the deal
   b. Being measured not on volume only, but on ROI or EVA to help us know exactly when to walk away from a deal, etc.

These moves may not be quick or easy, but they do add choices. If a deal is important enough, we invest time and effort to set the value negotiation stage. However, if we lack the resources for this, we now know to be extra careful.

And yet, the stage is never completely set before the negotiation starts. Part of the stage is also built as we progress. So if the negotiation turns out well, there may be no need for additional work. On the other hand, if the negotiation starts to derail, we can always remember to reset the stage.

## Be Prepared

Our busy schedules and competing demands cause us to enter many negotiations almost unaware and often underprepared. Probably the easiest to understand of the four elements of negotiation power, preparation is extremely important. **Preparation is the exercise to ready oneself for a negotiation.**

How is preparation different from the other three building blocks of negotiation power? Preparation involves what is going to be said or done in a negotiation meeting. Unlike the often long-term focus of assumptions and boundaries, preparation works on our next transaction. Different from the outward exercise of setting the stage, preparation is more of an internal task. Still, preparation includes all of the above in a broader sense. Indeed, changing our assumptions, negotiating boundaries and setting the stage are all steps to get us ready for future negotiations.

Preparation helps us cover all bases to maximize our ability and knowledge to perform at our best. In preparation, we anticipate our negotiation needs and moves as well as theirs. But can this not be exhausting and endless? Correct. Like packing for a long trip, we aim to bring all that is relevant. Yet we are careful not to overpack as it reduces our efficiency. Especially when time and attention are scarce, managing our preparation makes efficient use of valuable resources.

In preparing for a negotiation, we think through our interests, options and legitimacy in a relaxed and risk-free environment. We carefully craft or even role-play our communication and relationship moves. Once within context, we define our goals, strategize and anticipate our critical moments. We guarantee that we will have what we need when we need it in the negotiation. Preparation reduces the work and improvisation needed and thus our exposure under the more challenging environment of the negotiation process. Preparation minimizes risk and maximizes reward by clarifying our different choices and paths. Since we prepare to fulfill our NBS, a simple way of looking at it is:

- How can we build an interdependent JVP **relationship**?
- What value negotiation **communication** process can we proactively develop for this particular negotiation?

- Do we understand all the **interests** at play?
- What creative and mutual-gains **options** can we generate?
- What persuasive (i.e., meaningful) **legitimacy** can we establish?
- How can we put together well-crafted **commitments** to help them say "yes"?
- Do we have a good **BATNA** as a backup plan?

When preparing, it is important to remember that fire is not fought with fire, but with water, foam or air. Thus, to try to match fire with fire is to generate a power-driven win-lose conflict. Furthermore, many who bargain do so under the belief that they have more power. To counter with a similar power move (escalation) is to play on their turf and reduce our chances of success. We specifically want to avoid this conflict and proactively redirect the negotiation towards value. To do so, we seek to understand our power sources as well as theirs.

A power source is an existing and available condition (resource, relationship, process, etc.) that facilitates negotiators getting what they want. Most bargainers believe negotiation has a single power source: the BATNA. **Negotiation has several power sources** which are not to be compared. We do not need to have more of something than them to consider it a power source. If we are both fast, speed is a power source for both of us even if they are faster than us. When we seek power sources, we are not building power distances, but rather our negotiation power (the ability to get what we want).

Do I only need to identify my power source? No, since a power source is just a potential, and it is how we use it that makes the difference. We may possess little of a certain power source, but this may be enough if we tap into it well. It is no guarantee that someone with a lot of time to think will come up with good options. Someone else with less time but more creativity may come up with more or better options.

A quick scan of the seven negotiation elements can illustrate some negotiation power sources:

### Relationship
- Do we have high interpersonal skills?
- Is it easy to make people comfortable around us? Or to trust us?

### Communication
- Are we good listeners and do we convey our ideas persuasively?
- Are there process steps that play to our skills or proposals? Can we build them?

### Interests
- Do we have control over or access to a lot of resources, including the ones they need?
- Do they have interests we can generate options for?

### Options
- Are we creative to come up with innovative yet practical solutions?
- How flexible are we ready to be with our options?

**Legitimacy**
- Are there many standards of fairness that support our case?
- Do we have or can we easily get the necessary information or expertise?

**Commitment**
- Is time an issue for us?
- Do we have latitude in our decision-making? Do we have authority?

**Alternatives**
- Do we have a wide network of people we can rely on?
- Do we have or can we easily get other offers?

Notice how these are power sources, not power moves. We can have these power sources available to us and, deliberately or mistakenly, never use them. Or we may use them wrongly and have them backfire. The wrong use of a power source usually happens through an exaggerated or abusive use of it. An abusive use of a power source is usually in creating or increasing a power distance. Say we have too much money (control over a resource) and we try to impose our will over them. They may reject our demands not based on rational gains, but just to teach us a lesson.

This case is well-illustrated by the ultimatum game. In this famous game, two players are given a sum of money to divide. The proposer suggests a split and the responder can accept or reject the deal. If the responder rejects it, no one gets anything. In game theory, the rational solution is for the proposer to offer the smallest amount and the responder to accept it. Being guaranteed of something, even if small, is better than nothing. In practice, when the proposer suggests a lopsided split, he is perceived to have abused his power. In these cases, the responder normally rejects the proposal as unfair.

While in the short term our power sources are somewhat of a given, they can evolve in the long term. Several, for example, can be changed through active moves to set the stage (we can expand our network). Some power sources originate from us as individuals or institutions. Our high interpersonal skills or our company's brand recognition can help initiate relationships quickly. Others will be contextual: we may have a specific valuable resource or information for a certain negotiation, which is meaningless to another.

# Conclusion

Clara Lee and Ninie Ming were MBA colleagues hired by a German company to work in Asia. After receiving the offer, they learned they were the first two hires in Asia under the new Leadership program. Though happy with getting an offer, Clara and Ninie were unhappy about the compensation package. They actually thought that no MBA holders from the top schools would accept such a package. However, they decided to avoid bargaining directly on salary.

When they met with the HR staff, they chose to adopt collaborative roles and frame the negotiation as a JVP, specifically as MBA holders giving suggestions on how to improve the package to attract the top talent (including themselves). This was carefully crafted based on the interest learned from HR in previous conversations. Their options involved monetary and non-monetary adjustments and many involved mutual-gains solutions. While willing to listen, HR said:

> I love these ideas, but right now this comes from HQ and I have no authority to change it. I already told them that I believe this package to be low. They, however, told me that since the market is down they want to get good talent for an affordable price. I will understand if you believe this is not enough for you.

While Clara had alternatives and walked away, Ninie accepted it as she had none. They could have negotiated with HQ, but assumed it would be too much effort and chose not to. After working on all four building blocks of power, we may still not get what we want. At least at this stage, we can indeed say that we did everything we could. The exercise of maximizing our negotiation power gives us the serenity to accept what we cannot change or control. Even then, it gives us the understanding that we can control much more than we initially expected.

On some occasions, we may not have had enough time to invest. On others, we may have chosen to invest less time. We may have even done all we could and still it was not enough. Sometimes, it is just not meant to be and that is okay. No one wins all the time.

Accepting this in turn helps us to appreciate our many trade-off choices more explicitly. Instead of claiming that we failed because we had no choice, we may now recognize the consequences of our choices. Perhaps we chose not to set the stage properly because it was too costly and uncertain. This recognition gives us the understanding that there is just so much we can do at times. It also helps us to understand where to improve next time.

The way Ms. Kim negotiated exemplifies the use of all four building blocks of negotiation power. The fact that she did it so consistently with value negotiation expands her power further. How we negotiate today lays the ground for our future negotiations. It is not just reputation, but also development of negotiation skills, a nework of potential future negotiation partners and the confidence from past successes. These are all power sources that can help us in our next negotiation.

Becoming a value negotiator with maximum negotiation power is a long-term endeavor. To prepare for this journey, we recommend starting through preparation as the simplest and most practical block to implement. In the short term, concentrate on setting the stage. With time and attention, our assumptions change as we see innovative and empowering results. We then feel more competent to negotiate boundaries we could not before.

# Negotiation Ethics

Usually, the ethical challenge happens when our economic and moral interests conflict. If there is a moral but no economic interest or vice-versa, then the choice is simple. Instead of having to choose between ethics and economics, value negotiation attempts to tailor options that eliminate the very source of the conflict.

We strongly believe this whole book provides systematic advice to help negotiate ethically. In our eyes, the win-win attitude applied through the value negotiation system lends itself to an ethical approach. A negotiation independent from power, where negotiators confidently work together towards value, produces fewer ethically questionable situations. Additionally, a negotiator well-versed in value negotiation is also better prepared to maneuver away from choices that challenge ethics.

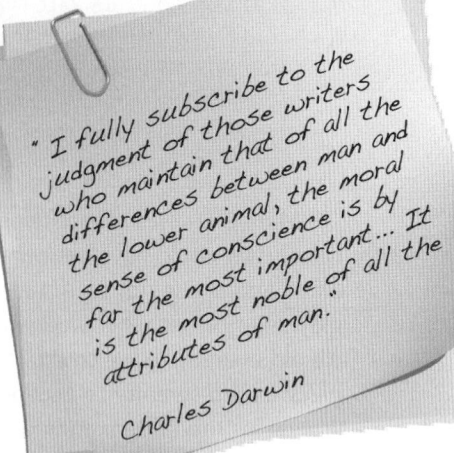

By no means do we expect to exhaust a topic as vast as negotiation ethics here. However, being such an important issue, we felt we could not finish this book without having an open discussion about it. Actually, Professors Menkel-Meadow and Wheeler have written extensively on the subject. In their book *What's Fair: Ethics in Negotiation,* they identify five ethical tensions:

> "I fully subscribe to the judgment of those writers who maintain that of all the differences between man and the lower animal, the moral sense of conscience is by far the most important... It is the most noble of all the attributes of man."
>
> Charles Darwin

1. **Truth-telling in negotiations** – Are we speaking the truth?
   - *Situation* – When purchasing a TV, Tom lied to the salesperson that his son had a genetic disease to gain empathy and a discount.
2. **Bargaining tactics** – Are we choosing tactics and behaviors that take advantage of power or information asymmetries?
   - *Situation* – Tom then went to another store and used his discount gained on that lie to pressure the competitor to offer him an even cheaper price.
3. **Negotiating relationships** – Are we choosing to treat them as partners, enemies or adversaries in a game?
   - *Situation* – When Tom lost his expensive rental car key ($1,200), the rental agency replaced his car, reimbursed his taxi ride and did not charge for the key. However, when they did not show up to tow the car (maybe by mistake), Tom used this to make them feel guilty.
4. **Negotiation and agents** – Are we representing our interests or that of our client?
   - *Situation* – Ten minutes before a store was about to close on Halloween, the saleswoman was eager to leave. Tom offered $10 to buy all the 31 remaining bags of candy that were normally priced at $1 per bag. The saleswoman took the deal. Was she really working in the store owner's best interest or hers in selling the candy and leaving early? We don't know.

5. **Social influences and impact** – Are we satisfying the interests of the negotiators around the table at the expense of others and of society at large?
   - *Situation* – Tom offered to buy a leather jacket and pay in cash. For doing so, he received a $150 discount. It seems like value creation: cash payment for a discount. However, the salesman justified the discount by saying: "We will mark the coat as stolen. It is very simple. My boss will not care."

These tensions pose ethical choices when pursuing value. While some tensions vary in relevance depending on culture, the differences are usually one of degree. Cultures often differ most on where they draw the ethical line, not if the line is drawn at all. Few cultures will disagree strongly on the core ethical decisions. However, deriving a single definition of right and wrong is at the very least a risky endeavor.

For example, lying is an ethical problem in most cultures. Most parents around the world tell their children not to lie. Most religions will tell their followers not to lie. What is considered a lie, however, changes from culture to culture. In most cultures, it includes saying something to blatantly mislead the other. In a few cultures, lying extends to not voluntarily sharing information that could be important to the other. All cultures seem to unite in valuing and promoting ethical behaviors.

We do not believe we can or need to teach readers on what is right or wrong. Most of us know it. We know that unethical behaviors are the "easy" way and rarely turn out to be the right way. Here, we think about what ethics means for each of us so we can successfully negotiate ethically.

# From Value to Skills

While we believe that almost everyone has already engaged in some form of lying, we also believe that most of us would have preferred not to do so. We probably only did so from ignorance on how to guarantee our economic gains in an ethical way.

When discussing ethics in the classroom, two questions seem to always come up:

1. Do we lie (manipulate, coerce, etc.) in negotiations?
   - We always try our best not to since lies are a very risky tactic. We do not claim to be perfect. As humans, we accept that we make mistakes, including ethical ones. As negotiators, we are disappointed with ourselves and continuously strive to improve next time.

2. How can we best lie (manipulate, coerce, etc.) if we have to?
   - Why do we feel like we have to or want to in the first place? Is it to get more rewards? To prevent a risk? Do we not know of any better way to go forward besides lying? If we do, what prevents us from choosing it?

Ethics is not just a matter of knowing **what** to do. As noted above, most people have a decently good idea about it. Ethics for many of us is a matter of knowing **how** to do it. For example, we know we should tell the truth and we prefer to. But will we still tell the truth if it means revealing our lack of alternatives or losing our jobs? The uncertainty of success and the fear of failure push many into making win-lose unethical choices.

Conversely, we believe that the courage to behave ethically comes with the confidence that we can do it successfully. Negotiating ethically is a combination of values (what to do) and skills (how to do). Actually, negotiation and specifically value negotiation can be the ultimate tool to manage ethical dilemmas. As a process to overcome conflict of interests, negotiation can impart skills to behave ethically and satisfy economic interests.

## Ethics is Value

Ethics are often threatened by a lack, misuse or abuse of power to satisfy positions. The use of power in negotiations communicates a lack of principles, which invites a win-lose process and unethical behaviors. Negotiators often respond to the ethical dilemmas as if it is an all-or-nothing decision: "Anything goes!" or "We would never do this." These responses are usually associated with the negotiator's ethical approach (Table 15.3):

| Ethical dilemmas | Win-Win??? | Win-Lose |
| --- | --- | --- |
| 1. Truth-telling | 1. Speak the truth | 1. Lie, deceive or hide information |
| 2. Bargaining tactics | 2. Collaborate | 2. Act power-focused, explore information asymmetries or manipulate |
| 3. Negotiating relationships | 3. Treat them as partners | 3. Treat them as enemies or adversaries |
| 4. Negotiation and agents | 4. Do whatever is in the best interest of our client no matter the price | 4. Protect our own interests even at the clients' expense |
| 5. Social influences and impact | 5. Never influence or impact others negatively | 5. Only worry about our own gains |

**Table 15.3**
Win-win and win-lose response to ethical dilemmas

In the above table, what may be the problem with the win-win column? Perhaps it is too absolute? The behaviors seem independent of a risk-and-reward consideration as ethics seems to trump all other interests. This is an unnecessarily high price to pay to be ethical. Despite our good intentions, if we follow this advice we will be taken advantage of when dealing with someone who follows the win-lose column. The supposedly win-win column looks more like a lose-win column.

For most, the choice for or against ethical behaviors is a question between competitive advantage and integrity. It is a matter of being able to secure the gains necessary for survival or success versus living up to a higher standard no matter the price. Most do not see another way than to reluctantly break their ethical lines or sacrifice their other interests. This seems like a win-lose, zero-sum frame to ethics and value.

Actually, ethics is for many a source of value. Most negotiators would value or prefer negotiating ethically if they can do so without sacrificing other interests. Isn't that what we have been trying to do since the beginning of this book?

To negotiate so as to satisfy as many interests as possible with minimal or no sacrifices (or waste of value).

Every move in value negotiation is an attempt to make power irrelevant and create value. This consistent effort creates an environment conducive to ethics without the need to sacrifice other interests. Value negotiators reject the yes-or-no dichotomy of having to decide between telling the truth or not to. Instead, we negotiate to find the best ways to behave ethically such as how to safely say the truth. A value negotiator will behave in the following ways (Table 15.4):

| Ethical dilemmas | Choose to | Not to |
| --- | --- | --- |
| 1. Truth-telling | 1. Carefully exchange the truth | 1. Lie, deceive or hide information |
| 2. Bargaining tactics | 2. Act value-focused, diagnose and separate the three negotiations consistently | 2. Act power-focused, explore information asymmetries or manipulate |
| 3. Negotiating relationships | 3. Proactively invite them to negotiate as partners | 3. Treat them as enemies or adversaries |
| 4. Negotiation and agents | 4. Negotiate with clients to allow us to better and safely perform our duties | 4. Protect our own interests even at the clients' expense |
| 5. Social influences and impact | 5. Be cautious about our social influences and impact | 5. Only worry about our own gains |

And the value negotiator will also not just: a) tell the truth without caution, b) collaborate or treat them as partners independently of how they behave; c) follow orders from clients; or d) accept the situation as it is. This is the difference between blindly following our ethics and negotiating both our ethics and other interests. Ethical value negotiation is not easily applied.

**Table 15.4**
Value negotiation responses to ethical dilemmas

## Be Prepared to be Courageous

If we find ourselves underprepared in a high-stakes negotiation, we are much more prone to ethical mistakes. Courage to pursue our ethics goes hand in-hand with the confidence to perform well within our ethical space. Our confidence to negotiate is proportionally stronger the more prepared we are.

Some may say: "I never lie." Others will confess: "I lie if I need to safeguard my client's interests." Others may feel compelled: "I only lie because everyone else around me does." But does the person who never lies also volunteer information that may be helpful to the other? Would the person who lies on behalf of the client refrain from it if the client requested? If we lie because others do, do we stop when they do?

> "They tell us that the only thing we have to fear is fear itself, but I don't believe that," he said. Then, a moment later, he added: "Oh, the fear is there, alright. It comes to us in many different forms, at different times, and overwhelms us. But the most frightening thing we can do at such times is to turn our backs on it, to close our eyes. For then we take the most precious thing inside us and surrender it to something else. In my case, that something was the wave."
> 
> Haruki Murakami

For any of us who eventually behaves unethically, we tend to rationalize our behavior in ways that justify it. This defense mechanism helps us live with our decisions when they conflict with our beliefs. It makes us feel innocent or blameless, but it also frees us of any responsibility. Consequently, we ignore our ethical challenges and stop working to manage them. Thus, we need courage to look ourselves in the mirror whenever we act unethically, and recognize we need to change. Only then will we be able to really want and know what to change.

Perhaps harder than having the courage to acknowledge our ethical mistakes is to recognize our own bounded ethicality. Bounded ethicality makes us believe we are behaving ethically (or within our own preferred ethics) when we are not. Some common bounded ethicality traps are:

- "I deserve more than them!" – Claiming more credit or value than we deserve from overestimating our own contributions as compared to others.
  - *Risk minimization* – Focusing on legitimacy for value-claiming.
- "I trust these people more than the others!" – Most of us unconsciously behave more positively towards people similar to us than those different from us.
  - *Risk minimization* – Starting the negotiation with the zero-trust discipline.
- "I have their best interests at heart!" – When representing a client or organization, we start to believe what is good for us is also good for them even if this is not true.
  - *Risk minimization* – Transparently sharing process intentions and consulting frequently with the client on their interests.
- "Let's create value!" – When we create value in the negotiation by claiming it from or at the expense of others outside of the negotiation (i.e., parasitic value creation).
  - *Risk minimization* – Consider how society, the environment and third parties would judge our options. Think social responsibility.

Once we recognize our own ethical mistakes and our bounded ethicality, we can better negotiate ethically. Then, we can start by creating the right environment to negotiate. We prepare and understand our interests well, including that of behaving ethically. We are free of time constraints or other value-creation enemies. We are able to walk away if we need to. We anticipate critical moments so that we are under less pressure. In sum, preparing a value negotiation is about preparing ourselves to negotiate ethically.

# Ethical Value Negotiation

To start our ethical value negotiation, we would like to address three questions:

- Are they being unethical?
- Does that justify reciprocation?
- How do we convince them to reciprocate ethics?

The first question is, in our experience, a tricky one. When something seemingly unethical happens, we may assume that it is indeed unethical. This assumption may well be a defense mechanism of expecting the worst-case scenario to be prepared for it. However, in accepting this assumption, we close ourselves to learning.

We may believe that they are lying, only to find out they actually have new information that we lack. Are they lying? We may never know. But as we ask questions, we reinforce our suspicions enough to arrive at a safe, though imperfect, conclusion.

The second question of whether their unethical behavior justifies reciprocation has the resonance of a philosophical question. If we combat fire with fire, we are just going to burn everything down and nothing will be left. The risks of behaving unethically because the other side has done so are high, as we may escalate a dangerous game. They may be good at it, while we may damage our reputation or just lose the value of behaving ethically. It distracts us from our value-focus and minimizes our learning. Finally, we would be reacting to them, thus losing our leadership and the chances of building a good outcome.

If we keep our proactive process leadership in an ethical way, we are likely to inspire them to reciprocate. Why should we reciprocate unethical behaviors if we do not want to? Why not help them to feel safe to reciprocate ethical behaviors instead? Most people will act ethically if they are confident of succeeding without unethical means.

The third and final question has many answers. Below we try to give some, and it will become clear how they all point to value negotiation strategies. Before we do so, we want to give a warning. When negotiating ethically, we should avoid judging or patronizing the other party. Otherwise, we risk projecting our judgments onto them or communicating a belief that we are better than them. Either way, we risk a negative emotional backlash. Not only does this encourage unethical behaviors, but they may also try to prove that they are superior.

1. **Truth-telling** – Carefully exchange the truth
   a. *What do we do?* We transparently lead the process, learn and diagnose, and proactively manage the information disclosure tension. These behaviors avoid lying or hiding information, moving towards a transparent yet safe communication.
   b. *What if they don't?* If they ask us for information that puts us at a disadvantage (e.g., no alternatives), we negotiate ourselves out of it by saying:
      - "Why is this important for you?"
      - "I am not sure this information will help us keep on working as a team. If I have a good BATNA, you may feel threatened. If I don't, you may feel tempted to take advantage of me. Can I recommend we talk about what you really want out of this negotiation instead?"

2. **Bargaining tactics** – Act value-focused, diagnose and separate the three negotiations consistently
   a. *What do we do?* We commit to a value negotiation approach to the three negotiations. Thus, we negotiate the substance fairly, the relationship collaboratively and the communication transparently.

b. *What if they don't?* If they insist on bargaining, we can act against:
     - Power moves – Insist on value creation and legitimate value claiming.
     - Manipulation – Persistently separate relationship from substance.
     - Information asymmetries – Carefully lead a dialogue pattern.

3. **Negotiating relationships** – Proactively invite them to negotiate as partners
   a. *What do we do?* We start with the zero-trust discipline, and open positively but not naïvely. Then, we advance in a dialogue pattern and forgive past actions if they start to treat us as a partner.
   b. *What if they don't?* If they treat us as enemies or adversaries, we can:
      - Reinforce interdependence to collaborate independently of trust (or create an environment for future trust).
      - Make deals based only on legitimacy to protect us from prejudice or discriminatory behaviors.
      - Transparently lead a value negotiation process to prove that we are trying to help all parties win.

4. **Negotiation and agents** – Negotiate with clients to allow us to better and safely perform our duties
   a. *What do we do?* We proactively provide all the information they need to make good decisions or requests. We negotiate our mandate if it puts us in situations that could tempt us to act unethically or against our personal interests.
   b. *What if they don't?* If our agents do not represent us well or our clients are non-collaborative, we can:
      - Engage our agents on contingency contracts aligned with our most important interests.
      - Consistently send our clients simple decisions to be made on the more relevant interests with background information.
      - Negotiate with either agent or client the behaviors we expect from them to be able to work better together.

5. **Social influences and impact** – Be cautious about our social influences and impact
   a. *What do we do?* We try to eliminate internal and external value-creation enemies to all parties. This will give us the focus to create value for the parties involved without extracting value from those not present.
   b. *What if they don't?* If others attempt to create value which may be at our expense or a third party's expense, we can:
      - Invite the third party to or represent them at the negotiation.
      - Gain access to the negotiation (if we are not already there).
      - Prepare someone who is in the negotiation to represent us.

At the end of the day, there are no negotiation solutions for all problems or ethical tensions. We have tried to elaborate on how value negotiation can make us more ethical, and thus more successful, individuals. Sometimes, it all boils down to making some hard choices: which interests are more important to us. Sometimes, we have to walk away from a deal to protect our ethics. We do not have to close a deal that sacrifices such important interests as self-respect and self-identity.

Being a value negotiator should help us influence others to behave ethically as well. We then create a safe value-focused environment where all negotiators can satisfy their interests, including ethical ones.

# summary

## Power

Power in negotiations is our use of power to force or manipulate others into giving in. Negotiation power is our ability to get the value we want in a negotiation. There are four main levers to increase negotiation power:

1. Empowering assumptions – Our premises or beliefs positively frame the way we think and act
2. Negotiable boundaries – Start with the assumption that all issues are negotiable
3. Active leverage – Set the stage before and between meetings to enhance our ability to negotiate for value
4. Negotiation preparation – Our exercise to ready ourselves for a negotiation

## Ethics

Ethics in negotiations is not just a matter of knowing what to do, but also how to do it. Negotiation, particularly value negotiation, can help us manage ethics and other interests to overcome conflicts. Most negotiators see value in negotiating ethically and would pursue it as an important interest.

The five ethical tensions are:

1. Truth-telling in negotiations – Are we speaking the truth?
2. Bargaining tactics – Are we choosing tactics and behaviors that take advantage of power or information asymmetries?
3. Negotiating relationships – Are we choosing to treat them as partners, enemies or adversaries in a game?
4. Negotiation and agents – Are we representing our interests or those of our client?
5. Social influences and impact – Are we satisfying the interests of the negotiators around the table at the expense of others and of society at large?

A win-win ethical negotiation is not just behaving ethically without consideration of the risk to other interests. An ethical value negotiator:

1. Carefully exchanges the truth
2. Acts value-focused, diagnoses and separates the three negotiations consistently
3. Proactively invites them to negotiate as partners
4. Negotiates with clients to better and safely perform his duties
5. Is cautious about his social influences and impact

We are all prone to falling victim to bounded ethicality and ethical mistakes. Though part of human nature, we should not just accept this as a given, but rather strive for improvement. Common bounded ethicality traps are:

- "I deserve more than them!" – Overestimating and over-claiming our fair share
- "I trust these people more than the others!" – Unconscious discrimination
- "I have their best interests at heart!" – Starting to believe what we want to believe
- "Let's create value!" – Value creation to the detriment of third parties

At the end of the day, both power and ethics are matters of choice and within our control.

# questions

## Easy

1. What is the difference between power in negotiation vs. negotiation power?
2. Why are alternatives usually associated with power in negotiations? Are they the only source? Are they a good source?
3. What are the four levers to increase negotiation power? Explain in your own words what you understand by them.
4. What is the difference between a crippling assumption and a physical limitation? Is lack of time a crippling assumption or a physical limitation?
5. What is the difference between setting the stage and negotiation preparation?
6. Why do we need courage to be ethical? How do we increase our courage?

## Medium

1. Why do negotiators seek power? Is this effective? What are the risks?
2. What are power sources? Why are they an important concept? How do they help us negotiate better? How are they different from power moves?
3. Are all four negotiation power levers part of negotiation preparation? Why?
4. What are the five ethical tensions in negotiation? Define them in your own words. Why do we call them "tensions"?
5. What is the difference between speaking the truth and carefully speaking the truth?
6. What are ethical mistakes and how are they different from bounded ethicality? Describe in your own words the four examples used in this chapter.

## Difficult

1. Ms. Kim chose not to cancel her check. Would you have done the same? Why did she do it? What risks did she run? Did she do anything to minimize them? What else could she have done to minimize such risks? Why did it work in the end?
2. Is negotiation power a choice or an ability?
3. We could argue that there are only three ethical tensions: Substance, Relationship and Communication. How would you recommend we fit the five ethical tensions into the three negotiations? Why did you classify them this way?
4. Why do ethics have value? Give at least three reasons.
5. What would be the risks if we behaved in the following way in regards to the five ethical tensions?
   a. Speak the truth
   b. Collaborate
   c. Treat them as partners
   d. Do whatever is in the best interest of our client no matter the price
   e. Never influence or impact others negatively
6. How do the crippling assumptions below hinder our negotiation power?
   a. My counter-party is my enemy
   b. There is no use in talking to them
   c. This is a zero-sum negotiation
   d. Whoever has more power wins

# scenarios

## Easy

1. Would our helping to craft the requirements for their bidding process such that these become closer to our own options than those of our competitors be coherent with the philosophy behind setting the stage? What are the ethical concerns? What would be your recommendation?

2. *So if someone is on higher ground, we try to also climb the hill before we negotiate. If we have the higher ground, we descend before the negotiation, even if just for a while to deal with them.*

   Do you agree with this statement? Why?

## Medium

What are the risks of setting the stage? Please analyze one question per element below:

**Relationship**
- Who can we talk to or negotiate with before this negotiation?
- Who can we bring into this negotiation?

**Communication**
- What time or place to meet that will help create the right atmosphere?
- What messages can we send before we meet to facilitate our negotiation?

**Interests**
- Can we guarantee or at least protect access over resources we need?
- How can we learn their interests ahead of time?

**Options**
- What steps can we take to make options that do not currently exist viable?
- How can we test or check feasibility of our key options in advance?

**Legitmacy**
- What different frames of fairness have they used or accepted in the past?
- Which evidence do we need to produce to enhance our case?

**Commitment**
- How can we put in place a process that facilitates value negotiation?
- How can we buy ourselves more time if we need to?

**Alternatives**
- How can we improve our BATNA so that leaving is a realistic choice?
- How can we worsen their BATNA if they threaten to use it?

## Difficult

Use the questions below in a negotiation that is presently non-negotiable for you to make it into a negotiable situation:

**Relationship**
- Who among them is more likely to listen to us?
- Who do they listen to besides us?

**Communication**
- Can we invite them into a simple, transparent and balanced process?
- When and where can we best meet to talk? (Less time pressure or distractions)

**Interests**
- Why are they not interested?
- Can we lower the potential cost or increase the potential reward to enter a negotiation?
- If they do not care about the substance, what do they care about to at least talk to us?

**Options**
- Can we explore a few ideas without any commitments?
- What advice would they give us in a similar situation?

**Legitimacy**
- What persuaded them to negotiate a similar issue in the past?
- Is there a reason why they should do the same today?

**Commitment**
- Who can open doors that are currently shut?
- How can we make it easier for them to agree to talk?

**Alternatives**
- What external elements can turn this into a negotiable issue?
- Do we really need to negotiate this?

Once done, reflect on the use of the questions. Which question was insightful in this case? What other questions did you find yourself asking? Which questions led nowhere in this case? Why do you think that is?

# bibliography

A surprising finding on new business mortality rates. (1993, June 14). *Business Week*. Retrieved from http://www.businessweek.com/archives/1993/b332312.arc.htm

Adair, W., Brett, J., Lempereur, A., Okumura, T., Shikhirev, P., Tinsley, C., et al. (2004). Culture and negotiation strategy. *Negotiation Journal*, 20(1), 87-111.

Adler, R.S. & Silverstein, E.M. (2000) When David Meets Goliath: Dealing with Power Differentials in Negotiations. *Harvard Negotiation Law Review*, 5, 77-110..

Aggressive. (n.d.). In Merriam-Webster's Online dictionary. Retrieved July 23, 2009, from http://www.merriam-webster.com/dictionary/aggressive

Allred, K. G. (2000). Distinguishing best and strategic practices: A framework for managing the dilemma between claiming and creating value. *Negotiation Journal*, 16(4), 387-397.

Ames, D. R. (2004). Inside the mind reader's tool kit: Projection and stereotyping in mental state inference. *Journal of Personality & Social Psychology*, 87(3), 340-353.

Ames, D. R. (2004). Strategies for social inference: A similarity contingency model of projection and stereotyping in attribute prevalence estimates. *Journal of Personality & Social Psychology*, 87(5), 573-585.

Amir, O., Ariely, D., & Carmon, Z. (2008). The dissociation between monetary assessment and predicted utility. *Marketing Science*, 27(6), 1055-1064.

Are you overly committed to the deal? (2008, April). *Negotiation*, 11, 6-7.

Are you really ready to negotiate? (2007). *Negotiation*, 10(9), 1-4.

Argyris, C. & Schon, D. A. (1978) *Organizational Learning: A Theory of Action Perspective*. Reading, Mass: Addison-Wesley.

Aristotle. (350 B.C.E). *Poetics*. Retrieved April 23, 2009, from http://classics.mit.edu/Aristotle/poetics.html

Aristotle. (350 B.C.E). *Rethoric*. Retrieved April 23, 2009, from http://classics.mit.edu/Aristotle/rhetoric.html

Armstrong, K. (2007). *The great transformation: The beginning of our religious traditions*. New York: Anchor.

Asiamah, F. (2009, Feb 20) Ghana: GBC gets ADR centre. Retrieved March 11, 2009, from http://allafrica.com/stories/200902200562.html

Associated Press. (2008). *"Timeline: Microsoft courts Yahoo"* Retrieved June 14, 2009, from http://www.cnbc.com/id/24446884/

Avruch, K. (2000). Culture and negotiation pedagogy. *Negotiation Journal*, 16(4), 339-346.

Axelrod, R. (1984). The evolution of cooperation. New York: Basic Books.

Babcock, L. & Laschever, S. (2008) *Ask for it: how women can use the power of negotiation to get what they really want*. New York: Bantam Books.

Babcock, L., & Laschever, S. (2007). *Women don't ask: The high cost of avoiding negotiation--and positive strategies for change*. New York: Bantam Books.

Balachandra, L., Barrett, F., Bellman, H., Fisher, C., & Susskind, L. (2005). Improvisation and mediation: Balancing acts. *Negotiation Journal*, 21(4), 425-434.

Balachandra, L., Bordone, R. C., Menkel-Meadow, C., Ringstrom, P., & Sarath, E. (2005). Improvisation and negotiation: Expecting the unexpected. *Negotiation Journal*, 21(4), 415-423.

Balachandra, L., Crossan, M., Devin, L., Leary, K., & Patton, B. (2005). Improvisation and teaching negotiation: Developing three essential skills. *Negotiation Journal*, 21(4), 435-441.

Barkat, J. S. (2002). Building on the strengths of different approaches. *Negotiation Journal*, 18(4), 359.

Baron, J. (2007). *Thinking and deciding* (4th ed.). New York, Cambridge University Press.

Barrett, F. J. (2004). Critical moments as "Change" in negotiation. *Negotiation Journal*, 20(2), 213-219.

Bauer, F. (2000). The practice of one ombudsman. *Negotiation Journal*, 16(1), 59-79.

Bazerman, M. (2002). *You can't enlarge the pie: Six barriers to effective government* Cambridge, MA: Basic Books.

Bazerman, M. H. (1994). *Negotiating rationally*. New York: Free Press.

Bazerman, M. H. (2005). *Judgment in managerial decision making* (6th ed.) New York: Wiley.

Bazerman, M. H., & Gillespie, J. J. (1999). Betting on the future: The virtues of contingent contracts. *Harvard Business Review*, 77(5), 155-160.

Bazerman, M. H., & Watkins, M. D. (2008). *Predictable surprises: The disasters you should have seen coming, and how to prevent them*. Boston, MA: Harvard Business School Press.

Bendor, J., Kramer, R. M., & Stout, S. (1991). When in doubt... COOPERATION IN A NOISY PRISONER'S DILEMMA. *Journal of Conflict Resolution*, 35(4), 691-719.

Benjamin, G. A., Margulis, J., & Benjamin, G. A. (2001). *The angel investor's handbook: How to profit from early-stage investing*. Princeton, NJ: Bloomberg Press.

Benoliel, M., & Cashdan, L. (2004). *Done deal: Insights from interviews with the world's best negotiators*. Avon, MA: Adams Media Corporation.

Blackshaw, I. S. (2003). Mediating sports disputes: National and international perspectives (book). *Negotiation Journal*, 19(2), 184-184.

Blaker, M., Giarra, P., & Vogel, E. (2003). Case studies in japanese negotiating behavior (book). *Negotiation Journal*, 19(2), 184-184.

Blount, S. (2000). Whoever said that markets were fair? *Negotiation Journal*, 16(3), 237-252.

Blount, S., & Larrick, R. P. (2000). Framing the game: Examining frame choice in bargaining. *Organizational Behavior & Human Decision Processes*, 81(1), 43.

Bond Jr., C. F., & DePaulo, B. M. (2006). Accuracy of deception judgments. *Personality & Social Psychology Review (Lawrence Erlbaum Associates)*, 10(3), 214-234.

Bond Jr., C. F., & DePaulo, B. M. (2008). Individual differences in judging deception: Reply to O'sullivan (2008) and pigott and wu (2008). *Psychological Bulletin*, 134(4), 501-503.

Bond Jr., C. F., & Depaulo, B. M. (2008). Individual differences in judging deception: Accuracy and bias. *Psychological Bulletin*, 134(4), 477-492.

Bond Jr., C. F., & Uysal, A. (2007). On lie detection "wizards.". *Law & Human Behavior,* 31(1), 109-115.

Bond Jr., C. F., Berry, D. S., & Omar, A. (1994). The kernel of truth in judgments of deceptiveness. *Basic & Applied Social Psychology,* 15(4), 523-534.

Bond Jr., C. F., Omar, A., Pitre, U., Lashley, B. R., Skaggs, L. M., & Kirk, C. T. (1992). Fishy-looking liars: Deception judgment from expectancy violation. *Journal of Personality & Social Psychology,* 63(6), 969-977.

Bond, J.,Charles F., & DePaulo, B. M. (2006). Accuracy of deception judgments: Appendix A. *Personality & Social Psychology Review,* 10(3), -1-18.

Bond, J.,Charles F., & DePaulo, B. M. (2006). Accuracy of deception judgments: Appendix B. *Personality & Social Psychology Review,* 10(3), -1-32.

Bordone, R. C. (2000). Teaching interpersonal skills for negotiation and for life. *Negotiation Journal,* 16(4), 377-385.

Bordone, R. C. (2006). Divide the pie--without antagonizing the other side. *Negotiation,* 9(11) , 4-6.

Bordone, R. C. (2007). Dealing with a spoiler? negotiate around the problem. *Negotiation,* 10(1), 4-6.

Bordone, R. C. (2007). Listen up! your talks may depend on it. *Negotiation,* 10(5), 9-11.

Bordone, R. C., & Moffitt, M. L. (2006). Create value out of conflict. *Negotiation*, 9(6), 3-5.

Bordone, R. C., & Todd, G. (2005) Have You Negotiated How You'll Negotiate?!. *Negotiation,* 8(9), 7.

Bourdeaux, C., Rosemary O'Leary, & Thornburgh, R. (2001). Control, communication, and power: A study of the use of alternative dispute resolution of enforcement actions at the U.S. environmental protection agency. *Negotiation Journal,* 17(2), 175-191.

Bowling, D., & Hoffman, D. (2000). Bringing peace into the room: The personal qualities of the mediator and their impact on the mediation. *Negotiation Journal,* 16(1), 5-28.

Brams, S. J., & Taylor, A. D. (1996). *Fair division: From cake-cutting to dispute resolution.* Cambridge: Cambridge University Press.

Brandenburger, A. M., & Nalebuff, B. J. (1997). *Co-opetition: A revolution mindset that combines competition and cooperation : The game theory strategy that's changing the game of business..* New York: Doubleday.

Break down "sacred" barriers to agreement.(2009). *Negotiation,* 12, 3-5.

Brett, J. M. (2007). *Negotiating globally: How to negotiate deals, resolve disputes, and make decisions across cultural boundaries.* (2nd ed.). San Francisco: Jossey-Bass.

Brockner, J., De Cremer, D., Van, D. B., & Ya-Ru Chen. (2005). The influence of interdependent self-construal on procedural fairness effects. *Organizational Behavior & Human Decision Processes,* 96(2), 155-167.

Buckingham, M., & Clifton, D. O. (2001). *Now, discover your strengths.* New York: Free Press.

Cambria, J., DeFilippo, R. J., Louden, R. J., & McGowan, H. (2002). Negotiation under extreme pressure: The 'mouth marines' and the hostage takers. *Negotiation Journal,* 18(4), 331.

Campbell, J. (1968). *The hero with a thousand faces.* Princeton: Princeton University Press.

Campbell, J. (1988). *The power of myth.* New York: Doubleday.

Capra, F. (2000). *The tao of physics: An exploration of the parallels between modern physics and eastern mysticism* (25th anniversary edition.) Boston: Shambhala Publications, Inc.

Carmon, Z., & Ariely, D. (2000). Focusing on the foregone: How value can appear so different to buyers and sellers. *Journal of Consumer Research,* 27(3), 360-370.

Carmon, Z., Wertenbroch, K., & Zeelenberg, M. (2003). Option attachment: When deliberating makes choosing feel like losing. *Journal of Consumer Research,* 30(1), 15-29.

Carnegie, D. (1998). *How to win friends & influence people.* New York: Pocket.

Carrie Menkel-Meadow. (2001). Negotiating with lawyers, men, and things: The contextual approach still matters. *Negotiation Journal,* 17(3), 257-293.

Chancealot, S. (no date) *Neg-Hits.* Retrieved August 16, 2009 from http://www.sosuave.com/articles/neghits.htm

Chen-Bo Zhong, Dijksterhuis, A., & Galinsky, A. D. (2008). The merits of unconscious thought in creativity. Psychological Science, 19(9), 912-918.

Chiarella, Tom (2005, January 31) *Haggling for Hot Dogs.* Esquire, Retrieved September 20, 2009 from http://www.esquire.com/features/money/ESQ0205NEGO_114_1

Cialdini, R. B. (2007). Influence: *The psychology of persuasion.* New York: Harper Paperbacks.

CNET editors. (2008). *"News.com special coverage: Microsoft's big bid for Yahoo".* Retrieved June 15, 2009, from http://news.cnet.com/Microsofts-big-bid-for-Yahoo/2009-1028_3-6228762.html

Cobb, S. (2000). Negotiation pedagogy: Learning to learn. *Negotiation Journal,* 16(4), 315-319.

Cohen, H. (1982). *You can negotiate anything.* New York: Bantam.

Cohen, J. R. (2002). The ethics of respect in negotiation. N*egotiation Journal,* 18(2), 115-120.

Cohen, R. (2001). Resolving conflict across languages. Negotiation Journal, 17(1), 17-34.

Coleman, P. T., & Ying Ying, J. L. (2001). A systematic approach to evaluating the effects of collaborative negotiation training on individuals and groups. *Negotiation Journal,* 17(4), 363-392.

Collins, J. (2001). *Good to great: Why some companies make the leap... and others don't* New York: HarperBusiness.

Condlin, R. J. (1991) Bargaining in the dark: the normative incoherence of lawyer dispute bargaining role. *Maryland Law Review* 51(1).

Congleton, R. D., & Sweetser, W. (1992). Political deadlocks and distributional information: The value of the veil. *Public Choice,* 73(1), 1-19.

Cook, G. (2006, February 17), Thought for thinkers - 'Follow your gut,' study advises on big decisions. *Boston Globe.* Retrieved from http://www.boston.com/news/nation/articles/2006/02/17/thought_for_thinkers/?page=1

Cooper, C. (2008). *"No love lost from Jerry Yang when it comes to Microsoft".* Retrieved June 15, 2009, from http://news.cnet.com/8301-10784_3-9867893-7.html

Courtney, H., Kirkland, J. & Viguerie, P. (1997) Strategy under uncertainty. *Harvard Business Review,* 75(6), 67-79.

Covey, S. R. (2004). *The 7 habits of highly effective people* New York: Free Press.

Craver, C.B. (2003) Negotiation Styles: The Impact on Bargaining Transactions, *Dispute Resolution Journal,* 58 (1), 48-55.

d'Ambrumenil, P. (1997). M*ediation And Arbitration London:* Cavendish Publishing Limited.

Davidson, D. (2008). *"Yahoo! set for shake-up as executives leave in droves".* Retrieved June 15, 2009, from http://www.brandrepublic.com/News/823508/Yahoo-set-shake-up-executives-leave-droves/?DCMP=ILC-SEARCH

De Dreu, C. K. W., Giebels, E., & Van, d. V. (1998). Social motives and thrust in integrative negotiation: The disruptive effects of punitive capability. *Journal of Applied Psychology,* 83(3), 407-422.

De Meyer, A., Loch, C. H. & Pich, M. T.. (2002). Managing project uncertainty: from variation to chaos. *MIT Sloan Management Review,* 43(2), 60-67.

Decaro, J. D. (2000). *La cara humana de la negociación.* Bogotá, Colombia: McGraw-Hill Companies.

Diagnose. (n.d.). In Merriam-Webster's Online dictionary. Retrieved July 23, 2009, from http://www.merriam-webster.com/dictionary/diagnose

Dijksterhuis, A. (2004). Think different: The merits of unconscious thought in preference development and decision making. *Journal of Personality & Social Psychology,* 87(5), 586-598.

Dijksterhuis, A. (2007). *"New insights on the benefits of unconscious thought"* Advances in Consumer Research - North American Conference Proceedings, 34, 694-695.

Dijksterhuis, A., Smith, P. K., Van Baaren, R. B., & Wigboldus, D. H. J. (2005). The unconscious consumer: Effects of environment on consumer behavior. *Journal of Consumer Psychology* (Lawrence Erlbaum Associates), 15(3), 193-202.

Dixit, A. K., & Nalebuff, B. J. (1993). *Thinking strategically: The competitive edge in business, politics, and everyday life.* New York: W.W. Norton & Co.

Doctoroff, S. (1998). Reengineering negotiations. *Sloan Management Review,* 39(3), 63-71.

Donohue, W. A. (2004). Critical moments as "Flow" in negotiation. *Negotiation Journal,* 20(2), 147-151.

Drolet, A., Larrick, R., & Morris, M. W. (1998). Thinking of others: How perspective taking changes negotiators' aspirations and fairness perceptions as a function of negotiator relationships. *Basic & Applied Social Psychology,* 20(1), 23-31.

Druckman, D. (2004). Departures in negotiation: Extensions and new directions. *Negotiation Journal,* 20(2), 185-204.

Economies of scale (n.d.). Retrieved April 4, 2009, from Wikipedia: http://en.wikipedia.org/wiki/Economies_of_scale

Economies of scope (n.d.). Retrieved April 4, 2009, from Wikipedia: http://en.wikipedia.org/wiki/Economies_of_scope

Eiran, E., Kaufmann, C., Sher, G., Lustick, I., & Greenberg, J. (2005). Political dimensions of the israeli settlements issue: Historic opportunities and challenges. *Negotiation Journal,* 21(2), 193-208.

Eliasson, J. (2002). Perspectives on managing intractable conflict. *Negotiation Journal,* 18(4), 371.

Epley, N., Caruso, E. M., & Bazerman, M. H. (2006). When perspective taking increases taking: Reactive egoism in social interaction. *Journal of Personality & Social Psychology,* 91(5), 872-889.

Epley, N., Mak, D., & Idson, L. C. (2006). Bonus of rebate?: The impact of income framing on spending and saving. *Journal of Behavioral Decision Making,* 19(3), 213-227.

Epley, N., Mak, D., & Idson, L. C. (2006). Erratum: Bonus of rebate?: The impact of income framing on spending and saving. *Journal of Behavioral Decision Making,* 19(4), 407-407.

Ertel, D. (1999). Turning negotiation into a corporate capability. *Harvard Business Review,* 77(3), 55-70.

Falcao, H (2006, April 06) An Open channel of communication: FT mastering financial management series. *Financial Times.* http://www.ft.com/cms/s/2/4fd011c0-f57d-11da-bcae-0000779e2340.html

Falcao, H. (2006). Keep your customers cool. *World Business,* 7, 26-31.

Falcao, H. (2006). Learning to negotiate with a female touch. *World Business,* 2, 30-35.

Fearless. (n.d.) Retrieved April 4, 2009, from Wikipedia: http://en.wikipedia.org/wiki/Fearless_(2006_film)

Fein, A. J., & Anderson, E. (1997). Patterns of credible commitments: Territory and brand selectivity in industrial distribution. *Journal of Marketing,* 61(2), 19.

Fein, S. (1996). Effects of suspicion on attributional thinking and the correspondence bias. *Journal of Personality & Social Psychology,* 70(6), 1164-1184.

Ferreira, G. (2009, May 1). A 'Operação Adriano'. Extra Online. Futebol, Coisa & Tal: *O blog do Gilmar Ferreira.* Retrieved May 08, 2009. Message posted from http://extra.globo.com/blogs/futebol/posts/2009/05/01/a-operacao-adriano-182090.asp

Ferris, F. D. (2001). The things negotiators do with money. *Negotiation Journal,* 17(1), 47-58.

Fisher, R. (1969) *International conflict for beginners.* New York: Harper & Row

Fisher, R. (1983). Negotiating power. *American Behavioral Scientist,* 27(2), 149.

Fisher, R. (1994) Deter, Compel, or Negotiate? *Negotiation Journal* 10(17), 32.

Fisher, R., & Brown, S. (1989). *Getting together: Building relationships as we negotiate.* New York: Penguin.

Fisher, R., & Ertel, D. (1995). *Getting ready to negotiate.* New York: Penguin.

Fisher, R., & Shapiro, D. (2006). Address the concern, not the emotion. *Dispute Resolution Journal,* 61(1), 44-89.

Fisher, R., & Shapiro, D. (2006). *Beyond reason: Using emotions as you negotiate.* New York: Penguin.

Fisher, R., & Sharp, A. (1999). *Getting it done: How to lead when you're not in charge.* New York: Harper Paperbacks.

Fisher, R., & Ury, W. L. (1991). *Getting to yes: Negotiating agreement without giving in.* New York: Penguin.

Fisher, R., Kopelman, E., & Schneider, A. K. (1996). *Beyond Machiavelli : Tools for coping with conflict.* New York: Penguin.

Fisher, R., Schneider, A. K., Borgwardt, E., & Ganson, B. (1996). *Coping with international conflict: A systematic approach to influence in international negotiation.* Upper Saddle River, NJ: Prentice Hall.

Fishman, C. (2003). The Wal-mart you don't know. *Fast Company,* (77), 68.

Flax, J., & Chaisiri, J. (2004). Cross-cultural issues in a life sciences company. *Negotiation Journal,* 20(1), 79-86.

Fonstad, N. O., McKersie, R. B., & Eaton, S. C. (2004). Interest-based negotiations in a transformed Labor–Management setting. *Negotiation Journal,* 20(1), 5-11.

Forester, J. (2004). Responding to critical moments with humor, recognition, and hope. Negotiation Journal, 20(2), 221-237.

Fortgang, R. S. (2000). Taking stock: An analysis of negotiation pedagogy across four professional fields. *Negotiation Journal,* 16(4), 325-338.

Fortgang, R. S., Lax, D. A., & Sebenius, J. K. (2003). Negotiating the spirit of the deal. *Harvard Business Review,* 81(2), 66-75.

Fragale, A. R. (2006). The power of powerless speech: The effects of speech style and task interdependence on status conferral. *Organizational Behavior & Human Decision Processes,* 101(2), 243-261.

Frankl, V. E. (2006). *Man's search for meaning.* Boston: Beacon Press.

Fried, I. (2008). *"Microsoft: We only wanted to buy Yahoo if quickly".* Retrieved June 15, 2009, from http://news.cnet.com/8301-13860_3-9968527-56.html?tag=txt

Friedman, G. J. (1993). *A guide to divorce mediation: How to reach a fair, legal settlement at a fraction of the cost.* New York: Workman Publishing Company.

Fukushima, S. (1999). What you bring to the table: Transference and countertransference in the negotiation process. *Negotiation Journal,* 15(2), 169-180.

Gadlin, H. (2000). The ombudsman: What's in a name? *Negotiation Journal,* 16(1), 37-48.

Galinsky, A. D., Maddux, W. W., & Ku, G. (2006). The view from the other side of the table. *Negotiation,* 9, 1-4.

Gardner, H. (2000). Using multiple intelligences to improve negotiation theory and practice. *Negotiation Journal,* 16(4), 321-324.

Gigerenzer, G. (2008). *Gut feelings: The intelligence of the unconscious.* New York: Penguin.

Gladwell, M. (2005). Blink: *The power of thinking without thinking.* Boston: Little, Brown and Company.

Gladwell, M. Outliers: *Why some people succeed and some don't.* Boston: Little, Brown & Co., 2008.

Golann, D. (2004). Death of a claim: The impact of loss reactions on bargaining. *Negotiation Journal,* 20(4), 539-553.

Goldberg, S. B., Sander, F. E. A., Rogers, N. H., & Cole, S. R. (2007). *Dispute resolution: Negotiation, mediation, and other processes* (5th ed.). Austin, Texas: Wolters Kluwer Law & Business.

Goldman, J. (2008). *"Yahoo Disputes Microsoft's Non-Negotiation Claims".* Retrieved June 15, 2009, from http://www.cnbc.com/id/24457487

Goleman, D. (1995). *Emotional intelligence: why it can matter more than IQ.* New York: Bantam.

Goleman, D. (2007). *Social intelligence: The new science of human relationships.* New York: Bantam.

Gordon, M., & Ertel, D. (2007). *The point of the deal: How to negotiate when yes is not enough.* Cambridge, MA: Harvard Business School Press.

Gray, B. (2003). Negotiating with your nemesis. *Negotiation Journal,* 19(4), 299-310.

Gray, E. B. (1999). What's in a name? A lot when "non-" is involved. *Negotiation Journal,* 15(2), 103-106.

Green, G. M., & Wheeler, M. (2004). Awareness and action in critical moments. *Negotiation Journal,* 20(2), 349-364.

Greene, R. (2000). *The 48 laws of power.* New York: Penguin.

Greene, R. (2003). *The art of seduction.* New York: Penguin.

Guglielmo, S., Monroe, A. E., & Malle, B. F. (2009). At the heart of morality lies folk psychology. *Inquiry,* 52(5), 449-466.

Guthrie, C. (2007). Option overload? manage the choices on the table. *Negotiation,* 10, 7-9.

Hackley, S., Bazerman, M., Ross, L., & Shapiro, D. L. (2005). *Psychological dimensions of the Israeli settlements issue: Endowments and identities,* 21 (2), 209-219.

Hammond, J. S., Keeney, R. L., & Raiffa, H. (1998). Even swaps: A rational method for making trade-offs. *Harvard Business Review,* 76(2), 137-150.

Hammond, J. S., Keeney, R. L., & Raiffa, H. (2002). Smart choices: *A practical guide to making better decisions.* New York: Broadway Books.

Hammond, J. S., Keeney, R. L., & Raiffa, H. (2006). The hidden traps in decision making. *Harvard Business Review,* 84(1), 118-126.

Harding, C. (2004). Improvisation and negotiation: Making it up as you go along. *Negotiation Journal,* 20(2), 205-212.

Hastie, P. R., & Dawes, D. R. M. (2001). *Rational choice in an uncertain world: The psychology of judgement and decision making.* Thousand Oaks, California: Sage Publications, Inc.

Hawawini, G., & Viallet, C. (2006). *Finance for executives: Managing for value creation* (3rd ed.). New York and London: South-Western College Publishing.

Headd, B. (2003). Redefining business success: distinguishing between closure and failure. *Small Business Economics, Springer,* 21(1), 51-61.

Heath, C., & Heath, D. (2007). *Made to stick: Why some ideas survive and others die.* New York: Random House.

Heath, C., & Larrick, R. P. (1999). Goals as reference points. *Cognitive Psychology,* 38(1), 79.

Heifetz, R. (1998). *Leadership without easy answers.* Boston: Harvard University Press.

Helft, M. & Sorkin, A. (2008). *"Eyes on Google, Microsoft Bids $44 Billion for Yahoo".* Retrieved June 15, 2009, from http://www.nytimes.com/2008/02/02/technology/02yahoo.html

Henderson, M. D., Trope, Y., & Carnevale, P. J. (2006). Negotiation from a near and distant time perspective. *Journal of Personality & Social Psychology,* 91(4), 712-729.

Hernan Cortes. (n.d.). Retrieved July 23, 2009, from Wikipedia: http://en.wikipedia.org/wiki/Hernan_Cortes

Herne, K., & Suojanen, M. (2004). The role of information in choices over income distributions. *Journal of Conflict Resolution,* 48(2), 173-193.

Herrman, M. S., Hollett, N., Dawn, G. E., Gale, J., & Foster, M. (2002). Supporting accountability in the field of mediation. *Negotiation Journal,* 18(1), 29-49.

Hobson, C. A. (1999). E-negotiations: Creating a framework for online commercial negotiations. *Negotiation Journal,* 15(3), 201-218.

Hofstadter, D. (1996) *Metamagical themas: questing for the essence of mind and pattern.* New York: Basic Books

Hogarth, R. M., & Kunreuther, H. (1995). Decision making under ignorance: Arguing with yourself. *Journal of Risk & Uncertainty,* 10(1), 15-36.

How body language affects negotiation.(2008). *Negotiation,* 11, 4-7.

How short-term focus contributes to future disasters.(2008). *Negotiation,* 11, 6-7.

How to win an auction--and avoid the sinking feeling that you overbid.(2008). *Negotiation,* 11, 1-3.

Huberman, B. A., Loch, C. and Onculer, A. (2004) Status as a valued resource. *Social Psychology Quarterly* 67(1), 103-114.

Imperador Adriano está de volta ao Flamengo com sonho de 'reconquistar a felicidade'. (2009, May 07). *O Globo.* Retrieved May 08, 2009, from http://oglobo.globo.com/esportes/mat/2009/05/07/imperador-adriano-esta-de-volta-ao-flamengo-com-sonho-de-reconquistar-felicidade-755743344.asp

Is time on your side?(2007). *Negotiation,* 12-12.

Jackman, J. M., & Strober, M. H. (2003). Fear of feedback. *Harvard Business Review,* 81(4), 101-107.

Josephs, R. A., Larrick, R. P., Steele, C. M., & Nisbett, R. E. (1992). Protecting the self from the negative consequences of risky decisions. *Journal of Personality & Social Psychology,* 62(1), 26-37.

Kahneman, D., & Tversky, A., (Eds.). (2000). *Choices, values, and frames.* New York: Cambridge University Press.

Kaiser, K. (2009). The value creation imperative: a user guide for managers in the new world. *INSEAD Working Paper Collection,* (53).

Kaiser, K., & Young, S. D. (2009). Blue line management: what value creation really means. *INSEAD Working Papers Collection,* (37), 2-13.

Kaiser, K., & Young, S. D. (2009). Need cash? Look inside your company. *Harvard Business Review,* 87(5), 64-71.

Kaplan, R. S.; Norton, D. R.. (1996). Using the balanced scorecard as a strategic management system. *Harvard Business Review*, 74(1), p75-85.

Kaplan, R. S.; Norton, D. R.. (2005). The balanced scorecard: measures that drive performance. *Harvard Business Review,* 83(7/8), p172-180.

Kaplan, R. S.; Norton, D. R.. (2007). Using the balanced scorecard as a strategic management system. *Harvard Business Review,* 85 (7/8), p150-161.

Karelaia, N. (2006). Thirst for confirmation in multi-attribute choice: Does search for consistency impair decision performance? *Organizational Behavior & Human Decision Processes,* 100(1), 128-143.

Kim, P. H., Pinkley, R. L., & Fragale, A. R. (2005). Power dynamics in negotiation. Academy of Management Review, 30(4), 799-822.

Kim, W. C. & Mauborgne, R.. (1997). Value innovation: the strategic logic of high growth. *Harvard Business Review,* 75(1), p103-112

Kolb, D. M. (2000). More than just a footnote: Constructing a theoretical framework for teaching about gender in negotiation. *Negotiation Journal,* 16(4), 347-356.

Kolb, D. M. (2004). Staying in the game or changing it: An analysis of moves and turns in negotiation. *Negotiation Journal,* 20(2), 253-268.

Kolb, D. M. (2004). The shadow negotiation and the interest-based approach at kaiser permanente. *Negotiation Journal,* 20(1), 37-46.

Kolb, D. M., & Carnevale, P. J. (2007). When dividing the pie, smart negotiators get creative. *Negotiation,* 10, 9-11.

Kolb, D. M., & Williams, J. (2001). Breakthrough bargaining. Harvard Business Review, 79(2), 88-97.

Kotler, P., & Armstrong, G. (1996). *Principles of marketing (7th ed.).* Englewood Cliffs, **NJ: Prentice Hall College Div.**

Kotter, J. P. (2007). Leading change. *Harvard Business Review,* 85 (1), p96-103.

Kramer, R. M. (1999). Trust and distrust in organizations: Emerging perspectives, enduring questions. *Annual Review of Psychology,* 50(1), 569.

Kramer, R. M. (2002). When paranoia makes sense. *Harvard Business Review,* 80(7), 62-69.

Kramer, R. M. (2003). The harder they fall. *Harvard Business Review,* 81(10), 58-66.

Kramer, R. M. (2006). The great intimidators. *Harvard Business Review,* 84(2), 88-96.

Kramer, R. M. (2009). Rethinking trust. *Harvard Business Review,* 87(6), 68-77.

Kramer, R. M., Pommerenke, P., & Newton, E. (1993). The social context of negotiation. *Journal of Conflict Resolution,* 37(4), 633-654.

Kray, L. J., Thompson, L., & Galinsky, A. (2001). Battle of the sexes: Gender stereotype confirmation and reactance in negotiations. *Journal of Personality & Social Psychology,* 80(6), 942-958.

Ku, G., & Malhotra, D. (2001). The on-line auction phenomenon: Growth, strategies, promise, and problems. *Negotiation Journal,* 17(4), 349-361.

Lakoff, G., & Johnson, M. (1980). *Metaphors we live by.* Chicago: University Of Chicago Press.

Lancepress. (2009, April 30). Kléber Leite: 'O Adriano será o mais barato'. Retrieved May 08, 2009, from http://oglobo.globo.com/esportes/mat/2009/04/30/kleber-leite-adriano-sera-mais-barato-755528804.asp

Landry, E. M., & Donnellon, A. (1999). Teaching negotiation with a feminist perspective. *Negotiation Journal,* 15(1), 21-30.

Langer, E. J. (2000). Can words cure cancer? *Psychology Today,* 33(4), 28.

Langer, E. J. (2001). When more is more. *Psychology Today,* 34(4), 70.

Langer, E. J. (2002). Why do we do the things we do? *Psychology Today,* 35(3), 76.

Larkin, I. (2007). Negotiations versus auctions: New advice for buyers. *Negotiation,* 10, 9-11.

Larrick, R. P., & Blount, S. (1997). The claiming effect: Why players are more generous in social dilemmas than in ultimatum games. *Journal of Personality & Social Psychology,* 72(4), 810-825.

Larrick, R. P., & Boles, T. L. (1995). Avoiding regret in decisions with feedback: A negotiation example. *Organizational Behavior & Human Decision Processes,* 63(1), 87-97.

Larrick, R. P., & Wu, G. (2007). Claiming a large slice of a small pie: Asymmetric disconfirmation in negotiation. *Journal of Personality & Social Psychology,* 93(2), 212-233.

Larrick, R. P., Nisbett, R. E., & Morgan, J. N. (1993). Who uses the cost-benefit rules of choice? Implications for the normative status of microeconomic theory. *Organizational Behavior & Human Decision Processes,* 56(3), 331.

Larson, D. A. (2004). Online dispute resolution: Technology takes a place at the table. *Negotiation Journal,* 20(1), 129-135.

Latif, U. (2008). *"What Microsoft Wants from Yahoo".* Retrieved June 15, 2009, from http://www.techuser.net/microsoft-yahoo.html

Lax, D. A., & Sebenius, J. K. (1987). *Manager as negotiator: Bargaining for Cooperation and Competitive Gain.* New York: Free Press.

Lax, D. A., & Sebenius, J. K. (2002). Dealcrafting: The substance of three-dimensional negotiations. *Negotiation Journal,* 18(1), 5-28.

Lax, D. A., & Sebenius, J. K. (2006). *3-d negotiation: Powerful tools to change the game in your most important deals.* Boston, MA: Harvard Business Press.

Leary, K. (2003). A special section: Negotiating and psychoanalysis: Some common aspects of practice. *Negotiation Journal,* 19(4), 311-313.

Leary, K. (2004). Critical moments in negotiation. *Negotiation Journal,* 20(2), 143-145.

Lévi-Strauss, C. (1968). *The savage mind (nature of human society).* Chicago: University of Chicago Press.

Levitt, S. D., & Dubner, S. J. (2009). *Freakonomics: A rogue economist explores the hidden side of everything (P.S.).* New York: William Morrow/HarperCollins.

Lewicki, R. J. (2007). Walk the lime: Ethical dilemmas in negotiation. *Negotiation,* 10, 4-6.

Lewicki, R. J., McAllister, D. J., & Bies, R. J. (1998). Trust and distrust: New relationships and realities. *Academy of Management Review,* 23(3), 438-458.

Lewicki, R., Barry, B., & Saunders, D. (2006). *Essentials of negotiation* (4th ed.) Boston: McGraw-Hill/Irwin.

Lewicki, R., Saunders, D., & Barry, B. (2009). *Negotiation* (6th ed.) Boston: McGraw-Hill/Irwin.

Lieberfeld, D. (1999). Conflict "ripeness" revisited: The south african and Israeli/Palestinian cases. *Negotiation Journal,* 15(1), 63-82.

Lieberfeld, D. (2003). Nelson mandela: Partisan and peacemaker. *Negotiation Journal,* 19(3), 229-250.

Liew, C. (2008) *Development of Mediation in Singapore.* Retrieved March 11, 2009, from http://www.ausdispute.unisa.edu.au/apmf/2008/papers/43-%20Slide%20Carol%20Liew.pdf

Linsky, M., & Heifetz, R. A. (2002). *Leadership on the line: Staying alive through the dangers of leading.* Boston: Harvard Business Press.

List of mergers and acquisitions by Microsoft. Retrieved June 15, 2009, from Wikipedia: http://en.wikipedia.org/wiki/List_of_companies_acquired_by_Microsoft_Corporation

Loch, C. H., De Meyer, A., & Pich, M. T. (2006). Managing the unknown: a new approach to managing high uncertainty and risk in projects. London: J. Wiley and Sons.

Loewenstein, J., & Thompson, L. (2000). The challenge of learning. *Negotiation Journal,* 16(4), 399-408.

Lum, G., Tyler-Wood, I., & John, A. W. (2002). Expand the pie: How to create more value in any negotiation. Washington, DC: Castle Pacific Publishing.

Lytle, A. L., Brett, J. M., & Shapiro, D. L. (1999). The strategic use of interests, rights, and power to resolve disputes. *Negotiation Journal,* 15(1), 31-52.

Machiavelli, N. (2008). *The Prince.* New York: Oxford University Press.

Maddux, W. W., Mullen, E., & Galinsky, A. D. (2008). Chameleons bake bigger pies and take bigger pieces: Strategic behavioral mimicry facilitates negotiation outcomes. *Journal of Experimental Social Psychology,* 44(2), 461-468.

Maister, D. H., Green, C. H., & Galford, R. M. (2001). *The trusted advisor.* New York: Free Press.

Malenka, D. J., Baron, J. A., Johansen, S., Wahrenberger, J. W. and Ross, J. M. (1993) The framing effect of relative and absolute risk. Journal of General Internal Medicine, 8(10), 543–548

Malenka, D. J., Baron, J. A., Johansen, S., Wahrenberger, J.W., Ross, J. M. (1993). The framing effect of relative and absolute risk. *Journal of General Internal Medicine,* 8(10),:543-548

Malhotra, D. (2004). Risky business: Trust in negotiations. Negotiation, 7(2), 3-5.

Malhotra, D. (2007). Leverage time to your advantage. *Negotiation,* 10, 9-11.

Malhotra, D. (2007). The perils of negotiating to win. *Negotiation,* 10, 1-4.

Malhotra, D. (2009). When contracts destroy trust. *Harvard Business Review,* 87(5), 25-25.

Malhotra, D., & Bazerman, M. (2008). *Negotiation genius: How to overcome obstacles and achieve brilliant results at the bargaining table and beyond.* New York: Bantam.

Malhotra, D., & Bazerman, M. H. (2007). Pitch your offer--and close the deal. *Negotiation,* 10, 1-4.

Malhotra, D., & Murnighan, J. K. (2002). The effects of contracts on interpersonal trust. *Administrative Science Quarterly,* 47(3), 534-559.

Malle, B. F. (1999). How people explain behavior: A new theoretical framework. *Personality & Social Psychology Review,* 3(1), 23.

Malle, B. F. (2006). The actor-observer asymmetry in attribution: A (surprising) meta-analysis. *Psychological Bulletin,* 132(6), 895-919.

Malle, B. F., & Knobe, J. (1997). Which behaviors do people explain? A basic actor--observer asymmetry. *Journal of Personality & Social Psychology,* 72(2), 288-304.

Mandel, D. R. (2006). Economic transactions among friends:Asymmetric Generosity But Not Agreement In Buyers' And Sellers' Offers. *Journal of Conflict Resolution,* 50(4), 584-606.

Mankiw, N. G. (2006). *Principles of microeconomics* (4th ed.) Mason, Ohio:Thompson South-Western.

Mark Weber, J., Malhotra, D., & Keith Murnighan, J. (2005). Normal acts of irrational trust: Motivated attributions and the trust development process. *Research in Organizational Behavior,* 26, 75-101.

Marsh, S. R. (2000) *Mediation Pitfalls And Obstacles.* Retrieved March 11, 2009, from http://www.adrr.com/adr1/essayc.htm

Marsh, S. R. (2000) Mediation pitfalls and obstacles. Retrieved on March 11, 2009, from http://www.adrr.com/adr1/essayc.htm

Marsh, S. R. (2000) *The Truths Behind Mediation.* Retrieved March 11, 2009, from http://www.adrr.com/adr3/other.htm#1a

Maslow, A. H. (1943). A theory of human motivation. *Psychological Review,* 50(4), 370-396.

McCormack, M. H. (1986). *What they don't teach you at Harvard Business School: Notes from a street-smart executive.* New York: Bantam.

McGinn, K. L., Lingo, E. L., & Ciano, K. (2004). Transitions through out-of-keeping acts. *Negotiation Journal,* 20(2), 171-184.

McKersie, R. B. (1999). What would you do about the other side dropping the ball? *Negotiation Journal,* 15(2), 113-116.

McKersie, R. B., Eaton, S. C., & Kochan, T. A. (2004). Kaiser permanente: Using interest-based negotiations to craft a new collective bargaining agreement. *Negotiation Journal,* 20(1), 13-35.

McNamee, S. (2004). Critical moments as "Transformations". *Negotiation Journal,* 20(2), 269-274.

Menkel-Meadow, C. & M. Wheeler, eds. (2004). *What's fair: Ethics for negotiators.* San Francisco: Jossey-Bass.

Menkel-Meadow, C. (2000). Teaching about gender and negotiation: Sex, truths, and videotape. *Negotiation Journal,* 16(4), 357-375.

Menkel-Meadow, C. (2004). Critical moments in negotiation: Implications for research, pedagogy, and practice. *Negotiation Journal,* 20(2), 341-347.

Menkel-Meadow, C. (2007). Know when to show your hand. *Negotiation,* 10(6), 1-4.

Menkel-Meadow, C. J., (2001) Aha? Is Creativity Possible in Legal Problem Solving and Teachable in Legal Negotiation? *Harvard Negotiation Law Review,* 6, 97-144.

Metcalfe, D. (2000). Rethinking pareto-efficiency and joint feasibility. *Negotiation Journal,* 16(1), 29-33.

Microsoft. (2008). Microsoft comments on Yahoo! announcement [Press release]. Retrieved June 13, 2009, from http://www.microsoft.com/presspass/press/2008/apr08/04-09statementPR.mspx

Microsoft. (2008). Microsoft issues statement regarding Yahoo! [Press release]. Retrieved June 13, 2009, from http://www.microsoft.com/presspass/press/2008/jun08/06-12statement.mspx

Microsoft. (2008). Microsoft issues statement regarding Yahoo! [Press release]. Retrieved June 13, 2009, from http://www.microsoft.com/presspass/press/2008/may08/05-18statement.mspx

Microsoft. (2008). Microsoft proposes acquisition of Yahoo! conference call [Press release]. Retrieved June 13, 2009, from http://www.microsoft.com/presspass/press/2008/feb08/02-01Transcript.mspx

Microsoft. (2008). Microsoft responds to Yahoo! announcement [Press release]. Retrieved June 13, 2009, from http://www.microsoft.com/presspass/press/2008/feb08/02-11msft-response.mspx

Microsoft. (2008). Microsoft sends letter to Yahoo! Board of directors [Press release]. Retrieved June 13, 2009, from http://www.microsoft.com/presspass/press/2008/apr08/04-05LetterPR.mspx

Microsoft. (2008). Microsoft statement regarding Carl Icahn Letter [Press release]. Retrieved June 13, 2009, from http://www.microsoft.com/presspass/press/2008/jul08/07-07statement.mspx

Microsoft. (2008). Microsoft withdraws proposal to acquire Yahoo! [Press release]. Retrieved June 13, 2009, from http://www.microsoft.com/presspass/press/2008/may08/05-03letter.mspx

Microsoft. (2008).Microsoft proposes acquisition of Yahoo! For $31 per share [Press release]. Retrieved June 13, 2009, from http://www.microsoft.com/presspass/press/2008/feb08/02-01CorpNewsPR.mspx

Mills, E. (2006). *"Yahoo CEO to be paid $1 salary".* Retrieved June 15, 2009, from http://news.cnet.com/Yahoo-CEO-to-be-paid-1-salary/2100-1030_3-6079650.html?tag=lia;rcol

Mitchell, T. (2007, October 27). *The Man Who Broke the Mould. FT.com.* Retrieved from http://www.ft.com/cms/s/0/060e5b28-8429-11dc-a0a6-0000779fd2ac.html?nclick_check=1

Mitropoulos, D. (1999). The reporter's dilemma: News gathering as negotiation. *Negotiation Journal,* 15(3), 229-244.

Mnookin, R. (2005). Afterword to the conference report: Resolving the behind-the-table conflict. *Negotiation Journal,* 21(2), 259–262.

Mnookin, R. H. (1992). Creating value through process design: The IBM-fujitsu arbitration. *Arbitration Journal,* 47(3), 6-11.

Mnookin, R. H. (1993) Why Negotiations Fail: An Exploration of Barriers to the Resolution of Conflict. *Ohio State Journal on Dispute Resolution* 8(235) No. 2.

Mnookin, R. H. (2004). Turn disputes into deals. *Negotiation,* 7, 1-4.

Mnookin, R. H., Peppet, S. R., & Tulumello, A. S. (2004). *Beyond winning: Negotiating to create value in deals and disputes.* Cambridge, MA: Belknap Press of Harvard University Press.

Mnookin, Robert H. (1993) *Why Negotiations Fail: An Exploration of Barriers to the Resolution of Conflict.* Ohio Sate Journal on Dispute Resolution 8, 235.

Moffit, Michael. (1997) *Casting Light on the Black Box of Mediation: Should Mediators Make Their Conduct More Transparent?* Ohio State Journal on Dispute Resolution 13, 1.

Musashi, M. (2005). *The book of five rings.* Boston: Shambhala Publications, Inc.

Nadler, J. (2007). Build rapport--and a better deal. *Negotiation,* 10, 9-11.

Nascimento, A., Bloch, A., Motta, A. A., Mansur, C. E., Calazans, F., Amato, G., Pimentel, J., Rodrigues, J. L., Gueiros, P. M., de Aguiar, T. (2009, May 03). Adriano e os pingos nos is. *O Globo.* Retrieved May 08, 2009, from http://oglobo.globo.com/esportes/mat/2009/05/03/adriano-os-pingos-nos-is-755667914.asp

Neale, M. A., & Bazerman, M. H. (1983). The role of perspective-taking ability in negotiating under different forms of arbitration. *Industrial & Labor Relations Review,* 36(3), 378-388.

Neale, M. A., & Bazerman, M. H. (1992). Negotiating rationally: The power and impact of the negotiator's frame. *Academy of Management Executive,* 6(3), 42-51.

Negotiating without a net: A conversation with the NYPD's Dominick J. Misino.(2002). *Harvard Business Review,* 80(10), 49-54.

Nelken, M. L., (1996) Negotiation and Psychoanalysis: If I'd Wanted to Learn About Feeling, I wouldn't have Gone to Law School. J*ournal of Legal Education* 46(420).

Nelson, D., & Wheeler, M. (2004). Rocks and hard places: Managing two tensions in negotiation. *Negotiation Journal,* 20(1), 113-128.

Nicholas, T. N. (2005) *Fooled by randomness.* New York: Random House.

Nicholson, C. Y., Compeau, L. D., & Sethi, R. (2001). The role of interpersonal liking in building trust in long-term channel relationships. *Journal of the Academy of Marketing Science,* 29(1), 3.

Nisbett, R. (2004). *The geography of thought: How Asians and Westerners think differently...and why.* New York: Free Press.

Nolan-Haley, J. (2003). New problem-solving scholarship: An historical tale with a happy ending. *Negotiation Journal,* 19(2), 169-182.

Nordgren, L. F., & Dijksterhuis, A. P. (2009). The devil is in the deliberation: Thinking too much reduces preference consistency. *Journal of Consumer Research,* 36(1), 39-46.

Nucci, A. R. (1999). The demography of business closings. *Small Business Economics,* 12(1), 25-39.

O'Connor, K. M., & Adams, A. A. (1999). What novices think about negotiation: A content analysis of scripts. *Negotiation Journal,* 15(2), 135-148.

O'Laughlin, M. J., & Malle, B. F. (2002). How people explain actions performed by groups and individuals. *Journal of Personality & Social Psychology,* 82(1), 33-48.

Olsen, S. & Kawamoto, D. (2007). *"Will Yahoo's board get a makeover?"* Retrieved June 15, 2009, from http://news.cnet.com/Will-Yahoos-board-also-get-a-makeover/2100-1030_3-6192587.html?tag=lia;rcol

Öncüler, A., & Onay, S. (2009). How do we evaluate future gambles? experimental evidence on path dependency in risky intertemporal choice. *Journal of Behavioral Decision Making,* 22(3), 280-300.

Option. (n.d.). In The Free Dictionary. Retrieved July 23, 2009, from http://financial-dictionary.thefreedictionary.com/Option

Paquet, R., Gaétan, I., & Bergeron, J. (2000). Does interest-based bargaining (IBB) really make a difference in collective bargaining outcomes? *Negotiation Journal,* 16(3), 281-296.

Parkhe, A. (1998). Building trust in international alliances. *Journal of World Business,* 33(4), 417.

Parks, C. D., Henager, R. F., & Scamahorn, S. D. (1996). Trust and reactions to messages of intent in social dilemmas. *Journal of Conflict Resolution,* 40(1), 134-151.

Pease, B., & Pease, A. (2006). *The definitive book of body language.* New York: Bantam.

Pease, B., & Pease, A. (2006). *The definitive book of body language.* New York: Bantam.

Peppet, S. R. (2002). Teaching negotiation using web-based streaming video. *Negotiation Journal,* 18(3), 271-283.

Peters, D. (1993) Forever Jung: Psychological Type Theory, the Myers Briggs Type Indicator and. Learning Negotiation. *Drake Law Review* 42(1).

Peters, H. E., Argys, L. M., Maccoby, E. E., & Mnookin, R. H. (1993). Enforcing divorce settlements: Evidence from child support compliance and award modifications. *Demography,* 30(4), 719-735.

Picard, C. (2002). Common language, different meaning: What mediators mean when they talk about their work. *Negotiation Journal,* 18(3), 251-269.

Pich, M.T., Loch, C.H. and De Meyer, A. (2002). On uncertainty, ambiguity and complexity in project management. *Management Science,* 48(8), 1008-1024.

Pirsig, R. M. (2000). *Zen and the art of motorcycle maintenance: An inquiry into values.* New York: Harper Perennial.

Pirson, M., & Malhotra, D. (2008). Unconventional insights for managing stakeholder trust. *MIT Sloan Management Review,* 49(4), 43-50.

Plato, Cooper, J. M., & Hutchinson, D. S. (1997). *Plato complete works* Hackett Pub Co.

Plato. (360 B.C.E). *Sophist.* Retrieved April 23, 2009, from http://classics.mit.edu/Plato/sophist.html

Plato. (360 B.C.E). *The Republic.* Retrieved April 23, 2009, from http://classics.mit.edu/Plato/republic.html

Plato. (360 B.C.E). *The Republic.* Retrieved April 23, 2009, from http://classics.mit.edu/Plato/symposium.html

Plato. (380 B.C.E). *Laches, or Courage.* Retrieved April 23, 2009, from http://classics.mit.edu/Plato/laches.html

Plato. (n.d.). *Apology.* Retrieved April 23, 2009, from http://classics.mit.edu/Plato/apology.html

Pruitt, D. G., & Kimmel, M. J. (1977). Twenty years of experimental gaming: Critique, synthesis, and suggestions for the future. *Annual Review of Psychology,* 28, 363.

Putnam, L. L. (2004). Transformations and critical moments in negotiations. *Negotiation Journal,* 20(2), 275-295.

Rackham, N. (1988). *SPIN selling* McGraw-Hill.

Raiffa, H. (1985). *The art and science of negotiation.* Cambridge, MA: Belknap Press of Harvard University Press.

Raiffa, H. (2007). *Negotiation analysis: The science and art of collaborative decision making.* Cambridge, MA: Belknap Press of Harvard University Press.

Rainsberger, P. K. (2008, September). *XVIII. Standards Defining the Concept of Bad Faith Bargaining.* Retrieved November, 08, 2008, from http://labored.missouri.edu/research/pdf/2005-18.pdf

Ratner, R., Soman, D., Zauberman, G., Ariely, D., Carmon, Z., Keller, P., et al. (2008). How behavioral decision research can enhance consumer welfare: From freedom of choice to paternalistic intervention. *Marketing Letters,* 19(5), 383-397.

Reeder, G. D. (2009). Mindreading and dispositional inference: MIM revised and extended. *Psychological Inquiry,* 20(1), 73-83.

Reeder, G. D. (2009). Mindreading: Judgments about intentionality and motives in dispositional inference. *Psychological Inquiry,* 20(1), 1-18.

Reeder, G. D., Kumar, S., Hesson-McInnis, M., & Trafimow, D. (2002). Inferences about the morality of an aggressor: The role of perceived motive. *Journal of Personality & Social Psychology,* 83(4), 789-803.

Reeder, G. D., Vonk, R., Ronk, M. J., Ham, J., & Lawrence, M. (2004). Dispositional attribution: Multiple inferences about motive-related traits. *Journal of Personality & Social Psychology,* 86(4), 530-544.

Reinhard, M., & Dickhäuser, O. (2009). Need for cognition, task difficulty, and the formation of performance expectancies. *Journal of Personality & Social Psychology,* 96(5), 1062-1076.

Reinhard, M., & Messner, M. (2009). The effects of source likeability and need for cognition on advertising effectiveness under explicit persuasion. *Journal of Consumer Behaviour,* 8(4), 179-191.

Richard Shell, G. (2001). Bargaining styles and negotiation: The Thomas-Kilmann conflict mode instrument in negotiation training. *Negotiation Journal,* 17(2), 155-174.

Rubin, J. Z., & Breslin, J. W., eds. (1991). *Negotiation theory and practice.* Cambridge: Program on Negotiation Books.

Russo, J. E., & Schoemaker, P. J. H. (2001). *Winning decisions: Getting it right the first time.* New York: Broadway Business.

Salacuse, J. W. (2001). Renegotiating existing agreements: How to deal with "Life struggling against form". *Negotiation Journal,* 17(4), 311-331.

Salacuse, J. W. (2003). *The global negotiator: Making, managing and mending deals around the world in the twenty-first century.* New York: Palgrave Macmillan.

Salacuse, J. W. (2007). Write first, talk later? using drafts to make deals. *Negotiation,* 10, 1-4.

Sander, F. E. A., & Bordone, R. C. (2005). Early intervention: How to minimize the cost of conflict. *Negotiation,* 8, 1-5.

Sander, F. E. A., & Bordone, R. C. (2005). Keep it out of court: Resolving differences in-house. *Negotiation,* 8(7), 3-5.

Sander, F. E. A., & Bordone, R. C. (2006). All in the family: Managing business disputes with relatives. *Negotiation,* 9(3), 3-5.

Savitsky, K., Epley, N., & Gilovich, T. (2001). Do others judge us as harshly as we think? overestimating the impact of our failures, shortcomings, and mishaps. *Journal of Personality & Social Psychology,* 81(1), 44-56.

Sayman, S., & Öncüler, A. (2009). An investigation of time inconsistency. *Management Science,* 55(3), 470-482.

Schelling, T. C. (1981). The strategy of conflict. Cambridge, MA: Harvard University Press.

Schelling, T. C. (2006). *Micromotives and macrobehavior.* New York: W.W. Norton & Co.

Schneider, A. K. (2002) Shattering Negotiation Myths: Empirical Evidence on the Effectiveness of Negotiation Style. *Harvard Negotiation Law Review,* 7, 143.

Schonfold, E. (2009). *"Google Gobbled Up 90 Percent Of All U.S. Search Growth In 2008".* Retrieved June 15, 2009, from http://www.techcrunch.com/2009/01/28/google-gobbled-up-90-percent-of-all-us-search-growth-in-2008/

Schwartz, B. (2005). *The paradox of choice: Why more is less.* New York: Harper Perennial.

Schweitzer, M. E. (2007). Call their bluff! detecting deception in negotiation. *Negotiation,* 10(3).

Sebenius, J. K. (2001). SIX HABITS OF merely effective NEGOTIATORS. *Harvard Business Review,* 79(4), 87-95.

Sebenius, J. K. (2002). Caveats for cross-border negotiators. *Negotiation Journal,* 18(2), 121-133.

Sebenius, J. K. (2002). Negotiating lessons from the browser wars. *MIT Sloan Management Review,* 43(4), 43-50.

Sebenius, J. K., Eiran, E., Feinberg, K. R., Cernea, M., & McGovern, F. (2005). Compensation schemes and dispute resolution mechanisms: Beyond the obvious. *Negotiation Journal,* 21(2), 231-244.

Securities and Exchanges Commission (2001, April 19). *Insider Trading.* Retrieved May 18, 2008, from http://www.sec.gov/answers/insider.htm

Seligman, M. (2004). *Authentic happiness: Using the new positive psychology to realize your potential for lasting fulfillment.* New York: Free Press.

Sellier, A. L., & Chattopadhyay, A. (2009). Valuing time: Moderate download times can improve online goal pursuit. *Journal of Consumer Psychology* (Elsevier Science), 19(2), 236-245.

Senger, J. M. (2002). Tales of the bazaar: Interest-based negotiation across cultures. *Negotiation Journal,* 18(3), 233-250.

Shapiro, D. L. (2000). Supplemental joint brainstorming: Navigating past the perils of traditional bargaining. *Negotiation Journal,* 16(4), 409-419.

Shell, G. R. (1991) When is it Legal to Lie in Negotiations. *Sloan Management Review,* 32, 93-101.

Shell, G. R. (2006). *Bargaining for advantage: Negotiation strategies for reasonable people* (2nd ed.). New York: Penguin.

Shell, G. R., & Moussa, M. (2007). *The art of woo: Using strategic persuasion to sell your ideas*. New York: Portfolio.

Shelton, R. L. (2000). The institutional ombudsman: A university case study. *Negotiation Journal,* 16(1), 81-98.

Shooting the messenger (n.d.). Retrieved March 07, 2009, from Wikipedia: http://en.wikipedia.org/wiki/Shooting_the_messenger#cite_note-0#cite_note-0

Should you make the first offer? (2008). *Negotiation,* 11, 3-4.

Shyaka, A. (2004). *The Rwandan Conflict: Origin, Development, Exit Strategies. A Study ordered by: The National Unity and Reconciliation Commission*. Retrieved March 08, 2009, from http://www.grandslacs.net/doc/3833.pdf

Sinaceur, M., & Neale, M. (2005). Not all threats are created equal: How implicitness and timing affect the effectiveness of threats in negotiations. *Group Decision & Negotiation,* 14(1), 63-85.

Sinetar, M. (1988). Building trust into corporate relationships. *Organizational Dynamics,* 16(3), 73-79.

Singer, L. (1994). *Settling disputes: Conflict resolution in business, families, and the legal system* (2nd ed.). Boulder, Colorado: Westview Press.

Smith, T. H. (2005). Metaphors for navigating negotiations. *Negotiation Journal,* 21(3), 343-364.

Smyth, L. F. (2002). Identity-based conflicts: A systemic approach evaluation project. *Negotiation Journal,* 18(2), 147-161.

Soll, J. B., & Larrick, R. P. (2009). Strategies for revising judgment: How. (and how well) people use others' opinions. *Journal of Experimental Psychology / Learning, Memory & Cognition,* 35(3), 780-805.

Sophocles. (1909–14) Antigone, translated by E. H. Plumptre. Vol. VIII, Part 6. *The Harvard Classics. New York: P.F. Collier & Son,* Retrieved March 07, 2009, from www.bartleby.com/8/6/.

Soto, H. D. (2003). *The mystery of capital: Why capitalism triumphs in the west and fails everywhere else*. New York: Basic Books.

Stedman, B. E. (1999). A multi-option system helps get to the bottom of "big dig" conflicts. *Negotiation Journal,* 15(1), 5-10.

Stern, D. N. (2004). The present moment as a critical moment. *Negotiation Journal,* 20(2), 365-372.

Stieber, C. (2000). 57 varieties: Has the ombudsman concept become diluted? *Negotiation Journal,* 16(1), 49-57.

Stone, D., Patton, B., Heen, S., & Fisher, R. (2000). *Difficult conversations: How to discuss what matters most*. New York: Penguin.

Strauss, N. (2005). *The game: Penetrating the secret society of pickup artists*. New York: Regan Books / Harper Collins.

Stuart Jr., H. W. (2004). Surprise moves in negotiation. *Negotiation Journal,* 20(2), 239-251.

Subramanian, G. (2007). Negotiate conditions -- and bring value to the deal. *Negotiation,* 9-11.

Surowiecki, J. *The wisdom of crowds*. New York: Anchor Books.

Suspicion. (n.d.). *In Merriam-Webster's Online dictionary*. Retrieved July 23, 2009, from http://www.merriam-webster.com/dictionary/suspicion

Susskind, L. (2004). Ten propositions regarding critical moments in negotiation. *Negotiation Journal,* 20(2), 339-340.

Susskind, L. (2007). A question of ethics. *Negotiation,* 10, 8-8.

Susskind, L. (2007). Find the sweet spot in your next deal. *Negotiation,* 10, 7-9.

Susskind, L. (2007). Finding a good negotiation coach. *Negotiation,* 10, 4-6.

Susskind, L., & Field, P. (1996). *Dealing with an angry public: The mutual gains approach to resolving disputes*. New York: Free Press.

Susskind, L., Levine, H., Aran, G., Kaniel, S., Sheleg, Y., & Halbertal, M. (2005). Religious and ideological dimensions of the israeli settlements issue: Reframing the narrative? *Negotiation Journal,* 24(3), 221 – 246.

Susskind, L., Mnookin, R., Rozdeiczer, L., & Fuller, B. (2005). What we have learned about teaching multiparty negotiation. *Negotiation Journal,* 21(3), 395-408.

Sutherland, A. (2009). *What shamu taught me about life, love, and marriage: Lessons for people from animals and their trainers*. New York: Random House.

Taleb, N. (2007). *The black swan: The impact of the highly improbable*. New York: Random House.

Taleb, N. Fooled by randomness: *The hidden role of chance in life and in the markets*. New York: Random House.

Tamra, P. d., Fast, L. A., Weiss, J. N., & Jakobsen, M. S. (2001). Changing the debate about "Success" in conflict resolution efforts. *Negotiation Journal,* 17(2), 101-113.

Tang, W., Bearden, J. N., & Tsetlin, I. (2009). Ultimatum deadlines. *Management Science,* 55(8), 1423-1437.

Tenbrunsel, A. E., & Diekmann, K. A. (2007). When you're tempted to deceive. *Negotiation,* 10, 9-11.

Tenbrunsel, A. E., & Messick, D. M. (1999). Sanctioning systems, decision frames, and cooperation. *Administrative Science Quarterly,* 44(4), 684-707.

Text of Bush Speech Giving Saddam 48-hour Ultimatum. (2003, March 18). *People's Daily Online*. Retrieved June 26, 2009, from http://english.peopledaily.com.cn/200303/18/eng20030318_113478.shtml

Thaler, R. H. & Sunstein, C. R. (2009) *Nudge : Improving Decisions About Health, Wealth, and Happiness*. New York: Penguin.

The crucial first five minutes. (2007). Negotiation,10(10), 1-3.

The Office of Advocacy of the U.S. Small Business Administration. (2004). The small business economy: a report to the president. *Washington: United States Government Printing Office.* Retrieved from http://www.sba.gov/advo/stats/sb_econ2004.pdf

The robin hood effect in negotiation. (2009). *Negotiation,* 11, 5-5.

The Yahoo-Microsoft negotiation: What to consider before you say no.(2008). *Negotiation,* 11, 7-7.

Thomas, K. W. (2002). *Thomas-kilmann conflict mode instrument CPP,* Inc.

Thompson, L. L. & Hastie, R. (1990) Social perception in negotiation. *Organizational Behavior and Human Decision Processes,* 47(1), 98-123.

Thompson, L. L. (2008). *Mind and heart of the negotiator,* the (4th ed.). Upper Saddle River, NJ: Prentice Hall.

Threat response at the bargaining table.(2008). *Negotiation,* 11, 6-7.

Threat. (n.d.). *In Merriam-Webster's Online dictionary.* Retrieved July 23, 2009, from http://www.merriam-webster.com/dictionary/threat

Threat. (n.d.). Retrieved July 23, 2009, from Wikipedia: http://en.wikipedia.org/wiki/Warning

Trump, D. J. & Schwartz, T. (2004) *Trump: The Art of the Deal.* New York: Ballantine Books

Turner, P. (forthcoming) *Murphy for Entrepreneurs.* Provided by the author.

Twemlow, S. W., & Sacco, F. C. (2003). The management of power in municipalities: Psychoanalytically informed negotiation. *Negotiation Journal,* 19(4), 369-388.

Tzu, S. (2005). The art of war. Boston: Shambhala Publications.

Uncover hidden value with a post-settlement settlement.(2009). Negotiation, 12, 3-3.

Ury, W. (1993). *Getting past no.* New York: Bantam.

Ury, W. (2007). *The power of a positive no: Save the deal save the relationship and still say no.* New York: Bantam.

Ury, W. L. (2000). *The third side: Why we fight and how we can stop.* New York: Penguin.

Ury, W. L., Brett, J. M., & Goldberg, S. B. (1988). *Getting disputes resolved: Designing systems to cut the costs of conflict.* San Francisco: Jossey-Bass.

Van Boven, L., Gilovich, T., & Medvec, V. H. (2003). The illusion of transparency in negotiations. *Negotiation Journal,* 19(2), 117-131.

Waal, F. B. M. d. (1990). *Peacemaking among primates.* Cambridge, MA: Harvard University Press.

Wade-Benzoni, K., Hoffman, A. J., Thompson, L. L., Moore, D. A., Gillespie, J. J., & Bazerman, M. H. (2002). Barriers to resolution in ideologically based negotiations: The role of values and institutions. *Academy of Management Review,* 27(1), 41-57.

Wagner, M. L. (2000). The organizational ombudsman as change agent. *Negotiation Journal,* 16(1), 99-114.

Wanis-St. John, A. (2003). Thinking globally and acting locally. N*egotiation Journal,* 19(4), 389-396.

Warning. (n.d.). *In Merriam-Webster's Online dictionary.* Retrieved July 23, 2009, from http://www.merriam-webster.com/dictionary/warning

Warning. (n.d.). Retrieved July 23, 2009, from Wikipedia: http://en.wikipedia.org/wiki/Threat

Wathieu, L., Brenner, L., Carmon, Z., Chattopadhyay, A., Wertenbroch, K., Drolet, A., et al. (2002). Consumer control and empowerment: A primer. *Marketing Letters,* 13(3), 297-305.

Watkins, M. (1999). Getting to wye. *Negotiation Journal,* 15(1), 53-62.

Watkins, M. (1999). Negotiating in a complex world. *Negotiation Journal,* 15(3), 229-244.

Watkins, M. (2001). Principles of persuasion. *Negotiation Journal,* 17(2), 115-137.

Watkins, M. (2002). *Breakthrough business negotiation: A toolbox for managers.* San Francisco: Jossey-Bass.

Watkins, M. (2003). *The first 90 days: Critical success strategies for new leaders at all levels.* Boston: Harvard Business School Press.

Watkins, M. (2006). *Shaping the game: The new leader's guide to effective negotiating.* Boston: Harvard Business School Press.

Watkins, M. D., & Bazerman, M. H. (2003). Predictable surprises: The disasters you should have seen coming. *Harvard Business Review,* 81(3), 72-80.

Watkins, M., & Rosegrant, S. (2001). *Breakthrough international negotiation: How great negotiators transformed the world's toughest post-cold war conflicts.* San Francisco: Jossey-Bass.

Watkins, M., Edwards, M., & Thakrar, U. (2001). *Winning the influence game: What every business leader should know about government.* New York: Wiley.

Weber, J. M., Kopelman, S., & Messick, D. M. (2004). A conceptual review of decision making in social dilemmas: Applying a logic of appropriateness. *Personality & Social Psychology Review (Lawrence Erlbaum Associates),* 8(3), 281-307.

Weber, J. M., Malhotra, D., & Murnighan, J. K. (2001). *An attributional impetus model of trust development* Academy of Management.

Weiss, J. N. (2003). Trajectories toward peace: Mediator sequencing strategies in intractable communal conflicts. *Negotiation Journal,* 19(2), 109-115.

Welsh, N. A., & Coleman, P. T. (2002). Institutionalized conflict resolution: Have we come to expect too little? *Negotiation Journal,* 18(4), 345.

Wertenbroch, K., Soman, D., & Chattopadhyay, A. (2007). On the perceived value of money: The reference dependence of currency numerosity effects. *Journal of Consumer Research,* 34(1), 1-10.

Wetlaufer, B. (1996) The limits of integrative bargaining. *Georgetown Law Journal* 85(369).

Wetlaufer, G. B. (1996). The Limits of Integrative Bargaining. *Georgetown Law Journal,* 85, 369-93.

Wheeler, M. (2004). Anxious moments: Openings in negotiation. *Negotiation Journal,* 20(2), 153-169.

When negotiation is not the answer.(2008). *Negotiation,* 11, 5-7.

When you have a failure to communicate.(2008). *Negotiation,* 11, 1-4.

White, J.J. (1984). The Pros and Cons of Getting to Yes. *Journal of Legal Education* 34,115-24.

White, M. (2008). *"We have met the enemy... and he is us".* Retrieved October 28, 2007. Message posted to http://www.igopogo.com/we_have_met.htm

Whlte, S. B., Valley, K. L., Bazerman, M. H., Neale, M. A., & Peck, S. R. (1994). Alternative models of price behavior in dyadic negotiations: Market prices, reservation prices, and negotiator aspirations. *Organizational Behavior & Human Decision Processes,* 57(3), 430-447.

Why your negotiating behavior may be ethically challenged--and how to fix it.(2008). *Negotiation,* 11(4), 1-5.

Why your next negotiation power trip could backfire.(2007). *Negotiation,* 10, 4-5.

Wikipedia.org. (2009). *"List of acquisitions by Yahoo".* Retrieved June 15, 2009, from http://en.wikipedia.org/wiki/List_of_acquisitions_by_Yahoo!

Will your proposals hit the mark? (2008). *Negotiation,* 11(5), 1-4.

Williams, L. (1964, December 22). NLRB kills Boulwarism and closes an era. Retrieved May 9, 2008. Message posted to http://www.lindseywilliams.org/index.htm?Editorial_Archives/1964_12-_NLRB_Kills_Boulwarism_and_Closes_an_Era.htm~mainFrame

Winship, C. (2004). Veneers and underlayments: Critical moments and situational redefinition. *Negotiation Journal,* 20(2), 297-309.

Wondolleck, J. M., & Ryan, C. M. (1999). What hat do I wear now?: An examination of agency roles in collaborative processes. *Negotiation Journal,* 15(2), 117-134.

Wright, R. (1994). *The moral animal: Evolutionary psychology and everyday life.* New York: Pantheon Books.

Wu, J., & Laws, D. (2003). Trust and other-anxiety in negotiations: Dynamics across boundaries of self and culture. *Negotiation Journal,* 19(4), 329-367.

Yahoo! (2008). Yahoo! Announces Microsoft talks have concluded [Press release]. Retrieved June 14, 2009, from http://yhoo.client.shareholder.com/press/releasedetail.cfm?ReleaseID=316365

Yahoo! (2008). Yahoo! Board of Directors responds to latest Microsoft letter [Press release]. Retrieved from http://yhoo.client.shareholder.com/press/releasedetail.cfm?ReleaseID=303369

Yahoo! (2008). Yahoo! Board of Directors says Microsoft's proposal substantially undervalues Yahoo! [Press release]. Retrieved June 14, 2009, from http://yhoo.client.shareholder.com/press/releasedetail.cfm?ReleaseID=291270

Yahoo! (2008). Yahoo! Board of Directors to Evaluate Unsolicited Proposal from Microsoft [Press release]. Retrieved June 14, 2009, from http://yhoo.client.shareholder.com/press/releasedetail.cfm?ReleaseID=291270

Yahoo! (2008). Yahoo! Issues statement in response to Microsoft [Press release]. Retrieved June 14, 2009, from http://yhoo.client.shareholder.com/press/releasedetail.cfm?ReleaseID=308131

Yahoo! (2008). Yahoo! Mails letter to stockholders [Press release]. Retrieved from http://yhoo.client.shareholder.com/press/releasedetail.cfm?ReleaseID=294288

Yahoo! (2008). Yahoo! Remains open to value maximizing transactions. [Press release]. Retrieved June 14, 2009, from http://yhoo.client.shareholder.com/press/releasedetail.cfm?ReleaseID=310948

Yahoo! (2008). Yahoo! Responds to Carl Icahn's intention to nominate candidates for election to Yahoo!'s board of directors [Press release]. Retrieved June 14, 2009, from http://yhoo.client.shareholder.com/press/releasedetail.cfm?ReleaseID=310754

Yahoo! (2008). Yahoo! Responds to Carl Icahn's letter of June 4, 2008 [Press release]. Retrieved June 14, 2009, from http://yhoo.client.shareholder.com/press/releasedetail.cfm?ReleaseID=314081

Yahoo! (2008). Yahoo! Responds to Carl Icahn's letter of June 6, 2008 [Press release]. Retrieved June 14, 2009, from http://yhoo.client.shareholder.com/press/releasedetail.cfm?ReleaseID=314663

Ye, L. I., & Epley, N. (2009). When the best appears to be saved for last: Serial position effects on choice. *Journal of Behavioral Decision Making,* 22(4), 378-389.

Your good mood may work against you.(2007). *Negotiation,* 12-12.

Zeisberger, C., Falcao, H., & Gehlen, C. (2009). *Turning an elephant into a cheetah: the turnaround of Indian railways.* Fontainebleau: INSEAD Ref. 09/2009-5623.

# Index

## A
absolute goal, 54, 58
acceptance, 211, 219, 354, 358, 359
accepting or rejecting an offer, 98–100 see also commitment
active listening, 59, 153–154, 160–161
adverse terms, 172
alliances, 21
allocation of resources, 16
alternatives, 56, 61, 67, 100–102, 108, 191–192, 325–341, 353
anchoring, 270, 289–290
angel investors, 221
anticipate pitfalls, 175–179
artificial limits, 256–258
aspiration price, 267–272
assumptions, 151, 354–355
    crippling, 354–355
    empowering, 354–355
attributions, 151–152
attribution trap, 151
authority, 219, 275
availability bias, 274

## B
bargaining, 65–68, 206, 266, 272–273, 303
bargaining concepts, 267–272, 336, 369
bargaining style, 67, 68, see negotiation style
bargaining tension, 67-68
BATNA, 56, 61, 100–102, 325–327, 351
    as a win-win tool, 340–341
    estimating, 327
    external, 330
    internal, 330
BATNA, handling their, 327–332
    around negotiation, 330–332
    inside negotiation, 327–330
BATNA, using your, 330–340
best option on the table (BOpoT), 301, 304–305, 308, 310, 311, 313, 327, 329–330, 335–336
body language, 190, 195–198
body alignment, 197
Boulware, Lemuel, 70–73, 75, 76, 80, 281
Boulwarism, 71–74, 75, 80
bounded ethicality, 368
brainstorming, 193, 194, 254–255

## C
caring, 129, 131
collaboration, 19–20, 23, 24, 40, 69, 117, 119, 126, 154, 158
collaborative roles, 124–127, 190
coming up with solutions, 94–95, see also options
commitment, 61, 98–100, 108, 246, 250–251, 301–320, 355
    early process commitment, 100
communication, 91, 138, 147–179, 192–198
    three-way, 152–179
    two-way, 59, 91, 152–154
communication control, 91
communication foundation, 37–38
communication negotiation, 71, 73–74, 80–82, 192–195
    strategic directive, 80
    temptation, 80
    trade-off, 80
concessions, 253–254, 270–272
    reactive, 253
conducive environment, 187–189
Cortes, Hernan, 341
Counteroffer, 96–98
critical moments, 87–102, 127
Currently Perceived Choice (CPC), 311–312, 315
custody battle, 249
cycle of inference, 150

## D
Darwin, Charles, 15–16, 302, 348, 364
deadlines, 315–318
deciding to walk away, 100–102, see also alternatives
deciding what you want, 216–221
decision short-cuts, 275
decision trees, 306
decision weights, 304–306
decision-making bias, 274–275
defection, 38–41
defining the process, 91–92, see also communication
dehumanization, 121–122
diagnostics, 5, 89–90, 92, 93, 95, 97–98, 99–100, 101–102, 127, 145, 159, 188–189, 225, 239–240, 242, 245, 248, 257, 286–287, 290–291, 328, 329–330, 331–332, 333
dialogue pattern, 76–78, 152–179
disbelief, 119, 124
distributive negotiation, 113
distributive phase, 265, see also value claiming
dovetailing, 238, 240

## E
early process commitment, 100
emotions, 20, 136–137, 163–165, 170–171, 281
empathy, 219, 257, 364
ethical value negotiation, 368–370
ethics, 347–370
    courage to pursue, 367
evolutionary theory, 16
eye contact, 197

## F
facial expressions, 190, 195, 197
fairness, 278–282
    fair outcome, 280–282
    fair process, 278–280
Fisher, Roger, 2, 55, 166, 214, 222, 313, 356
focal points, 277–278
    qualitative, 277–278
    quantitative, 277
four Ps, 192–195
    people, 192
    process, 193
    product, 192
    purpose, 192
framing, 212, 249, 274
Fujimori, Alberto, 122-123

## G
generalizations, 155-156
gifts, 148–149, 179, 253

## H
Haggling, 65, 289, see win-lose process
hiring process, 129

## I
impasse, overcoming an, 315–320
information asymmetry, 80, 147–150, 254–255
information disclosure tension, 223–226
initiating interaction, 88–90, see also relationship
insider trading, 81
intangible issues, 55
integrative negotiation, 113
intent-impact gap, 38, 151
interdependence, 89–90, 117–118
interest categorization, 222, 237, 238

interest exchange, 223, 225-226, 227, 228
interest prioritization, 218, 222
interests, 92-94, 191, 214–215
    communication, 219, 224
    considering all, 94
    relationship, 72, 74, 79, 116, 219
    substance, 79, 218, 219, 234
interests preparation, 215–223
interrogation temptation, 156
intimacy, 129
intuition, 302–303
issues, 211-214

## J

joint problem-solving process, 112, 119
joint value pursuit (JVP) frame, 119–120, 141, 170, 190
    statements, 119
judgmental heuristics, 275–276, see decision short-cuts

## K

knowledge curse, 274

## L

ladder of inference, 176–179
leadership in negotiation, 40, 91–92
legitimacy, 56, 60, 96–98, 282–287
leverage, 358–360
liking, 129, 190, 275
logrolling, 241

## M

Mahuad, Jamil, 122, 123
making an offer, 99, see also legitimacy
manipulation, 54, 73, 96, 168–170, 175, 370
marketing, 14
Maslow's hierarchy of needs, 217–218
Maximizer, 54
Mediation, 149
    success rate of, 149
messengers, 120
meta-messages, 166
multi-issue complexity, 250
mutual-gains options, 94–95, 238–240

## N

naïve, 5, 19, 20, 24, 76, 282
narrow scope, 121, 258–260
needs, 33, 34, 131, 217–218
neg, 351–352
negotiation
    definition, 13–14
    seven elements of, 55-56
Negotiation Balanced Scorecard, 58, 304, 308, 352
negotiation bridge, 110
negotiation complexity, 54–55
negotiation dance, 270–272
negotiation power, 117, 351–363
negotiation style
    hard, 67, 68
    soft, 67, 68
negotiation tension, 67–68
negotiations; mixing the, 78–79
negotiations; trading between, 79–80

## O

offer, 6–7, 72, 96–100, 270–272, 287–292
    external criteria, 97
    neutral criteria, 97
    objective criteria, 96
omissions, 155–156, 162, 306–307
opening counteroffer, 96–98, 289–292
opening offer, 96–98, 270–272, 287–292
opening statement, 190–191
option generation; package approach, 246–247
options, 56, 60, 94–95, 240, 247–248
    contingent, 243–246
    tailored, 237, 252
overconfidence, 274, 275

## P

paraphrasing, 165–166
Pareto efficiency; see Pareto improvement
Pareto frontier, 31–33, 236, 240
Pareto improvement, 31–33, 238, 241, 251, 257
Pareto optimality; see Pareto improvement
Partnership, 131, 132, 286
passive acceptance, 358, 359
Pastrana, Andres, 78, 89
Patton, Bruce, 2, 55, 214
perceptions, 119, 150–151, 154, 155, 175, 281
persuasion, 139–140, 168
Pick-Up Artists (PUA), 351–352
positional bargaining, see win-lose process
positional bargaining process, 66, 254
positional offer, 66
positions, 59–60, 66, 67, 92–93, 94, 226–230
Positive No, 310, 340
positive-sum, 31, 33
power difference, 17–18, 73, 341
power distance, 252–253
power in negotiation, 352–355
power moves, 76–77, 226
power sources, 73, 353, 361–362, 363
power, demonstrating, 16
preparation, 360–362
prisoner's dilemma, 38, 40
proactive learning, 154, 159–167, 189
proactive reciprocation, 40

## Q

questions, types of
    check-in, 162
    clarification, 162
    closed, 156–158, 162–163
    conducting, 161
    confirmation, 161
    leading, 157–159
    learning, 155–157

## R

rational behavior, 136–137
reality testing, 328–330
reciprocal altruism, 19, 24
reciprocation, 19, 20, 40, 117, 135, 136, 275
regret, 306–308
    commission, 307
    omission, 307
relationship foundation, 33–36
relationship length
    long-term, 35–36
    short-term, 35–36

relationship negotiation, 73, 78–80
   strategic directive, 78
   temptation, 78
   trade-off, 78
relationship value, 15, 116
relationships, 33–36, 78–80, 115–141, 187–192
relative goal trap, 53–54
reliability, 129, 245, 328, 329–330
reservation price, 267–268
resistance, 17, 23–25, 252, 292, 317
resource constraints, 255–256
   absolute, 255–256
   relative, 255–256
Revolutionary Armed Forces of Columbia (FARC), 78, 89
Reward, 6–7, 111, 223, 241
Rhythm, 198
Risk, 6–7, 17–18, 24, 40–41, 69–70, 114, 124, 139–140, 204, 223–224, 241, 243–246, 281
risk analysis, 139
rules, 303–304

## S

sales, 14
satisficer, 54
saying no, 309–310
saying yes, 311–314
scarcity, 276
setting the stage, see leverage
seven elements of negotiation, 55–56
short-term concern, 17, 352
sit side-by-side, 123–124
small talk, 189–190
social proof, 275
Southampton team, 21
strategic directives, 75, 78, 80
Strauss, Neil, 351–352
substance negotiation, 73, 75–78
   strategic directive, 75
   temptation, 75
   trade-off, 75
substance value, 15
sunk costs, 274
survival of the fittest, 15
suspicion, 94, 134
sustainable agreement, 61, 282

## T

take it or leave it (Tioli), 66, 68, 71, 72, 73, 80
talking about value, 92–94, see also interests
tangible issues, 55
temptations, 75, 78, 80, 125, 203–204, 210, 211, 246
tentative commitments, 251
threat, 336–337
time alternative, 337–340
Tit-for-Tat, 18–23
   advantages of, 19–20
   criticisms of, 20–21
trade-offs, 55, 75, 78, 80, 363
trades, 240–243, 254
   multi-issue, 243
transactions, 115–116, 131
transparent advocacy, 168–179
transparent process leadership, 91–92, 158
trust, 33–35, 89–90, 127–141
   categories of, 129
trust-building, 127–141

## U

ultimatum game, 362
unconditionally constructive behavior (UCB), 135, 136, 141, 147, 282
understanding, 13–25
Ury, William, 2, 55, 214, 310
us vs. them, 118, 121–122, 123, 258, 293

## V

value
   focus on, 20, 75–76, 224
value claiming, 265–293
   negotiating legitimacy, 285–287
   preparing legitimacy, 284
   risks, 272–276
value creation, 235–260
   external enemies, 255–260
   internal enemies, 252–255
   obstacles to, 241, 252
value discovery, 113, 205–230, 237
value foundation, 30–33
value maximizing, 18, 20, 91
value negotiation, 1–12, 70, 71, 367, 368–370
   core assumptions, 6
   process, 110, 111
value pursuit, 110, 203–204
value tension, 207–211

## W

wait-and-see strategy, 40
walking away, 335–340
warning, 101, 336–337
we mentality, 118, 121–127
weakness, perception of, 119
win-lose approach, 16–18
   fallacies, 273
   process, 66
win-win approach, 23–25, 269
win-win strategy, 69–70
   interest-based, 69
   mutual gains, 70
   principled, 70
   value negotiation, 70
working relationship, 58–59, 89, 117, 140

## Y

Yesable Future Choice (YFC), 311, 312–314

## Z

zero-sum, 30–31, 273
zero-trust, 132–135
Zone of Possible Agreement (ZOPA), 268–270